RUSSIANS: THEN AND NOW

RUSSIANS: THEN AND NOW

A SELECTION OF RUSSIAN WRITING

FROM THE SEVENTEENTH CENTURY

TO OUR OWN DAY

edited by

AVRAHM YARMOLINSKY

THE MACMILLAN COMPANY, NEW YORK

First Printing

Library of Congress catalog card number: 63-8394

Printed in the United States of America

ACKNOWLEDGMENTS

"Here's winter," translated by Babette Deutsch (with minor changes), and twenty stanzas from "Eugene Onegin," translated by Babette Deutsch, are reprinted from *The Poems, Prose and Plays of Alexander Pushkin*, edited by Avrahm Yarmolinsky. Copyright 1936 by Random House, Inc., reprinted by permission.

"Sergeant Prishibeyev," "Anna on the Neck," and "At Christmastime" by Chekhov, translated by Avrahm Yarmolinsky, are from *The Portable Chekhov*, edited by the same. Copyright 1947 by The Viking Press, Inc., and reprinted by their permission.

Kochetkov's "The Battle Raged" and "Quatrain," Tvardovsky's "To My Critics," Slutzky's "Housing Construction," Tatyanicheva's "July" and "The bear has shifted," Yevtushenko's "I lie upon damp earth," and Akhmatova's "From an Airplane" are all from *Anthology of Russian Verse, 1812-1960*, edited by Avrahm Yarmolinsky. Copyright © 1962 by Avrahm Yarmolinsky. Copyright 1949 by The Macmillan Company. Reprinted by permission of Doubleday & Company, Inc.

Derzhavin's "On the Emperor's Departure, December 7, 1812," Pushkin's "Evil Spirits," Lermontov's "My Country," Tyutchev's "Sorry hamlets" and "Not with the mind," Nekrasov's "Freedom" and "Newlyweds," Belyi's "Once more I pray," Blok's "To sin, unshamed," Bunin's "Russian Spring," Mandelstamm's "On every still suburban street" and "The air strikes chill," Voloshin's "Crimean Twilight," Yesenin's "Autumn" and "Transfiguration," Pasternak's "The Urals for the First Time," Khodasevich's "It scarcely seems worthwhile," Akhmatova's "Lot's Wife," selection from Mayakovsky's "At the Top of My Voice," Orlov's "Pause on the March," and Dolmatovsky's "Frost" are reprinted with permission of the publisher from *A Treasury of Russian Verse*, edited by Avrahm Yarmolinsky. Copyright 1949 by The Macmillan Company.

"Platon Karatayev" is taken from Louise and Aylmer Maude's translation of *War and Peace* by Tolstoy, and is reprinted by permission of Oxford University Press; the excerpt has been slightly revised by the editor.

iv

ACKNOWLEDGMENTS

Babel's "A Letter," Zoschenko's "The Cap," Olesha's "Love," and Koltzov's "Ivan Vadimovich, a Man in the Swim," are from *Soviet Short Stories*, edited by Avrahm Yarmolinsky, Anchor Books, Doubleday and Company, copyright © 1960 by Avrahm Yarmolinsky. Reprinted by permission of the publisher.

The editor's biographical notes on Tolstoy and Chekhov, and his translation of "The New Day" by Vasily Grossman (from *Stalingrad*), are from *The Heritage of European Literature*, edited by Weatherly, Wagener, Zeydel, and Yarmolinsky, Ginn and Company, 1949, Vol. 2; these texts have been revised. The following selections were first published in *The Heritage of European Literature*: Babel's "A Letter," Zoschenko's "The Cap," Olesha's "Love," Lermontov's "My Country," Tyutchev's "Sorry hamlets," Nekrasov's "Newlyweds," Bunin's "Russian Spring," Voloshin's "Cimmerian Twilight," Yesenin's "Transfiguration," Akhmatova's "Lot's Wife," and Dolmatovsky's "Frost." They are reprinted by permission of Ginn and Company.

Yevtushenko's "I lie upon damp earth" was first published in *The Atlantic Monthly*, June 1960, under the title "Pioneers." "From an Airplane" by Akhmatova was first published in *The Virginia Quarterly Review*, Summer 1961, under the title "Versts by the Hundred."

The translation of Yevgeny Zamyatin's "Comrade Churygin Has the Floor" is by Bernard G. Guerney; it has been revised by the editor.

The translation of the excerpt from the Epilogue to Pasternak's *Doctor Zhivago* is by Max Haywood and Manya Harrari, and is reprinted by permission of Pantheon Books Inc.

NOTE

The verse translations are by Babette Deutsch. The editor is responsible for the translations of the prose selections other than those cited in the Acknowledgments.

Several selections have been given titles by the editor; these titles are set in parentheses.

For help in the preparation of this book, the editor is deeply indebted to his wife, Babette Deutsch.

CONTENTS

CONTENTS

II: Under the Hammer and Sickle

CONTENTS

FOREWORD

This book is of Russians, by Russians, if not for Russians. The editor's purpose is to afford outsiders glimpses of the people through the eyes of the country's most perceptive and articulate writers. Here is what amounts to a literary sample-case. The collection is made up of imaginative prose supplemented with semidocumentary and expository pieces. Verse is represented by some thirty lyrics, chosen with a view to helping the reader get the "feel" of Russia, and by a sequence of stanzas from Pushkin's *Eugene Onegin*. This narrative, which combines the magic of poetry with the solid substance of fiction, may be regarded as the matrix of the Russian novel. Fortunately for the anthologist, the art of the short story has been sedulously cultivated both in Russia that was and in Russia that is, so that many of the inclusions are complete in themselves. There are also excerpts taken, not without reluctance, from items too large to be got in whole. The period covered ranges over three centuries.

Of the two nearly equal sections into which the text falls, the first is devoted to the age of the Empire, the second to the Soviet era, the Revolution forming the Great Divide. Except for the pages from *Doctor Zhivago* by Boris Pasternak, all the material in Part Two was published in the Soviet Union. No apology is needed for the disproportionate share of space given to the decades that witnessed the making of the new society on which the eyes of the world are fixed. A note, largely biographical, is devoted to each of the authors represented by a prose piece, and, among poets, to Pushkin. Unless mentioned there, the date of publication or composition (the latter in brackets), if ascertainable, follows the text. Pains have been taken to surmount the barrier of language as far as possible. In many cases new translations have been made especially for this book. Several items have never before appeared in English.

Part I opens with three Russian folktales that are among the earliest to have been recorded. These are followed by excerpts from the first Russian autobiography—a seventeenth century text—and several items dating from or relating to the next century, an age of apprenticeship. The remaining pages offer a selection from the work of the major literary figures, beginning with Pushkin, a contemporary of Keats and Shelley, and concluding with Gorky, a writer rooted in the old order and straddling the line separating it from the new. These nineteenth century authors, working a realistic vein, explored, each in his own way, the life of the mind as well as that of the senses. The best of their novels, stories, poems, by virtue of a warm humanity, of questionings, keen insights, a sensitiveness to the burden of the mystery, have a universal appeal. They are also national, local, of the moment, of the place within the native setting.

To a greater extent than is usual with writers, Pushkin and, more especially, his heirs are chroniclers of their times, deeply concerned observers of the society in which they moved. Though engaged with the inner man, they were very much aware of external circumstance, and solicitous for the correctness of factual data down to the merest minutiae. "To reproduce the truth, the reality of life accurately and powerfully," wrote Turgenev, "is the greatest happiness for a writer, even if the truth does not coincide with his sympathies." Dostoevsky, who was a sensationalist and who called himself a realist in the higher sense, also evidences regard for the authenticity of factual particulars. When Raskolnikov faints in the police station, he is handed a glass of "yellow" water: in the 1860's this was the color of Petersburg drinking water. Dr. Zhivago, in Pasternak's novel, speaks of Tolstoy's "unequivocal faithfulness to facts." In concluding his second Sevastopol story, Tolstoy wrote: "The hero of my tale, whom I love with all the powers of my soul . . . is the truth."

The piece was published without delay, but with changes made by the chief censor in order to eliminate anything casting discredit on "our officers, the brave defenders of Sevastopol," to use his own words. Needless to say, freedom of the printed word was severely limited in old Russia, particularly before Alexander II came to the throne. It was generally taken for granted, however, that State control of literature was, in the nature of things, purely negative, prohibitory, confined to thou-shalt-nots. The idea of virtually dictating to poets and novelists what and how they should write was alien to the official mind.

This mischievous idea became operative under the Soviet regime. Back in the days when Lenin headed an underground revolutionary faction, he insisted that Party press—that is, newspapers, pamphlets, leaflets—should be subject to strict Party discipline. After the Bolsheviks seized power, this principle was applied to belles-lettres as well. Speaking to a German comrade in 1920, Lenin observed that an artist had "the right to create freely." But at once he hedged: Communists, he added, could not "stand with folded arms" and let artistic activities develop at random; they must "steer the process according to plan, and shape its results." Heirs to the utilitarian aesthetics championed by nineteenth century Russian radicals, the Bolsheviks held that literature was a potent social force, and so were intent on using it to further the Revolution. They repudiated the laissez-faire policy in the cultural domain as in all other fields. The tutelage over arts and letters was erected into a cardinal dogma of Marxism-Leninism. It has persisted to this day.

The dogma was soon guiding administrative action. Writing in 1923, Victor Shklovsky, a perceptive and outspoken critic, observed: "The greatest misfortune of Russian art is that it is not allowed to function organically, the way the heart beats in the human breast. Instead, it is regulated like train traffic." As a matter of fact, for some time a concessive spirit prevailed in high places with respect to literature. Protests against government interference with arts and letters appeared in the press. Aesthetic theories, the Marxist conception of literature, and like matters were aired in public debates in which officials participated. A variety of literary organizations and loose coteries enlivened the scene. The Party took a tolerant attitude toward all of them, including a group that advocated the artist's right to autonomy and political neutrality. One who examines the literature for clues to Soviet life finds that during the first decade of the new era writers were not prevented from presenting certain aspects of Soviet reality with a large measure of objectivity, candor, and stylistic freedom. That the regimentation of writing was then far from complete is indicated by the material in this book that dates from that decade. Here are the unflinching sketches by Babel and Zamyatin, Zoshchenko's wry pages, Olesha's mingling of whimsy and metaphysics, Yesenin's extravagant hosannah to the Revolution, along with Khodasevich's shy welcome to its promise, amid the miseries of upheaval, and Anna Akhmatova's nostalgic lines about the irrecoverable past. In the years to come, nearly all these writers were to suffer for their nonconformism, two of them expatriating themselves, two being proscribed, one perishing in a concentration camp.

It was in the late twenties, after Stalin had consolidated his dictatorial position, that the situation changed. With the launching of the first Five Year Plan in 1928, the strategic retreat from "socialism" under the New Economic Policy was over, and the Revolution was again on the offensive. Writers found themselves in uniform. The assumption was that art can be directed toward specific practical ends by fiat. According to a formula attributed to Stalin, writers are "engineers of human souls." It was held that they have the power immediately and directly to mold men's minds and influence their behavior. But if they were valued, they were not trusted. Since their skill could be used for good or ill, they needed "guidance" by the Party and by "Comrade Stalin personally," a formula that eventually became ritualistic.

In 1932, by a stroke of the pen, the Central Committee dissolved all literary organizations and replaced them by a single Union of Soviet Writers, which is still in existence. The Party thus acquired an agency that it employed to centralize and tighten control over literary production. Membership in the union, which has always been nominally voluntary but to a professional writer indispensable, involved allegiance to the Party program and acceptance of "socialist realism" as the one "basic method" of writing. It meant that a member agreed to turn out work "socialist in content and realistic in form." Central to this quasi-official formula was the proposition that the Soviet writer was not an impartial onlooker, but a militant partisan, obligated to use his pen in fighting for the new order and helping to build it according to Party blueprints. This was to be done chiefly by educating, that is, indoctrinating, the public in the spirit of what went by the name of socialism. Before long the shoddy doctrine hardened into a body of conventions and prescriptions. A handful of authors either withdrew into silence or, like Sholokhov, managed to ignore some of the regulations with impunity. By and large, writers accommodated themselves, some quite readily, to what were in substance Party directives. Fear was, no doubt, a large factor, particularly since a number of authors were among the victims of the terror that raged in the late thirties.

The literature produced in the quarter of a century before Stalin's death (in 1953) makes a sorry showing. It is mediocre, depressingly wanting in diversity, disingenuous. Back in 1924, Zamyatin with his usual bluntness declared in print that the writers of the day had become "confirmed liars." This quondam overstatement does credit to his prescience. Much of the output is crude, clumsy propaganda for official policies, such as the Plan. No opportunity is missed to glorify the Party, its leader, the devotion of the people to both. "Socialist realism" at once prescribes veracity and requires the writer to picture Soviet life in glowing colors. The argument is that the writer may do so in good conscience, since his gaze is rightly fixed, not on the drab present, but on the glorious future forecast by the science of Marxism-Leninism with the certainty of an astronomer's prediction of an eclipse. In fiction there is a prevalence of stock sentiments and stereotyped situations and characters. The heroes are models of Bolshevik virtues for the citizens to emulate. Villains are remnants of the capitalist past, invariably "unmasked" and either cast into outer darkness or experiencing a remarkable change of heart. The mandatory atmosphere is cheery, bracing; the tears shed are mostly tears of joy over the victory, say, of a team of plasterers in a socialist competition. The style is of the kind accessible to mass audiences—conventional, commonplace, innocent of subtlety. Not seldom does criticism come close to being an arm of the intelligence service engaged in ferreting out ideological errors and seditious intentions. Sholokhov's novel *Virgin Soil Upturned*, from which an excerpt is given here, is an example of "socialist realism" of the better-than-average variety. It gives a fairly good idea of what was going on in the Cossack villages during the expropriation of the kulaks in connection with the start of rural collectivization. Occasionally a readable novel dealing with the civil war or the economic reconstruction finds its way into print, as well as an apolitical piece of verse that touches the heart. A lampoon, like that by the ardent Communist Mikhail Koltzov, is an exceptional phenomenon.

With the outbreak of war in 1941, those members of the profession who were not in the armed forces used their pens to "arm the souls" of their fellow citizens with "fiery love" of the fatherland and "searing hatred of the enemy." So the Writers' Union was to phrase it in an address to Stalin. The sentiments were genuine. For a change, writers were able to say what they truly felt, and some said it well. During the early phase of hostilities, when the German troops occupied a large section of the country, reaching the suburbs of Moscow, the Party, in the interests of morale-building, put up with such deviations from "socialist realism" as an appeal to religious sentiment. Both in imaginative literature and in reportage— the latter is exemplified in these pages by Grossman's sketches of the Battle of Stalingrad (now Volgograd)—the conflict was truthfully pictured as a people's war not unlike the one fought in 1812 against the invaders led by Napoleon. As the Red Army took the offensive and the chances of victory increased, however, signs foreshadowing a return to strict ideological orthodoxy began to appear.

Peace put finis to tolerance. In 1946, by way of intimidating the literati, the poet Anna Akhmatova was proscribed by the Central Committee of the Party for the sins of pessimism, decadence, and aestheticism. As noted elsewhere, the popular humorist Zoshchenko, too, suffered proscription. The old demands on literature were repeated with a new sternness. Furthermore, writers were required to depict the victory as due to the Party's infallible ladership and Stalin's military genius. Naturally they were called upon to do their part in the cold war. On the whole, these promptings, whether explicit or not, were heeded. There was no shortage of contributions to what is now called the "cult of personality." (Such euphemisms are typical of the rot that is eating away Soviet language.) Novelists, poets, playwrights outdid themselves in glorifying the people's heroism in battle and in the peaceful labors of reconstruction. They extolled the invincibility of the Soviet order and its moral superiority entitling that order to remake mankind in its image. At the same time they labored to breed contempt for and hatred of the country's wartime allies, especially the United States. Never before was there such uninhibited perversion of the truth in depicting Russia's past and present and in presenting the foreign scene. In the stifling atmosphere that prevailed during the interval between the end of the war and that of Stalin, Soviet writing reached its lowest ebb. It was a degraded, emasculated, eviscerated literature, cut off from the intellectual life abroad, and largely out of touch with the realities at home.

It is a matter of common knowledge that Stalin's death marked the beginning of a new era. Although the fundamental principles of the system have remained intact, the regime has become less oppressive. Not that it has surrendered its tutelage over literature. The new Communist Program, approved by the Congress of the Party in October, 1961, re-affirms the thesis that "socialist realism" is the basis of Soviet art. Literature has not been emancipated. The role assigned to it is still that of a handmaiden of the State. Yet there has undoubtedly been a loosening of the straitjacket in which the writers had been confined under Stalin. Those in authority are less hidebound in interpreting the aesthetic canon. The principal organ of the Party printed an address that Leonid Leonov delivered in November, 1960, on the occasion of the fiftieth anniversary of Tolstoy's death, in the course of which the veteran novelist said: "A true work of art, a work of literature in particular, is an invention in form and a discovery in substance." This proposition is hardly in line with the regimentation of imaginative writing. Now and then, however, a voice from the summit of power carries a note of threat against authors who go too far in their heterodoxy.

In fact, much recent work is cast in the old, prescribed mold. But prose and verse of a different order are coming to the fore. A number of stories and poems give the impression that their authors, not all of them be-longing to the younger generation, have never heard of "socialist realism." No moral is spelled out, no message obtrudes, no ready-made solutions are offered to the problems that inhere in the human condition. Chekhov's ghost presides over the most sensitive stories. Some, like those by Nagibin and Kazakov, are devoid of any political or social charge. They are concerned with wholly private matters, especially emotional involvements between men and women. The style of Kazakov's "Autumn in Oak Woods" also deviates from the norm when it strays in the direction of naturalism or sophistication. During Stalin's last years the taboo on frank treatment of erotic experience was enforced with particular strict-ness. In this one respect the story is orthodox: sex is slurred over, and awk-wardly at that.

As might be expected, the sphere of private preoccupations by no means monopolizes the writers' attention. Nekrasov's narrative deals with a public theme, one that has long dominated fiction: the late war. Here is an ac-count of life and death at the front, without any heroics, without obeisance to the Party leadership, and showing none of the obsessive chauvinism that Stalin's decease has not exorcised. The climax would probably not have cleared the barrier of censorship in former years. A story printed at about the same time is almost certain not to have been published before the "thaw"; indeed, it would probably not have been committed to writing. It deals understandingly with a Red Army soldier who went over to the Germans. There is no window-dressing, no prettify-ing of Soviet actualities in the somber pages of "Journey to the Old Home," by Zhdanov, which is printed here. Both the sketch by Agapov (1934) and the *ocherk* (documentary) by Melnikov (1961) are concerned with the Communist League of Youth. But while the first is an exercise in glorification, with a digression into metallurgy and a paean to the automobile, the second focuses on human beings and, though a blithe, buoyant piece, draws a picture in which there is shade as well as light.

For several years now variations have been endlessly repeated on this official theme: having achieved socialism, as was inevitable, we, examplars of the new humanity, who identify the public interest with our personal interests, have entered upon the next phase of our glorious undertaking—we have begun to build communism. A tale by Sergey Antonov, published in 1960, too long for inclusion here, sounds a jarring note in this myriad-voiced chorus. The author has a teamster deliver himself of the following tirade: "Generally speaking, man is a slimy creature. Everybody thinks only of himself and has no thought for others. So it has been, so it will be. People shout: 'We are building communism!' but at the same time they try to grab as much as possible, to make their pile as quickly as possible, taking according to their needs, as if communism were already here. Look into men's souls—greed, cowardice, lies."

The revelation of Stalin's monstrous crimes at the Party Congress in 1956 caused what has been called his "second death." Ever since then there has been a thin, intermittent stream of prose and verse reflecting the mood of a nonconformist generation, in revolt against fetishes and slogans, hypocrisy and mendacity, the shamming to which most of the citizenry are forced to resort, as the protagonist of Pasternak's novel has it. These works expose, occasionally with unprecedented boldness, some of the darker aspects of Soviet life: bureaucratic dry rot, widespread corruption, ruthless careerism, the arrogance and vulgarity of the parvenu upper class. The muckraking is not an attack on the system, however, but on the abuses to which it is subjected, not on communism, but on its betrayal. The critical voices are those of prophets within the Law. Lenin is worshiped as the symbol of communism in its pristine purity, and the Party "was and is the embodiment of the intelligence, the conscience, and the honor of our epoch," in the words of a commentator on literature, writing in 1956. There are, no doubt, those who do not share this enthusiasm, holding that the evils of Soviet life, including the debasement of arts and letters, are the product of the order spawned by the Revolution. But the voicing of such views is not suffered. Witness the fate of Pasternak's novel, some pages of which are printed here. This is not the only recent work of literature to have been withheld from the public at home and eventually published abroad.

In fine, the post-Stalin years have brought novelists, poets, playwrights a limited and precarious freedom of expression, granted by the authorities, not wrested from them; tolerated, not approved. The situation is one of unstable equilibrium. It seems unlikely—though the wish may be father to the thought—that there will be a return to the old stringency. Increased contacts with the outside world appear to have pricked writers to demand more of themselves. Certainly there are now Soviet authors who show an unmistakable concern for depth, objectivity, candor. In a speech at the Congress of the Party held in 1961, Tvardovsky, an eminent poet, who is also the editor of the leading Moscow monthly, deplored the craven timidity of his fellows and the lack of fidelity to the realities of life in their work. And he quoted Tolstoy's declaration, cited earlier in this Foreword, about truth as the hero of his tale. Tvardovsky's lines "To My Critics," printed here, testify further to his sympathy with Tolstoy's stand.

Truth, if not the whole truth, is beginning to find utterance in imaginative writing. Here is a lantern that glimmers through the fog of pretension and propaganda. Soviet literature, its grave shortcomings notwithstanding, can scarcely be disregarded in an attempt to form an idea of Russia's national ethos, admittedly a nebulous concept, half fact, half fiction; or to reduce her immense diversity to a more or less coherent image, however blurred and changeful. It is the editor's hope that the material presented in this book can to some small degree help the reader to capture this image.

AVRAHM YARMOLINSKY

January, 1962

I: Under The Double-Headed Eagle

THREE FOLKTALES

The hero of these tales is Ivan the Terrible (1530–1584). What must have endeared the dread Czar to the common people was the implacable—and futile—war he waged on the boyars. The stories are among the several Russian folktales that were the first to be set down in writing. Curiously enough, this pioneer effort was made, not by a native, but by an Englishman, one Samuel Collins (1619–1670). A holder of the degree of Doctor of Medicine from the University of Padua, he spent nine years in Moscow as physician to Czar Alexis Mikhailovich, father of Peter the Great. The text of the tales, in an English version, appears in *The Present State of Russia*, Collins' memoir, which came out under a London imprint the year after the author's death.

(The Czar and the Bast Shoes)

When *Juan* went his progress, many of the Commons as well as Gentry presented him with fine Presents. A good honest Bask [bast] shoe-maker, who made shoes of Bask for a *Copeak* a pair, consults with his wife what to present his Majesty; says she, a pair of fine *Lopkyes* [*lapti*], or shoes of Bask; that is no rarity (quoth he); but we have a huge great Turnip in the Garden, we'll give him that, and a pair of *Lopkyes* also. This they did; and the Emperour took the present so kindly, that he made all his Nobility buy *Lopkyes* of the fellow at five shillings a pair, and he wore one pair himself. This put the man in stock, whereby he began to drive a Trade, and in time grew so considerable, that he left a great estate behind him. His family are now Gentlemen, and call'd *Lopotsky's*. There is a tree standing near his *quondam* house, upon which it is a custom to throw all their old *Lopkyes* as they pass by, in memory of this Gallant.

A Gentleman seeing him so well paid for his Turnep, made account by the rule of proportion to get a greater Reward for a brave Horse;

1

but the Emperour suspecting his design, gave him nothing but the great Turnep, for which he was both abash'd and laugh'd at.

(A Lesson in Hospitality)

Juan in a disguise sought a lodging in a Village nigh the City, none would let him in but a poor man whose wife was then in Travel, and deliver'd whilst he was there; away he went before day, and told the man he would bring him some Godfathers next day; accordingly he and many of his Nobility came and gave the poor Fellow a good largess, and burn'd all the houses in the Village but his, exhorting them to charity, and telling them, because they refused to admit Strangers into their houses, they should be forced to seek their Fortunes, and try how good it was to lie out of door in Winter.

(The Czar and the Thief)

Sometimes he [Czar Ivan] would associate with Thieves in a disguise, and once he advis'd them to rob the Exchequer, for (says he) I know the way to it; but one of the Fellows up with his Fist, and struck him a hearty good blow on the Face, saying, Thou Rogue, wilt thou offer to rob his Majesty who is so good to us; let us go rob such a rich *Boyar* who has cozen'd his Majesty of vast sums. At this *Juan* was well pleased, and at parting changed caps with the fellow, and bid him meet him next morning in the *Duaretz* [*Dvoretz*—palace] (a place in the Court where the Emperour used often to pass by) and there (said he) I will bring thee a good cup of *Aqua-vitae* and *Mead*. The thief came accordingly, and being discover'd by his Majesty, was call'd up, admonish'd to steal no more, preferr'd in the Court, and serv'd for a discoverer of Thieves.

ARCHPRIEST AVVAKUM
(c. 1620–1682)

In the mid-seventeenth century the Russian Church suffered a schism. On ascending the patriarchal throne in 1652, Nikon abruptly proceeded to make changes in the ritual and the liturgy, so as to eliminate the deviations from the Greek model that had grown up over the centuries. A number of clerics and lay people, in defiance of ecclesiastical authority backed up by the State, refused to accept these novelties, and formed a separate Church community, which came to be known as that of Old Believers or Old Ritualists and which is still in existence.

Avvakum stands out among the founders of this body of adherents to the time-hallowed observances. He was a traditionalist with the temperament of a rebel, a fanatic capable of tenderness, humility, good sense. A born apostle, he held inviolate every jot and tittle of what he believed to be the letter of the Law, and he lived and died a martyr to his faith. He epitomized the Muscovite mentality in his conservatism, his xenophobia, his concern for the punctilios of ritual, his arrogant conviction that Russia alone had maintained Christianity in its pristine purity. This last belief, which originated back in the fifteenth century, was to persist into the nineteenth; it was championed by the Slavophiles, and dominated Dostoevsky's thinking.

First the ecclesiastical and later the secular powers sought to silence the archpriest by periods of incarceration and of exile to remote corners of the land. The last fifteen years of his life he spent uninterruptedly in prison. From there he continued to denounce the ordinances of "the wolf and renegade" Nikon in writings that were smuggled out of the dungeon and circulated in manuscript. Chief among them was an account of his life, composed in 1672–1673. It is a pious narrative, abounding in the supernatural, which is accepted as a matter of course on the grounds that "God is an old hand at miracles." Yet it is less a work of edification, like the hagiographical literature current in Muscovy, than an impassioned piece of invective and propaganda, intended to hearten the hard-pressed true believers and persuade them to remain faithful to their cause even unto death. The earliest Russian attempt at an autobiography, it is couched in a style that is free from the baroque grandilioquence of the lives of saints and that owes much to the living speech of the folk, direct, homely, trenchant, occasionally coarse.

After a preamble, devout and diffuse, the Life opens thus:

FROM THE Autobiography

I was born in the region of Nizhny Novgorod, beyond the Kudma River, in the village of Grigorovo. My father, Peter by name, was a priest; my mother's name was Maria, in religion, Martha. My father was addicted to strong drink; my mother was given to fasting and praying. From the first she taught me the fear of God. As for me, one day I saw a dead cow at a neighbor's, and that night I rose and wept copiously for my soul before the icon, remembering death, for I, too, must die, and from then on it became my custom to pray every night. Then my mother was widowed and we were driven out by our kin.

My mother resolved to marry me off. For my part, I besought the most Holy Mother of God to give me a wife who would help me to win salvation. Now, in the same village there was a maiden, an orphan, too, who was wont to frequent the church—her name was Anastasia. Her father had been a blacksmith, Marko by name, and exceeding rich. But after his death all his possessions were wasted. So she lived in poverty and prayed to God that she should be united to me in matrimony, and so it was, by God's will. Thereupon, my mother, having taken the veil, departed to God, in a state of grace. And I removed to another village. At the age of twenty-one I was ordained deacon and, two years later, priest. After eight years I was raised to the rank of archpriest by Orthodox bishops.

Not long thereafter Nikon became patriarch. His first step was to forbid genuflections in church and to order making the sign of the cross with three fingers instead of two, as was the custom. The traditionalists were deeply troubled. Such a break with familiar ritual seemed to them to verge on apostasy. Some of them, including Avvakum, met in Moscow and took counsel. He writes:

We saw that winter was coming; our hearts froze, and our legs trembled. Neronov [Avvakum's father confessor] entrusted his church to me, retired to the Chudov monastery and spent a week in a cell, praying. While he was praying there, he heard a voice from the icon:

"The hour of suffering has come; it behooves you to suffer without weakening." Weeping, he related this to me and also to Bishop Paul of Kolomna, the same that Nikon afterward burned at the stake in Novgorod, then to Daniel, the archpriest of Kostroma, and to all the brethren.

Opposition to the reforms brought on severe repressions. Avvakum was arrested, put in chains and imprisoned, beaten and spat upon, then transferred to Siberia with wife and children. There he continued to preach against the innovations, and was ordered to join, with his family, a military expedition to the wilderness of the Amur region. It was commanded by Afanasy Pashkov, a monster of brutality. The archpriest managed to earn the man's implacable hostility by speaking up against him, and was knouted mercilessly and left to lie all night long, chained hand and foot, on the deck of a barge under an autumnal downpour. More tortures followed. For a time Avvakum and his family faced starvation, keeping alive by eating carrion, such as what the wolves had left, and his two little sons died. On one occasion he was taken to a fort and thrown into a cold prison cell. Here is a description of the beginning of his stay there:

At this time winter dwells in that land, but God kept me warm without clothes! I lay like a little dog on the straw, and some days they brought me food, some days they did not. And the blackguards made game of me: one day they would give me only bread, another—raw ham, or butter without bread. I ate like a dog, too. I did not wash, I could not make my bows; I would only look at Christ's cross and say my prayers. My guards, five men, were not far off. There was a chink in the wall—every day a little dog came up and looked at me. Just as Lazarus lay at the rich man's gate and the dogs comforted him by licking his sores, so I talked with my little dog; but passers-by gave me a wide berth and dared not look at the prison. There were many mice, and I would strike at them with my skullcap: the fools would not give me a stick. All the time I lay on my belly: my back was full of sores [from the flogging]. There were many fleas and lice. I wanted to beg Pashkov's pardon, but God's will prevented me—it had been ordained that I should suffer.

In the eighth winter of his stay in Siberia, Avvakum, with his family and other companions, began trekking back to European Russia. Below is an account of an early incident of the journey, which lasted three years:

For five weeks we traveled in dog sledges over naked ice. For the children and our things he [Pashkov] gave me two nags; myself and the archpriestess [as he refers to his wife] toiled along on foot, stumbling on the ice. A barbarous land, hostile natives; we dared not lag behind the horses, and yet could not keep up with them, hungry and jaded as we were. My poor archpriestess would tramp and tramp along, and then drop—how often! On one occasion she fell, and a weary old man stumbled over her and fell, too; both of them screamed and were unable to get up. The man cried, "Forgive me, good Mother!" and she, "You've crushed me, Father!" I came up to her, and she, poor soul, said to me reproachfully: "How long will this suffering last, Archpriest?" And I said, "Markovna, till our death!" And she, sighing: "So be it, Petrovich; let us trudge on."

We had a little black hen, and by God's will she laid two eggs a day to feed the children, helping us in our need; God had arranged it thus. In the dog sledge she was crushed to death, for our sins. To this day I am sorry for that hen whenever I think of her. I know not if it was a hen or a miracle: all year round she laid two eggs a day; we would not have given her up for a hundred rubles, we would have spat on them. That little bird, God's animate creature, fed us; she would take her meals with us, pecking at the porridge of pine bark in the pot, or at the fish if we chanced to have fish, and in exchange she gave us two eggs daily. Glory be to God, who does all things for the best.

When, the following year, the travelers reached the towns in western Siberia inhabited by Russians, Avvakum realized that the outlook for the cause of ancient piety was poor, and he was sore at heart. He writes:

Aggrieved, I sat down and reflected: What am I to do? Should I continue preaching God's word or go into hiding? For wife and children tied me down. And, seeing me sad, my archpriestess accosted me with deference, and said: "What troubles you, my lord?" And I spoke to her at length thus: "Wife, what shall I do? The winter of heresy is here. Am I to speak or hold my peace? You have tied me down." But she said to me: "Lord, have mercy! What are you saying, Petrovich? . . . I and the children bless you: dare to preach God's word as heretofore and do not feel anxious about us; so long as God wills it, we shall live together, and if we are parted, remember us in your prayers. Christ will not abandon us! Get thee gone, get thee gone to church, Petrovich; expose the whoredom of heresy!" I bowed low before her for those words, and, shaking off the blindness of discouragement, I began to preach and teach God's word in the towns and everywhere as heretofore, and I boldly exposed the Nikonian heresy as well.

Back in Moscow in 1664, the archpriest was well received in high places. The innovations introduced by the Patriarch had been accepted by a large section of the clergy and the laity, but the opposition was not without open adherents and secret sympathizers, the Czarina among them. After a short armistice Avvakum resumed the fight, and by order of the Czar was exiled with his family to Mezen, a tiny settlement on the shores of the White Sea. Two years later he was brought back to the capital. He was shifted from one monastic prison to another, maltreated, and finally unfrocked. "My excommunication by the renegades I trample underfoot," he wrote subsequently; "and with their anathema—it's wrong to say—I wipe my arse." Not that he blames those who have offended against him: it is all the work of the Devil. He adds:

It is plain, my hearer, our misfortune is unavoidable, impossible to escape it! God allows offenses to the end that the elect become known, that they may be burned, that they may be made white, that those who have been tried may be manifest among you. Satan, by begging, has managed to get radiant Russia* from God, so as to stain it red with the blood of martyrs. A good notion, Devil—and we rejoice in suffering for the sake of Christ, our light!

In the summer of 1667 Avvakum was taken from prison to the Kremlin to face a conclave of the princes of the Church, including two Greek patriarchs, "the army of the Antichrist," as he put it. Some of those present attacked him with their fists; others argued with him—all in vain. Subsequently, further attempts were made to persuade him to give up his stand, but he was adamant. Thereupon he was deported to Pustozero, a hamlet on the Arctic Ocean, his family remaining at Mezen. Exiled with him were two other schismatics: Lazarus, a priest, and Epiphanius, a monk. Both had had a part of their tongues cut out. On reaching the hamlet, the three men, together with a fourth Old Believer, were placed in a prison, "an earthen coffin." In the third year of their incarceration a voivode, whom Avvakum calls "Pilate," questioned the prisoners to discover if they had had a change of heart. They proved obdurate. The archpriest writes:

* "Radiant Russia," a "quasi-official phrase" (Pierre Pascal), first occurring in a fifteenth century tale composed in Novgorod.—A. Y.

They led us to a scaffold and, having read the order, took me back to the dungeon. The order was to put me in a subterranean prison and to keep me on bread and water. I spat on that; I wanted to starve myself to death, and I refused food for eight days or more, but the brethren bade me eat again.

And they took Lazarus, the priest, and cut out his whole tongue from his throat; a little blood came and then stopped flowing. And, behold, he spoke again without his tongue. Then, placing his right hand on the block, they cut it off at the wrist, and the hand that had been cut off, lying on the ground, of itself joined its fingers [for the sign of the cross] after the traditional use, and for a long time lay thus before the people. Even in death the poor thing confessed the Savior's sign staunchly. I myself marveled at this miracle: the lifeless convicting the living.

The same punishment was meted out to Epiphanius. In his case, the reader is told, the tongue that had been cut out was replaced by a new one.

Avvakum and his comrades were supposed to be in strict isolation, but owing to the sympathy of the common folk, including the guards, were able to communicate with their well-wishers and fellow zealots. Thus the threescore homilies, tracts, and epistles the archpriest had composed got into the hands of his fellow schismatics. Those were bitter years for them. Thousands of the faithful were hanged or perished at the stake. Some chose the "fiery death" voluntarily. To avoid arrest a group would crowd into a wooden hut, set it on fire, and allow themselves to be burned. To his sorrow Avvakum learned that his two grown sons had escaped the gallows by submitting. "It is for my sins that this weakness has been permitted," he writes. "Well, so be it! Christ can save and pardon us all."

When the news of the death of Czar Alexis reached the archpriest's prison, he addressed a missive to the monarch's son and successor urging him to abolish the Nikonian reforms, which his father had supported. He had heard from Christ, he added significantly, that the deceased Czar was "in torments." Czar Theodor's response was to order Avvakum and his fellow prisoners to be executed by fire "for severe disparagement of the Czar's house." Accordingly, they were placed in a log cabin and burned alive.

VASILY KLYUCHEVSKY
(1842–1911)

This profile is a slightly abridged chapter from *A Course of Russian History,* based on the lectures delivered at the University of Moscow by the great historian. Klyuchevsky combined a mastery of sources, a broad view of the historical process, and liberal principles with a literary gift unique in Russian historiography. In the interest of clarity several sentences, in brackets, have been inserted in the text.

(Peter the Great)

Peter was a giant nearly seven feet tall, towering a full head above any crowd in which he found himself. When he gave the ritual kiss of greeting at Easter, he had to stoop continually until his back ached. Nature had granted him great physical strength, and constant handling of ax and hammer developed his muscular power and dexterity. Not only could he twist a silver plate into a roll, but also cut with a knife a piece of cloth thrown into the air. The fourteenth child of Czar Alexis and his second wife, who was a Naryshkina, Peter did not inherit the debility that marked the Romanov line. He took after his mother. The Naryshkins were distinguished for vivacity and mental agility. In later years they produced a succession of wits, and indeed one became a jester at the court of Catherine the Great.

[From 1682 until he came of age, in 1689, Peter shared the throne with his half-brother Ivan under the regency of their sister Sophia.] According to an ambassador who was presented to the two czars in 1683, Peter, then eleven years old, was a handsome, lively boy. While Czar Ivan sat like a wax figure on his silver throne beneath icons, a fur-trimmed, gem-studded crown pushed down over his lowered eyes that looked at no one, Peter, perched next to him on an identical throne, wearing an identical crown, and glancing about him eagerly, found it hard to sit still. Later on, the agreeable impression that he made was marred by the signs of a serious nervous disorder, which resulted from his having witnessed, as a child of ten, a bloody mutiny in the Kremlin, or from all too frequent plunges into dissipation that, since he had not fully matured, played havoc with his health. More probably, it was the effect of both causes. He was going on twenty when he began to suffer from a tremor of the head, and in moments of agitation or concentrated thought his handsome features were distorted by convulsions. This, together with a birthmark on his right cheek and the habit of sawing the air with his arms as he walked, made him a marked figure. Owing to these peculiarities, of which the Dutchmen who visited Moscow had gossiped to their countrymen, he was readily recognized as the Russian Czar when in 1697, in the guise of a Muscovite carpenter, he entered a barbershop in Saardam to get a shave. His lack of self-restraint lent his large, restless eyes a look so piercing and sometimes even so wild as to make the fainthearted quake. . . .

Peter was a guest in his own house. He grew up and matured on the road and working in the open. If at the end of his life he had taken time to cast a retrospective look upon it, he would have realized that he had always been on the move. During his reign he had traveled over the broad expanse of Russia from one end to the other, from the Neva to the Pruth, from Archangel to Azov, Astrakhan, and Derbent. Continual travel bred a roving spirit in him, a need for constant change of scene, for fresh impressions. Haste became his habit. He was always in a hurry about everything. His customary gait was so rapid, what with his great stride, that an ordinary person walking with him could only keep up with him by runs and leaps. It was difficult for him to sit in one place for any length of time; at banquets he often jumped up from his chair and ran into another room to stretch his legs. It is not surprising that in his youth he was very fond of dancing. He was a frequent and merry guest on festive occasions at the homes of courtiers, merchants, and master craftsmen, and he danced a great deal and rather well, although he had never taken dancing lessons, but had picked up the art "solely by practice" at the soirées given by Admiral Lefort [the Genevan who was one of Peter's close associates].

If Peter was not traveling or feasting or sleeping or making a tour of inspection, he was sure to be building something. His hands were eternally busy, and never free from calluses. He engaged in manual labor whenever an occasion offered. Whenever, as a young man without any experience, he happened to be visiting a factory or mill, he would promptly take his place beside the workmen. It was difficult for him to remain a mere spectator of other men's work, particularly if it was new to him: he wanted to try his hand at it, and instinctively reached out for the tool. He developed great resourcefulness and dexterity; having looked closely at the exercise of a new kind of skill, he immediately grasped the trick of it. In time his penchant for handicrafts, for industrial arts, turned into a habit, an addiction. He was impelled to learn and master every new technique before he troubled to consider whether or not he could put it to any use. Over the years he acquired an immense mass of technical knowledge. During his first trip abroad—he was then twenty-five—the German princesses concluded from their talks with him that he had mastered fourteen crafts. Afterward he was at home in any workshop, any factory. Wherever he stayed he left mementos in the shape of things that he had made with his own hands: snuffboxes, dishes, chairs, boats. One wonders how he managed to get the time to make these innumerable objects.

His success in mastering crafts made him confident that he could handle any tool: he considered himself an experienced surgeon and a good dentist. Such of his intimates as happened to need surgical attention dreaded the thought that the Czar would get wind of their illness and would appear with his instruments to offer his services. It is said that he left behind a sackful of teeth that he had pulled, a monument to his prowess as a dentist.

But what he prized above all else was shipbuilding. He would turn his back upon business of State no matter how important, if he had the slightest opportunity to wield an ax in a dockyard. Until late in life, whenever he was in Petersburg, he did not let a day pass without spending an hour or two at the Navy Yard. Indeed, he achieved great skill in naval construction: his contemporaries considered him the best shipwright and shipmaster in Russia. Not only could he design and supervise the construction of a ship; he could also build one with his own hands, from the laying of the keel to the finishing touches. He was proud of his skill in this craft, and spared neither money nor effort to establish and develop it in Russia. This descendant of plainsmen, born in the Kremlin, hundreds of miles away from salt water, grew up to be a true mariner, to whom sea air was as necessary as water is to a fish. To this air, as well as to constant physical activity, he himself ascribed a beneficial effect upon his health, which was continually being harmed by all manner of excesses. Hence also his gargantuan, truly seamanlike appetite. He could eat always and everywhere. Whenever he came to visit, whether before or after dinner, he was ready to sit down at table. As a rule he rose early, between four and five in the morning, dined between eleven and twelve, and directly thereafter took a nap. Even as a guest at a banquet, he did not refuse himself these forty winks, and refreshed thereby, he would return to the banquet hall, ready to eat and drink again. . . .

Peter could not bear the pomp and circumstance of the Kremlin palace. Imperious and domineering, he felt lost amid solemnities. He would breathe heavily, turn crimson and perspire when he had to give audience to an ambassador and, flanked by his courtiers, stand before the throne in sumptuous regal trappings listening to the dignitary's bombastic twaddle. He tried to order his daily life in the simplest and most thrifty fashion. The monarch who was considered to be one of the wealthiest and most powerful in the world was often seen in shoes that were down at heel and in socks darned by his wife or daughters. In the morning he received visitors in his private quarters wearing a plain old nankeen dressing gown. On going out for a walk or a drive, he wore a simple kaftan made of coarse cloth, and seldom changed. In summer, if he was going no great distance, he did not wear a hat. He drove out in a one-horse chaise or, if in a carriage and pair, the vehicle was one in which many a Moscow merchant would have disdained to appear. On solemn occasions, when he was invited to a wedding, for example, he would rent a carriage from Jaguzinski, the Procurator General of the Senate, who was the glass of fashion.

A native of the boundless Russian plain, Peter found the air in a narrow German valley, hemmed in by mountains, oppressive. On the other hand, although he grew up in the open and was accustomed to spacious ways, he could not abide a high-ceilinged room. Whenever he found himself in such a chamber, he would order a linen canopy to simulate a low ceiling. Perhaps because he had spent his childhood in a village, where he lived in a little old frame house that, according to a foreign memoirist, was worth less than a hundred thalers, the winter and summer palaces that he built for himself in Petersburg were small and the rooms narrow. He could not bear living in a large house.

Having given up the Kremlin palaces, he also put aside the sumptuous ceremonial that had surrounded the Muscovite czars. In all Europe, only the court of the niggardly Friedrich Wilhelm I of Prussia could perhaps rival the Petersburg court in simplicity. Not for nothing did Peter compare himself to that king, saying that both of them disliked luxury and extravagance. In his reign there were no Chamberlains or Gentlemen of the Bedchanmber. The court attendants were usually a dozen young noblemen of low rank, called orderlies. Peter disliked livery and uniforms trimmed with expensive gold braid, nor did he tolerate expensive plate. The regular budget of the court, which formerly had absorbed hundreds of thousands of rubles, did not exceed 60,000 rubles per annum in his time. In his last years, however, the Empress Catherine, his second wife, maintained a brilliant court that could hold its own with the establishment of any German prince of the period. Himself impatient of regal glitter, Peter wished to surround Catherine with it, perhaps in order to make his entourage forget her origin. [She is believed to have been a Livonian peasant girl, who, having been taken prisoner, was a cross between a servant and a concubine to two high-ranking Russian generals in succession, until, in 1703 or thereabouts, Peter made her his mistress. She remained his lifelong companion and bore him twelve children. Eventually he married her and had her crowned; and after his death, in 1725, she succeeded him on the throne.]

Simplicity and lack of ceremony also marked Peter's relations with people. In his dealings with them he mingled the manners of a Russian magnate with the rough-and-ready ways of a journeyman. When paying a visit he would sit down on any chair that happened to be vacant; if he was hot, he would take off his kaftan in everybody's presence without embarrassment; when he was invited to be "marshal" (master of ceremonies) at a wedding, he would perform his duties in a businesslike and scrupulous fashion, and then, placing his marshal's baton in a corner, he would go up to the buffet and, taking the roast from the plate in his hands, proceed to consume it without further ado. His habit of doing without knife and fork at table astonished the German princesses who supped with him at Koppenbrügge. Peter was not noted for fine manners or courtesy. At the winter assemblies which he established in Petersburg and which drew the *beau monde* to the mansion of one or another dignitary, he would sit down to play chess with a common sailor and drink beer with him, meanwhile puffing at a long Dutch pipe stuffed with cheap tobacco, without paying any attention to the ladies who were dancing in the same room or the next.

When, the day's labors over, he either went visiting or received guests at home, he liked to have cheerful faces about him and to listen to free talk over a glass of Hungarian wine. He would take part in the conversation, striding up and down the room and not forgetting his drink. He did not tolerate a sneer, a rude remark, or anything that might spoil the talk or lead to a quarrel. A culprit was immediately punished by the imposition of a "drinking fine": he was forced to down three glasses of vodka in succession or to empty an "eagle," a large pitcher, in order that he might not "twaddle too much or try to pick a quarrel." During these informal interchanges ticklish subjects were, of course, avoided, although the lack of constraint that characterized Peter's entourage inclined the unwary or the plainspoken to blurt out what came into their heads.

Peter loved and esteemed the naval lieutenant Mishukov for his seamanship, and indeed this was the first Russian to whom the Czar entrusted a frigate. At a banquet in Kronstadt, Mishukov, who was seated next to the sovereign and who had imbibed freely, grew thoughtful and suddenly burst into tears. Astonished, the Czar inquired sympathetically what was wrong. Thereupon Mishukov sobbed out for all to hear that the hall in which they were seated, the capital nearby, the Baltic navy, ships and seamen, finally, he, Mishukov himself, the commander of the frigate, who was deeply sensible of the Czar's favor, all were the creation of the sovereign, and that recalling this fact, and realizing that the Czar's health was failing, he could not restrain his tears.

"In whose care will you leave us?" he cried.

"What do you mean? I have an heir: the Czarevich!" replied Peter. [After having been tried for treason and condemned to die, the Czarevich is believed to have been tortured to death in 1718.]

"Oh, but he's stupid," Mishukov blurted out; "he'll ruin everything!"

Peter rather liked the old mariner's frank expression of what was indeed the bitter truth, but the man had to be upbraided for the crudity of his language and the impropriety of his remarks.

"Fool!" said Peter with a grin, rapping him on the head. "That sort of thing isn't said publicly."

Accustomed to behaving in a simple and direct fashion, he demanded energy, forthrightness, and frankness from others, too, and did not tolerate evasiveness. Nepluyev relates in his memoirs that on returning from Venice, after completing his studies in navigation there, he was examined by the Czar himself and then put in charge of the ships that were being built in the capital, so that he came in almost daily contact with Peter. He had been advised to be prompt and always to tell the Czar the truth. Having stayed up late one night at a name-day celebration, he overslept and appeared at his post when Peter was already on the spot. Dreading the Czar's wrath, his first thought was to go home and send word that he was ill, but he changed his mind and decided to acknowledge his fault.

"Well, my friend, I am here ahead of you," said Peter.

"My fault, Sire," replied Nepluyev. "Last night I was visiting and got home late."

Taking him gently by the shoulders, so that Nepluyev quaked and nearly dropped, Peter said:

"Thanks, my boy, for telling me the truth. You're forgiven. Who isn't a sinner before God? Who isn't his grandmother's grandson? And now let's go and pay our respects to the mother of a new baby."

They drove out to the house of a carpenter whose wife had just been delivered of a child. The Czar gave her five *grivnas* [*grivna*—a copper coin] and kissed her, ordering Nepluyev to do likewise. Nepluyev gave her one *grivna*.

"Well, brother," said the Czar, laughing, "I see you don't hand out money as freely as they do abroad."

"I can't give so much, Sire. I am a poor man, with a wife and children to support, and if it weren't for the salary that you allow me, I would have nothing to eat here away from home."

Whereupon Peter inquired how many "souls" he owned and where his estate was situated. Meanwhile the carpenter brought out two glasses of vodka for the guests on a wooden tray. Peter drank a glass and munched a piece of carrot pie. Nepluyev would not eat or drink, but Peter insisted:

"Drink as much as you can. Do not offend our host." And, breaking off a piece of pie, he added: "Here, eat it, it's good Russian food, no Italian stuff."

Kindhearted by nature, Peter was a harsh ruler, with no respect for human dignity, either his own or that of others. His environment as a growing child could not foster that respect. As he grew older, he learned to master his cruder impulses, but sometimes they got the better of him. As a young man, his favorite, Menshikov, more than once felt the force of Peter's fist on his long face. At a certain banquet a foreign artilleryman, who was a chatterbox and a bore, flaunted his knowledge before Peter without allowing him to put a word in edgewise. Peter kept on listening to the braggart, but finally, unable to bear it any longer, spat straight into the man's face and quietly walked away.

The simplicity of his demeanor and his habitual joviality rendered relations with him as difficult as did his fits of temper and the spells of bad humor, which were announced by convulsions. When these occurred, those about him, noticing the approaching storm, immediately summoned Empress Catherine. She made him sit down, took his head in her hands, and began stroking it gently. He would soon fall asleep, and everyone near the couple held his breath while Catherine clasped the Czar's head in her hands. An hour or two later he would wake up as though nothing had happened. But even when he was not subject to these morbid fits, Peter's lack of delicacy spoiled ease and freedom of intercourse with him. In his good moments he liked to make merry and play pranks, but these often exceeded the bounds of propriety and were even cruel.

On State occasions in summer he liked to see the high society of the capital seated about him on plain wooden benches at rustic tables in the oak grove that he had himself planted in the Summer Garden in front of his palace. He would chat with lay dignitaries about

16

politics and with clerics about Church affairs, and as a genial host took pains to regale his guests. But his hospitality had certain drawbacks. Used to raw vodka, he demanded that his guests, not excepting the ladies, should also drink it. Terror would seize the company when the smell of the liquor filled the place as the Guards appeared in the Garden carrying great tubs of it. Sentries stationed at the exits were under orders not to let anyone out, and majors of the Guard were especially appointed to see that everyone drank the Czar's health. Happy was the man who managed to slip out of the Garden. The ecclesiastics alone, many of them reeking with the smell of horseradish and onions, did not turn their faces from the bitter cup, but sat cheerfully at their tables. On one occasion, some foreigners passing by the Garden during a festival noticed that the churchmen were the most besotted, a fact which amazed a Protestant minister who had not imagined that the Russian clergy would imbibe thus publicly. When in 1721, at a wedding of the elderly widower, Count Yury Trubetzkoy, to a twenty-year-old daughter of the Golovin house, a course was served with side dishes of aspic, Peter ordered the bride's father, who was very fond of this delicacy, to open his mouth, and proceeded to shove chunks of aspic down his throat, and even pried the man's mouth wider when he did not open it wide enough. At the same time the groom's daughter, Princess Cherkasskaya, a very wealthy and fashionable lady, standing behind the chair of her brother, a cultivated youth who was acting as best man, at a sign from the Empress began to tickle him, and he roared like a calf being slaughtered, to the loud amusement of the entire company, the choicest in the capital.

Toward the end of the Swedish War a considerable number of annual court festivals, including the victory celebrations, were instituted, and from 1721 on there was the annual commemoration of the Nystadt Peace that had concluded the hostilities. But Peter particularly liked to make merry on the occasion of a launching: he rejoiced over a new ship as over a newborn child. In those days there was as heavy drinking everywhere in Europe as there is nowadays, and in higher circles, particularly at court, it was perhaps even heavier. In this respect the Petersburg court was not behind its foreign models. Thrifty in everything else, Peter did not spare expense when it came to toasting a newly built craft. The entire *beau monde* of the capital, both men and women, was invited to the festivities on board. It was a drinking bout of truly oceanic proportions, to which could be applied, or from which comes, the saying about a man being "half seas over." They would drink until old man Apraksin, the Lord High Admiral, would begin to shed bitter tears and complain that there he was, in his old age, an orphan, without a mother, without a father, while his Serene Highness, Prince Menshikov, Minister of War, would roll under the table, and Princess Dasha, his wife, would come running from the ladies' quarters, all atremble, and dash water on her insensible spouse and try to resuscitate him by massage. But the orgies did not always end as peacefully as all that. Sometimes Peter would have a fit of temper and run off to the ladies' quarters, forbidding his companions to leave until his return, and indeed placing sentries at the exits. While Catherine was soothing the irritated Czar and getting him off to sleep, and all during his slumbers, the guests kept their seats, drank, and yawned.

The Nystadt Peace was celebrated by a masked ball that lasted for seven days. Peter was beside himself with joy that the long war [it lasted twenty-one years] had come to an end, and, forgetting his age and his ailments, he sang and danced on the tables. The celebration took place in the Senate House. In the midst of the banquet Peter went off to take a nap on his yacht, which was tied up nearby on the Neva, ordering his guests to wait for his return. Although the wine flowed freely and there was noisy jollification, this did not prevent them from feeling bored and getting tired of the interminable and obligatory merrymaking—a heavy fine was imposed on those who failed to attend. Thousands of masks were milling around, drinking and dancing, for an entire week, and people were overjoyed when the festivities came to an end.

These formal entertainments were oppressive and fatiguing enough. Even worse were the carousals, also official, which were improper to the point of obscenity. Perhaps Peter was moved by a need for unbridled diversion after his strenuous labors, perhaps he failed to consider the consequences of his behavior. He sought to give the debauchery a bureaucratic cast and erect it into a permanent institution. It was thus that what was officially styled the Booziest, Craziest, Most Clownish Synod came into exitence. It was presided over by the Grand Clown, who bore the title of Papal Prince or the Most

Reverberant and Most Clownish Patriarch of Moscow, Kokuy, and Yauza.* Under him was a conclave of twelve cardinals, all confirmed drunkards and gluttons, and a large staff of bishops, archimandrites, and other church dignitaries of the same propensities, with utterly unprintable titles. Peter had the rank of Archdeacon. He personally drafted the statutes of the Order, and did so with the same care and thoughtfulness that he devoted to the composition of his State documents. The statutes prescribed to the last detail the manner in which the Papal Prince was to be elected and installed, as well as the procedure of ordaining the various members of the bibulous hierarchy. The first commandment of the Order was to get drunk daily and not to go to bed sober, and its purpose was to glorify Bacchus by excessive drinking. It had its authorized form of worship ("the service of Bacchus and honorific treatment of strong drinks"), its vestments, its prayers and canticles. There were even Most Clownish Bishopesses and Abbesses. As the catechumen in the primitive Church was asked before baptism, "Dost thou believe?" so the candidate for admission to the Order was asked, "Dost thou drink?" Those who sinned by sobriety were excommunicated from all the pothouses of the realm, and heretics who dared to oppose drinking were anathematized. In a word, it was a most indecent parody of the Church hierarchy and the divine service. The pious regarded it as leading to damnation and tantamount to apostasy, while opposition to this infamous travesty was the road to martyrdom.

At Yuletide a crowd of some two hundred people would drive through the streets of Moscow or the new capital in scores of sleighs, burlesquing the celebration of the Nativity, and the performance would last through the night. The procession was headed by the mock patriarch in his prescribed vestments with a tin miter on his head and a scepter in his hand. Behind him at breakneck speed dashed sleighs crammed with other members of the Order bawling songs and hallooing. The heads of the houses the celebrants deigned to visit were obliged to pay for the distinction and to entertain the guests. The amount of liquor consumed on such an occasion, observes a contemporary, was appalling. Again, during the first week in Lent the blasphemous confraternity would get up a procession of penitents: for the edification of the faithful they would parade wear-

* Kokuy—a small town in Siberia; Yauza—a tributary of the Moscow River.—A. Y.

ing sheepskins turned inside out and riding asses or oxen or seated in sleighs drawn by pigs, bears, and goats. In 1699, during Carnival, the Czar concluded a sumptuous court banquet with a service to Bacchus. The mock patriarch [the post was then occupied by Nikita Zotov, the man who had taught Peter his letters] kept drinking and blessing with crossed tobacco pipes the guests who knelt before him, in mockery of the ceremony in which a bishop blesses the congregation with two- and three-branched candlesticks. Then, crosier in hand, the prelate executed a dance. Only one of those present, a foreign envoy, could not endure the spectacle, and withdrew from the gathering of Orthodox clowns.

In parodying the Church ritual Peter and his associates did not revile the Church or indeed the ecclesiastical hierarchy as an institution, but simply vented their spleen on a class, many members of which they found objectionable. It is not surprising that Peter was untroubled about the effects and consequences of the orgies. The reactionary clergy could be unpleasant; it was not dangerous.

The majority of the Church hierarchy deserved the reproach the opponents of reform leveled at Hadrian, the last patriarch [after his death in 1700 his high office remained vacant and was subsequently abolished]; namely, that he knew on which side his bread was buttered, that he lived but to eat and sleep, that his sole concern was to keep his cassock and his white cowl, and that hence he never spoke out against the ungodly. The clergy constituted no serious threat to Peter. The resentment of the masses, among whom it was already being whispered that the throne was occupied by the Antichrist, was a graver matter. Here Peter relied upon the knout and the torture chamber. Such measures were a matter of course in those days. Moreover, Peter's improper diversions were only an exaggeration of a tendency common to the folk. Who does not know the Russian habit of poking fun at sacred objects and garnishing idle banter with a verse from Scripture? Equally familiar is the attitude toward the clergy and Church ritual in popular legend. The clerics had only themselves to blame for this. While they demanded strict outward observance of the Church ritual, they failed to inspire respect for it because they lacked respect for it themselves. Peter resembled his people in this regard: he was devout; he deplored the ignorance of the clergy and the low estate of the Church; he knew and honored the rites; on holidays he would join the ranks of the choristers and mingle his strong voice with theirs, and yet he included in the program of the celebration of the Peace of Nystadt the obscene wedding of the aged Buturlin, who held the post of mock patriarch, to the widow of his predecessor. By order of the Czar, the ceremony took place in the presence of the court in a setting of burlesque solemnity at the Trinity Cathedral. This was not deliberate anticlericalism, but the coarseness of highly stationed merrymakers, symptomatic, it is true, of the serious decline of Church authority.

Nature had not deprived Peter of the ability to enjoy more civilized amusements. He had a normal responsiveness to beauty, and he spent much money and effort in obtaining good paintings and statues from Germany and Italy, thus laying a foundation for the art collection that is now housed in the Hermitage. He had a special predilection for architecture, as is testified by the pleasure palaces that he erected in the suburbs of his capital and for the building of which he imported at great cost eminent masters from the West. Such was for example the celebrated Le Blond, "a veritable marvel," as Peter called him, whom he lured from the French court with the offer of an enormous salary. The Peterhof palace, *Mon Plaisir*, with the fine carvings that embellish its study, its splendid view of the sea, and its shady gardens, which was designed by that architect, elicited the praise of many foreign visitors.

Not that Peter was an admirer of the classical style. What he looked for in art was something cheerful and enlivening. His Peterhof palace was decorated with admirable Flemish paintings of seascapes and rustic scenes, mostly in a jovial vein. Peter had an appreciation of landscape, especially if the sea figured in it. He squandered large sums on his suburban palace, with its artificial terraces, cascades, fountains, and flower gardens. He had a strong aesthetic sense, but it was limited to certain kinds of art, as might be expected of a man of his character and habits. Having the skilled craftsman's sharp eye for details and his ability to estimate distances precisely, he possessed a keen sense of form and symmetry. The plastic arts had a particular attraction for him, and he enjoyed poring over complicated blueprints; but he confessed that he did not care for music, and at a ball he was irked by the orchestra.

At times, serious talk was heard at the boisterous gatherings of

Peter and his boon companions. As the wars went on and as domestic reforms developed, Peter and his co-workers more often gave thought to the meaning of their labors. Such conversations afford us a closer view of the men, and mitigate the unfavorable impression created by their intemperate and disorderly assemblies. While the tobacco smoke billowed and the glasses clinked, political ideas were set forth which showed these leaders in a happier light. On one occasion, in 1722, having tossed off a number of glasses of Hungarian wine, Peter grew chatty with the group of foreigners whom he was entertaining. He spoke of the first years of his reign when he had had to create a regular army and navy and at the same time instruct his coarse and idle people in the sciences and implant in them the sentiments of valor, loyalty, honor. All this, he said, had cost him a terrible effort, but now, glory be to God, the critical period was over and he could take things more easily, and he added that in order to know his people, a ruler must spare no pains.

He was talking of things that he had long been pondering. He seems to have originated the image of himself that posterity continued to elaborate. According to his contemporaries, he appears to have thought of himself as a sculptor under whose hands a human figure was emerging from the crude block of marble that was Russia. One is led to believe that by the end of the Swedish War, Peter and his associates were aware that in spite of the military successes and internal reforms achieved, their task was still unfinished, and they were occupied with the question of what remained to be done. . . . [But time was running out for the Czar: he then had only four years left him.]

Peter spent his life in ceaseless and intense physical activity, and was constantly assailed by a stream of external impressions. And so he became alert to stimuli from without, and developed an amazing capacity for observation and a strikingly practical turn of mind. He took no interest in general ideas; in everything, he grasped the details more quickly than the general plan; he was more keenly aware of ends and means than of consequences; he was a doer, not a thinker. These aspects of his character were reflected in his conduct both as man and ruler. He grew up in an environment unfavorable to the development of a statesman: the court and the family circle of Czar Alexis were made up of nonentities and were dominated by feuds and petty interests. Court intrigues and palace revolutions were Peter's early political schooling. Because his sister's malice forced him out of this milieu, he broke away from the political notions that belonged to it. In itself this break was no great loss to Peter: political thinking in the Kremlin in the seventeenth century was a hodgepodge of ceremonial usages and seignorial habits inherited from the former dynasty, and of delusions and ambiguities that prevented the czars of the new dynasty from understanding their position in the realm. Peter's misfortune was that he was left without any political outlook at all, but merely with a vague and hollow sense that his power, though it might be threatened, had no limits.

For a long time his mind remained a vacuum, politically speaking. The rough manual work with which he had occupied himself from boyhood on, interfered with reflection and drew his thoughts away from the subjects essential to a political education. Peter was developing into a ruler without the rules that spiritualize and justify power, a ruler wanting in elementary political concepts, and not subject to any restraints imposed by society. Foreigners who came in contact with the twenty-five-year-old Czar were struck by the fact that he combined moral instability and lack of judgment with the extraordinary abilities and skill of a technician, and it seemed to them that nature had fitted him to be a good carpenter rather than a great sovereign. Deprived of moral guidance in his impressionable years, and with a constitution early undermined by physical excesses, incredibly coarsened by his upbringing and way of life and brutalized by the experiences of his youth, Peter was at the same time extraordinarily energetic, alert, and observant. These natural gifts somewhat compensated for the defects and vices bred in him by his environment. Bishop Burnet noted that as early as 1698 Peter was making an earnest effort to overcome his passion for drink. No matter how little attention he paid to the political order and the manners and customs of the West, he could not help noticing that the Western nations were growing stronger and better educated through means other than the knout and the torture chamber, while the cruel lessons driven home to him by the Turks and the Swedes at Azov, at Narva, and on the Pruth gradually forced on him the awareness of his unperparedness as a statesman, and this led him to undertake his political self-education. He began to see the great gaps in his training and to think about his empire and his people, law and justice, the sovereign and his obligations. He was capable of conceiving his duty as a ruler to be that of selfless service, but he could not break his gross habits, and if the misfortunes of his early years helped him to escape from the political affectations of the Kremlin, he could not rid himself of what was in his blood: the instinct of arbitrary power, the sole guiding principle of Muscovite policy. To the end of his days he was unable to understand either the logic of his people's history or the physiology of their life. He should not be blamed, however, for this failure; it was shared even by that statesmanlike sage Leibnitz, who was his counselor. The latter believed, and apparently assured Peter, that it would be the easier to implant the sciences in Russia, the less ready the country was to receive them.

All Peter's activities as a reformer were guided by belief in the necessity for and the omnipotence of coercion by authority: he hoped to force upon the people the blessings they lacked; he believed that it was possible to divert the stream of national life from the bed it had shaped for itself in the course of history and to drive it into a new channel. And so, while concerned for the welfare of his people, he bore hard upon them, taxing their strength to the utmost; he spent blood and treasure recklessly, prodigally. He was an honorable and sincere man, severe and exacting with himself, just and benevolent toward others; but he was accustomed to dealing with materials and tools rather than with human beings, and therefore he treated human beings as if they were tools. He knew how to make use of them; he estimated shrewdly what they were good for; but he did not like to, or know how to, enter into their situation or to husband their strength; he lacked his father's sympathetic nature. Peter knew people, but he was not able to understand them, or he did not always wish to do so. This aspect of his character is reflected in his relations with his family. The man who had sufficient knowledge of his empire to rebuild it from top to bottom was ignorant of the small corner that was nearest him: his own home, and he lived there as a guest. He did not get on with his first wife; he had reasons to complain of his second; and he was completely at odds with his son, failing to guard him from hostile influences, which led to the Czarevich's death, and thus endangered the very existence of the dynasty.

And so Peter turned out to be quite different from his predecessors, although one can recognize a kinship between him and them, although he did not break the chain of historic continuity. Peter was a great manager, who understood the economic interests of his domain better than anything else and who was particularly concerned about the sources of State revenue. His predecessors, the czars of the Rurik dynasty and the early Romanovs, had likewise been excellent managers, but they had been stay-at-homes, who did not soil their hands with toil, delegating it to others. Peter was a rolling stone, a self-taught man, a jack-of-all-trades, a czar who was a laborer.

MIKHAIL (MIKHAILO) LOMONOSOV
(1711–1765)

The son of an illiterate peasant who was a well-to-do White Sea fisherman, Lomonosov grew up to be a veritable "universal man," the type that was the glory of the Renaissance. He broke fresh ground in, or made significant contributions to, numerous branches of science and technology, and he was also an economist, a historian, a grammarian, a rhetorician. A pioneer in fashioning modern literary Russian, he formulated the principles of Russian prosody, composed tragedies in verse, wrote odes, chiefly for court occasions, also devising fireworks for them, and he produced pictures in mosaic. Admitted to the Academy of Sciences at the age of thirty-one, he added much to its luster. The first Russian university, which was established in Moscow, owes its existence to his initiative. The letters below offer a glimpse of the man. The dates are Old Style.

Five Letters

TO IVAN IVANOVICH SHUVALOV

This communication is addressed to the statesman and Maecenas who is reputed to have been Empress Elizabeth's lover. The first rector of the University of Moscow, and for some years the president of the newly established Academy of Arts, he was the patron of Lomonosov during the last fifteen years of his life. The Empress had made a generous gift of land and serfs to Lomonosov (for details see the letter to Euler), and Shuvalov had evidently expressed apprehension, his or another's, that this new wealth might temper his protégé's ardor for the sciences:

MY DEAR SIR, IVAN IVANOVICH!

Your Excellency's gracious letter assures me, to my great joy, of your unchanged favor, which for many years I have counted as a great blessing.

Could the sublime generosity of our incomparable Empress, which

I owe to your fatherly concern for me, weaken my love and zeal for the sciences, if the extreme poverty which I voluntarily endured for their sake could not turn me from the pursuit of learning? Your Excellency, do not account me self-vaunting if I make bold to speak in my defense.

While I was studying at the Spassky School,* I was subject on all sides to forces that tended to pull me away from learning, forces that at the age at which I was then, were well-nigh insuperable. On the one hand, my father was saying that I, his only son, had abandoned the property, large by local standards, that he had accumulated for me by sweating blood, and that, after his death, would be pillaged by strangers. On the other hand, there was my unspeakable poverty: with a daily allowance of three kopecks, all I could have by way of food was half a kopeck's worth of bread and half a kopeck's worth of kvass; the rest had to buy paper, shoes, and other necessities. I lived like this for five years, yet did not forsake study. On the one hand, they wrote me that, knowing my father to be well-to-do, substantial householders at home were ready to marry off their daughters to me— I had had such offers before I left the village; on the other hand, my schoolmates, little boys, would shout and point their fingers at me: "Look at that blockhead, come to study Latin at twenty!" Soon thereafter I was transferred to St. Petersburg and then sent abroad,† my allowance being forty times what it had been previously. Far from drawing me away from study, this proportionately increased my eagerness for it, though there is a limit to my strength.

I most humbly beg Your Excellency to rest assured that I shall do everything within my power to allay the anxiety of those who, knowing my zeal, urge me not to overexert myself, and, further, that I shall labor to bring shame upon those who speak ill of me, and teach them not to measure the strength of others by the yardstick they use for their own. They should remember, too, that the Muses are not wenches who can be raped at any time. They fall in love with whomever they please.

If there still be such as hold that a man of learning must be poor, I offer them the example of Diogenes, who lived with dogs in a

---

* This so-called Slavo-Greco-Latin Academy was attached to a Moscow monastery.—A. Y.

† After a year at the secondary school attached to the Academy of Sciences, Lomonosov, in 1736, entered the University of Marburg.—A. Y.

27

barrel and who bequeathed a few witticisms to his countrymen to swell their pride; and, on the other hand, the examples of Newton, of the wealthy Lord Boyle, who achieved all his glory in the sciences through the use of great sums of money, of [Christian] Wolff, who, by lectures and through gifts, accumulated over 500,000 [thalers?] and besides won the title of Baron; of [Hans] Sloan, in England, who left so great a library that no private person was in a position to buy it, and hence Parliament paid twenty thousand pounds for it.

I shall not fail to carry out all your commands, and I remain, with profound esteem, Your Excellency's most humble servant,

MIKHAILO LOMONOSOV

St. Petersburg, May 10, 1753

TO THE SAME

Following in the footsteps of Benjamin Franklin, Lomonosov and the other academician mentioned below, Georg Wilhelm Richmann, were experimenting with atmospheric electricity:

My dear sir, Ivan Ivanovich!

Consider it a miracle that I am now writing to Your Excellency, for the dead do not write. I still do not know if I am alive or dead; at least I have doubts on the subject. The fact is that Professor Richmann was killed by a thunderbolt in exactly the same circumstances in which I was at the time. This day, July 26, between noon and 1:00 P.M. a stormcloud rose in the North. It thundered terrifically, but there was not a drop of rain. I looked at my storm machine and saw no trace of electric force. But just as the food was placed on the table, I did notice that the wire emitted electric sparks, and by that time my wife and others had come into the room. Both I and they kept touching the wire and the rod attached to it, for I wanted to have witnesses of the varied colors of the fire, about which the late Professor Richmann had disagreed with me. Suddenly there was a violent peal of thunder at the very moment when my hand touched the iron, and sparks crackled. Everyone ran away from me, and my wife begged me to step aside. Curiosity kept me at the machine another two or three minutes, until I was told that the cabbage soup would get cold, and besides, the electrical force had almost spent itself.

I had not been at table more than a few minutes when suddenly the door was opened by the late Richmann's servant, who was in tears and breathless with terror. I thought that someone had attacked him while he was on his way to my house. "The professor," he was barely able to bring out, "has been struck by a thunderbolt." Upon making my way to his house with the utmost speed, I saw him lying lifeless. The poor widow and her mother were as pale as he. I was so overcome by my own narrow escape, by the pallor of his countenance, by the weeping of his wife and children that I could not utter a word as I looked at the face of the friend with whom only an hour before I had sat at the Academy and discussed our impending public report. The first discharge from the strip of iron with the attached thread struck his head, and a cherry-colored spot was visible on his forehead; the thunder's electrical force had passed through him from head to foot and into the boards of the floor. His foot and toes were blue, and the shoe was torn but not burned.

We tried to restore the circulation of the blood, because he was still warm, but his head was injured, and there was no hope. And so, by an experiment with lamentable consequences he has established that the thunder's electrical force can be deflected onto an iron rod, but one which must stand in an empty spot, where the thunder may strike where it will. Mr. Richmann died a beautiful death, in the execution of his professional duties. His memory will live always. [The writer then implores his patron to secure for the widow, who was left with three small children, a pension that would enable her to educate her five-year-old son, "so that he may become a lover of the sciences like his father."] Meanwhile, that this accident may not be used as an argument against the pursuit of the sciences, I beg Your Excellency to favor them, as well as

Your Excellency's most humble servant, who writes in tears,

MIKHAILO LOMONOSOV

St. Petersburg
July 26, 1753

TO LEONARD EULER

At the time, the great mathematician was teaching in the Berlin Academy of Sciences, to which he had been attached since 1741, when he left the Russian Academy. After opening the letter, written in Latin, with apologies for his failure to keep up his part in the correspondence, Lomonosov proceeds:

For three years I was wholly absorbed in physico-chemical experiments relating to the theory of colors. And my labors have not been fruitless, for, aside from the results I obtained in dissolving and precipitating minerals, nearly 3,000 experiments with the production of colored glass not only yielded an enormous amount of material for the construction of a true theory of colors but also led me to engage in the making of mosaics. The sample that I prepared, namely, an image of the Holy Virgin, I presented to the Empress on her birthday in 1752. She was pleased with it, and this encouraged me further. On December 16 of that year, by order of the Senate, I was granted the exclusive privilege of manufacturing objects made of colored glass for a period of thirty years, and I was given 4,000 rubles for the establishment of a glass factory. Furthermore, the Empress' generosity surpassed all my hopes and merits. On March 16, 1753, the most gracious Empress presented me with 226 peasants and 25,000 acres, comprising fields, pastures, fisheries, streams, and four villages, one of them bordering on the sea, within forty to fifty miles of Petersburg. A house and a glass factory have been erected on the property, and now I am building a dam, a mill, and a sawmill; over this rises a meteorological observatory, a description of which I shall publish, with God's help, next summer.

And so you understand, O most celebrated man, that it was not because I had cooled toward you that I interrupted our correspondence for so long. I have always prized our friendship very highly. And so pray accept in a calm and friendly fashion the fitful character of our correspondence, and consider also this extenuating circumstance: here I am forced to be not only a poet, orator, chemist, and physicist, but also to devote myself wholeheartedly to history. Last spring I spent some time in Moscow waiting for the deed conveying the gift to be signed, and the Most August Empress, having honored me with a most gracious audience, remarked, among other things, that she would be pleased if I were to write a history of the Fatherland in my style. Therefore, when, on my return to Petersburg, I was composing my recent oration ["On Aerial Phenomena Caused by the Electric Force"], in the very process of work I often caught myself wandering mentally among Russian antiquities. For that reason I have omitted not a few arguments in favor of the contention that in a complete calm the upper layer of the atmosphere not infrequently must descend to the lower. Nor did I touch upon many matters that would have demolished [Newton's] theory that comets' tails consist of vapor. I confess that I have omitted all this so that, in attacking the writings of great men, I should not appear to be indulging in vainglory rather than seeking the truth. For the same reason I have long refrained from offering my thoughts about monads to the erudite world for discussion. I firmly believe that my arguments would completely destroy this mystical doctrine, but I do not wish to sadden the old age of a man whose kindnesses toward me I cannot forget;* otherwise I would not be afraid to incense the monadist hornets throughout Germany.

Farewell, incomparable man, and do not desist from honoring me with your favor and friendship.

MIKHAILO LOMONOSOV

12

Petropolis, Feb. 23, 1754

TO IVAN IVANOVICH SHUVALOV

This communication, somewhat abridged, has to do with the final incident in the long-standing feud between Lomonosov and his former disciple, the playwright and poet Alexander Sumarokov (1718–1777). The latter was ranked by some of his contemporaries above Corneille, and likened to Racine and Shakespeare, while Pushkin dismissed him as "a feeble pupil of foreign masters." Lomonosov's "rightful requests" were for a higher rank and the vice-presidency of the Academy of Sciences. Ivan Taubert was an Academician, and so was Gerhard Friedrich Miller. His duties included editing the Academy's monthly periodical.

MY DEAR SIR, IVAN IVANOVICH!

No one has ever hurt my feeling more than Your Excellency. You summoned me today, and I had thought that this meant a favorable response to my rightful requests. Suddenly I heard the words, "Make your peace with Sumarokov"; that is, do something ludicrous and shameful, form a bond with a man who is avoided by all, who does nothing but abuse everyone and sing his own praises and who sets his poor doggerel above all human knowledge. He berates Taubert and Miller only because they do not print his works, and not

---

* The reference is to Christian Wolff, Lomonosov's teacher at Marburg, who died two months later, at the age of seventy-five.—A. Y.

because this is against the public interest. I ignore all his malice and do not crave any vengeance—God has not given me a vindictive heart. Only, I can by no means be on friendly terms with him, having learned from experience what it is to [relieve yourself] in nettles. Not wishing to offend you in the presence of many gentlemen, I acceded to this request of yours, but, I assure you, this will not happen again. And if, despite my zeal in your service, you will be wroth, then I shall rely on the help of the All-High, who has been my protector and has never abandoned me when I shed tears before him in a just cause. Your Excellency, now having a chance to serve the fatherland by aiding the sciences, you can do better than seek to make peace between me and Sumarokov. I do not wish him ill. I have no thought of vengeance for the wrongs done me. I merely beg the Lord to keep me from having dealings with him. If he has any knowledge and skill, let him benefit the fatherland; I too am ready to exert myself as far as my small talent allows. But I cannot, nor do I wish to, have any traffic with a man who denigrates all branches of knowledge of which he knows nothing. And here is my true opinion, which I offer you in cold blood: I do not wish to play the fool at the table of the noble and the wealthy, indeed even for the Lord God Himself, as long as he does not take away the intelligence which He has given me. . . .

Your Excellency's humbled and obedient servant,

MIKHAILO LOMONOSOV

January 19, 1761

TO M. V. GOLOVINA

The sister to whom Lomonosov was writing a month before his death about her eight-year-old son was a simple woman who had married within her class. The boy eventually studied under Euler, and became a mathematician.

MY DEAR SISTER, MARIA VASILYEVNA, may you live long, with husband and children.

I am very glad to tell you that Mishenka has reached St. Petersburg in good health and that he reads and writes unusually well for a child. As soon as he arrived, a new French suit was made for him, shirts were sewn, and he is dressed from head to foot, and wears his hair the way we do, so that he would not be recognized at Matigory [his native village]. What surprises me most is that he is not bashful and that he has at once become accustomed to us and to our food, as though he had always lived with us, and he shows no sign of being homesick or crying. The day before yesterday I placed him in the school that is attached to the Academy of Sciences, and of which I am in charge. This school is attended by forty children, whose fathers are nobles or at any rate not peasants; there he will board and study under proper supervision, and on holidays and Sundays he will have dinner and supper in my house and stay overnight. I have ordered that he should be taught Latin, arithmetic, penmanship, and dancing. Last evening I visited the school purposely to see him having supper with the other scholars and to find out who is his roommate. Believe me, dear sister, that I look out for him as a good uncle and godfather should. My good woman, too, and my daughter, love him and provide him with everything that he needs. I have no doubt that study will make him happy. And with true love I remain

your brother,

MIKHAILO LOMONOSOV

March 2, 1765
St. Petersburg

I often see the governor of your province here, and I have asked him, for friendship's sake, not to refuse you his favors. In case of need or even if there is no need, you may pay your respects to His Excellency, either your husband or you yourself.

My wife and daughter greet you.

SERGEY AKSAKOV
(1791–1859)

Born into an old, modestly circum-
stanced family of landed gentry, Aksakov grew to be a man of moderate
views. In his youth and early middle age he held minor government posts,
that of censor among them, while also dabbling in literature. During his
last two decades, spent on his estate near Moscow, he took time off from
the occupations of a gentleman farmer to write his memoirs in two volumes, which brought him enduring fame. Leaning on his own recollections and on stories heard from his parents, he chronicled candidly the
lives of three generations of Aksakovs, calling them Bagrovs. The pages
that follow are a chapter from A *Family Chronicle* (1856), translated into
English as A *Russian Gentleman*. The place described in this account is
a newly colonized section of southeastern Russia, the time, the early years
of the reign of Catherine II.

FROM A Family Chronicle
(ONE OF GRANDFATHER'S GOOD DAYS)

At the end of June the weather was very hot. After a stifling night a
fresh breeze, such as always drops when the sun grows hot, set in
from the east. At sunrise Grandfather woke up. It was particularly
hot in his bedroom, because it was small and, though the old-
fashioned window with its small panes was raised as high as it
would go, there was a curtain of loosely woven homespun cloth
around the bed. This precaution was essential: without a curtain the
wicked mosquitoes would have kept him awake and worn him out.
They flew about in swarms, each thrusting its long sting through the
thin fabric, and kept up their tiresome serenade all night long. It
sounds absurd, but it would not be right to conceal the fact that I
like the shrill voice and even the sting of the mosquitoes: they con-
jure up for me the sultry summer, the glorious sleepless nights, the
banks of the Buguruslan, overgrown with green bushes and loud

34

with the song of the nightingales. I remember the thrill of my young heart and the sweet unaccountable sadness, for which I would now give all that remains of life's dying fire.

Grandfather woke up, wiped the sweat off his high forehead with a hot hand, raised the curtain, put out his head, and burst into laughter. His two servants, Vanka and Nikanorka, were snoring away, stretched out on the floor in an attitude at once ludicrous and picturesque. "How they snore, the dog's litter!" he said, and smiled again. Stepan Mikhailovich was something of an enigma: you might have expected that such a vigorous verbal opening would be followed by a jab in the sleepers' ribs with his cudgel (it always stood by his bed), a kick, or even a greeting with a chair. But not so: Grandfather had smiled on waking, and remained in this mood throughout the day. He got up quietly, crossed himself once or twice, thrust his bare feet into rust-colored leather slippers and then, wearing only a shift of coarse linen woven by the serfs—Grandmother would not let him have shirts of fine linen—he went out on the porch, where the pleasant morning freshness enveloped him.

Just now I said that Arina Vasilyevna would not let her husband have shirts of fine linen, and the reader will rightly remark that this is out of keeping with the relationship between the two. But I can do nothing about it—I apologize, but such was the case: the woman's will triumphed over the man's, as always! Pummeled more than once because of the coarse linen, Grandmother persisted in supplying him with it, and in the end succeeded in overcoming the old man's aversion to it. On one occasion he resorted to a heroic measure: he chopped up all the objectionable linen with an ax on the threshold of his room, in spite of the fact that Grandmother howled and implored him to give *her* a beating rather than destroy his own belongings. . . . But even this measure failed. Coarse linen reappeared, and the old man submitted. I apologize for having interrupted my narrative in order to refute the reader's imaginary remark.

Without disturbing anyone, Grandfather fetched a felt mat kept in the storeroom, spread it out on the top step of the porch and, as was his custom, sat down to watch the sun rise. Daybreak fills any man's heart with gladness without his realizing it, as it were. Grandfather felt added joy as he looked at his farmyard, already fully provided with all the necessary farm buildings. True, the yard was not fenced in, and the livestock, turned out of the peasants' yards before being herded together and driven out to graze, would visit it in passing, as happened on this morning and as always happened in the evening. Several muddy pigs were rubbing and scratching themselves against the very porch on which Grandfather was sitting, and, grunting the while, were feasting on crayfish shells and all manner of leavings which had been unceremoniously thrown out close to the steps. Cows and sheep, too, wandered in and, of course, left unsightly tokens behind them. But Grandfather found nothing unpleasant about it. On the contrary, he feasted his eyes on the healthy cattle, seeing it as a sure sign of the well-being of his peasants. Soon the loud cracking of the cowherd's long whip drove the visitors away.

Now the servants began to wake up. Spiridon, the sturdy stableman, led out three colts, one after another, two skewbald and one bay, tied them to a post, rubbed them down, and then exercised them on a long halter, while Grandfather admired their points. In anticipation he also admired the stock he hoped to raise from them—an enterprise in which, indeed, he fully succeeded. Then the old housekeeper emerged from the cellar where she slept, and went down to the river to wash. She sighed and groaned, according to her inveterate habit, then, turning to the east, said a prayer, and proceeded to clean and rinse pots and dishes. Swallows and martins twittered gaily as they circled in the sky; quails called jerkily and loudly in the fields; the songs of larks reverberated in the air; corncrakes, straining their voices, vocalized hoarsely in the bushes. The whistling of swamp hens, the mating calls and bleatings of snipe came from the marsh nearby; warblers mocked the nightingales. From behind the hill, the sun rolled out—a bright ball! Smoke rose above the peasants' huts, its blue columns bent in the breeze, as though a row of riverboats had hoisted their flags; and the peasants were making for the fields.

Grandfather now felt the urge to wash in cold water and then have his tea. He roused his two servants from their slumbers. They jumped up in fright, but their master's cheerful voice soon reassured them.

"Vanka, I'll wash now!" he declared. "Nikanorka, wake up Aksyutka and the mistress, and have them make tea!"

There was no need to repeat these orders: clumsy Vanka dashed to the spring, carrying a bright copper basin, while nimble Nikanorka roused homely young Aksyutka, who, straightening her kerchief, waked Arina Vasilyevna, her stout old mistress. In a few minutes the entire household was up and everyone knew that the old master had got out of bed on the right side. A quarter of an hour later a table, covered with a white homespun cloth with a pattern in it, stood near the porch, and Aksyutka was bustling about the table, where a samovar in the form of a large copper teapot was boiling. Arina Vasilyevna greeted her husband, not moaning and groaning as she found it necessary to do on certain mornings, but in a loud, cheerful voice, and inquired how he had slept and what dreams he had had. Grandfather affectionately reciprocated the salutation of his spouse, calling her Arisha. He never kissed her hand, but would give her his own to kiss as a token of favor. Grandmother blossomed out and, her obesity and clumsiness vanishing, took on a youthful look. Forthwith she fetched a stool and sat down on the porch beside Grandfather, which she dared not do if he failed to greet her cordially. "Come, Arisha, let's have tea together," said Stepan Mikhailovich, "before it gets hot. The night was stifling, but I slept so soundly that I had no dreams. And how did you sleep?" Such a question was a sign of signal attention, and Grandmother hastened to reply that when Stepan Mikhailovich had a good night she too slept well, but that Tanyusha* had been restless all night. Tanyusha was the youngest daughter, and, as often happens, the old man loved her more than his other daughters. He was disturbed by the report, and ordered them not to rouse her but let her sleep until she woke up by herself. Tatyana had been awakened, together with Alexandra and Yelizaveta, and was already dressed, but no one dared to apprise Grandfather of the fact. Tanyusha quickly undressed, got into bed, had the shutters of her room closed and, though she could not get to sleep, lay in the dark for nearly two hours, and Grandfather was pleased that she had had a good sleep. The only son, who was nine,† was never wakened early.

The two elder daughters appeared at once. Affectionately, Grandfather gave them his hand to kiss and called them by their pet names. They were rather clever girls, and Alexandra combined cunning with her father's vivacity and violent temper, but lacked his good qualities.

* A pet name for Tatyana.—A. Y.
† The memoirist's father.—A. Y.

Grandmother, a simple soul, was entirely at the mercy of her daughters. If she sometimes dared to be crafty in dealing with her husband, it was because they put her up to it. Her stratagems rarely succeeded, because she was clumsy and because Grandfather saw through her. He knew that his daughters were ready to deceive him at the slightest opportunity, and only out of boredom or to protect his peace of mind did he allow them to think—when he was in a good mood—that they were making a dupe of him. But in his first fit of temper he would tell them what he thought of their behavior in the plainest terms, and sometimes even gave them a beating. Being true descendants of Eve, they were not discouraged. When the hour of wrath was over, and the clouds had lifted from their father's face, they resumed their sly schemes, and not seldom succeeded in them.

When he had had his tea and chatted about this and that with his family, Grandfather got ready to drive out to the fields. He had previously ordered Vanka to hitch up his horse, and the old bay gelding was already standing at the porch, harnessed to a long peasant carriage, very comfortable, with sides made of netted rope and a plank covered with felt for a seat. Spiridon, the coachman, was attired very simply: he was barefoot and wore only a long shirt with a narrow red woolen belt, from which hung a key and a copper comb. On a previous trip Spiridon had driven out bareheaded, but Grandfather had scolded him for it, and now he wore some sort of cap, woven out of broad strips of bast. Grandfather laughed at his headgear, put on his *field* caftan of unbleached linen homespun and a cap, and got into the carriage, spreading under him his long coat, which he took in case of rain. Spiridon, too, folded his coat thrice and placed it on his seat. The coat was made of peasant cloth dyed bright red with madder, which grew profusely in the fields. So much of it was used by the Bagrovo house serfs that they were called "madderites" by the neighbors. I myself heard the nickname fifteen years after Grandfather's death.

In the fields he found everything to his satisfaction. He examined the rye, which was shedding its blossoms and stood like a wall as high as a man. A gentle breeze raised violet-blue waves on it, now lighter, now darker in the sun. The sight of such a field gladdened the master's heart! Grandfather inspected the young oats, the emmer, and all the spring crops. Then he made for the fallow and had himself driven back and forth over those acres. That was his way of testing the quality of the plowing: any spot that had not been touched by the plow jolted the light carriage, and if Grandfather was out of sorts, he stuck a stick or a twig in that spot, sent for the *starosta* [village elder] and immediately meted out punishment. But this time all went well. Grandfather may have encountered bad spots, but he did not notice, or chose not to notice them. He also drove out to the hayfields on the steppe, where he admired the thick, tall grass that was to be mown in a few days. He paid a visit to the peasants' fields as well, to find out for himself who had a good crop and who had not, and he tested their fallow land. He noticed everything and forgot nothing. Driving past a field long untilled, and seeing a patch of wild strawberries nearly ripe, he alighted and, with Vanka's help, picked many big delicious berries and took them home for his Arisha. In spite of the heat, he stayed out until almost midday.

As soon as Grandfather's carriage was seen descending the hill, dinner was set on the table, and the entire family waited for the master on the porch. "Well, Arisha," he said cheerfully, "what crops God is giving us! Great is the Lord's mercy! And here are some strawberries for you." Grandmother melted with joy. "The berries are almost ripe," he went on; "starting tomorrow, send people out to pick them." As he spoke, he walked into the hall. The smell of hot cabbage soup, wafted from the dining room, assailed his nostrils. "Ah, it's ready!" said Grandfather, even more cheerfully, "Thanks!" And, without going to his own chamber, he went straight into the dining room and sat down at table.

I must say that this was his custom: whenever he returned from the fields, early or late, dinner had to be on the table, and Heaven help the household if they failed to notice his return and serve the meal on time. There were occasions when such a blunder had sad consequences. But on this blessed day, everything went off without a hitch. Nikolka, a strapping house serf, took his stand behind Grandfather with a whole birch bough in order to keep the flies off him. Hot cabbage soup, which a Russian will not refuse in the sultriest weather, Grandfather scooped up with a wooden spoon, for a silver one would burn his lips. The cabbage soup was followed by iced fish salad, with vegetables, transparent cured filet of sturgeon, salted sturgeon, yellow as wax, crayfish, as well as other light dishes. All this was washed down with iced kvass and home-brewed beer. The meal was a jolly one, with much talking, joking, and laughing, but there had been dinners eaten in dreadful silence and mute expectation of a fit of temper. All the servants' little sons and daughters knew that the old master was having his midday meal in a cheerful mood, and they crowded into the dining room, hoping for bounty. They were not disappointed. Grandfather was generous, for five times the amount of food that the family could eat had been prepared.

Immediately after dinner he lay down to sleep. The flies were chased out of the bed curtain, it was drawn round him, and the edges were tucked under the mattress. Soon mighty snoring announced that the master was fast asleep. All the members of the household retired to their quarters to rest. Having gorged themselves on the remains of the master's meal, Vanka and Nikanorka stretched out on the floor in the hall at the very door of Grandfather's bedroom. They had slept before dinner too, but now again dozed off at once, but the stuffy air and the hot sunlight that streamed through the window soon wakened them. Their throats parched by sleep and heat, they were anxious to cool them with the master's iced beer, and here is the trick the bold loafers played: they got hold of Grandfather's dressing gown and nightcap that were lying on a chair near the door, which had been left ajar. Nikanorka put them on and sat down on the porch, while Vanka ran to the cellar with a jug, roused the housekeeper, who, like everyone in the house, was fast asleep, and demanded some cold beer for the master, who had waked up. When she expressed some doubt as to whether the master was up, Vanka pointed to the figure in the dressing gown and nightcap sitting on the porch. The beer was drawn, ice added, and Vanka promptly dashed off with the booty. The two emptied the jug, sharing the contents in a brotherly fashion, replaced the dressing gown and nightcap, and waited a whole hour for the master to wake up.

He opened his eyes in a frame of mind even more cheerful than in the morning, and his first words were, "Cold beer!" The scamps took fright. Vanka hurried off to the housekeeper, who guessed at once that the servants themselves had drunk the contents of the first jug. She produced the beverage, but followed the servant to the porch where the real master sat in his dressing gown. The deception was uncovered at once, and, trembling with fear, Vanka and Nikanorka fell at their master's feet. And what do you think Grandfather did? He burst out laughing, sent for his wife and daughters, and, still laughing boisterously, told them of his servants' escapade. The poor devils recovered their composure, and one of them even grinned. Grandfather noticed this and very nearly waxed angry. He began to frown, but the jolly day had left his heart so serene that the wrinkles on his forehead were smoothed out and, merely casting a threatening glance, he said:

"Well, God will forgive you this time, but if it happens again . . ." There was no need to finish the sentence.

It is to be marveled at that the servants of a master so furiously hot-tempered and so cruel in his fits of anger would dare play such an impudent prank. But I noticed many times in the course of my life that the domestics of the strictest masters were capable of perpetrating the most daring pranks. Grandfather had other experiences of the like kind. One day the same Vanka, while sweeping his master's bedroom before making the bed, was tempted by the soft down of the featherbed and the pillows, and decided to have a taste of luxury. He lay down on the master's bed and dropped off. Grandfather himself found him there fast asleep, and—only burst into laughter. True, he gave him a hard one with his cudgel, but he did this just for fun, to amuse himself at Vanka's fright. . . .

He woke up at five in the afternoon and, after drinking cold beer, asked for tea, in spite of the burning heat, for he believed that a hot drink made sultry weather more tolerable. But first he went down to bathe in the cool waters of the Buguruslan, which flowed past the windows of the house. On his return he found his whole family waiting for him at the tea table, which was set in the shade with the same samovar and the same Aksyutka. Having had his fill of his favorite sweat-producing beverage, with heavy cream and the browned skin of milk, Grandfather proposed that the entire family make a pleasure trip to the mill. Naturally, all welcomed the suggestion with joy, and Alexandra and Tatyana took fishing rods along, for they were fond of angling.

Two long carriages were instantly made ready. Grandfather and Grandmother seated themselves in one of these, placing between them their sole heir, the precious scion of their ancient noble line; the other carriage was occupied by their three daughters and the lad,

Nikolashka, who was to dig for worms on the dam and bait the hooks for the young ladies. When they reached the mill, a bench was brought out for Grandmother, and she seated herself in the shade of the mill barn, not far from the millpond, where her younger daughters were getting ready to fish. And Yelizaveta, the eldest, partly because of her interest in such matters and partly to please her father, went with him to inspect the mill and the mortar. The little boy now watched his sisters fishing—he himself was not allowed to fish in deep places—now played beside his mother, who did not take her eyes off him for fear that the child would tumble into the water.

Both pairs of millstones were working, one husking wheat for the master's table, the other grinding a neighbor's rye, and millet was being pounded in the mortar. Grandfather was an expert in everything concerning a farm. He knew all about the construction and working of a mill, and explained it all in detail to his alert and intelligent daughter. He instantly perceived all the defects in the machinery or in the position of the millstones. He ordered one of them lowered half a notch, and the flour came out finer, to the customer's great satisfaction. When he came to the other stone, his ear detected that one of the cogs of the gear was wearing out. He ordered the stream turned off, and the miller jumped down, examined and felt the gear, and said:

"You're quite right, Stepan Mikhailovich, sir, one cog is a little worn."

" 'A little,' you say," Grandfather retorted, though without displeasure; "if I hadn't come, the gear would have broken this very night."

"My fault, Stepan Mikhailovich, I've been remiss," said the miller.

"Well, God will forgive you. Get a new gear, and replace the cog in the old one, and mind the new cog is of the same size as the others—that's the main thing!"

A new gear, fitted and tested beforehand, was brought. It was put in to replace the old one, was greased with tar where necessary, the stream was turned on, not all at once, but gradually, also by Grandfather's order—and the millstone began to hum, grind smoothly and evenly, with no interruptions or knocks. Then Grandfather and his daughter went over to the mortar. He took a handful of pounded millet, spread out his palm, blew the chaff from it, and said to the customer, a Mordvinian of his acquaintance:

"Don't be anxious, neighbor. Look, there isn't a single grain that hasn't been pounded. If you keep the mortar going any longer, you'll lose some of the millet."

The Mordvinian tried it himself, and saw that Grandfather was right. He thanked Grandfather, nodded his head by way of a bow, and ran to turn off the stream.

Grandfather and his pupil then made their way to the poultry yard. He found everything there in excellent condition. The yard held a great multitude of geese, ducks, turkeys, and hens; they were looked after by an elderly peasant woman and her granddaughter. As a token of special favor, Grandfather gave both of them his hand to kiss and ordered that the poultry-wife should be given twenty pounds of wheat flour for pies every month, in addition to her regular allowance of victuals. Grandfather rejoined his wife in excellent spirits and satisfied with everything: his daughter had proved keen-witted, the mill worked well, the poultry-wife took good care of the fowls.

The heat had long since abated; the coolness that the water gave off added to that of the approach of evening. From the long cloud of dust that moved down the road toward the village came the bleating and lowing of the herd. The sun was sinking behind a steep hill. Standing on the dam, Grandfather admired the broad pond that lay motionless as a mirror in the frame of its gently sloping banks. Fish glided and splashed ceaselessly, but Grandfather was not a fisherman.

"Time to go home, Arisha," he said; "I reckon the starosta is waiting for me."

His younger daughters, seeing that he was in a good humor, asked permission to continue fishing. They said that at sunset fish took the bait better and that they would return on foot in half an hour. Grandfather was agreeable, and left for home with Grandmother in one of the carriages, while Yelizaveta and her little brother seated themselves in the other carriage.

Grandfather was not mistaken: the starosta was waiting for him beside the porch, and with him were several peasants and peasant women. The starosta, who had already seen the master, knew that he was in a good mood, and had told some of the peasants about it.

Those who had unusual requests to make of him took advantage of this favorable opportunity. None of them was disappointed: Grandfather let one peasant have grain, in spite of the fact that the man had not paid his old debt, as he could have done; he permitted another serf to marry off his son before winter, and not to the girl chosen by the master; he gave a soldier's wife, whom he had ordered out of the village for some offense, leave to go on living with her father, and so forth. Moreover, everyone was offered home-brewed vodka in a silver cup more capacious than an ordinary tumbler. Thereupon Grandfather, speaking briefly and clearly, gave the starosta orders relating to the farm, and went in to supper, which had been waiting for him for some time. The evening meal differed little from the midday dinner, and everyone must have eaten more heartily because it was not so hot. After supper Grandfather was in the habit of sitting for half an hour or so on the porch, wearing only his shirt, to enjoy the coolness of the evening, while letting his family retire. This time he stayed there somewhat longer than usual, laughing and joking with his servants. He made Vanka and Nikanorka wrestle and punch each other, and teased them so that they pummeled one another in earnest and even pulled each other's hair. But when Grandfather had laughed his fill, a peremptory word from him made them come to their senses, and part.

A glorious brief summer night enfolded all of Nature. The glow of sunset was not yet extinguished; it would linger on till it was replaced by the glow of dawn. Hour by hour the depths of the heavenly vault waxed darker; hour by hour the stars shone more brightly; voices, and the cries of the night birds, resounded more loudly, as if they came closer to man! In the damp mist of night the noise of the mill and the mortar seemed nearer. . . . Grandfather rose from the porch, and, facing the starry sky, crossed himself once or twice. Then, though the air in his room was stifling, he lay down on the hot feather bed there and ordered the curtain drawn round him.

ALEXANDER RADISHCHEV
(1749–1802)

Ten months after the fall of the Bastille and half a dozen years before the death of Catherine II, a volume entitled A *Journey from Petersburg to Moscow* appeared in the Russian capital. Ostensibly an innocuous travel book, duly provided with the official imprimatur, it was in effect a political tract bordering on the seditious. Exalting the spirit of freedom, it inveighs against autocratic government, social injustice, religious intolerance, censorship. Above all, it calls for the abolition of serfdom.

The author was a middle-aged civil servant of gentle birth. Having studied law at the University of Leipzig, Alexander Radishchev had embraced the ideas that were to throw up barricades on the streets of Paris, and on his return home he continued to keep in touch with Western thought. He busied himself with the *Journey* on and off for nearly a decade, and had it printed on his private press by his own serfs. Within a few weeks of publication all available copies of the books were seized and destroyed by the police, while the author was arrested and promptly condemned to capital punishment. The sentence was commuted to exile, and shortly after the death of the Empress, Radishchev was allowed to leave Siberia. Eventually he was, indeed, appointed to serve on a government commission. A year later he committed suicide.

Although the *Journey* did not become accessible to the public until the early years of the present century, it proved to be a truly seminal work. The liberals honored it as the earliest plea for democratic reforms; radical opinion prized it as the starting point of the native revolutionary tradition. On September 22, 1918, a statue of Radishchev was unveiled in Petrograd, the first of the monuments erected at Lenin's behest to mark the victory of the Revolution.

FROM A Journey from Petersburg to Moscow

(ON SERFDOM)

The passage from the *Journey* that follows finds the traveler walking beside his carriage to get a respite from its jolting.

A few steps from the road I saw a peasant plowing a field. The weather was hot. I looked at my watch. It was twenty minutes of one.

I had set out on Saturday. It was now Sunday. The plowman, of course, belonged to a landed proprietor, who would not let him discharge his obligations by paying quitrent. The peasant was plowing with great care. Naturally, the field was the one he tilled for himself. He turned the plow with surprising ease.

"God help you," I said, walking up to the plowman, who, without stopping, was finishing the furrow he had started. "God help you," I repeated.

"Thank you, master," the plowman said to me, shaking the plowshare and transferring the plow to a new furrow.

"You are, of course, a Schismatic, since you plow on a Sunday."

"No, master, I make the right sign of the cross," showing me the three fingers put together.* God in His mercy does not bid us starve to death, as long as one has strength and a family."

"Have you no time to work during the week, so that you cannot rest even on Sunday, and during the hottest part of the day at that?"

"There are six days in a week, master, and six times a week we go to work for the master; and in the evening, if the weather is good, we cart the hay left in the woods to the master's courtyard; besides, on holidays women and girls go walking in the woods to pick mushrooms and berries. God grant," he went on, crossing himself, "that it rains this evening. If you have peasants of your own, master, they are praying to the Lord for the same thing."

"I have no peasants, my friend, and for that reason no one curses me. Do you have a large family?"

"Three sons and three daughters. The eldest is going on ten."

"How then do you manage to provide bread for them, if you have only the holidays free?"

"Not only the holidays, the nights, too, are ours. If a man isn't lazy, he won't starve to death. You see, one horse is resting; when this one gets tired, I'll hitch up the other; so the work gets done."

"Do you work the same way for your master?"

"No, master, it would be a sin to work the same way. On his fields he has a hundred hands for one mouth, and I have two for seven mouths, so you figure it out for yourself. You may work your fingers to the bone for the master, but you will get no thanks. He won't pay

* Schismatics (Old Believers) cross themselves with two fingers.—A. Y.

46

your poll tax, nor will he reduce his demands for livestock, fowls, linen, butter."

After saying that the peasants paying quitrent were better off than the rest and that the practice of leasing the serfs to outsiders was "a veritable invention of the devil," the plowman bade the stranger goodbye and started a new furrow.

Toward the end of his trip the traveler finds himself in a peasant cottage and has a close look at its interior. He writes:

Half of the four walls and the entire ceiling covered with soot; the floor full of chinks and coated with at least two inches of dirt; an oven without a chimney, but the best protection against cold, and smoke filling the hut every morning winter and summer; window openings covered with stretched bladders admitting a dim light at midday; two or three pots (happy the cottage, if one of them every day holds meatless cabbage soup!). A wooden bowl and beakers called plates; a table hewn with an ax, which is scraped on holidays. A trough to feed pigs and calves, if there are any; people sleep together with them, swallowing air in which a burning candle appears to be in a fog or behind a curtain. If they are lucky, a tub of kvass resembling vinegar, and in the courtyard a bath house, in which cattle sleep if people are not steaming in it. A homespun hempen shirt, footwear given by nature, onuchi* and bast shoes to go out in.

It is here that the source of the State's wealth, strength, might is justly held to lie; but here are also seen the weakness, deficiencies, abuse of the laws, their rough side, so to speak. Here the greed of the gentry, our plundering and tormenting are seen, and the helpless condition of the poor. Greedy beasts, insatiable leeches, what do we leave for the peasant? What we cannot take away: air. Yes, air alone. Not seldom do we take away from him not only bread and water, gifts of the earth, but also the very light. The law forbids taking his life. That is, all at once. But there are many ways of taking it from him gradually! On the one side well-nigh omnipotence, on the other, defenseless infirmity. For as regards the peasant, the landlord is legislator, judge, executor of his own verdict, and, if he so desires, a plaintiff against whom the defendant dare say nothing. This is the

---

* Onucha: a rag wrapped around the foot.—A. Y.

47

lot of one put in irons; this is the lot of one locked up in a vile dungeon; this is the lot of an ox under the yoke. . . .

On an earlier occasion the author, quoting from a manuscript that he pretends to have found, warns his compatriots thus:

Do you not know, dear fellow citizens, what ruin faces us, in what danger we stand? All the coarsened feelings of slaves, not softened by the beneficent effect of freedom, will strengthen and perfect their inner fervor. A torrent that is barred in its course becomes the stronger, the firmer the obstacle it meets. Once it has burst the dam, nothing will be able to check its flood. Such are our brothers whom we keep in fetters. They are waiting for a favorable chance and hour. The bell rings. And lo, the bane of bestiality spreads incontinently. We shall see swords and poison round about us. Death and conflagration will be the recompense for our harshness and inhumanity. And the slower and more stubborn we are about freeing them from their shackles, the more violent will they be in their revenge. Call back to your memory the happenings of former times. Delusion had made the slaves how fiercely eager to destroy their masters! Enticed by a crude impostor,* they followed him, and wished nothing more than to free themselves from the yoke of their masters; in their ignorance they thought of no other way of doing it than to kill them. They spared neither sex nor age. They sought the exhilaration of vengeance more than the benefit of shaking off their fetters.

This is what faces us; this is what we must expect. Destruction is mounting gradually, and already danger is hovering over our heads. Time has already raised its scythe; it is waiting for an opportune moment; and the first smooth-tongued talker or lover of mankind who comes to awaken the unfortunates will hasten the sweep of the scythe. Beware!

Stopping off in a village, the traveler listens to the story of a serf who has been the victim of lawlessness and unspeakable brutality on the part of his master, and sees three shackled peasants who had been sold by their owner because he needed money for a new carriage and who are being drafted into the army. He is moved to exclaim:

* The allusion is to Pugachev, who headed a peasant rebellion in 1772–1775.—A. Y.

Oh, would that the slaves, burdened with heavy fetters, raging in their despair, with the iron barring their liberty, crush our heads, the heads of their inhuman masters, and redden their fields with our blood! What would the State lose thereby? Soon great men would spring from their midst to replace the slain tribe; but they would be of a different mind and deprived of the right to oppress. This is no reverie; the gaze penetrates the dense curtain of time concealing the future from our eyes; I look across a whole century.

GAVRIIL DERZHAVIN
(1743–1816)

On the Emperor's Departure, December 7, 1812*

Lo, my prophetic dreams are very truth at last:
France bows to Russia's might and Europe is laid low.
The glory we may claim no nation yet surpassed!
The gift of peace 'tis in our power to bestow.
Be the Greek Alexander renowned as great in war,
But who brings peace on earth, his soul is greater far!

[1812]

* On that day Alexander I, receiving word that the Russian army
had entered Vilna (now Vilnius), left the capital for Kutuzov's headquarters to hearten the troops by his presence.—A. Y.

ALEXANDER PUSHKIN
(1799–1837)

This author occupies a preeminent place in Russian letters. Pushkin is paid homage by his compatriots not only as their greatest poet but also as the father of their literature in its modern phase. His work is cherished as the most precious part of the nation's cultural patrimony.

Though, like most of his fellow writers, he belonged by birth and upbringing to the thin upper crust of society, he had genuine democratic and libertarian sympathies. A man of passionate temperament and clear intelligence, he hated servility, stupidity, injustice, but he was not by nature a rebel. In his youth he composed a number of subversive pieces, including an ode to freedom, and the authorities transferred the *enfant terrible*—he was a minor functionary—to a town on the southern periphery of the empire, in the hope that there he would sober down. Subsequently the secret service found that in one of his letters he had described "pure atheism" as a "most plausible" doctrine. He was banished to his family estate and put under police surveillance, which was to last the rest of his life. The reputation he enjoyed at this time was that of the Byron of Russia. His romantic malaise did not last. The works of his later years are in the realistic vein. They are marked by sanity and balance, implying a serene acceptance of the human condition.

Considering that Pushkin's life was cut short by a duel, the body of his writings is rather ample. It has also great diversity. His efforts in the field of imaginative prose broke new ground, but his more significant achievements were in the medium of verse. In addition to composing lyrics and ballads, he made poems out of material that he found in other literatures—his mind was anything but parochial. He modeled his blank-verse drama *Boris Godunov*, a closet piece, on the historical plays of "our father, Shakespeare," to use his phrase. He owed something to foreign models (Byron's *Beppo* and *Don Juan*) in fashioning *Eugene Onegin*, the masterpiece, published in 1833, which most fully and happily exemplifies Pushkin's powers. This "novel in verse" is a story of unrequited love, frustration, and failure, set against the deftly drawn Russian scene of the post-Napoleonic years. Rather than *The Captain's Daughter*, a prose romance, *Eugene Onegin* is the fountainhead of the realistic fiction that is Russia's main contribution to world literature.

FROM **Eugene Onegin**

(A RUSSIAN DANDY)

As the "novel" opens, the protagonist, Onegin, a blasé young fop born and bred in the capital, has just waived the debt-ridden inheritance left him by his wastrel father and is on his way to see his affluent country uncle, who is on his deathbed and whose sole heir Eugene is. The stanzas that follow are in the nature of a flashback. The few that are omitted are those in which Pushkin recalls his youthful pleasure in the stage and, apropos of the ball, apostrophizes the ladies' seductive little feet:

A servant of the Czar, his father
Would always give three balls a year;
He lived in debt and he would rather
Be ruined than retrench, 'twas clear.
Fate guarded Eugene, our young waster;
While in due time *Monsieur* replaced her,
At first *Madame* controlled the child.
The charming lad was somewhat wild.
Monsieur l'Abbé, a Frenchman, seedy,
Thought sermons fashioned to annoy;
He spared the rod to spoil the boy,
And in a voice polite but reedy
Would chide him, would forgive him soon,
And walk him in the afternoon.

When Eugene reached the restless season
Of seething hopes and giddy play
And melancholy minus reason,
Monsieur was sent upon his way.
Onegin's free, restraints abolished;
A London dandy's not more polished
Than he, well-groomed and clipped and curled,
Making his bow to the great world.
In French he could converse politely,
As well as write; and how he bowed!
In the mazurka, 'twas allowed,

No partner ever was so sprightly.
What more is asked? The world is warm
In praise of so much wit and charm.

Since but a random education
Is all they give us as a rule,
With us to miss a reputation
For learning takes an utter fool.
Onegin, wiseacres aplenty
Called learned, although not yet twenty,
And some harsh judges found, forsooth,
A very pedant in the youth.
A gifted talker, he could chatter
With easy grace of this and that,
But silent as a sage he sat
When they discussed some weighty matter,
And with the spark of a *bon mot*
He set the ladies' eyes aglow.

As Latin's held not worth attention,
His knowledge of the tongue was slight:
Of Juvenal he could make mention,
Decipher epigraphs at sight,
Quote Virgil, not a long selection,
And always needing some correction,
And in a letter to a friend
Place a proud *vale* at the end.
He had no itch to dig for glories
Among time's ruins, thought it just
That dusty annals turn to dust,
But knew the most amusing stories
That have come down the years to us
Since the dead days of Romulus.

The art of verse, that lofty pleasure
He scorned; our Eugene never knew
Trochaic from iambic measure,
In spite of all our efforts, too.

Theocritus and Homer bored him;
If true delight you would afford him,
You'd give him Adam Smith to read.
A deep economist, indeed,
He talked about the wealth of nations;
The state relied, his friends were told,
Upon its staples, not on gold—
The subject filled his conversations.
His father listened, frowned and groaned,
And mortgaged all the land he owned.

All Eugene knew is past relating,
But for one thing he had a bent,
And I am not exaggerating
His principal accomplishment;
From early youth his dedication
Was to a single occupation;
He knew one torment, one delight
Through empty day and idle night:
The science of the tender passion
That Ovid sang, that brought him here,*
And closed his turbulent career
In such a miserable fashion—
Ovid, who found, so far from Rome,
In these bare steppes an exile's home.

He early played the gay deceiver,
Concealed fond hopes, feigned jealousy,
With glib words won the unbeliever,
Seemed sunk in gloom, or bold and free,
Would turn quite taciturn with languor,
Then flash with pride and flame with anger,
Show rapture or indifference,
Or burn with sudden eloquence!
The letters that he wrote so neatly,

* The place mentioned in the original is Moldavia. Ovid was
banished to a town not far from the mouth of the Danube for
an unknown reason. When Pushkin was writing these stanzas,
he was staying in neighboring Bessarabia.—A. Y.

So easily, with passion seethed.
One thing alone he loved, he breathed,
And thus forgot himself completely.
His eyes, how tender, quick and clear,
Or shining with the summoned tear!

He knew the ruses that would brighten
The eyes of the ingenuous young;
He could pretend despair, to frighten,
Or use the flatterer's smooth tongue;
He'd catch the moment of emotion,
And out of an old-fashioned notion
The strait-laced innocent beguile
With skill and passion, touch and smile.
He would implore the shy confession,
Catch the first stirrings of the heart,
Secure a tryst with tender art,
And at the following sweet session
Would, tête-à-tête, where no one heard,
Instruct the fair without a word.

In no time he learned how to flutter
The heart of the confirmed coquette!
What biting words the rogue would utter
Of those he wished her to forget!
None was so quick as he at trapping
A rival, or to catch him napping.
You men who lived in wedded bliss
Remained his friends, I grant you this.
The married rakes, no longer naughty,
Would show him every friendliness;
Suspicious age could do no less,
Nor yet the cuckold, stout and haughty,
Whose satisfactions were, through life,
Himself, his dinner, and his wife.

After an evening's dissipations
He will lie late, and on his tray

Find notes piled high. What? Invitations?
Three ladies mention a soirée,
Here is a ball, and there a party;
His appetite for pleasure's hearty—
Where will my naughty lad first call?
Tut! he'll find time for one and all.
Meanwhile, in morning costume, gaily
Donning his wide-brimmed Bolivar,
He joins the throng on the *boulevard*,
To promenade, as all do daily,
Until Breguet's* unsleeping chime
Announces it is dinner-time.

At dusk a sleigh's the thing; bells tinkle;
"Make way! Make way!" the drivers roar;
On Eugene's beaver collar twinkle
Like silver dust the specks of hoar.
Off to Talon's,† no hesitating:
His friend, Kaverin, must be waiting.
And now he has arrived: pop goes
A cork, the comet's vintage‡ flows.
A bleeding roast beef's on the table,
And truffles, luxury of youth,
French dishes for the gourmet's tooth,
A Strasbourg pie, imperishable;
Here's every dainty that you please:
Gold pines and live Limburger cheese.

Glass after glass is drained in drenching
The hot fat cutlets; you would say
They've raised a thirst there is no quenching.
But now it's time for the ballet.
The theater's wicked legislator,
Who unto every fascinator
In turn his fickle homage brings,

* A repeater named for a famous watchmaker.—A. Y.
† A fashionable restaurant.
‡ There was an exceptionally fine vintage in 1811, a year
marked by the appearance of a comet.—A. Y.

56

And boasts the freedom of the wings,
Onegin flies to taste the blisses
And breathe the free air of the stage,
To praise the dancer now the rage,
Or greet a luckless Phèdre with hisses,
Or call the actress he preferred
Just for the sake of being heard.

The house rocks with applause; undaunted,
And treading toes, between the chairs
Onegin presses; with his vaunted
Aplomb, he lifts his eyeglass, stares
Askance at fair, unwonted faces,
Remarks the jewels and the laces,
And notes complexions, with a sneer
Briefly surveying every tier.
He bows to sundry friends; his mocking
Slow eyes come last to rest upon
The lighted stage, and with a yawn
He sighs: "They're past the age—it's shocking!
I've haunted the ballet—what for?
Even Didelot becomes a bore."

The imps and cupids, quick as monkeys,
Upon the boards still flutter free,
While in the lobby sleepy flunkeys
Are guarding fur coats faithfully;
Within, you hear the feet still pounding,
The coughs, the shouts and hisses sounding,
The noses blown, and without pause,
Above it all, the wild applause.
The carriage horses, chilled with waiting,
Impatient, twitch beneath the lamp,
The coachmen round the bonfires tramp,
Their masters wearily berating.
But our Onegin's out of range
Of curses: he's gone home to change.

Shall I depict less with a prudent
Than with a wholly faithful pen
The cabinet where fashion's student
Is dressed, undressed and dressed again?
All that the London fashions hallow
And that for timber and for tallow
Is shipped across the Baltic Sea
To please capricious luxury,
And all that Paris, mercenary
As she is modish, can devise
By way of costly merchandise
To tempt the gay voluptuary,
Whatever imports are the rage
Adorn the cell of our young sage.

Here's bronze and china in profusion,
And Turkish pipes of amber rare,
And, for the senses' sweet confusion,
Perfumes in crystal cut with care;
Steel files and combs of various guises,
And brushes, thirty shapes and sizes,
That teeth and nails may both be served,
Are here, with scissors straight and curved,
Rousseau (forgive me if I chatter)
Could not conceive how pompous Grimm
Dared clean his nails in front of him—
The fluent madcap!—but no matter:
In this case it is not too strong
To call that friend of freedom wrong.

A man of sense, I am conceding,
May pay attention to his nails;
Why should one quarrel with good breeding?
With most folk custom's rule prevails.
My Eugene was Chaadayev* second:

* Pyotr Chaadayev, 1794–1856, an aristocratic Muscovite,
was a close friend of Pushkin's. A Russian diplomat is said to
have remarked that, if he had his will, he would make
Chaadayev keep touring the most populous regions of Europe

With every jealous word he reckoned,
He was a pedant, nothing less,
In the particulars of dress.
To prink and preen he'd need no urging,
But spend three hours before the glass,
Till from his dressing-room he'd pass
Like Aphrodite thence emerging,
Did giddy deity desire
To masquerade in male attire.

---

so as to show Europeans *"un russe parfaitement comme il faut."*
This Moscow Beau Brummel was one of the most cultivated
Russians of his time, and an original religious thinker.

In 1836 a Moscow magazine printed an essay of his in which
Russia was described as a nation cut off from the Christian
world, existing in a vacuum, without a past or a future, "a gap
in the moral order," a country that no one would notice if it
did not stretch from the Bering Strait to the Oder. Forthwith
the periodical in which the essay had appeared was suppressed,
its editor deported, the censor who had passed the piece dismissed. As for the author, by the Czar's order he was declared
insane and placed under the care of a physician attached to the
police.

The ill-fated piece was the first of a series of essays, all of
them written some years previously. The irony of the situation
was that meanwhile Chaadayev's thinking had undergone a
complete change. The sterility of Russia's past now seemed to
him a pledge of the predestined greatness of her future. Someday, he predicted, Russia would become the intellectual center
of Europe. Her long isolation, he now concluded, meant that
Providence had placed the country outside the field of national
interests and had "entrusted" to it, he wrote, "the interests of
all mankind." Furthermore, it was the Russians who were
destined to establish the kingdom of God on earth, a consum-
mation toward which, he believed, all creation moved. They
would achieve this by turning from their ascetic, individualistic
Christianity to the "social" Christianity practiced in the
Catholic West, and since this would involve an abrupt break
with the past, theirs was the path of revolution.

The scope of Chaadayev's views was broader than it has been
possible to indicate here. Forbidden to publish, he was reduced
to spreading them in private letters and by word of mouth in
Moscow drawing rooms. He did write an unfinished paper,
entitled "The Apologia of a Madman." It was published only
posthumously together with his other essays. His ideas were
known beyond his immediate circle, however, even in his lifetime, and had considerable resonance, particularly when trans-
posed to a secular key.—A. Y.

But never mind, let's rather hurry
Off to the ball as is required,
Whither Onegin in a flurry
Is dashing in a cab he hired.
Along dark streets wrapped deep in slumber
Gay carriages, a goodly number,
Shed rainbow lights across the snow
From their twin lanterns as they go.
With lampions bright on sills and ledges
The splendid mansion shines and gleams,
And silhouetted by the beams,
Across the pane a shadow edges:
The profile that a move will blur
Of lovely lady, modish sir.

Straight past the porter, like an arrow
Our hero took the marble stair,
But then he paused, and with his narrow
White hand he swiftly smoothed his hair,
And entered. Here the throng is trooping;
The orchestra's already drooping;
A gay mazurka holds the crowd;
The press is thick, the hubbub loud.
The Horse Guard's spurs clank as he dances;
And hand meets hand, and hearts beat high;
The ladies' little feet fly by,
Pursued in flight by flaming glances;
While wildly all the fiddles sing
To drown the jealous whispering.

And what of my Onegin? Drowsing,
He's driven from the ball to bed:
The drum is heard, the city's rousing,
For Petersburg's no sleepyhead.
The peddler plods, the merchant dresses,
On into town the milkmaid presses,
Bearing her jar o'er creaking snows;
And to his stand the cabby goes.

The cheerful morning sounds awaken;
The shutters open; chimneys spout;
The baker's wicket opens out,
A loaf is proffered, coins are taken,
A white cap shows, all in a trice:
The baker's German and precise.

The ball's wild gaiety was wearing,
So turning morning into night,
To darkness' kind abode repairing,
Now sleeps the scion of delight.
By afternoon he will be waking,
He'll then resume till day is breaking
The merry and monotonous round,
And then once more till noon sleep sound.

"Here's winter"

Here's winter. Far from town, what shall we do? I question
The servant bringing in my morning cup of tea:
"How is the weather—warm? Not storming? The ground's covered
With freshly fallen snow?" Come, is it best to be
Astride a horse at once, or shall we, until dinner,
See what our neighbor's old reviews may have to say?
The snow is fresh and fine. We rise, and mount our horses,
And trot through fields agleam with the first light of day.
We carry whips; the dogs run close behind our stirrups;
With careful eyes we search the snow, we scour the plain
For tracks, ride round and round, and tardily at twilight,
After we've missed two hares, at last turn home again.
How jolly! Evening comes: without, a storm is howling;
The candlelight is dim. The heart is wrenched with pain.
Slow drop by drop I drink my boredom's bitter poison.
I try a book. The eyes glide down the page—in vain:
My thoughts are far away . . . and so I close the volume,
Sit down, take up my pen, force my dull Muse to say
Some incoherent words, but melody is wanting,
The sounds won't chime. . . . The devil! Where now is the way

I had with rhyme? I can't control this curious handmaid:
The verse is shapeless, cold, so lame it cannot walk.
So I dismiss the Muse: I am too tired to quarrel.
I step into the parlor where I hear them talk
About the sugar-works, about the next election;
The hostess, like the weather, frowns, her only arts
Are plying rapidly her long steel knitting needles
And telling people's fortunes by the king of hearts.
How dismal! Thus the days go by, alike and lonely.
But if, while I play draughts at twilight in my nook,
Into our dreary village a closed sleigh or carriage
Should just by chance bring guests for whom I did not look:
Say, an old woman and two girls, her two young daughters
(Tall, fair-haired creatures, both), the place that was so dull,
So Godforsaken, all at once is bright and lively,
And suddenly, good heavens, life grows rich and full!
Attentive sidelong looks, and then a few words follow,
There's talk, then friendly laughter, and songs when lamps are lit,
And after giddy waltzes there are languid glances,
There's whispering at table, gay and ready wit;
Upon the narrow stairs a lingering encounter;
When twilight falls, a girl steals from her wonted place
And out onto the porch, bare-throated, chest uncovered—
The wind is up, the snow blows straight into her face!
Unhurt by northern blasts the Russian rose will blow.
How hotly a kiss burns in keen and frosty weather!
How fresh a Russian girl blooming in gusts of snow!

[1829]

Evil Spirits

The clouds are scurrying and spinning;
The moon, in hiding, casts her light
Upon the flying snow; the heavens
Are troubled, troubled is the night.
I drive across the naked country,
The bells go ding! and ding, again!

Lonely and lost, I gaze in terror
Upon the unfamiliar plain.

"Drive faster, fellow!" "There's no help, sir,
The horses find the going rough;
The blizzard pastes my eyes together;
The roads are buried, sure enough.
There's not a track for me to follow;
We've lost our way. What shall we do?
The devil's leading us in circles
And right across the meadows, too.

"There, there he is! He's playing with us;
He spat at me, you might have seen;
He's here, befuddling the poor horses,
He'll push them into a ravine;
Now he pretends that he's a milepost
Where there was never such a mark;
He flashed by like a spark and vanished,
Vanished into the empty dark."

The clouds are scurrying and spinning;
The moon, in hiding, casts her light
Upon the flying snow; the heavens
Are troubled, troubled is the night.
We have no strength to go on circling;
The bell is silent suddenly;
The horses halt. . . . What is that yonder?
Who knows? A stump? A wolf, maybe?

The storm is vicious now, it's howling;
The restive horses snort, oh, hark!
It's he who dances in the distance,
Alone his eyes burn in the dark;
Once more the horses hurry onward,
The bells go ding! and ding, again!
Those throngs I see are evil spirits
Gathered upon the whitening plain.

Innumerable, various, horrid,
Demoniac creatures are in flight,
Whirled round like leaves in deep November
Under the wild moon's troubled light. . . .
What numbers! Whither are they driven?
Their chant has such a plaintive pitch:
Is it a house sprite they are burying
Or do they marry off a witch?

The clouds are scurrying and spinning;
The moon, in hiding, casts her light
Upon the flying snow; the heavens
Are troubled, troubled is the night.
A dizzy host of swarming devils
Goes rushing through the topless sky;
It tears the heart of me to hear them,
Their desolate, long, lamenting cry.

[1830]

ALEXANDER HERZEN
(1812–1870)

Born out of wedlock to a wealthy Russian nobleman and a middle-class German girl from Stuttgart, Herzen spent his early years in a Moscow mansion swarming with house serfs, when he was not summering on one of his father's estates. The boy was attended by servants, instructed by private tutors, including a former Jacobin, and generally treated as a son of the house. Yet he was not unaware of his irregular status, and this may have fostered a rebellious disposition in him.

At the University of Moscow the youth was the soul of a tiny circle of disaffected students. The failure of the Paris insurrection of July, 1830, and of the Warsaw rising later in the year shook their faith in political revolution, and young Herzen, for one, embraced the "socialism" preached by the disciples of Fourier and Saint-Simon. At the age of twenty-two, a year after his graduation from the university, he was imprisoned and subsequently deported to a distant province on suspicion of having engaged in subversive activities. Exile fed his hatred of the existing order: he found it as inept as it was corrupt and brutal.

It was nearly eight years before he was permitted to reside in Moscow and visit Petersburg, while remaining under strict police surveillance. He had been trying his hand at dramatic and autobiographical sketches. Now he turned to essays in a philosophical vein—aligning himself with the Hegelian left—and wrote several novels. He also took a prominent part in the debates of Russia's past and future in which the intellectual elite of both capitals engaged. All these activities left him deeply frustrated. He could not bear the suffocating atmosphere of the police state ruled by Nicholas I. Early in 1847, not long after the death of his father, who left him a sizable fortune, he took his family with him across the western frontier.

Herzen remained abroad to the end of his days, dying in Paris. No longer tongue-tied by authority, the expatriate, a flaming, somewhat erratic spirit, became a prolific publicist. A deeply interested and sharply critical observer of the foreign scene, he commented on it in effervescent pages. Yet his native land was the nub of his thinking and writing. He undertook to speak for his muzzled compatriots. In 1853, having removed from the Continent to England, with the aid of several other émigrés he established in London the Free Russian Press for the printing of literature to be smuggled into the empire. This press turned out a number of leaflets, including his appeal to the gentry to take the initiative in freeing the serfs, as well as three journals that he launched after Alexander II came to the throne. In the pages of *The Bell*, a periodical devoted to the "liberation of Russia," he effectively attacked the abuses of the administration, and less successfully prodded the Czar to follow a liberal course in his reforms.

Furthermore, Herzen lost no opportunity of preaching what he termed "communism in bast shoes" or "Russian socialism." A nebulous, semi-anarchistic doctrine that owed nothing to Marxism and claimed no credentials except the sanction of reason and justice, it called for an end to economic exploitation and the centralized State. He gave wide currency to the idea that by virtue of the muzhik's age-old collective way of life (something of a myth), Russia was in a unique position to assure the triumph of the new order in the fullness of time. This thesis, largely a product of wishful thinking, became the cardinal dogma of the incipient Russian revolutionary movement. Curiously enough, Herzen took great pains to tell his readers that ideological dogmatism out of touch with experience was apt to beget a regime as oppressive as the tyranny of brute force. A consistent libertarian by instinct and conviction, he suspected that freedom was as seriously threatened from the Left as from the Right. Moreover, in early middle age he lost his faith in violence as an instrument of social melioration. Indeed, years later he did not hesitate to describe himself as a gradualist. Nevertheless, Lenin gave him a place of honor among the men who prepared the way for the Russian Revolution. It is certain that Herzen labored for a revolution quite unlike the one led by the Bolsheviks.

The latest edition of Herzen's writings, begun in 1954 under a Moscow imprint, is planned to run to thirty volumes. Four of them contain his memoirs. This work, which shows his gifts at their fullest and for which he is best known, occupied him, on and off, for sixteen years. Its title may be freely translated as *Reflections and Things Past*. It is of signal literary distinction and great documentary value, a complex whole made up of frank self-analytical autobiography and shrewd observations on many subjects, of descriptive and argumentative passages, of a portrait gallery of Russians and Europeans, especially revolutionaries, with digressions into politics and economics, history and prophecy.

The passage, abridged, that is offered below comes from the account of Herzen's childhood and early youth that forms Part I of the memoirs. Written in 1852–1853, it was first published in London two years later under the imprint of the Free Russian Press. December 14, 1825 (O.S.) is the date of the army putsch directed against the autocratic regime, which took place in Petersburg at the accession of Nicholas I to the throne.

Another equally futile and amateurish attempt, which was begun in the South a fortnight later, collapsed early in January, but the leaders of both abortive uprisings have gone down in history as Decembrists.

FROM Reflections and Things Past

(DECEMBER FOURTEENTH)

One winter morning the senator [Herzen's uncle] called, not at his customary hour; looking worried, he made his way with hurried steps into my father's study and locked the door, having motioned me to remain in the drawing room.

Luckily I did not have to rack my brain for a long time guessing what was the matter. The door of the anteroom opened slightly, and a red face, half hidden by the wolf-skin collar of the livery overcoat, appeared, and I was called in a whisper; it was the senator's footman.

"You haven't heard?" he asked.

"What?"

"The Czar died at Taganrog."

The news startled me; I had never thought of the possibility of the Czar's death. I had grown up in an atmosphere of great respect for Alexander, and I recalled sadly how I had seen him not long before in Moscow. Out walking, we had met him beyond the Tver Gate. He was riding at a quiet trot in the company of two or three generals, returning from Khodynka, where there had been maneuvers. His face looked friendly, its features soft and rounded, the expression tired and melancholy. When he drew alongside us, I took off my hat and raised it; he bowed to me with a smile. What a contrast from Nicholas, who always looked like a partly bald Medusa with cropped hair and moustaches! In the street, at the palace, with his children and ministers, with courtiers and ladies-in-waiting he constantly tried to discover if his eyes had the rattlesnake's power of freezing the blood in the beholder's veins. If Alexander's outward gentleness was a mask, isn't such hypocrisy better than the frank arrogance of despotism?

While vague thoughts passed through my mind, while portraits of Constantine, the new Emperor, were being sold in the shops, while notices were issued requesting the populace to take the oath of allegiance to him, and good people were hastening to comply, the rumor spread that Constantine had refused the crown. Thereupon the same footman of the senator's, who was very fond of political rumors and who had ample opportunities of gathering them in the anterooms of senators' apartments and government offices, to which he drove from morning till night—he did not enjoy the favor accorded the horses, which were changed after dinner—this footman informed me that there had been a mutiny in Petersburg and that "field guns" had been fired in Galerny Street.

The following evening Count Komarovsky, a general of the corps of gendarmes, was visiting us. He told us of the insurgent troops drawn up in battle formation on St. Isaac's Square, of the attack by the loyal Horse Guards, of the death of Count Miloradovich.* Then came arrests: "So-and-So has been taken," "So-and-So has been seized," "So-and-So has been brought from the country." Frightened parents trembled for their children. Dark clouds blanketed the sky.

In Alexander's reign political penalties were rare. True, he had Pushkin exiled for his verse, and Labzin, secretary of the Academy of Arts, for having proposed to make the Czar's coachman, Ilya Baikov, a member of the academy,† but there was no systematic persecution. The secret police had not yet grown into an autocratic corps of gendarmes, but consisted of an office headed by [Ivan] de Sanglain, a garrulous old follower of Voltaire, a wit and a humorist like Jouy.‡ Under Nicholas he himself was subjected to police surveillance, and was considered a liberal, though he remained what he had been; this alone is a measure of the difference between the two reigns.

Nicholas was completely unknown until he ascended the throne; under Alexander he counted for nothing and interested no one. Now all rushed to make inquiries about him. The Guard officers alone could supply an answer. They hated him for his cold cruelty, his petty pedantry, his vindictiveness. One of the first stories that made the

---

* The governor general of the capital, a veteran of the Napoleonic wars, shot by the mutineers.—A. Y.

† The president of the academy proposed to make Count Arakcheyev [the brutal martinet and obscurantist invested by the Czar with unlimited authority] an honorary member. Labzin inquired what services the count had rendered the arts. The president was at a loss, and replied that Arakcheyev was "the person closest to the Czar." "If this is a sufficient reason," the secretary observed, "then I propose that the Czar's coachman, Ilya Baikov, be admitted to the academy: he is not only close to the sovereign but sits in front of him." Author's note.

‡ Victor de Jouy, 1764–1846, a French man of letters.—A. Y.

round of the town eloquently confirmed the Guards' opinion of him. It was related that on one occasion at a drill the Grand Duke had so far forgotten himself that he tried to collar an officer. The latter reacted by saying: "Your Highness, I have a sword in my hand." Nicholas drew back, said nothing, but never forgot the retort. After December Fourteenth he twice inquired if that officer was involved in the mutiny. Fortunately, he was not.

The tone of society was changing before our eyes; the rapid moral deterioration was a melancholy proof of how little the sense of personal dignity was developed among Russian aristocrats. No one (women excepted) dared show sympathy, say a warm word about relatives, friends, whose hands had been shaken only the previous day, and who had been seized overnight. On the contrary, there appeared savagely enthusiastic supporters of slavery, some for sordid reasons, others, worse still, from disinterested motives.

Women alone did not take part in the shameful repudiation of their own people. At the cross, too, only women stood, and at the blood-stained guillotine there appeared now Lucille Desmoulins, that Ophelia of the Revolution, who haunted the ax, waiting her turn, now George Sand, who gave the hand of sympathy and friendship to the youthful fanatic Alibaud.*

The wives of the men condemned to hard labor lost all civil rights, abandoned wealth and social position, and chose to live in the terrible climate of eastern Siberia under the still more terrible oppression of the local police. . . .

The accounts of the uprising, of the trial of the ringleaders, the terror in Moscow, made a strong impression on me. A new world, which was becoming more and more the center of my moral existence, was opening up before me. I do not know how it came about, but although I had scarcely any comprehension, or a very vague one, of what it was all about, I sensed that I was not on the side of grapeshot and victory, prisons and fetters. The execution of Pestel† and his comrades completely awakened my soul from its childish sleep.

* Lucille, the wife of Camille Desmoulins, protested against the death sentence passed by the revolutionary tribunal on her husband, was arrested and beheaded eight days after his execution. Louis Alibaud (1810–1836) was executed for attempting the life of Louis Philippe.—A. Y.

† Colonel Pavel Pestel, one of the five leaders of the rising who were hanged.—A. Y.

Everyone expected some mitigation of the fate of the condemned men, since the coronation was near at hand. Even my father, in spite of his cautiousness and skepticism, said that the death penalty would not be carried out, that all this was done merely in order to impress people. But, like everyone else, he did not know the young monarch. Nicholas left Petersburg and, without entering Moscow, stopped at Peter's Palace.* The Muscovites scarcely believed their eyes, reading in the *Moscow Gazette* the terrible news of July 14.†

The Russian people had become unused to executions. After Mirovich, who was beheaded instead of Catherine II, and after Pugachev‡ and his comrades there were no executions. Men died under the knout, soldiers were made to run the gauntlet (contrary to law) until they dropped dead, but capital punishment *de jure* did not exist. The story goes that under Paul there was a minor mutiny of the Don Cossacks in which two officers were involved. The Czar ordered them court-martialed and gave full authority to the hetman or some general. The court condemned the officers to death, but no one dared to confirm the sentence, and the hetman submitted the case to the monarch. "They are a lot of milksops," said Paul; "they want to put the blame for the execution on me, many thanks," and he commuted the sentence to penal servitude.

Nicholas introduced the death penalty into our punitive practice, at first illegally, and later legitimized it by putting it into his Code.

The day after the terrible news broke there was a religious service in the Kremlin.§ It celebrated Nicholas' victory over the five; Metropolitan Filaret thanked God for the murders. The entire Imperial Family [the Czar was not present], as well as the senators and ministers, attended the service, and all around a vast area was packed with masses of Guards who, kneeling and bareheaded, took part in the prayers; cannon thundered from the heights of the Kremlin. Never have gallows been solemnized with such pomp; Nicholas understood the importance of his victory!

* The building is situated just outside Moscow.—A. Y.

† The hangings took place on July 13th.—A. Y.

‡ Lieutenant Vasily Mirovich was executed in 1764 for an attempt to make a palace revolution in favor of Ivan VI, legitimate heir to the throne, who was kept in prison and died there under obscure circumstances. The memoirist presumably credits the report that Catherine was responsible for his death. Pugachev, who led a bloody *jacquerie*, was beheaded in 1775.—A. Y.

§ The rest of the paragraph and the one following are printed in the original text as a footnote.—A. Y.

As a boy of fourteen, lost in the crowd, I was present at this service, and right there, before the altar defiled by the bloodstained prayers, I swore to avenge the executed, and dedicated myself to fight against this throne, this altar, these cannon. I have not avenged them; the Guards and the throne, the altar and the cannon—all that remains, but for thirty years I have stood under the same banner, which I have never once deserted.

The execution celebrated, Nicholas made his triumphant entry into Moscow. I saw him there for the first time. He was on horseback beside the carriage that was occupied by the Dowager Empress and the young Czarina. He was handsome, but his good looks breathed a chill; no other face betrayed so implacably a man's character. The sharply retreating forehead, the lower jaw, developed at the expense of the skull, indicated iron will and feeble intelligence, cruelty rather then sensuality. But the most telling feature was his eyes, without any warmth, without any mercy, wintry eyes. I don't believe he ever loved a woman passionately, as Paul loved Princess Gagarina [née Anna Lopukhina, his mistress], as Alexander loved all women, except his wife—Nicholas was "favorably inclined toward them," nothing more. . . .

Although political reveries occupied me day and night, my ideas were not distinguished by any particular perspicacity. They were so confused that I actually imagined that the aim of the Petersburg insurrection was, among other things, to put Constantine on the throne, while limiting his power. Hence for a whole year I revered that eccentric. At the time he was more popular than Nicholas—why, I do not know, but the masses for whom he had never done anything, and the soldiers to whom he had done nothing but harm, liked him. I clearly remember how during the coronation he walked frowning beside pale Nicholas, a hunched figure in the Lettish Guards' uniform with its yellow collar, his bushy brows pale-yellow and his shoulders raised to his ears. After taking the place of the bridegroom's parent in Nicholas' marriage to Russia, he went away to complete the work of exasperating Warsaw, and was not heard of till November 29, 1830.* . . .

It goes without saying that solitude weighed upon me more than before; I wanted to communicate my thoughts and reveries to some-

* The date of the Polish rebellion.—A. Y.

one, to check them, to hear them corroborated; I was too proudly aware of being a "subversive" to say nothing about it or to speak of it at random.

My first choice was my Russian tutor.

I. E. Protopopov was full of that high-minded and vague liberalism that often vanishes with the first gray hair, with marriage and a position, but ennobles a man nevertheless. He was touched, and as he was leaving embraced me with the words, "God grant that these feelings may ripen and grow strong in you." His sympathy was a great joy to me. After this, he began bringing me dog-eared copies, written in a small hand, of Pushkin's poems, such as "Ode to Freedom" and "The Dagger," and "Musings" by Ryleyev.* I would copy them secretly. (Now I print them openly!)

Of course, my reading, too, underwent a change. Politics moved into the forefront, and above all the history of the Revolution; all I knew about it was from the tales of Madame Proveau [Herzen's German nurse, married to a French gardener]. In our basement library I discovered a history of the 1790's by a royalist. It was so biased that even I, at fourteen, did not believe it. I happened to hear old Bouchot [Herzen's French tutor] say that he had been in Paris during the Revolution, and I was eager to question him. But Bouchot was a morose, sullen man, with a huge nose and spectacles; he never indulged in unnecessary conversation with me; he conjugated verbs with me, dictated sentences, scolded me, and left, leaning on a stout knotty stick.

"Why was Louis XVI executed?" I asked him once in the middle of a lesson.

The old man looked at me, lowering one eyebrow and raising the other, pushed his spectacles up on his forehead like a visor, took out an enormous blue handkerchief and, wiping his nose, brought out with dignity:

"*Parce qu'il a été traître à la patrie.*"

"If you had been one of the judges, would you have signed the verdict?"

"With both hands."

This lesson was worth more than all the subjunctives; it was enough for me: clearly the king deserved to be executed—it served him right.

* One of the five Decembrists who were hanged.—A. Y.

72

Old Bouchot disliked me, and thought that I was an empty-headed, mischievous boy because I did not do my assignments properly. He often said, "You'll turn out a good-for-nothing." But when he noticed my sympathy for his regicidal ideas, his harshness gave place to mercy, he excused my mistakes, described episodes of the year 1793 and how he had left France when "the dissolute and the cheats" got the upper hand. He would end a lesson with the same dignity and without a smile, but would say indulgently, "I really did think that you'd turn out a good-for-nothing, but your noble feelings will save you."

MIKHAIL LERMONTOV
(1814–1841)

My Country

I love my country, but that love is odd:
My reason has no part in it at all!
Neither her glory, bought with blood,
Nor her proud strength holds me in thrall;
No venerable customs stir in me
The pleasant play of revery.
Ask me not why I love, but love I must
Her fields' cold silences,
Her somber forests swaying in a gust,
Her rivers at the flood like seas.
I love to rattle on rough roads at night,
My lodging still to find, while half awake
I peer through shadows left and right
And watch the lights of mournful hamlets quake.
I love the smoke above singed stubble rising;
I love a caravan that winds forlorn
Across the steppe; I love surprising
Two birches white above the yellow corn.
A well stocked barn, a hut with a thatched roof,
Carved shutters on a village window: these
Are simple things in truth,
But few can see them as my fond eye sees.
And on a holiday, from dewy dusk until
Midnight, it is a boon for me
To watch the dancers stomping to the shrill
Loud babble of the drunken peasantry.

[1841]

74

NIKOLAY GOGOL
(1809–1852)

While Pushkin paved the way for the Golden Age of Russian imaginative prose, it fell to Gogol, a thoroughly assimilated Ukrainian, to usher it in. A well-born provincial, come to the capital to find scope for his literary ambitions, he was in his middle twenties when he achieved fame as the author of some miscellaneous essays, a dozen stories, and a historical romance. His early fiction is marked by good-natured humor, a feeling for landscape, and a mingling of realism and fantasy, occasionally weird. Many of these pages evoke the scenery, the daily routine, the customs, the folklore of his native Little Russia. This regionalism, which has not worn well, is absent from the pieces Gogol wrote for the stage, to which he ascribed a function far above that of entertainment. He composed several comedies, the chief of which, known in English as *The Inspector General*, opened in Petersburg on May 1, 1836 (N.S.), and continues to draw audiences, even abroad, to this day.

The work that shows forth Gogol's genius most fully and that occupied him much of his adult life is *Dead Souls*. It began as a picaresque tale based on an anecdote. Soon, however, it assumed in his mind the dimensions of a narrative that was to mirror all Russia. Eventually he came to see his novel as a kind of *Pilgrim's Progress*, indeed, another *Divine Comedy*, tracing the rebirth of a soul and leading to nothing less than the country's regeneration, the author thus fulfilling his high mission on earth. He succeeded in completing to his satisfaction only Part I of what he called his "epic."

The novel opens with the arrival of Collegiate Councilor Chichikov in a provincial city. As he is of a prepossessing appearance, has an ingratiating manner, and gives the impression of a man of substance, he succeeds in establishing himself in the good graces of the local officials and their ladies. Actually, he is a shady character who had been repeatedly bounced from posts in the civil service for corrupt practices. It is these catastrophes that he has in mind when he hints to people that he has suffered much in the cause of justice. The amiable swindler has hit on a fraudulent scheme to get rich quick, which he proceeds to carry out. He visits several landed proprietors in the neighborhood and buys up for a song their runaway "souls" (male serfs), as well as those who are dead but for whom their owners must pay the poll tax until the next census, when the deceased are removed from the register. His intention is to mortage these insubstantial goods for real cash and thus make a fortune. Chichikov's excursions provide the author with an opportunity to draw several masterly portraits or, rather, caricatures, of small provincial gentry. Like the city functionaries, they are a sorry lot of dolts and knaves. The protagonist himself is a consummate study of the acquisitive man uninhibited by moral scruples, no melo-dramatic villain, no lost soul, such as Dostoevsky will imagine, but the embodiment of smug mediocrity. Gogol refuses to be harsh in judging his antihero and, in fact, is at pains to extenuate his failings.

Returning to town from his trip, and feeling tired, Chichikov goes to bed after a light supper, and falls soundly asleep. While he slumbers, the author takes advantage of the pause to reflect on the unhappy case of the writer, who, like himself, chooses his characters from among the low and paltry specimens of humanity, and who views life through tears unper-ceived by the world that sees only his laughter. Waking up, Chichikov proceeds to draw up the deeds of purchase, and as he looks over the lists of the "souls" he has acquired, he falls to musing about the lot each one of these serfs had been fated to endure. Emerging from his reverie, he heads for the government bureau to register the papers.

The purchase having been duly legalized, the report is bruited about that Chichikov is a millionaire, and he becomes the darling of the town society. Before long, however, rumors of the ghoulish nature of his trans-actions transpire, and precipitate a general upheaval. Greatly perturbed, the officials foregather in the house of the chief of police to discuss the question of who Chichikov really is and what is to be done about him. In the course of the deliberations Ivan Andreyevich, the postmaster, an-nounces that Chichikov is none other than Captain Kopeikin. As no one present has heard of the captain, the postmaster relates the following story. A ruthlessly expurgated version of it appears in the first edition of the novel. The text given here is the one that failed to pass the censor and was not published until 1889. The end, which is bracketed, is taken from an early variant of *Dead Souls*:

FROM *Dead Souls*

THE TALE OF CAPTAIN KOPEIKIN

"After the campaign of 1812, my good sir," so the postmaster began, although not one sir, but six were sitting in the room, "after the campaign of 1812 Captain Kopeikin was sent back home together with the wounded. At Krasnoe, or perhaps it was at Leipzig, but, just imagine it, my good sir, both an arm and a leg of his had been shot away. Well, at the time, don't you know, no arrangements whatever had been made for the care of the wounded. The Invalid Fund, you can imagine, was established, in a sense, much later. Captain Kopeikin sees that he'll have to get himself some work, but the only arm he has, you understand, is his left. He goes home to see his father, but his father says: 'I can't feed you, I have barely enough bread, you can imagine, for myself.' So my Captain Kopeikin decides to make his way to Petersburg, my good sir, to beg the Sovereign for some kind of a favor on the grounds that he had, so to speak, sacrificed his life, shed his blood, in a sense.

"Well, in some way or other, don't you know, by getting rides in carts or government conveyances—in a word, my good sir, he drags himself to Petersburg somehow. Well, you can imagine how a nobody like that, I mean Captain Kopeikin, all of a sudden finds himself in the capital, the like of which, so to speak, does not exist in the whole universe! Suddenly there is a world before him, a kind of vista of life, so to speak, a fabulous Scheherazade. Suddenly some kind of Nevsky Prospect, you can imagine, or some, you know, Gorokhovaya Street, deuce take it, or some sort of Liteinaya Street; over there some kind of spire, up in the air; bridges hanging in a devilish sort of way, you understand, without any, that is, contact—in a word, sir, Semiramis, no less. He messes around looking for a lodging, but the prices are highway robbery: curtains, blinds, all sorts of deviltry, you understand, carpets, in a word, prime Persia; you step on money, so to speak. Well, simply, you walk, that is, along the street and already your nose smells thousands. And my Captain Kopeikin's entire bankroll, you understand, consists of ten-odd fivers. Well, somehow or other he finds shelter in an inn for a ruble a day, including dinner: some kind of cabbage soup and a piece of Swiss steak.

"Well, he sees that a long stay is out of the question. He makes inquiries as to where he may apply. They say there's some kind of high commission, an office, sort of, you know, headed by General-in-Chief So-and-So. At the time, you must know, His Majesty was not yet in the capital, the troops, you understand, had not yet returned from Paris, everybody was abroad. Getting up early in the morning, my Kopeikin somehow scratches his beard with his left hand—paying a barber, you understand, would have run up an account, so to speak— pulls on his miserable uniform and hobbles off on his wooden leg to see, just imagine, the Chief, the bigwig himself. He asks where the General lives. "There"—the policeman points to a house on the

Palace Quay—a peasant shanty, you understand. The little window-panes, you can imagine, are mirrors ten foot high, so that the vases and everything in the rooms seem to be outside, as it were—your hand can reach them from the street, so to speak; priceless marbles, metal fancy goods; a doorknob is the kind of thing that you first have to run to a retail shop to buy a groat's worth of soap and scrub your hand for an hour or two before you can get up the courage to take hold of it—in a word, the polish on everything is such that it makes your head swim, as it were. Why, the doorman alone looks like a generalissimo: a gilded mace, a count's physiognomy, the looks of some well-fed fat pug or other, cambric cuffs—what the devil!

"Somehow my Kopeikin drags himself on his peg leg to the waiting room, huddles himself, you know, in a corner, so as not to shove his elbow, you can imagine, into some America or India—some kind of gilded porcelain vase, you understand. Of course, he has his fill of standing, because he has come at a time when the General has, in a manner of speaking, hardly got out of bed, and his valet may have brought him some kind of silver washtub, you understand, for various ablutions of sorts.

"My Kopeikin waits three or four hours, and finally in comes an adjutant or some other official on duty. 'The General,' says he, 'will come out right away.' By now there are as many people in the waiting room as beans on a plate. And they are none of them small fry like us but brass of the fourth and fifth grade, colonels, and here and there fat macaroni glitters on an epaulet—in a word, Generals. Suddenly, you understand, there is a barely noticeable stir in the room, like some kind of thin ether. Here and there you hear a shushing, and finally the stillness is terrifying. The Great Man enters. Well, you can imagine: a statesman! His face, so to speak . . . well, in keeping with his title, you understand . . . with his high rank . . . wears that kind of expression, you understand. Naturally, all at once everything in the room, you can imagine, stands at attention, trembling, awaiting the decision of Fate, as it were.

"The Minister, or whoever the great man is, goes over to one petitioner, to another: 'What brings you here? And you? What do you wish? What is your business?' Finally, my good sir, he reaches Kopeikin. Plucking up courage, Kopeikin brings out: 'Your Excellency, this is how it is: I shed my blood, lost an arm and a leg, so to say, I cannot work; I make bold to ask the Monarch's favor.' The Minister sees a man with a wooden leg and the right sleeve empty, pinned to his uniform. 'Very well,' says he, 'come back in a few days.'

"My Kopeikin left in a state bordering on rapture: for one thing, he had been honored by an audience, so to speak, with a big cheese; for another, because now finally the matter of the pension would, in a way, be settled. In high spirits, you understand, he hopped along the sidewalk. He stepped into the Palkin bar for a vodka, dined, my good sir, at the London, ordering a cutlet with capers and a capon with all the trimmings, and called for a bottle of wine; in the evening he went to a play—in a word, you understand, he had himself a time. On the street he caught sight of a shapely English lady, gliding along like a swan, you can imagine. My Kopeikin—his blood, you know, began to race—started after her on his peg leg, tap, tap. 'But no,' he decided, 'this is for later, when I get my pension; I've let myself go too far already.'

"Well, my good sir, three or four days later my Kopeikin appears at the Minister's again and waits till His Excellency comes out. 'This is how it is,' says he, 'I've come,' says he, 'to hear Your Exalted Excellency's order regarding the illnesses and wounds sustained . . .' and the life, you understand, in proper official style. The Great Man, just imagine, recognizes him immediately. 'Ah,' he says, 'very good,' he says, 'for the present I can tell you no more than that you have to wait for His Majesty's return; then doubtless instructions will be issued regarding the wounded, but without the Monarch's orders, so to speak, I can do nothing.' A bow, you understand, and—goodbye.

"Kopeikin, you can well imagine, left in a most unsettled state of mind. He had thought that the money would be handed over to him the very next day: 'Here it is, my dear fellow, eat, drink, and be merry'; instead he was ordered to wait—indefinitely. He walked down the steps as glum as an owl, looking, you understand, like a poodle a cook has doused with water, his tail between his legs and his ears drooping. 'Well, no,' he said to himself, 'I'll go again, explain that I'm down to my last morsel—if you don't help, I must starve to death, as it were.'

"In a word, my good sir, he gets to the Palace Quay again. They say: 'He's not receiving; come tomorrow.' The next day the same thing; the doorman simply does not even want to look at him. Meanwhile, you understand, there is a single solitary fiver left in his pocket. He used to eat cabbage soup, a piece of beef; now he is reduced to buying a herring or a pickle in the grocery and two groats' worth of bread—in short, the poor fellow is starving, while his appetite is simply wolfish. He goes past some sort of a restaurant—the chef there, you may well imagine, is a foreigner, a Frenchman with an open physiognomy, wears Dutch linen, a snow-white apron, and is busy turning out a *feenserve* or, say, cutlets with truffles—in short, a delicacy so whetting to the appetite that you are ready to eat yourself up. Or he may pass by the Milyutin stores, and there a salmon stares out of the window, in a manner of speaking; cherries at five rubles apiece; a mammoth watermelon, the size of a stagecoach, leans out of the window and is looking, so to speak, for a fool who would lay out a hundred rubles. In short, there is temptation at every step, his mouth waters, and meantime all he hears is 'tomorrow.' So picture his situation to yourself: on the one hand, so to speak, salmon and watermelon, and on the other, every day he is served the selfsame dish: 'tomorrow.'

"Finally, the poor fellow can bear it, in a manner of speaking, no longer. He decides to take the fortress by storm at all costs, you understand. He loiters at the entrance on the chance that another petitioner will appear, and then, indeed, together with some general or other, you understand, he slips into the waiting room with his wooden leg. The Great Man comes out as usual. 'What is your business? And yours? Ah!' he says, catching sight of Kopeikin, 'I have already informed you that you must await the decision.' 'For goodness' sake, Your Exalted Excellency, I haven't, so to speak, a crust of bread. . . .' 'But what's to be done? I am helpless in the matter; meanwhile try to help yourself, look for a means of livelihood yourself.' 'But, Your Exalted Excellency, you can judge for yourself, in a way, what means I can find, lacking an arm and a leg.' 'Well,' says the dignitary, 'you will agree that I cannot support you, so to speak, at my own expense; I have many wounded men; they all have an equal claim. . . . Arm yourself with patience. When His Majesty arrives, I can give you my word of honor that his mercy will not overlook you.' 'But, Your Exalted Excellency, I cannot wait,' exclaims Kopeikin, and he does it, as it were, rudely. By this time the dignitary is vexed, you understand. And, indeed, here are Generals all round waiting for decisions, orders; weighty business, so to speak, affairs of State, demanding most urgent attention—a minute's delay may cause trouble, and here is this importunate devil pestering him. 'Excuse me,' he says, 'I have no time. . . . More important affairs than yours are awaiting me.' It was a delicate, sort of, way of intimating that it was time for him to leave. But my Kopeikin—hunger, you know, was spurring him: 'Do what you please, Your Exalted Excellency, but I don't budge from the spot until you pass the resolution.'

"Well, now, just think of it: to talk like that to a top official, who has only to say the word and you turn topsy-turvy and go flying off where the devil himself won't find you. Why, among us, small fry, if a clerk were to talk like that to a clerk one grade higher, it would be put down as insolence. But there, what a difference, what a difference: a General-in-Chief and some kind of a Captain Kopeikin! Ninety rubles and zero! The General, you understand, does nothing more than stare, but his stare is a firearm—your heart is no more; it has sunk into your boots. But my Kopeikin, just imagine, does not budge; he stands rooted to the spot. 'Well?' says the General, and turns on the steam, as the saying goes. However, truth to tell, he treats Kopeikin mercifully enough. Another man would have given him such a fright that afterward the street would have danced upside down before his eyes, but he says only: 'Very good, if you find it too expensive to live here, and you cannot wait quietly in the capital until your future is settled, I will have you deported at government expense. Call a courier! Have this man taken to his legal place of residence!'

"Well, the government courier, you understand, is already right there, a strapping six-footer, you can imagine, with man-sized hands, shaped by Nature itself to impress drivers—in short, a dentist.* And so they grab the poor devil, my good sir, and get him into a carriage with the government courier. 'Well,' Kopeikin thinks, 'at least I won't have to pay my fare; that's something to be thankful for.' And so, my good sir, he is traveling under convoy, and as he travels, sort of, he reflects, so to speak: 'The General said that I should look for some means to help myself. Well,' says he, 'I'll find the means. . . .' he says.

* In colloquial use, one who is apt to punish a subordinate by knocking out his teeth.—A. Y.

"Well, where exactly he was taken is not known. Even rumors about Captain Kopeikin, you understand, sank in the river of oblivion, in some Lethe or other, as the poets call it. But, allow me, gentlemen, it's just here, it may be said, that the thread, the real plot of the tale begins. And so, what has become of Kopeikin is not known, but, just imagine, before two months had gone by, a gang of highwaymen appeared in the Ryazan forests, and the chieftain of this gang was, my good sir, none other than [our Captain Kopeikin. He had gathered together a whole band, you may say, from among deserters. This was, you can imagine, right after the war: people had got used to loose living, you know; all of them valued their lives at a kopeck, and snapped their fingers at everything, the daredevils. In short, my good sir, he simply had a whole army. The roads became impassable, and the band's attention, you understand, was, so to speak, centered on government property. If a man was traveling on private business, the Captain would just ask him what his business was and let him go in peace. But if it was some government conveyance, carrying provisions or money—in short, anything in the nature of State property, it was given no quarter. Well, you can imagine, the Treasury suffered a terrible loss. He'd hear that in some Crown village the time for paying taxes and quitrent to the Treasury was near, and he'd be right on the spot. At once he'd demand, in a sense, to see the headman: 'Let's have all those moneys, brother.' Well, the peasant sees a one-legged devil, with a firebird—red cloth—on his collar, devil take it, and smells a stiff punch. 'Here, Your Honor, take it, only let me be.' To himself he thinks: 'Must be a captain of rural police, or even worse.' Only, my good sir, Kopeikin receives the money properly, and to protect the peasant from any unpleasantness, you understand, he makes out a receipt on the spot to the effect that 'Such-and-Such, a Captain Kopeikin, has received all the payments due the Treasury in full, and besides he affixes his seal.' In short, my good sir, whenever he has a chance he robs the Treasury recklessly.

"Several times troops are dispatched to catch him, but my Kopeikin doesn't care a straw. The men around him are greedy wretches, you understand. But finally he takes fright, maybe because he sees that the mess he has made is, so to speak, no trifling matter, and that the measures taken against him are continually getting to be more of a threat. As he has in the meantime made quite a pile for himself, he crosses the frontier, my good sir, and makes his way, just imagine, straight to the United States of America. From there, my good sir, he writes a letter to His Majesty, which is more eloquent than anything you can imagine. The Platos and Demostheneses of antiquity—all of them are, you may say, a beadle, a rag, compared to him. 'Don't think, Sire,' he says, 'that I am this, and this, and this. . . .' How he rounds out those periods, you understand! 'Necessity,' says he, 'was the cause of my action, I had shed my blood, I hadn't, in a way, spared my life, and now I have no bread, as it were, to live on. Do not punish my comrades,' he says, 'for they are innocent, having been inveigled, so to speak, by me. Rather show a Monarch's mercy, so that in future, that is, should there be any wounded, for instance, some kind of provision, you can imagine, would be made for them.' In short, terribly eloquent.

"Well, His Majesty, you understand, was touched, so to speak. Really, his heart was aggrieved that a man had been driven, as it were, to such an extremity. Right off he issued instructions to stop prosecuting the culprits, and the strictest edict to form a committee for the exclusive purpose of improving the lot, that is, of all the wounded, and it was thus, my good sir, that the ground was laid for the Invalid Fund, which now fully provides, one may say, for the wounded. So that's who, my good sir, this Captain Kopeikin is. I believe that he ran through his money in the United States and has now returned to us to try, you understand, some new scheme, as it were, in the hope that it might succeed."]

"But allow me, Ivan Andreyevich," said the chief of police, suddenly interrupting the postmaster. "Captain Kopeikin, you said yourself, is minus an arm and a leg, while Chichikov . . ."

Thereupon the postmaster uttered an exclamation and slapped his forehead hard, calling himself a calf publicly within everyone's hearing. He could not understand how this circumstance had failed to occur to him at the start of the story, and conceded the complete justice of the saw: the Russian is wise after the event. A moment later, however, he began to use cunning, and tried to wriggle out of the difficulty by saying that mechanical contrivances had been greatly perfected in England, and, as you could see by the papers, someone had invented wooden legs, which at the mere touch of a spring carried a man God knows where, so that afterward there was no finding him anywhere. Nevertheless, they were all very much in doubt as to whether Chichikov was Captain Kopeikin, and found that the postmaster had gone too far.

Other surmises, including the one that Chichikov is Napoleon in disguise, are also rejected, and the officials are reduced to a state of utter bewilderment and anxiety. In fact, the public prosecutor is scared to death, literally. As Chichikov has also antagonized the ladies at a ball by rudely neglecting them for the governor's sixteen-year-old daughter, the town turns against him. He has his carriage repaired and the horses shod, and makes off forthwith. Then the author launches into a long, lyrical digression. He addresses Russia, hinting at a mysterious bond between himself and her, and asking where but in her vast expanse could a boundless idea be born and a titan arise. This rapturous passage is followed by an evocation of the delights of the open road.

Soothed by the even motion of his carriage, Chichikov drops off, and while he sleeps his career is traced, in a flashback, from his birth to the point at which the narrative began. After a while he awakens, the light britska speeds up, and the author indulges in another rhapsodic apostrophe, this time to the joy of the Russian heart—the swift troika. This is seen to be a symbol of Russia racing toward an unknown goal as the other nations, eyeing her askance, make way for her. On that proud note Part I of *Dead Souls* ends.

The book came out in 1842. In his last decade Gogol tried, on and off, to write a continuation of the novel. His intention seems to have been to project the moral regeneration of Chichikov and several other figures against the background of a brighter, indeed, glorious side of Russian life and Russian character. But perhaps because his talent was essentially satirical, he was unequal to the task he had set himself. He kept burning the manuscripts of the sequel, so that only fragments of it are extant, and *Dead Souls* remains a torso.

He put aside his novel to bring out, in 1847, a miscellany of essays and lay sermons that aroused dismay and indignation in the liberal camp. The views he championed in these unctuous pages were those of a narrow-minded pietist, a supporter of autocracy and serfdom as sacrosanct institutions. Nevertheless, *The Inspector General*, *Dead Souls*, "The Overcoat" (1842)—the short story which is one of the sources of the country's humane tradition—continued to be recognized as a severe, if indirect, attack on the established order. It is certain that Gogol's work was influential in directing Russian literature into the channel of social criticism.

FYODOR TYUTCHEV
(1803–1873)

"Sorry hamlets"

Sorry hamlets, niggard Nature,
Land that, patient, bears its yoke—
These are mine, this is my country,
Land of my own Russian folk!

Haughty foreign eyes can never
See your glory, never guess
The pure light that glimmers shyly
Through your humble nakedness.

Like a slave the King of Heaven
Tramped your roads on every hand;
Burdened with His cross He blessed you
Everywhere, my native land.

[1855]

"Not with the mind"

Not with the mind is Russia comprehended,
The common yardstick will deceive
In gauging her: so singular her nature—
In Russia you must just believe.

[1866]

IVAN GONCHAROV
(1812–1891)

Goncharov was the son of a well-to-do provincial merchant, but early came in close contact with the life of the landed gentry. After completing his studies at the University of Moscow, he held several civil-service posts, including that of censor. An unpolitically-minded individual, he was a congenital conservative. At the age of forty the comfort-loving, sluggish functionary found himself, to his consternation, making a voyage around the world as a member of an official mission to Japan. A travel book, *The Frigate Pallas* (1858), was the fruit of this experience. In addition to other prose, he wrote three novels. Of these, *Oblomov* stands out as a genuine achievement, a classic, at once national and universal. It was published in 1859, two years before the Emancipation. Immediately *oblomovism* became a byword for the indolence and torpor that a system based on serf labor bred in the masters. In all his fiction Goncharov chronicled the decay of the class of landed proprietors and the rise of an enlightened bureaucracy and bourgeoisie. He served literature like "a yoked ox," as he put it, working slowly, laboriously, and—in *Oblomov* at least—to great effect. Mental derangement darkened his last two decades.

FROM *Oblomov*

(THE COMPLETE SLUGGARD)

One morning Ilya Ilyich Oblomov was lying abed in his flat on Gorokhovaya Street in one of the big houses, the population of which is enough for a whole county town.

He was a man of thirty-two or -three, of medium height and pleasant appearance, with dark-gray eyes and a face that lacked any definite character in its features, any manifestation of thought. Reveries promenaded freely over his features, fluttered in his eyes, rested on his half-parted lips, hid in the furrows of his forehead, then vanished completely, and at such moments his whole face glowed with the even light of nonchalance. The nonchalance passed into the postures of his entire body and even into the folds of his dressing gown.

Sometimes his gaze was darkened by something like weariness or boredom. But neither fatigue nor ennui could for a moment banish the softness that was the predominant and basic expression not only of his face but of his whole soul, which shone openly and clearly in his eyes, his smile, every movement of his head and hand. A cold-hearted and superficial observer, having glanced at Oblomov, would say, "Must be a good-natured fellow, a simple soul!" A deeper and more likable person, after a long scrutiny of his face, would have walked away smiling, in a pleasantly thoughtful mood.

Oblomov's complexion was neither pink nor dark, nor positively pale, but indefinite, or perhaps seemed so because he had grown prematurely fat and flabby, owing to lack of exercise or fresh air, perhaps of both. In general, his body, to judge by the lusterless, excessive whiteness of his neck, his small, pudgy hands, his fleshy shoulders, seemed too soft for a man.

His movements too, even when he was troubled, were restrained by softness, and by an indolence that was not without something like grace. If care invaded his face, his gaze clouded over, lines appeared on his forehead, and his features showed the interplay of doubt, sadness, fear. But his alarm rarely crystallized into a definite thought, and even more rarely was transformed into an intention. It resolved itself into a sigh, and faded out in apathy and drowsiness.

How well the clothes that Oblomov wore indoors went with his placid features and soft body! He wore a dressing gown of Persian material, a real Oriental dressing gown, without the slightest hint of Europe, without tassels, velvet, waist, and very roomy, so that he could wrap it around him twice. The sleeves, in true Asiatic fashion, grew wider and wider from the fingers to the shoulders. Although this dressing gown had lost its pristine freshness and in places exchanged its original natural luster for an acquired one, it preserved the brilliance of Oriental color, and the material was as good as ever.

The dressing gown had a multitude of invaluable merits in Oblomov's eyes: it was soft and supple; he did not feel the touch of it; like an obedient slave, it submitted to the slightest movement of his body.

He never wore a necktie or a waistcoat in the house, because he disliked feeling cramped and constrained. He wore long, wide, soft slippers; when, without looking, he put his feet on the floor as he got out of bed, he invariably stepped into them.

For Ilya Ilyich lying down was not a necessity, as it is for a sick man or a drowsy one; nor was it a casual need, as for a tired person; nor a pleasure, as it is for a lazy one: It was a normal state. When he was at home—and he was nearly always at home—he was lying down all the time and invariably in the same room, the one in which we have found him and which served him as bedchamber, study, and parlor. There were three more rooms in the flat, but he seldom looked into them, perhaps in the morning, when his manservant swept the study, which he did not do every day. In those rooms there were slip-covers on the furniture, and the blinds were drawn.

The room in which Ilya Ilyich was lying at first glance looked splendidly appointed. In contained a mahogany desk, two couches upholstered in damask, a fine screen embroidered with birds and fruit not to be found in nature. There were also silk curtains, rugs, several pictures, bronzes and china, and much pretty bric-a-brac. Yet the experienced eye of a person of good taste would have had no difficulty noticing nothing but a perfunctory desire to comply with the conventions. Obviously Oblomov sought nothing else in furnishing his room. Refined taste would not have been content with these heavy, inelegant mahogany chairs and rickety chiffoniers. The back of one of the couches had broken down; some of the veneer had come unstuck. The pictures, the vases, the bric-a-brac were in equally bad taste.

The occupant of the flat himself regarded its appointments with such a cold and indifferent eye that he seemed to wonder who could have brought all that junk and set it up there. Because of Oblomov's lack of interest in his property, and perhaps because of an even greater indifference to the same object on the part of his servant Zakhar, the study, on closer inspection, struck you by its neglected and untidy state.

Cobwebs laden with dust festooned the pictures on the walls; the mirrors, instead of reflecting objects, could have served as tablets for indicating memoranda in the dust; the rugs were stained. A towel had been forgotten on the couch; almost every morning a plate with a salt cellar and a gnawed bone from the previous night's supper was seen on the table, which was strewn with bread crumbs.

Had it not been for this plate, for a freshly smoked pipe leaning against the bed, and the tenant of the rooms himself lying in it, you might have thought that no one lived there—so dusty and faded was everything and, generally speaking, so without living traces of a human presence. True, two or three open books and a newspaper were lying about on the chiffoniers; on the desk there was an inkwell with pens. But the pages at which the books were open had grown yellow and were covered with dust—evidently they had been left like that for a long time; the newspaper dated back to last year; and if a pen were to be dipped into the inkwell, only a frightened fly might dart out of it with a buzz.

Contrary to his habit, Oblomov had waked up very early, about eight o'clock. He was deeply worried about something. His expression kept changing from one of apprehension to one of anxiety and vexation. Clearly he was prey to an inner conflict, in which his intellect was not as yet engaged.

The fact is that the previous evening he had received an unpleasant letter from the steward of his estate. It is well known what disagreeable news a steward can send: bad harvest, serfs' unpaid dues, shrunken income, and the like. Although the steward had written the selfsame letters to his master the previous year and the year before that, the last letter had the strong effect of an unpleasant surprise.

This was no easy matter: it was necessary to think of how to go about taking certain measures. In justice to Ilya Ilyich it must be stated that he bestowed much care on his affairs. On receiving his steward's first unpleasant letter several years earlier, he had begun to consider various changes and improvements in the management of his estate. His plan provided for the introduction of all sorts of new measures affecting economy and order. It was, however, far from thoroughly thought out, and the steward's disagreeable missives kept repeating themselves year after year, urging him to action, and consequently disturbing his peace of mind. Oblomov realized that it was necessary to undertake something decisive even before his plan was completed.

As soon as he awoke he decided to get up, wash, and, after having his tea, do some hard thinking, weigh the pros and cons, take some notes and, in a word, attend to the matter properly.

He lay abed for about half an hour, tormented by this decision, but then it occurred to him that he could have his tea in bed as usual, all the more so since nothing prevented him from thinking while lying down, and then get busy.

This was what he did. After having his tea, he sat up in bed and was on the point of rising; looking at his slippers, he even put one foot out of bed and began lowering it toward them, but immediately drew it back again.

It struck half past nine. Oblomov started.

"What is the matter with me?" he said aloud with vexation. "This is shameful! It is time for me to set to work. If I don't get hold of myself, I'll . . . Zakhar!" he shouted.

From the room that was separated from Oblomov's study by a short passage came what sounded at first like the growl of a chained dog. This was followed by the sound of a pair of legs jumping off something. That was Zakhar, who had jumped off the *lezhanka*,* on which he generally sat dozing.

An elderly man, wearing a gray vest with brass buttons and a gray coat with a rent under the arm from which his shirt protruded, came into the room. His skull was as bare as a knee, but his light-brown side whiskers, streaked with gray, were so vast and thick that each of them was enough for three beards.

Zakhar did not try to change either the appearance the Lord had given him or the clothes he had worn in the country. His costume was made after the model he had brought from his master's estate. He liked the gray coat and vest because his semiformal attire vaguely reminded him of the livery he had worn in former times when he accompanied his late master and mistress to church or on a visit; in his memories this livery was the only thing that represented the dignity of the Oblomov house.

Nothing else reminded him of the peace and plenty of his master's life in the country. The old master and mistress were dead; the family portraits had remained in the old house and were probably lying about in the attic; the tales of the former way of life and of the family's importance were sinking into oblivion, and lived only in the

* The extension of a stove, used to lie or sit on.—A. Y.

memory of a few old men who had remained in the country. That is why the gray coat was dear to Zakhar. He saw in it a faint trace of past greatness. What further reminded him of it was something in Oblomov's countenance and manners that recalled his parents, and his whims, at which Zakhar grumbled both to himself and out loud, but which at heart he respected as a manifestation of the master's will and the master's prerogative. Without these whims he would not have felt that he had a master over him, as it were; without them nothing would have revived for him his youth, the village they had left long ago, the tales about the old house, the sole chronicle preserved by superannuated servants and nannies.

The Oblomov house had once been rich and famous in its section of the country, but later, goodness knows why, it began to go down in the world, and at last was imperceptibly lost among the newer families of the gentry. Only the servants who had grown gray preserved and handed on the memory of the past, treasuring it as a sacred thing. That is why Zakhar loved his gray coat so much. Perhaps he valued his side whiskers, too, because in his childhood he had seen many aged servants with this old-fashioned, aristocratic adornment.

Ilya Ilyich, deep in thought, did not notice Zakhar for a long time. Zakhar stood before him in silence. At last he coughed.

"What is it?" asked Oblomov.

"You called me, didn't you?"

"Called you? What did I call you for? I don't remember!" he answered, stretching. "Go to your room now, and I'll try to remember."

Zakhar left, and Ilya Ilyich went on lying in bed and thinking of the confounded letter.

Nearly a quarter of an hour passed.

"Well, enough lying in bed!" he said to himself. "I must get up. But no, let me read the steward's letter carefully once more, and then I'll get up. Zakhar!"

Again the same sound of a jump and louder growling. Zakhar entered, and Oblomov once more plunged into thought. Zakhar stood for a moment or two, looking at his master disapprovingly out of the corner of his eye, and finally walked toward the door.

"Where are you going?" Oblomov asked suddenly.

"You don't say a word, so why should I stand here for nothing?" Zakhar brought out in a hoarse whisper, his regular voice, he claimed, having been lost while he was riding to hounds with the old master, when a gust of wind had blown into his throat. He was standing in the middle of the room half turned away from Oblomov and still looking at him sideways.

"Have your legs grown so weak that you can't stand for a while? You see I'm worried, so you just wait! Haven't you been lying in your room long enough? Find the letter I got from the steward yesterday. What have you done with it?"

"What letter? I didn't see any letter," said Zakhar.

"But it was you who took it from the postman—such a dirty letter!"

"How should I know where it was put?" said Zakhar, tapping the papers and the various objects on the desk.

"You never know anything. Look there, in the basket. Or perhaps it dropped behind the sofa? Here, the back of the sofa hasn't been repaired yet. Why don't you call in a carpenter to repair it? You were the one who broke it. You don't think of anything!"

"I didn't break it," Zakhar declared. "It broke of itself; a thing can't last forever: it had to break someday."

Ilya Ilyich did not consider it necessary to dispute the point.

"Have you found it?" he merely asked.

"Here are some letters."

"It isn't one of them!"

"Well, there aren't any others," said Zakhar.

"Very well, go," Oblomov said impatiently. "I'll get up and find it myself."

Zakhar returned to his room, but just as he was about to lay his hands on the *lezhanka* in order to jump onto it, a hurried call was heard again:

"Zakhar, Zakhar!"

"Oh, Lord!" Zakhar grumbled, as he made his way back to the study. "This is torture! I wish I were dead! What is it now?" he asked, holding on to the door of the study with one hand and, as a sign of his disapproval, assuming a posture that allowed him to see his master only out of the corner of his eye and his master to see only one of his immense side whiskers, out of which you expect two or three birds to fly.

92

"My handkerchief, quick! You might have thought of it yourself—don't you see?" Oblomov observed sternly.

Zakhar showed no unusual annoyance or surprise at his master's command and reproach, probably finding both entirely natural.

"Who knows where your handkerchief is?" he grumbled, making the round of the room and feeling all the chairs, although one could see that there was nothing on them. "You keep losing things!" he observed, opening the door of the living room to see if the handkerchief was there.

"Where are you going? Look for it here! I haven't been in there since the day before yesterday. And hurry up!" Oblomov said.

"Where is the handkerchief? It isn't anywhere!" said Zakhar, making a helpless gesture and looking into every corner of the room. "Why, there it is," he wheezed angrily all of a sudden, "under you! One end of it is sticking out. You lie on the handkerchief and then you ask for it!"

And, without waiting for a response, he was about to go. Oblomov was somewhat taken aback by his own slip. But he quickly found other grounds for putting Zakhar in the wrong.

"You do keep the place clean! My God, the dust, the dirt! There, over there—have a look at the corners—you don't do a thing!"

"Don't do a thing, me," Zakhar began in an injured tone. "I try hard, I don't spare myself! I dust and sweep nearly every day."

He pointed to the middle of the room and the table at which Oblomov had dined.

"There, look there," he said, "everything's swept and tidied as if for a wedding. What more do you want?"

"And what's this?" Ilya Ilyich interrupted him, pointing to the walls and the ceiling. "And this? And this?"

He pointed to the towel left on the couch since the previous day and to a plate with a slice of bread on it, forgotten on the table.

"Well, this I might take away," Zakhar said, picking up the plate condescendingly.

"Only that? And the dust on the walls, the cobwebs?" said Oblomov, pointing to the walls.

"That I attend to before Easter week. I clean the icons then, and remove the cobwebs."

"And when do you dust the books, the pictures?"

"I do the books and pictures before Christmas. Anisya and I go over all the wardrobes and cupboards then. And how am I to clean the place now? You're always at home."

"Sometimes I go to the theater or pay a visit; you could do it then."

"What sort of cleaning can be done at night?"

Oblomov eyed him reproachfully, shook his head, and sighed. Zakhar looked out of the window unconcernedly, and sighed, too. The master seemed to reflect: "Well, brother, you are more of an Oblomov than I," while Zakhar all but said to himself: "Stuff and nonsense! You're good at spouting highfalutin and heart-wringing words, but you don't mind dust and cobwebs the least little bit."

"Do you know," said Oblomov, "that where there is dust there are moths? Sometimes I even see a bedbug on the wall!"

"I have fleas, too," Zakhar chimed in with indifference.

"Is that good? It's disgusting," Oblomov observed.

Zakhar smirked, and his grin was on such a generous scale that it extended to his eyebrows and side whiskers, which spread out as a result, while his face flushed red.

"Is it my fault that there are bedbugs in the world?" he said with naïve surprise. "Did I think them up?"

"It's because of dirt," Oblomov interrupted him. "You do gabble!"

"It wasn't me thought up dirt, either."

"You've got mice scurrying about in your room at night—I hear them."

"It wasn't me thought up mice, either. There's plenty of those creatures everywhere: mice, cats, bedbugs."

"How is it other people have no moths, no bedbugs?"

Zadhar's face expressed incredulity, or rather, calm certainty that this was not so.

"I've lots of everything," he said stubbornly. "You can't go after every bedbug; you can't crawl into its crack." He seemed to be thinking: "And what would sleeping be without a bug?"

"You just sweep and get the rubbish out of the corners—then there will be no creatures," Oblomov lectured him.

"Get it out today, and there'll be more of it tomorrow," Zakhar argued.

"No, there won't," his master interrupted, "there shouldn't be."

"There will be—I know," the servant insisted.

"If there is, sweep it out again."

"How's that? Clean all the corners every day?" asked Zakhar. "What will life be like, then? I'd rather the Lord took me."

"But why are other people's places clean?" Oblomov retorted. "Look at the piano tuner's across the street—it's a pleasure to see his rooms, and he has only one maid."

"And where would the Germans get any rubbish?" Zakhar suddenly retorted. "Look how they live! The whole family gnaws a bone all week long. A jacket passes from the father's back to the son's and from the son's to the father's again. His wife and daughters wear short dresses—they keep tucking their legs under them like geese. . . . Where would they get any rubbish? They don't have heaps of worn-out clothes lying in wardrobes for years, like us, or pile up a whole cornerful of crusts during the winter. They don't waste the crusts; they turn them into rusks and have them with beer!"

At the thought of such niggardly living Zakhar even spat through his teeth.

"Enough of your gabbing!" Ilya Ilyich retorted. "You'd better clean the place."

"Sometimes I'd like to, but you yourself don't let me," said Zakhar.

"There he's at it again. It's I who am in his way, you see."

"Of course it's you. You're always at home: how can I clean the place with you around? Go out for a whole day and I'll tidy up."

"What an idea! Go out, indeed! You'd better go to your room."

"But really!" Zakhar insisted. "Here, you go out this very day, and Anisya and me will tidy up the place. Just the two of us won't be able to manage; we ought to hire some charwoman to wash everything. . . ."

"Goodness, fancy that—charwomen! Off with you," said Ilya Ilyich.

By now he was sorry he had provoked this conversation with Zakhar. He kept forgetting that to touch on this delicate subject was to get involved in endless trouble. He would have liked to have his lodging clean, but he wanted this to happen somehow by itself, imperceptibly. But every time he asked Zakhar to dust, scrub the floors, and so forth, the man raised a rumpus. On such an occasion he argued that this necessitated a tremendous disturbance in the house, knowing full well that the mere thought of it terrified his master.

Zakhar left, and Oblomov sank into thought. A few minutes later the clock struck another half-hour.

"What's that?" Ilya Ilyich exclaimed, almost horrified. "It's eleven o'clock, and I haven't got up and washed yet! Zakhar! Zakhar!"

"Oh, my God! Well?" Zakhar's voice, followed by the well-known sound of a jump, came from the anteroom.

"Is my water ready?" asked Oblomov.

"Has long been ready!" answered Zakhar. "Why don't you get up?"

"Why didn't you tell me it was ready? I would have got up long ago. Go now, I'll follow you presently. I have something to attend to; I'll sit down to write."

Zakhar left, but a minute later returned with a scrap of paper and a greasy notebook filled with writing.

"Here, if you're going to write, be good enough to check these bills at the same time—they've got to be paid."

"What bills? Who has to be paid?" Ilya Ilyich asked, displeased.

"The butcher, the greengrocer, the laundress, the baker; all of them are asking for money."

"All they care for is money!" Oblomov grumbled. "Why don't you give me a few bills at a time instead of all of them at once?"

"But you kept sending me away, saying, 'Tomorrow, tomorrow . . .'"

"Well, can't we let it go till tomorrow this time, too?"

"No. They badger me so; they won't give me credit any more. Today is the first of the month."

"Oh!" said Oblomov, wretched. "Fresh trouble! Well, why do you stand there? Put the bills on the desk. I'll get up right away, I'll wash, and then I'll look at them. So the water is ready?"

"It is," said Zakhar.

"Well, now . . ."

With a groan he started raising himself in his bed, preparing to get up.

"I forgot to tell you," Zakhar began, "this morning, while you were still asleep, the landlord's agent sent the janitor to say that we must move—they need the flat."

"Well, what of it? If the flat is needed, of course we'll move. Why do you pester me? It's the third time you're telling me about it."

"They're pestering me, too."

"Tell them we'll move."

"They say you promised to about a month ago, but you haven't moved, they say; they'll inform the police, they say."

"Let them inform!" Oblomov said resolutely. "We'll move without further urging as soon as it gets warmer, in about three weeks."

"In three weeks! The agent says that in a fortnight the workmen will be here and start demolishing the place. Move, says he, tomorrow or the day after."

"Oh, they *are* in a hurry! Fancy that! Do you want us to move this minute? Don't you dare even remind me of the flat! I forbade you to do it once before, and you're at it again. Look out!"

"But what am I to do?" Zakhar spoke up.

" 'What am I to do?' That's how he talks his way out of it," answered Oblomov. "He's asking me! Is it any of my business? Don't bother me, and make any arrangements you please, as long as we don't have to move. Can't you put yourself out for your master?"

"But what can I do, Ilya Ilyich, sir?" Zakhar began, speaking gently in a husky voice. "The house isn't mine. How can we refuse to move from another man's house, if we are being driven out? If it were my house, I'd be only too glad . . ."

"Can't they be persuaded somehow? Tell them that we've lived here a long time, that we've paid rent punctually."

"I've told them."

"Well, and what did they say?"

"What? They keep saying: 'You must move out; we've got to make alterations in the flat.' They want to convert this flat and the doctor's into one big apartment in time for the wedding of the landlord's son."

"My God!" Oblomov exclaimed in vexation.

He turned over and lay on his back.

"You ought to write to the landlord, sir," said Zakhar. "Perhaps he wouldn't disturb you, but start work in the other flat." He pointed vaguely to the right.

"Very well, when I get up, I'll write. Go to your room, and I'll think. You can't do anything," he added, "and I have to attend to this rubbish, too, myself."

Zakhar left, and Oblomov started thinking. But he found it hard to decide what to fasten his thoughts on: the steward's letter, the moving, the bills. He was submerged in a flood of mundane cares, and continued to lie there, turning from side to side.

Now and then nothing but abrupt exclamations were heard: "Oh, my God! There's no escaping life; it gets at you everywhere."

It is uncertain how long he would have remained in this state of indecision had there not been a ring at the door.

"A visitor already!" said Oblomov, wrapping himself in his dressing gown. "And I am not up yet—it's a crying shame. Who can it be so early?"

And, still lying in bed, he looked curiously at the door.

Oblomov receives several callers, and it is only when the last of them comes in, a rascally fellow who habitually sponges on him, that he exchanges his bed for an armchair, without abandoning his dressing gown. He has his hair pomaded and combed by Zakhar, but delays washing. As it is the first of May, the visitors try to persuade him to join the fashionable parade that marks the day and otherwise bestir himself sociably, but they all fail. Oblomov is left alone and is now reposing on a sofa, plunged in reveries of blissful, perpetually sunny days. He sees himself living a life of sweet idleness and quiet pleasures on his ancestral domain, the father of a loving family, the center of a group of friends settled in the neighborhood, the master of contented serfs, industrious and paying their dues punctually.

He breaks off daydreaming to have a bit of lunch, and then exasperates Zakhar by calling him "venomous" for bringing up the subjects of the moving and the bills again. At that point his doctor drops in. He tells Oblomov that if he keeps up his present mode of living for another two or three years he will die of a stroke, and prescribes outdoor exercise, a gay social life, foreign travel, possibly a pleasure trip to America. Oblomov is distressed. To make matters worse, after the medico's departure Zakhar once more reminds his master that they must leave their present quarters. Addressing his servant, Oblomov expatiates on the horrors of moving:

"Now do you see for yourself what trouble you were trying to get your master into?" Oblomov asked reproachfully.

"I see," Zakhar whispered meekly.

"Then why did you propose that we move? Is there a human being strong enough to stand all that?"

"I thought that other people, who are no worse than us, do move, and so we can, too," said Zakhar.

"What? What?" Ilya Ilyich asked suddenly in amazement, rising from his armchair. "What did you say?"

Zakhar was taken aback, not knowing how his remark could have moved his master to that violent exclamation and behavior.

"Other people are no worse!" Oblomov repeated horrified. "So that's what you have come to! Now I shall know that to you I am the same as *other people!*"

Oblomov bowed to Zakhar ironically, and his expression left no doubt that he was deeply offended.

"For goodness' sake, Ilya Ilyich, I didn't liken you to anyone else, did I?"

"Out of my sight!" Oblomov said peremptorily, pointing to the door. "I can't bear to look at you. Ah! *Other people?* Very well!"

With a deep sigh Zakhar retired to his room.

"What a life!" he growled, seating himself on the *lezhanka.*

"My God!" Oblomov, too, moaned. "Here I wanted to give the morning over to serious work, and now I'm put out for the whole day. And who has done it? My own tried, devoted servant! And what he said! How could he?"

For a long time Oblomov was unable to regain his composure; he lay down, got up, paced the room, lay down again. That Zakhar should have reduced him to the level of *other people* struck him as a violation of his right to Zakhar's preference for his master's person over all and sundry. He probed the meaning of Zakhar's words, considered the difference between other people and himself, to what extent the comparison was possible and justified, and how gravely Zakhar had offended him. Finally he speculated as to whether Zakhar had offended him. Finally he speculated as to whether Zakhar had insulted him consciously; that is, whether the man was convinced that he, Oblomov, was the same as *other people,* or whether he had spoken thoughtlessly. In short, Oblomov's self-esteem was wounded, and he decided to enlighten Zakhar on the difference between himself and *other people,* and bring home to him all the infamy of his attitude.

"Zakhar!" he drawled solemnly.

Hearing the call, Zakhar did not noisily jump off the stove, as usual, did not growl, but slid down slowly and, his arms and thighs brushing against everything, walked out quietly, reluctantly, like a dog who recognizes by his master's voice that his mischief has been discovered and that he is being summoned to receive punishment.

Zakhar opened the door halfway, but hesitated to enter.

"Come in!" Ilya Ilyich called.

Although the door opened easily, Zakhar did not open it wide enough to be able to pass through and so, getting stuck in the doorway, did not enter.

Oblomov was sitting on the edge of the bed.

"Come here!" he persisted.

Zakhar disengaged himself from the doorway with difficulty, but immediately closed the door and put the weight of his back against it.

"Here!" Oblomov ordered, pointing to a place beside him.

Zakhar took half a step forward and stopped a dozen feet from the spot indicated.

"Closer!" said Oblomov.

Zakhar pretended to take a further step, but merely swayed, stamped his foot, and remained standing where he was. Seeing that this time he could not entice Zakhar to come any closer, Oblomov let him stand where he was and looked at him for some time reproachfully without a word.

Embarrassed by this mute contemplation of his person, Zakhar pretended not to notice his master, and stood there, turned away from him more sharply than usual and not even glancing at him sideways. He stared stubbornly to the left, where he beheld a sight long familiar to him: the cobwebs fringing the pictures and the spider—a living witness to his negligence.

"Zakhar!" Oblomov spoke up in a quiet and dignified tone.

Zakhar did not respond. "Well," he seemed to be saying to his master, "what do you want? Another Zakhar? I'm standing here, am I not?" And he shifted his gaze past his master to the right. There, too, he was reminded of himself by the mirror covered with a thick layer of dust as with muslin: through it, as through a mist, his own morose, unsightly countenance looked back at him distrustfully and unsociably. Annoyed, he turned away from that sad and all too familiar object and decided to fix his gaze for a moment on Ilya Ilyich. Their eyes met.

Zakhar could not bear the reproach in his master's eyes, and dropped his own. In the dust-laden, stained carpet he read again a sad testimonial to his zeal in his master's service.

"Zakhar!" Oblomov repeated with feeling.

"What is it, sir?" Zakhar inquired in a barely audible whisper, and shuddered slightly with the foreboding of a pathetic harangue.

"Give me some kvass," said Oblomov.

Zakhar felt relieved; overjoyed, he dashed to the sideboard like a boy and brought some kvass.

"Well, how do you feel?" asked Ilya Ilyich meekly, taking a sip from the glass and holding it in his hands. "Not so well, eh?"

Zakhar's sullen air was momentarily softened by a ray of repentance that lit up his face. He perceived the first signs of a reverent feeling for his master, which had awakened in his breast and touched his heart, and he suddenly began to look straight in his eyes.

"Are you aware of your misdemeanor?" asked Oblomov.

"What is this 'misdemeanor'?" Zakhar wondered bitterly. "Something heart-wringing, to be sure; you'll burst into tears willy-nilly when he starts raking you over the coals."

"Well, Ilya Ilyich," Zakhar began on the lowest note of his range, "I said nothing, except that—"

"No, wait a moment!" Oblomov interrupted. "Do you understand what you've done? Here, put the glass on the table and answer me!"

Zakhar made no reply, being utterly unable to understand what he had done, which did not prevent him from looking at his master with awe; he even hung his head a little, in acknowledgment of his guilt.

"Can you deny now that you are a venomous creature?" asked Oblomov.

Zakhar continued to hold his peace, and only blinked portentously two or three times.

"You have pained your master!" Ilya Ilyich said, in measured tones, gazing fixedly at Zakhar and savoring his discomfiture.

In his anguish Zakhar did not know what to do with himself.

"You have pained him, haven't you?" Oblomov persisted.

"I *have* pained him," Zakhar whispered, completely crushed by this new heart-wringing word. He looked to the right, to the left, and straight ahead, seeking salvation in something, and the cobwebs, the dust, his own reflection, the master's face, flickered before him again.

"If I could sink through the ground! Oh, why doesn't death come for me?" he thought, seeing that, do what he might, there was no escaping a pathetic scene. As it was, he felt that he was blinking more and more frequently and that at any moment tears would well up in his eyes. Finally he broke his silence,

"How have I pained you, Ilya Ilyich?" he asked, almost weeping.

"How?" Oblomov repeated. "But have you given thought to what *other people* are?"

He paused, continuing to gaze at Zakhar.

"Shall I tell you what they are?"

Zakhar turned like a bear in his lair and heaved a resounding sigh.

"*Other people*—those you have in mind—are a pack of riffraff, coarse, uneducated, living in an attic in filth and poverty; they can have a good sleep on a felt mat somewhere in a courtyard. What can happen to the likes of them? Nothing. They gobble potatoes and herring. Want chases them from place to place, and so they are on the run all day long. Very likely, they wouldn't hesitate to move to a new lodging. Lyagayev, for instance, would take his ruler under his arm and two shirts tied up in a handkerchief, and be on his way. 'Where are you going?' 'I'm moving,' he would say. That's what *other people* are like. In your opinion, am I like that, eh?"

Zakhar looked at his master, shifted from foot to foot, and was silent.

"What are *other people*?" Oblomov went on. "They are people who clean their boots themselves, who have to dress themselves. Such a one may sometimes have the appearance of a gentleman, but he is a fraud; he doesn't even know what a servant looks like; if there's no one to run an errand for him, he'll fetch and carry himself; he will poke the wood in the stove himself, sometimes even do a little dusting. . . ."

"Lots of Germans are like that," Zakhar observed sullenly.

"Right you are. And I? Do you think I am like the *others*?"

"You're quite different!" Zakhar said mournfully, still having no idea of what his master was driving at. "God knows what has come over you. . . ."

"I'm quite different, eh? Wait, give a thought to what you are saying! Consider how the *others* live. They slave away, rush, bustle," Oblomov continued; "if they don't work, they don't eat. The *others* bow, beg, abase themselves. . . . And I? Come, what do you think, am I one of the *others*, eh?"

"Pray, sir, don't go on wearing me out with heart-wringing words!" Zakhar implored. "Oh, my Lord!"

"I am one of the *others?* I don't rush about, don't work, do I? Do I have too little to eat? Do I look thin or wretched? Do I lack anything? I seem to have someone to wait on me, to do things for me. Never in my life have I pulled a sock on my foot myself, thank God! Why should I exert myself? What for? And to whom am I saying this? Haven't you taken care of me since childhood? You know all this; you have seen how tenderly I was brought up, that I have never suffered from cold or hunger, never known poverty; I haven't earned my bread and haven't engaged in any common labor. So how did you have the heart to liken me to *other people?* Am I as vigorous as they? Can I do what they do and endure what they can?"

Zakhar now completely lost the ability to understand what Oblomov was saying, yet his lips were swollen with inner agitation; the pathetic scene was thundering like a storm cloud over his head. He was silent.

"Zakhar!" Oblomov said again.

"What is your pleasure?" Zakhar hissed all but inaudibly.

"Give me more kvass."

Zakhar brought the kvass, and when Oblomov, having drunk it, handed the glass back to him, he quickly made for the door.

"No, no, you wait!" Oblomov began. "I am asking you: How could you have so terribly insulted the master whom you carried in your arms as a baby, whom you have served all your life, and who is your benefactor?"

Zakhar could bear it no longer: the word "benefactor" was the last straw. He began to blink more and more frequently. The less he understood the meaning of Oblomov's pathetic speech, the sadder he grew.

"It's all my fault, Ilya Ilyich," he began to wheeze contritely, "it's really because of my foolishness that I . . . ."

Not understanding what he had done, Zakhar did not know with what verb to wind up his speech.

"And I," Oblomov continued, in the voice of a man whose merits have not been rightly appreciated and who has in fact been insulted, "I worry day and night, I labor; sometimes my head is on fire; my heart sinks; I lie awake at night, tossing about, constantly thinking how to better things. . . . And for whom? Why, all for you, for the peasants, therefore for you, too. When you see me pull the blanket over my head, you probably think that I lie there like a log and sleep; but no, I don't sleep, I keep thinking hard all the time what do so that my peasants should suffer no hardships, so that they should not envy other masters' serfs, so that they should not complain of me to the Lord God on Judgment Day, but pray for me and think kindly of me. What ingratitude!" Oblomov concluded, in a bitterly reproachful tone.

The last *heart-wringing* words cut Zakhar to the quick. Little by little he began to sob. This time his wheezing and hissing merged into a note that no instrument, except perhaps a Chinese gong or an Indian tom-tom, could reproduce.

"Ilya Ilyich, sir! Don't keep it up!" he implored. "What on earth are you saying, the Lord bless you? Oh, Holy Mother of God! What a misfortune has suddenly befallen us against all expectation. . . ."

"And you," Oblomov continued, without listening to him, "you ought to be ashamed to say that! That is the kind of snake I've warmed in my bosom!"

"A snake!" Zakhar exclaimed, throwing up his hands, and bursting into weeping that sounded as if two dozen beetles had flown into the room and begun buzzing. "When did I mention a snake?" he said, amid his sobs. "I don't even dream of the foul creatures!"

The two had ceased to understand each other and now finally neither understood himself.

"How could you have brought yourself to say it?" Ilya Ilyich persisted. "And already in my plan I had assigned him a separate house, a kitchen garden, a ration of corn, and fixed a wage for him! You were to be my manager, chief steward, business agent! The peasants would bow to you from the waist; they would all call you Zakhar Trofimyich! Zakhar Trofimyich! And here he's still dissatisfied; he has been pleased to place me with *others!* Such is my reward! A fine way to honor his master!"

Zakhar continued sobbing, and Oblomov himself was moved. While reproving Zakhar, he became momentarily imbued with the consciousness of the benefits he had bestowed on the peasants, and he delivered his last reproaches in a trembling voice, with tears in his eyes.

"Well, go now, and God bless you!" he said to Zakhar in a conciliatory tone.

"Wait, give me some more kvass! My throat is parched. You yourself might have thought of getting me a drink—you heard that your master was hoarse. What you've brought me to! I hope you've understood your misdeed," said Oblomov, when Zakhar had brought the kvass, "and that in the future you won't compare your master with *others*. To redress the wrong, you arrange it somehow with the landlord that we don't have to move. That is how you protect your master's peace: you have upset me completely and deprived me of the possibility of having any new, useful ideas. And whom did you despoil? Why, yourself. I have devoted my whole being to all of you —for your sake I have retired from the service and live in seclusion. . . . Well, I forgive you! There, it's striking three! Only two hours before dinner, and what can you do in two hours? Nothing. And there is so much to do. Oh, well, I'll put off the letter [to the landlord] till the next mail, and sketch out the plan tomorrow. And now I shall lie down for a while: I am all worn out. Lower the blinds, shut the door tight, so that I am not disturbed; perhaps I shall sleep an hour or so; wake me up at half-past four."

Zakhar proceeded to seal his master hermetically in his study; first he covered him up and tucked the blanket under him; then he lowered the blinds, closed the door tight, and retired to his room.

"May you croak, you devil, you!" he grumbled, wiping away the traces of tears and climbing on the *lezhanka*. "A devil he surely is! A separate house, a kitchen garden, wages!" mumbled Zakhar, who had understood only the last words. "He's good at spouting heart-wringing words, he slashes your heart as with a knife. . . . Here is my house, my kitchen garden, here's where I'll turn up my toes!" he said, striking the *lezhanka* furiously. "Wages! If I didn't lay my hands on a few coppers now and then, I shouldn't have the wherewithal to buy tobacco or treat a chum! I wish you at the bottom of the sea! Why doesn't death come for me?"

Sleep is already beginning to numb Oblomov's body and mind when he is smitten by the thought that he has done nothing since waking up and has not even washed. Recalling the happenings of the day, especially his arguments with Zakhar, he is assailed by shame and horror. He asks himself what hostile fate has sapped his energies and caused his degradation. But this bitter self-awareness is momentary. Soon agitation gives way to his customary apathy, and after some sighs comes "the even snoring of a man peacefully asleep."

NIKOLAY NEKRASOV
(1821–1877)

Freedom*

Oh, Mother Russia, never yet have I
Traveled across your plains with heart so high!

I see a baby at its mother's breast
And by this stirring thought I am possessed:

Child, you were blest in these times to be born;
Please God, it will not be your lot to mourn.

Free, and in dread of no man from the start,
You will yet choose the work after your heart;

You may remain a peasant all your years,
Or soar, with only eagles for your peers.

Perhaps my dream will cause a doubtful smile:
Man's mind is subtle and is full of guile;

Though serfdom's nets are broken, well I know
New snares have been contrived, as time will show;

But these the people will more readily
Break loose from: Muse, greet freedom hopefully.
[1861]

* The emancipation of the serfs, promulgated by a ukase
dated Februray 19, 1861 (Old Style).—A.Y.

Newlyweds

So after the wedding, the husband
Must show off his goods to the bride:
"Look, woman, we've got a good cowshed,
But the cow—God would have it so—died!

"We've no featherbed and no bedstead,
But the bench here is warm, you can feel;
And though we've no calves, we've two kittens:
Just hark at them now, how they squeal!

"There are vegetables out in the garden:
Horseradish and onions I grew.
And if it is brassware you're wanting,
Here's a cross and a brass button, too."

[1866]

IVAN TURGENEV
(1818–1883)

"Within the limits of my power and ability, I strove conscientiously and impartially to represent and incarnate in appropriate types both what Shakespeare called 'the body and pressure of the time'* and the rapidly changing countenance of the educated Russians, who have been the predominant object of my observations." Thus wrote Turgenev toward the end of his life as he looked back at his novels. These form indeed a kind of imaginative social history of Russia during the middle decades of the past century, the age of halfhearted reforms that were changing the old order, threatened by rising political unrest. It is history in terms of the destinies of certain men and women of the privileged classes. The tales display a rare insight into behavior and feeling, the ability to evoke the very essence of a climactic moment or situation. The human dramas are played out against the background of the natural scene, and the vicissitudes of the individuals are set within the larger context of the fate of Russia itself, the huge, mute sphinx. Turgenev believed himself to be an objective, impartial observer of life, but his work reveals a clear-cut point of view: that of a good European, loving freedom "above all else," to use his own phrase, abhorring doctrinaire fanaticism, whether reactionary or radical, a gradualist pinning his faith to enlightenment, *civilization*, as the country's sole hope.

He had been rather slow in finding his true medium. When *Rudin*, his first novel, which was to be followed by half a dozen others, made its appearance in 1856, he considered himself to have practically reached the end of middle age. He had made no effort to obtain the academic post for which his university studies at home and in Berlin had prepared him, and after a short try he had given up a bureaucratic career. As a young gentleman of leisure with a taste for letters, he had composed verse and had also written for the stage. As a poet he was a failure, and, in 1850, shortly after completing A *Month in the Country*, his one lasting contribution to the Russian repertory, he decided that he was no playwright. By then he had to his credit a cycle of short stories and sketches, presented as the record of the author's experiences on his hunting trips. Together with other such pieces they came out in 1852 in a collection entitled A *Sports-*

* The quotation, given in the Russian text in English, telescopes the phrase in Hamlet: "to show . . . the very age and body of the time his form and pressure."—A. Y.

man's Sketches. These pages are a portrait gallery of peasants and their masters, and the subject of serfdom is repeatedly, if unobtrusively, touched upon. It is obvious that the author abominates the institution and is deeply sympathetic with its victims, but the book is not an abolitionist tract. Nevertheless, by revealing the humanity of the serfs, it must have helped to create an atmosphere favorable to the emancipation of the peasantry, which took place in 1861. It is noteworthy that for a decade prior to that historic date Turgenev was the owner—guilt-ridden, it is true —of a vast domain with two thousand "souls," which he had inherited from his ogreish mother.

A *Sportsman's Sketches* proved a signal success, and Turgenev was now launched on the career of a fiction writer. In the three decades left him he produced, in addition to his novels, dozens of shorter narratives. The later stories are, not surprisingly, reminiscent in character. Such is the piece, published in 1881, which is offered below. An uncle and aunt of his were the models from which he drew the couple, and the murder was an actual occurrence. In this instance, as in others, the author's imagination is illuminative rather than creative, to use George Moore's phrase.

"Old Portraits," like much of Turgenev's work, was written in Paris. He was a semiexpatriate whose art remained deeply rooted in the native soil. His main reason for spending a large part of his adult life abroad was in order to be close to Pauline Viardot, a prima donna of Spanish birth married to a Frenchman. He had fallen in love with her in his youth, and developed a lifelong attachment to her and her family. He died in a Paris suburb, with the widowed singer and her children at his bedside.

Old Portraits

About forty versts from our village there lived, many years ago, a cousin of my mother's, a retired officer of the Guards and a rather wealthy landowner, Alexey Sergeich Telegin. He lived on his estate, Sukhodol, which was his birthplace, did not go anywhere, and so did not visit us; but twice a year I used to be sent to pay him my respects—at first with my tutor, later alone. Alexey Sergeich always received me very cordially, and I used to stay three or four days at a time with him. He was an old man even when I first made his acquaintance; I was twelve, I remember, on my first visit, and he was then over seventy. He was born in the time of Empress Elizabeth —in the last year of her reign. He lived alone with his wife, Malanya Pavlovna; she was ten years younger than he. They had two daughters; but their daughters had been long married, and rarely visited

Sukhodol; they were not on the best of terms with their parents, and Alexey Sergeich hardly ever mentioned them.

I see, even now, the old-fashioned house, a typical manor house of the steppes. One-storied, with an immense attic, it was built at the beginning of this century, of amazingly thick pine logs—plenty of such logs were brought in those days from the Zhizdra forests; they have passed out of memory now! It was very spacious, and contained a great number of rooms, rather low-pitched and dark, it is true. The windows in the walls had been cut small for the sake of greater warmth. In the usual fashion (I ought rather to say, in what was then the usual fashion), the outbuildings and house serfs' huts surrounded the manorial house on all sides, and the garden was close to it—a small garden, but containing fine fruit trees bearing juicy apples and pipless pears. The flat steppe of rich black earth stretched for miles round. No lofty object for the eye; not a tree, nor even a belfry; somewhere, maybe, jutting up, a windmill with rents in its sails; truly, Sukhodol [Dry Plain]!

Inside the house the rooms were filled with ordinary, simple furniture; somewhat unusual was a little post that stood in the window of the drawing room, with the following inscription: "If you walk sixty-eight times around this drawing room you will have gone a verst; if you walk eighty-seven times from the farthest corner of the parlor to the right-hand corner of the billiard room, you will have gone a verst," and so on. But what most of all impressed a guest at the house for the first time was the immense collection of pictures hanging on the walls, for the most part works of the so-called Italian masters: old-fashioned landscapes of sorts, and mythological and religious subjects. But all these pictures were very dark, and even warped with age; in one, all that met the eye was some spots of flesh color; in another, undulating red draperies on an unseen body; or an arch that seemed to be suspended in the air; or a disheveled tree with blue foliage; or the breast of a nymph with an immense nipple, like the lid of a soup tureen; a cut watermelon, with black seeds; a turban, with a feather in it, above a horse's head; or the gigantic brown leg of an apostle, suddenly thrust out, with a muscular calf, and toes turned upward. In the parlor, in the place of honor, hung a portrait of Empress Catherine II, full length, a copy of the famous portrait by Lampi —an object of special reverence, one might say adoration, by the master of the house. From the ceiling hung glass chandeliers in bronze settings, very small and very dusty.

Alexey Sergeich himself was a stocky, paunchy little old man, with a chubby face of uniform tint, yet pleasant, with drawn-in lips, and very lively little eyes under high eyebrows. He wore his scanty hair combed back; it was only since 1812 that he had given up powdering. Alexey Sergeich invariably wore a gray redingote, with three capes falling over his shoulders, a striped waistcoat, chamois breeches, high boots of dark red morocco, with heart-shaped cutouts and tassels at the tops, a white muslin cravat, a jabot, lace cuffs, and he had two gold English watches, one in each pocket of his waistcoat. In his right hand he usually carried an enameled snuffbox with "Spanish" snuff, and his left hand leaned on a cane with a silver knob, worn smooth by long use. Alexey Sergeich had a little nasal, piping voice, and an invariable smile—kindly, but, as it were, condescending, and not without a certain complacent self-importance. His laugh, too, was kindly—a shrill little laugh that tinkled like glass beads. Courteous and affable he was to the last degree—in the old-fashioned manner of the days of Catherine—and he moved his hands with slow, rounded gestures, also in the old style. His legs were so weak that he could not walk, but ran with hurried little steps from one armchair to another, which he would suddenly sit down in, or rather fall softly into, like a cushion.

As I have said already, Alexey Sergeich went nowhere, and saw very little of his neighbors, though he liked society, for he was very fond of talking! It is true that he had plenty of society in his own house; various Nikanor Nikanoryches, Sevastey Sevasteiches, Fedulyches, Miheiches, all poor gentlemen in shabby Cossack coats and camisoles, often from the master's wardrobe, lived under his roof, to say nothing of the poor gentlewomen in cotton gowns, black kerchiefs thrown over their shoulders, and worsted reticules in their tightly clenched fingers—all sort of Avdotya Savishnas, Pelageya Mironovnas, and plain Feklushkas and Arinkas, who found a home in the women's quarters. No less than fifteen persons sat down to Alexey Sergeich's table. He was such a hospitable man!

Among all these dependents two were particularly conspicuous: a dwarf, nicknamed Janus, or the Double-Faced, of Danish—or, as some maintained, Jewish—extraction, and the mad Prince L. Contrary to what was customary in those days, the dwarf did nothing to amuse the master or the mistress, and was not a jester—quite the opposite: he was always silent, had an ill-tempered and sullen appearance, and scowled and gnashed his teeth directly a question was addressed to him. Alexey Sergeich called him also a philosopher, and even respected him; at table the dishes were handed to him first, after the guests and master and mistress. "God has afflicted him," Alexey Sergeich used to say; "such is His divine will; and it's not for me to afflict him further." "How is he a philosopher?" I asked him once. (Janus didn't take to me; if I went near him he would snarl hoarsely and mutter "Stranger! Don't pester me!") "Eh, God bless me! isn't he a philosopher?" answered Alexey Sergeich. "Look, little sir, how beautifully he holds his peace!" "But why is he double-faced?" "Because, little sir, he has one face on the outside—and so you, superficial observers, judge him by it. But the other, his real face, he hides. And that face I know, and no one else—and I love him for it. Because that face is good. You, for instance, look and see nothing, but I see without his saying a word: he is blaming me for something; for he's severe! And it's always with good reason. That, little sir, you won't understand; but you may believe an old man like me!"

The real history of the two-faced Janus—where he came from, and how he got into Alexey Sergeich's household no one knew; but the story of Prince L. was well known to everyone. A twenty-year-old youth, of a wealthy and distinguished family, he came to Petersburg to serve in a regiment of the Guards. At the first levee Empress Catherine noticed him, stood still before him, and, pointing at him with her fan, said aloud, addressing one of her courtiers, who happened to be near, "Look, Adam Vasilyevich, what a pretty fellow! A perfect doll!" The poor boy's head was completely turned; when he got home he ordered his coach out, and, putting on a ribbon of St. Anne, proceeded to drive all over town, as though he had really become the Empress' favorite. "Crush everyone who does not move out of the way!" he shouted to his coachman. All this was promptly reported to the Empress; the decree went forth that he should be declared insane and put under the guardianship of his two brothers; and they, without a moment's delay, carried him off to the country and flung him into a dungeon in chains. As they wanted to get the benefit of his property, they did not let the poor wretch out, even when he had come to his senses, and kept him locked up till he really did go out of his mind. But their villainy did not profit them. Prince L. outlived his brothers, and after many afflictions he came into the charge of Alexey Sergeich, whose kinsman he was. He was a stout, completely bald man, with a long, thin face and bulging blue eyes. He had quite forgotten how to talk—he simply uttered a sort of incomprehensible grumbling; but he sang old-fashioned Russian ballads beautifully, preserving the silvery freshness of his voice to extreme old age; and while he was singing he pronounced each word clearly and distinctly. At times he had attacks of a sort of fury, and then he became terrible: he would stand in a corner, with his face to the wall, and all perspiring and red —red all down his bald head and his neck—he used to go off into vicious guffaws, and, stamping his feet, order someone—his brothers probably—to be punished. "Beat 'em!" he growled hoarsely, coughing and choking with laughter; "flog 'em, don't spare them! Beat, beat, beat the monsters, my oppressors! That's it! That's it!"

On the day before his death he greatly astonished and frightened Alexey Sergeich. He came, pale and subdued, into his room and, bowing to him from the waist, first thanked him for his care and kindness, and then asked him to send for a priest, since death had come to him—he had seen death, and he must forgive everyone and establish his innocence. "How did you see death?" muttered Alexey Sergeich in bewilderment at hearing connected speech from him for the first time. "What was her appearance? Did she have a scythe?" "No," answered Prince L.; "a simple old woman in a jacket, but with only one eye in her forehead, and that eye without an eyelid." And the next day Prince L. did die, after having discharged all his duties and taken leave of everyone in a rational and touching manner. "That's just how I shall die," Alexey Sergeich would sometimes observe. And, as a fact, something of the same sort did happen with him—but of that later.

But now let us go back to our story. Of the neighbors, as I have said already, Alexey Sergeich saw little; and they did not care much for him, called him a queer fish, stuck up, a scoffer, and even a *Martinist,** who recognized no authorities, though they had no clear idea of the meaning of that word. To a certain extent the neighbors were right: Alexey Sergeich had lived in his Sukhodol for almost seventy years on end, and had had hardly anything whatever to do

* A Mason.—A. Y.

with the powers that be, the officials and the law courts. "Courts are for robbers, and orders for soldiers," he used to say; "but I, thank God, am neither robber nor soldier!" Rather queer Alexey Sergeich certainly was, but the soul within him was by no means a petty one. I will tell you something about him.

I never knew for certain what were his political opinions, if an expression so modern can be used in reference to him; but, in his own way, he was an aristocrat—an aristocrat rather than a country gentleman. More than once he expressed his regret that God had not given him a son and heir, "for the honor of our name, to keep up the line." In his own room there hung on the wall in a golden frame the family tree of the Telegins, with many branches and a multitude of little circles like apples. "We Telegins," he used to say, "are an ancient line, from long, long ago: however many of us Telegins there've been, we've never hung about great men's anterooms; never bent our backs, cooled our heels in shops, picked up a living in the courts, worn great lords' castoffs; we've never gone trailing off to Moscow, nor intriguing in Petersburg; we've sat at home, each on his roost, his own man on his own land . . . homebodies, sir! nest-building birds. I myself, though, did serve in the Guards—but not for long, thank you."

Alexey Sergeich preferred the old days. "There was more freedom in those days, more decorum; on my honor, I assure you; but since the year 1800" (why from that year, precisely, he did not explain) "the military, the soldiery, have got the upper hand. Our military gentlemen stuck some sort of plumes of cocks' feathers on their heads then, and turned into cocks themselves; began tying their necks up as tight as could be. They wheezed, their eyes bulged—how could they help it, indeed? The other day a police corporal came to me; 'I've come to you,' says he, 'honorable sir' (fancy his thinking to surprise me with that! I know I'm honorable without his telling me!), 'I've business with you.' And I said to him, 'My good sir, you'd better first unfasten the hooks on your collar, or else, God have mercy on us— you'll sneeze, and what will happen to you? What will happen to you? You'll burst open like a puffball, and I shall have to answer for it!' And they do drink, these military gentlemen—oh, oh, oh! I generally order Caucasian wine to be given them, because to them, good wine or poor, it's all the same; it runs so smoothly, so quickly, down their gullets—how can they tell the difference? And, another thing, they've started sucking at a pap bottle—smoking a tobacco pipe. Your military gentleman thrusts his nursing bottle under his moustaches, between his lips, and puffs the smoke out of his nose, his mouth, and even his ears—and fancies himself a hero! Take my sons-in-law—though one of them's a senator, and the other is some sort of curator—they suck the nursing bottles, and they reckon themselves clever fellows too!"

Alexey Sergeich could not endure smoking; and moreover, he could not bear dogs, especially small dogs. "If you're a Frenchman, to be sure, you may well keep a lapdog: you run and you skip about here and there, and it runs after you with its tail up, but what's the use of it to people like us?" He was exceedingly neat and fastidious. Of Empress Catherine he never spoke but with enthusiasm, and in exalted, rather bookish language: "A demigoddess she was, not a human being! Only look, little sir, at that smile," he would add, pointing reverently to Lampi's portrait, "and you will agree: a demigoddess! I was so fortunate as to be deemed worthy to behold that smile close in my lifetime, and never will it be effaced from my heart!" And thereupon he would relate anecdotes of the life of Catherine such as I never happened to read or hear elsewhere. Here is one of them. Alexey Sergeich did not permit the slightest allusion to the weaknesses of the great Czarina. "And, besides," he exclaimed, "can you judge her as other people?"

"One day while she was sitting in her peignoir during the morning toilette, she ordered that her hair be combed. And what do you think? The lady-in-waiting passed the comb through it, and sparks of electricity simply showered out! Then she summoned to her presence the court physician Rogerson, who happened to be on duty, and said to him: 'I am, I know, censured for certain actions; but do you see this electricity? Consequently, since such is my nature and constitution, you can judge for yourself, as you are a doctor, that it is unjust to censure me, and people ought to understand me!' "

The following incident remained indelible in Alexey Sergeich's memory. He was standing one day on guard indoors, in the palace—he was only sixteen at the time—and behold the Empress comes walking past him; he salutes. "And she," Alexey Sergeich would exclaim at this point with much feeling, "smiling at my youth and my zeal, deigned to give me her hand to kiss and patted my cheek, and asked who I was, where I came from, of what family, and then"—here the old man's voice usually broke—"then she bade me greet my mother in her name and thank her for having brought up her children so well. And whether I was on earth or in heaven, and how and where she deigned to vanish, whether she floated away into heaven or went her way into other apartments—to this day I do not know!"

More than once I tried to question Alexey Sergeich about those faraway times, about the people who made up the Empress' circle. But for the most part he edged off the subject. "What's the use of talking about old times?" he used to say. "It's only making yourself miserable, remembering that then you were a fine young fellow, and now you haven't a tooth left in your head. And what is there to say? Those were good old times . . . but there, let's be done with them! As for those folks—I know, you are asking, you troublesome boy, about the favorites!—haven't you seen how a bubble comes up on the water? As long as it lasts and is whole, what colors play upon it! Red and blue and yellow—a rainbow or diamond you'd say! Only, it soon bursts, and there's no trace of it left. And so it was with those folks."

"But how about Potiomkin?" I once inquired.

Alexey Sergeich looked grave. "Potiomkin, Grigory Alexandrovich, was a statesman, a theologian, a pupil of Catherine's, her cherished child, one may say . . . But enough of that, little sir!"

Alexey Sergeich was a very devout man, and, though it was a great effort, he attended church regularly. Superstition was not noticeable in him; he scoffed at omens, the evil eye and such "nonsense," but he did not like a hare to run across his path, and meeting a priest did not altogether please him. For all that, he was very respectful to clerical persons, and went up to receive their blessing, and even kissed the priest's hand every time, but was not willing to enter into conversation with them. "Such an extremely strong odor comes from them," he explained: "and I, poor sinner, am fastidious beyond reason; they've such long and oily hair, and they comb it out on all sides—they think they show me respect by so doing, and they grunt so loudly when they talk—from shyness, may be, or I dare say they want to show respect in that way too. And besides, they make you think of your last hour. And, I don't know how it is, but I still want to go on living. Only, you, little sir, don't you repeat my

116

words; we must respect the clergy—it's only fools that don't respect them; and I'm to blame for babbling nonsense in my old age."

Alexey Sergeich, like most of the noblemen of his day, had received very little education; but he had, to some extent, made good the deficiency by reading. He read only Russian books of the end of last century; the more modern authors he thought insipid and deficient in style. . . . While he read, they placed at his side a silver jug of frothing spiced kvass of a special sort, which spread an agreeable fragrance all over the house. He himself would put on the end of his nose a pair of big round spectacles, but in latter years he did not so much read as gaze dreamily over the rims of his spectacles, lifting his eyebrows, chewing his lips, and sighing. Once I caught him weeping, with a book on his knees, greatly, I own, to my surprise.

He had recalled these lines:

> "O wretched race of man, to thee
> Peace is unknown eternally!
> Unless 'tis time when once thou must
> Come to thy grave and swallow dust.
> Bitter this peace thou drinkest deep.
> Sleep, ye poor dead! Ye living, weep."

These lines were the composition of a certain Gormich-Gormitsky, a wandering poet, whom Alexey Sergeich had sheltered in his house, since he struck him as a man of delicate feeling and even subtlety; he wore slippers adorned with bows, spoke with a broad accent, and frequently sighed, turning his eyes to heaven. In addition to all these accomplishments, Gormich-Gormintsky spoke French decently, having been educated in a Jesuit college, while Alexey Sergeich only "followed French conversation." But once having got terribly drunk at the tavern, that same subtle Gormitsky went berserk; he gave a fearful thrashing to Alexey Sergeich's valet, the male cook, two laundry-maids who chanced to get in his way, and a carpenter from another village, and he broke several windowpanes, screaming furiously all the while: "There, I'll show them, these Russian loafers, roughhewn katzaps!"* And the strength the puny creature put forth! It was hard work for eight men to subdue him! For this display

---

* *Katzaps*: South-Russian term of opprobrium applied to Great Russians.—A. Y.

of violence Alexey Sergeich ordered the poet turned out of the house, after he had been put, as a precautionary measure, in the snow—it was wintertime—to sober him.

"Yes," Alexey Sergeich used to say, "my day is over; there was once a racehorse, but it has run its last race now. I used to keep poets at my expense, buy pictures and books of the Jews, keep geese of the best breeds, and clay-colored tumblers of pure blood. . . . I used to go in for everything! However, dogs I never did care for, because keeping them goes with drinking, foulness, and buffoonery! I was spirited, undaunted. That there should be anything of Telegin's and not first-rate . . . why, it was not to be thought of! And I had a splendid stud. And my horses came—from what stock do you think, young sir? Why, from the celebrated stables of Czar Ivan Alexeich, brother of Peter the Great. . . . It's the truth I'm telling you! All sleek fawn-colored stallions, their manes to their knees, their tails to their hoofs. . . . Lions! And all that was once—and is now—buried in oblivion. Vanity of vanities—all is vanity! But still—why regret it? Every man has his limits set him. There's no flying above the sky, no living in the water, no getting away from the earth. . . . We'll live a bit longer, anyway!"

And the old man would smile again and take a pinch of his Spanish snuff.

The peasants liked him; he was, in their words, a kind master, not easily angered. Only, they, too, repeated that he was a worn-out horse. In former days Alexey Sergeich used to go into everything him-self—he used to drive out to the fields, and to the mill, and to the dairy, and peep into the granaries and the peasants' huts; everyone knew his racing droshky, upholstered in crimson plush, and drawn by a tall stallion, with a broad white stripe on its forehead, called "Lantern," from the same famous stables. Alexey Sergeich used to drive it himself, the ends of the reins wound around his fists. But when his seventieth year came, the old man let everything go, and handed over the management of the estate to the steward Antip, of whom he was secretly afraid, and whom he called Micromégas (a reminis-cence of Voltaire!), or simply, robber. "Well, robber, what have you to say? Have you piled up a great deal in your barn?" he would ask with a smile, looking straight into the robber's eyes. "All, by your good favor, please your honor," Antip would respond cheerfully.

"Favor's all very well; only, you mind what I say, Micromégas: don't you dare lay hands on the peasants, my subjects! If they come to complain . . . I've a cane, you see, not far off!" "Your cane, your honor, Alexey Sergeich, I always keep well in mind," Antip Micromégas would respond, stroking his beard. "All right, don't forget it." And the master and the steward would laugh in each other's faces.

The servants, and the serfs in general, his "subjects" (Alexey Sergeich liked that word), he treated gently. "Because, think, little nephew: nothing of their own, but the cross on their neck—and that copper—and daren't covet other people's goods. . . . How can you expect sense of them?" It is needless to say that of the so-called "serf question" no one ever dreamed in those days; it could not agitate Alexey Sergeich: he was quite happy in the possession of his "subjects"; but he was severe in his censure of bad masters, and used to call them enemies of their class. He divided the nobles generally into three groups: the sensible, "who were rather few"; the prodigal, "of whom there are quite enough"; and the senseless, "of whom there are shoals and shoals."

"And if any of them is harsh and oppressive with his subjects"— he would say—"then he sins against God, and is guilty before men!"

Yes, the house serfs had an easy time of it with the old man; his other "subjects" of course, fared less well, in spite of the cane with which he threatened Micromégas. And what a lot there were of them, those house serfs, in his house! And for the most part sinewy, hairy, grumbling old fellows, with stooping shoulders, in long-skirted nankeen coats, with a strong, sour smell clinging to them. And in the women's quarters you heard nothing but the patter of bare feet, the swish of skirts. The chief valet was called Irinarkh, and Alexey Sergeich always summoned him in a long-drawn-out call: "I-ri-na-arkh!" The others he called: "Boy! Lad! Whoever of my subjects is there!" Bells he could not endure: "This is not an eating house, God forbid!" And what used to surprise me was that no matter when Alexey Sergeich called his valet, he always promptly made his appearance, as though he had sprung out of the earth, and with a scrape of his heels, his hands back, would stand before his master, a surly, almost angry, but devoted, servant!

Alexey Sergeich was generous beyond his means; but he did not like to be called "benefactor." "Benefactor to you, indeed, sir! . . . I'm benefiting myself, and not you, sir!" (When he was angry or indignant, he always addressed people with formality). "Give to a beggar once," he used to say, "and give him twice, and three times . . . and—if he should come a fourth time, give it to him still—only, then you might say too, 'It's time, my good man, you found work for something else than your mouth.'" "But, Uncle," you asked sometimes, "suppose even after that the beggar came again, a fifth time." "Oh, well, give again the fifth time." He used to have the sick who came to him for aid treated at his expense, though he had no faith in doctors himself, and never sent for them. "My mother," he declared, "used to treat illnesses of all sorts with olive oil and salt—she gave the stuff internally, and rubbed it on too—it always worked splendidly. And who was my mother? She was born in the days of Peter the Great—only fancy that!"

Alexey Sergeich was a Russian in everything; he liked only Russian dishes, he was fond of Russian songs, but the accordion—a factory gadget—he hated; he liked looking at the serf girls' dances and the peasant women's jigs; in his youth, I was told, he had been a fine singer and a dashing dancer; he liked steaming himself in the bathhouse, and steamed himself so vigorously that Irinarkh, who, serving him as attendant, lashed him with a bundle of birch twigs steeped in beer, rubbed him with a handful of tow, and then with a woolen cloth—the loyal Irinarkh used to say every time, as he crept off the shelf red as "a new copper statue": "Well, this time I, servant of God, Irinarkh Tolobeyev, have come out alive. How will it be next time?"

Alexey Sergeich spoke excellent Russian, a little old-fashioned, but savory and pure as spring water, continually interspersing his remarks with favorite expressions: "'Pon my honor," "Please God," "Howsoever that may be," "sir," "Little sir."

But enough of him. Let us talk a little about Alexey Sergeich's spouse, Malanya Pavlovna.

Malanya Pavlovna was born in Moscow. She had been famous as the greatest beauty in Moscow—*la Vénus de Moscou*. I knew her as a thin old woman with delicate but insignificant features, crooked teeth, like a hare's, in a tiny mouth, a multitude of finely frizzled little yellow curls on her forehead, and painted eyebrows. She invariably wore a pyramidal cap with pink ribbons, a high ruff round her neck, a short white dress and prunella slippers with red heels;

and over her dress she wore a jacket of blue satin, with a sleeve hanging loose from her right shoulder. This was precisely the costume in which she was arrayed on St. Peter's Day in the year 1789! As a still unmarried young woman, she went with her relations on that day to the Khodynka field to see the famous fisticuffs arranged by Count Orlov. "And Count Alexey Grigorevich" (oh, how often I used to hear this story!), "noticing me, approached, bowed very low, taking his hat in both hands, and said: 'Peerless beauty,' said he, 'why have you hung that sleeve from your shoulder? Do you, too, wish to try a tussle with me? I'm at your service; only I will tell you beforehand: you have vanquished me—I surrender! And I am your captive.' And everyone was looking at us and wondering." And that very costume she had worn continually ever since. "Only, I didn't wear a cap, but a hat *à la bergère de Trianon*; and though I wore powder, yet my hair shone through it, positively shone through it like gold!"

Malanya Pavlovna was foolish to the point of saintliness, as the saying goes; she chattered quite at random, as though she were hardly aware herself of what dropped from her lips—and mostly about Orlov. Orlov had become, you might say, the principal interest of her life. She usually walked, or rather swam, into the room with a rhythmic movement of the head, like a peahen, stood still in the middle, with one foot strangely turned out, and two fingers holding the tip of the loose sleeve (I suppose this pose, too, must once have charmed Orlov); she would glance about her with haughty nonchalance, as befits a beauty—and with a positive sniff, and a murmur of "What next!" as though some importunate gallant were besieging her with compliments, she would go out again, with a tap of her heels and a shrug of her shoulders. She used to take Spanish snuff out of a tiny *bonbonnière*, picking it up with a tiny golden spoon; and from time to time, especially when anyone unknown to her appeared, she would hold up—not to her eyes (she had splendid sight) but to her nose—a pair of eyeglasses in the shape of a crescent, with a coquettish turn of her little white hand, one finger held out separate from the rest.

How often has Malanya Pavlovna described to me her wedding in the Church of the Ascension, on Arbat—"Such a fine church!—and how all Moscow was there, and the crush was—awful! Carriages with teams harnessed tandem, golden coaches, outriders. . . . One outrider of

Count Zavadovsky got run over! And we were married by the bishop himself—and what a sermon he delivered! Everyone was crying—wherever I looked I saw tears. . . . And the governor general's horses were tawny, like tigers. And the flowers, the flowers that they brought! . . . Simply buried in flowers!" And how on that day a foreigner, a wealthy, tremendously wealthy person, had shot himself for love—and how Orlov too had been there . . . And going up to Alexey Sergeich, he had congratulated him and called him a lucky man. "A lucky man you are, you dunderhead!" said he. And how in answer to these words Alexey Sergeich had made a wonderful bow, and had swept the floor from left to right with the plumes of his hat, as if to say,

"Your Excellency, there is a line now between you and my spouse, which you will not overstep!" And Orlov, Alexey Grigorevich understood at once, and commended him. Oh! that was a man! Such a man! And how one day, Alexis and I were in his house at a ball—I was married then—and he wore the most marvelous diamond buttons! And I could not resist it, I admired them. "What marvelous diamonds you have, Count!" said I. And he, taking up a knife from the table, at once cut off a button and presented it to me and said: 'In your eyes, my dear, the diamonds are a hundred times brighter; stand before the looking glass and compare them." And I stood so, and he stood beside me. 'Well, who's right?' said he, while he simply rolled his eyes, looking me up and down. And Alexey Sergeich was very much put out about it, but I said to him: 'Alexis,' said I, 'please don't you be put out; you ought to know me better!' And he answered me: 'Don't disturb yourself, Mélanie!' And these very diamonds are now around my medallion of Alexey Grigorevich—you've seen it, I dare say, my dear—I wear it on feast days on a St. George ribbon, because he was a brave hero, a knight of St. George: he burned up the Turks."

For all that, Malanya Pavlovna was a very kindhearted woman and easily pleased. "She's not one to snarl or nag," the maids used to say of her. Malanya Pavlovna was passionately fond of sweets—and a special old woman who looked after nothing but jam, and so was called the jam maid, would bring her, ten times a day, a china dish with sugared rose petals, or barberries in honey, or pineapple sherbet. Malanya Pavlovna was afraid of solitude—dreadful thoughts are apt to come over you, she would say—and was almost always surrounded by companions, whom she would urgently implore: "Talk, talk! Why do you sit like that, simply keeping your seats warm!" and they would begin twittering like canaries. Being no less devout than Alexey Sergeich, she was very fond of praying; but as, in her own words, she had never learned to repeat prayers well, she kept for the purpose a poor deacon's widow who prayed with such relish! Never once stumbled over a word! And this deacon's widow certainly could utter the words of prayer in a sort of unbroken flow, not interrupting the stream to breathe out or to breathe in, and Malanya Pavlovna listened and was much moved. She had another widow in attendance on her—it was her duty to tell her stories at night. "But only the old ones," Malanya Pavlovna would beg—"those I know already; the new ones are all so fabricated."

Malanya Pavlovna was frivolous in the extreme, and at times she was queer too; some absurd notion would suddenly come into her head. She did not like the dwarf, Janus, for instance; she was always fancying he would suddenly get up and shout: "Do you know who I am? The prince of the Buriats! So you are to obey me!" Or else that he would set fire to the house in a fit of melancholy. Malanya Pavlovna was as generous as Alexey Sergeich; but she never gave money—she did not like to soil her hands—but kerchiefs, earrings, dresses, ribbons; or she would send out pies from the table, or a piece of roast meat, or a bottle of wine. She also liked feasting the peasant women on holidays; they would dance, and she would tap her heels and strike a pause.

Alexey Sergeich was well aware that his wife was a fool; but almost from the first year of his marriage he had schooled himself to pretend that she was very witty and fond of saying cutting things. Sometimes when her chatter began to get beyond bounds, he would threaten her with his little finger and say: "Ah, the tongue, the tongue! What it will have to suffer in the other world! It will be pierced with a red-hot pin!" Malanya Pavlovna was not offended, however, by this; on the contrary, she seemed to feel flattered to hear such words, as though she thought, "Well! is it my fault if I was born witty?"

Malanya Pavlovna adored her husband, and had been all her life the pattern of a faithful wife; but there had been a romance even in her life—a young cousin, a hussar, killed, as she supposed, in a duel on her account; but, according to more trustworthy reports, killed by a blow on the head with a billiard cue in a tavern brawl. A watercolor portrait of this object of her affections was kept by her in a secret drawer. Malanya Pavlovna always blushed up to her ears when she mentioned Kapiton—such was the name of the flame—and Alexey Sergeich would designedly scowl, shake his little finger at his wife again, and say: "No trusting a horse in the field nor a woman in the house. Don't talk to me of Kapiton, the Cupidon!" Then Malanya Pavlovna would be all of a flutter, and say: "Alexis, Alexis, shame on you! In your young days you flirted, I've no doubt, with all sorts of misses and madams—and so now you imagine—" "Come, that's enough, that's enough, my dear Malanya," Alexey Sergeich would interrupt with a smile. "Your gown is white—but whiter still your soul!" "Yes, Alexis, it is whiter!" "Ah, what a tongue, upon my honor, what a tongue!" Alexis would repeat, patting her hand.

To speak of "convictions" in the case of Malanya Pavlovna would be even more inappropriate than in the case of Alexey Sergeich; yet I once chanced to witness a strange manifestation of my aunt's secret feelings. In the course of conversation I once happened to mention the notorious Sheshkovsky.* Malanya Pavlovna suddenly turned livid, green, in spite of her makeup—and in a thick and perfectly unaffected voice (a very rare thing with her—she usually minced a little, showed off, and burred) she said: "Oh, what a man to mention! And toward nightfall, too! Don't utter that name!" I was astonished; what kind of significance could his name have for such a harmless and inoffensive creature, incapable—not merely of doing—even of thinking of anything not permissible? This terror, manifesting itself after almost half a century, aroused in me anything but cheerful reflections.

Alexey Sergeich died in his eighty-eighth year—in 1848, a year that disturbed even him. His death, too, was rather strange. He had felt well that morning, though by then he never left his easy chair. And all of a sudden he called his wife: "Malanya, my dear, come here."

"What is it, Alexis?"

"It's time for me to die, my dear; that's what it is."

"Mercy on you, Alexey Sergeich! Why so?"

"Because, first of all, one must know when to take leave; and, be-

---

* Chief of the secret service under Catherine II, her "private executioner," in Pushkin's phrase.—A. Y.

sides, the other day I was looking at my feet. . . . They are not mine—
say what you like! Look at my hands—they too are not mine! Look
at my stomach—that stomach's not mine! So really I'm using up
another man's life. Send for the priest; and meanwhile, put me to bed
—I shall not get up again."

Malanya Pavlovna was terribly upset; however, she put the old man
to bed and sent for the priest. Alexey Sergeich confessed, took the
sacrament, said goodbye to his household, and dozed off. Malanya
Pavlovna sat by his bedside.

"Alexis!" she cried suddenly, "don't frighten me, don't shut your
eyes! Are you in pain?"

The old man looked at his wife: "No, no pain . . . but it's difficult
. . . difficult to breathe." Then, after a brief silence: "Malanya
darling," he said, "so life has slipped by—and do you remember when
we were getting married . . . what a couple we were!"

"Yes, we were, my handsome, darling Alexis!"

The old man was silent again. "Malanya, my dear, shall we meet
again in the next world?"

"I will pray God for it, Alexis," and the old woman burst into
tears.

"Come, don't cry, silly; maybe the Lord God will make us young
again then—and again we shall be a fine pair!"

"He will make us young, Alexis!"

"With the Lord all things are possible," observed Alexey Sergeich.
"He is a wonder-worker—maybe He will make you a woman of
sense. . . . There, my love, I was joking; come, let me kiss your
hand."

"And I must kiss yours."

And the two old people kissed each the other's hand.

Alexey Sergeich began to grow quieter and to sink into unconscious-
ness. Malanya Pavlovna watched him tenderly, brushing the tears
off her eyelashes with her fingertips. For two hours she continued
sitting there.

"Has he dozed off?" the old woman with the talent for praying
inquired repeatedly in a whisper, peeping in behind Irinarkh, who,
immovable as a post, stood in the doorway, gazing intently at his
expiring master.

"He is asleep," Malanya Pavlovna would answer, also in a whisper. And suddenly Alexey Sergeich opened his eyes.

"My faithful companion," he faltered, "my honored wife, I would bow down at your little feet for all your love and devotion—but how to get up? Let me at least sign you with the cross."

Malanya Pavlovna moved closer, bent down. . . . But the raised hand fell back powerless on the quilt, and a few moments later Alexey Sergeich was no more.

His daughters with their husbands arrived only on the day of the funeral; they had no children, either of them. Alexey Sergeich did not treat them badly in his will, though he did not remember them on his deathbed. "My heart has hardened toward them," he once said to me. Knowing his kindly nature, I was surprised at his words. It is hard to judge between parents and children. "A great ravine starts from a little crack," Alexey Sergeich said to me once in this connection: "A wound a yard wide may heal, but cut off even a fingernail, it will not grow back again."

I fancy the daughters were ashamed of their eccentric old parents.

A month later Malanya Pavlovna too passed away. From the very day of Alexey Sergeich's death she had hardly risen from her bed, and had not put on her usual finery; but they buried her in the blue jacket, and with the Orlov medallion on her shoulder, but without the diamonds. These her daughters divided, on the pretext that the diamonds should be used in the settings of icons; in reality, they used them to adorn their own persons.

And so I can see my old friends before my eyes as though they were alive, and pleasant is the memory I preserve of them. And yet on my very last visit to them (I was a student by then) an incident occurred that jarred on the mood of patriarchal harmony always aroused in me by the Telegin household.

Among the house serfs there was a man no longer young, by the name Sukhoys' Ivan, a coachman or coachboy, as they called him on account of his small size. He was a fidgety little man, snub-nosed, curlyheaded, with an everlastingly smiling childish face and little eyes, like a mouse's. He was a great wag, a most amusing fellow; he was good at all sorts of tricks—he used to fly kites, set off fireworks, play all sorts of games, gallop standing on the horse's back, fly up higher than all the rest in the swing, even make Chinese shadows. No one could amuse children better; and he would gladly spend the whole day with them. When he started laughing, the whole house would liven up, his gaiety was so infectious. They would swear at him, but they laughed. Ivan danced marvelously, especially the "Fish Dance." When the chorus struck up a dance tune, the fellow would come into the middle of the ring and begin spinning and skipping and stamping, and then he would fall flat on the ground, and imitate the movements of a fish tossed out of the water onto dry land; he would bend this way and that way and positively kick the back of his head with his heels; and then he would get up and shriek—the earth seemed simply quivering under him. At times Alexey Sergeich, who, as I have said already, loved to watch dancing, could not resist shouting, "Call Ivan! The coachboy! Dance us the 'Fish,' smartly now"; and a minute later he would whisper rapturously, "Ah, what a fellow, damn him!"

Well, on my last visit, this Ivan came into my room, and, without saying a word, fell on his knees.

"Ivan, what's the matter?"

"Save me, sir."

"Why, what is it?"

And thereupon Ivan told me about his trouble.

He had been exchanged, twenty years ago, by the Sukhoy family for a serf of the Telegin's—simply exchanged without any formality or written deed. The man given in exchange for him had died, but the Sukhoys had forgotten about Ivan, and he had stayed on in Alexey Sergeich's house as his own serf; only his nickname had served to recall his origin. But now his former masters were dead; the estate had passed into other hands; and the new owner, who was reported to be a cruel man, a tormentor, having learned that one of his serfs was kept without any document by Alexey Sergeich, began to demand him back; in case of refusal he threatened legal proceedings, and the threat was not an empty one, as he had the rank of privy councilor, and had great weight in the province. Ivan had rushed in terror to Alexey Sergeich. The old man was sorry for his dancer, and he offered to buy Ivan from the councilor for a considerable sum. But the privy councilor would not hear of it; he was a Little Russian, and obstinate as the devil. The poor fellow would have to be given up.

"I've got used to this place, and I'm at home here; I've served here, here I've eaten my bread, and here I want to die," Ivan said to me—and there was no smile on his face now; on the contrary, it looked petrified. . . . "And now am I to go to this thug? Am I a dog that is chased from one kennel to another with a noose round its neck? . . . Save me, Master; beg your uncle, remember how I always amused you. . . . Or else there'll be trouble; it won't end without sin."

"What sort of sin, Ivan?"

"I'll kill that gentleman. I'll simply go and say to him, 'Master, let me go back; or else, mind, be careful of yourself. . . . I'll kill you.' "

If a siskin or a finch could speak, and had begun assuring me that it would peck another bird to death it would not have amazed me more than did Ivan at that moment. What! Sukhoys' Ivan, that dancing, jesting, amusing fellow, the favorite playfellow of children, and a child himself, that kindest-hearted of creatures a murderer! What nonsense! Not for an instant did I believe him; what astonished me beyond measure what that he was capable of saying such a thing. Anyway I went to see Alexey Sergeich. I did not repeat what Ivan had said to me, but earnestly begged him to do something to straighten matters out.

"My young sir," the old man answered, "I should be only too happy—but what's to be done? I offered this Little Russian a large compensation—I offered him three hundred rubles, 'pon my honor! But he—there's no moving him! What can you do? The transaction was not legal; it was done on trust, in the old-fashioned way. . . . And now see what mischief's come of it! The Little Russian fellow, you see, may take Ivan by force, for all I know: his arm is powerful, the governor eats cabbage soup at his table; the Little Russian fellow will send soldiers! And I'm afraid of those soldiers! In former days, to be sure, I would have somehow saved Ivan; but now, look at me, what a feeble creature I've become! How can I wage war?"

It was true; on my last visit I found Alexey Sergeich greatly aged; even the pupils of his eyes took on the milky color of babies' eyes, and on his lips his old voluntary smile was replaced by the forced, mawkish involuntary grin which even in sleep does not leave the lips of very feeble old people.

I told Ivan of Alexey Sergeich's decision. He stood still, was silent for a little, shook his head.

"Well," said he at last, "there's no escaping what is to be. Only, I'll keep my word. There's nothing left for me to do but to perform a stunt for the last time. Something for a drink, please!"

I gave him something; he got drunk and that day danced the "Fish Dance" so that the serf girls and peasant women positively shrieked with delight.

Next day I went home, and three months later, in Petersburg, I heard that Ivan had kept his word. He had been sent to his new master; his master had called him into his study, and explained to him that he would be made coachman, that a team of three ponies would be put in his charge, and that he would be severely dealt with if he did not look after them all, and was not punctual in discharging his duties generally. "I'm not fond of joking," he said. Ivan heard the master out, first bowed to him from the waist, and then announced that it was as His Honor pleased, but he could not be his servant.

"Let me off for a quitrent, Your Honor," said he, "or send me for a soldier; or else there will be trouble!"

The master flew into a rage. "Damn you! How dare you speak to me like that? In the first place, I'm to be called 'Your Excellency,'* and not 'Your Honor'; and secondly, you're overage, and not of a size to be sent for a soldier; and lastly, what do you threaten me with? Do you mean to set the house on fire?"

"No, Your Excellency, not set the house on fire."

"Murder me then, eh?"

Ivan was silent. "I'm not your servant," he said at last.

"Oh, well, I'll show you," roared the master, "whether you're my servant or not." And he had Ivan severely punished, but yet had the three ponies put into his charge, and assigned him as coachman in the stables. Ivan apparently submitted; he began working as coachman. He drove well, and he soon gained favor with the master, especially as Ivan was very quiet and unassuming in his behavior, and as he turned out the ponies as sound and sleek as cucumbers—they were quite a sight to see. The master took to driving out with him oftener than with the other coachmen. Sometimes he would ask him, "I say,

---

* A privy councilor had the rank of general, and so was addressed as "Your Excellency."—A. Y.

Ivan, do you remember how badly we got on when we met? You've got over all that nonsense, eh?" But Ivan never made any response to such remarks.

Now, one day just before Epiphany the master was driving to town with Ivan in his broad sledge drawn by a troika with bells. The horses began to walk up the hill, and Ivan got off the box and went behind the back of the sledge as though he had dropped something. There was a sharp frost; the master sat wrapped up, with a beaver cap pulled down over his ears. Then Ivan took an ax from under the skirt of his coat, came up to the master from behind, knocked off his cap, and saying, "I warned you, Pyotr Petrovich—you've yourself to blame now!" split his head at one blow. Then he stopped the ponies, replaced the cap on his dead master, and, getting on the box again, drove him to the town, straight to the police station.

"Here's the Sukhoy general for you, dead; I've killed him. As I warned him, so I did. Tie me up."

They took Ivan, tried him, sentenced him to the knout, and then to hard labor. The gay, birdlike dancer found himself in the mines, and there passed out of sight forever. . . .

Yes, willy-nilly—though in another sense—you repeat Alexey Sergeich's words: "Those were good old times . . . but let's be done with them!"

FYODOR DOSTOEVSKY
(1821–1881)

The son of a resident physician in a Moscow hospital for the poor, Dostoevsky was an intellectual proletarian who endured literary peonage most of his adult life. In addition to penury he suffered from epilepsy, and for years he was the victim of a ruinous gambling obsession. At the age of twenty-five he burst upon the literary scene with *Poor Folk*, a novelette, which was an immediate and dizzying success. It was followed by a number of short stories. In 1849, while working on a full-size novel, he was arrested for attending gatherings at which ideas subversive of Church and Throne were freely aired. Together with a score of other young men he was condemned to capital punishment, and only after he had stood on the scaffold in his shroud was it announced that for him, as for the others, death had been commuted to hard labor. He spent ten years in Siberia, first as a convict, later as a soldier.

Back in Petersburg, where he had been settled before his exile, Dostoevsky was not long in reestablishing his position as a man of letters. He was now a devoted subject of the Czar and a believer whose credo centered on Christ as the image of every perfection. What helped to bring him back into the public eye as a writer was *The House of the Dead*, his prison memoirs. They were serialized in 1861–1862 in the short-lived monthly he had launched soon after his return to the capital. The pages by which he is represented in this collection form a chapter in that factual and moving book. Then came the seminal *Notes from the Underground* (1864), an inquiry into the alienated and dehumanized personality. It may be regarded as a preamble to the novels: *Crime and Punishment* (1866), *The Gambler* (1866), *The Idiot* (1868), *Devils* (better known as *The Possessed*) (1871–1872), *A Raw Youth* (1875), *The Brothers Karamazov* (1879–1880). In his last years Dostoevsky did much forensic writing, which does not redound to his credit. It went to make up the contents of *A Writer's Diary*, his one-man monthly.

His early writings have to do with weak, flawed, sick souls. More than one of these pathetic or lugubrious stories are studies in insanity. The motifs of the morbid, the perverse, the aberrant, keep cropping up in his mature work as well. Whether or not they are within the normal range, his leading characters are drawn with immense imaginative power and an insight into the processes of the mind that anticipates some of the findings of modern psychology. The novels teem with emotional upheavals and deeds of violence, and rely heavily on the stock-in-trade of crude melodrama. Yet these turbulent thrillers are also the battlefield of ideas. These have their source in religious wellsprings, the concept of God having dominated Dosteoevsky's thinking.

Crime and Punishment was intended as a warning that unbelief held the threat of moral chaos. The author was committed to the proposition that man cannot be good or find life bearable without the certainty that God exists and that the soul is immortal. To the end he used his pen to combat what he called interchangeably nihilism or socialism. By this he meant the replacement of the existing order with a secular, soulless, rationally planned collective, built by human hands under the aegis of science. In such a society, he felt sure, the individual would lose the freedom to choose between good and evil, which is the essence of man's humanity and the only way to God. To this debasing materialistic doctrine he opposed the vision of mankind achieving unity not by force or out of self-interest but in the spirit of Christian loving-kindness and brotherhood. And, succumbing to the peculiarly Russian weakness for Messianism, he predicted that his compatriots were destined to bring about this divine event in the fullness of time, for—this was a cherished conviction with him—alone the Russian masses, uncorrupted by Western civilization, have preserved Christianity in all its purity.

He never tired of protesting that he was on the side of the angels. Faith, he held, has the power to exorcise a demon, to save the errant soul that has strayed into sin or crime, to make a divided self whole. But he usually had the good sense to refrain from depicting the event, relegating it to an indefinite future. He was not at heart a supporter of the Establishment. There is an air of impermanence about the world he imagined. He made a brave effort to limn a Christlike figure, a pious vagabond embodying the serene faith by which the common people lived, a saintly pillar of the Church, but he was immeasurably more effective in giving body and breath to a criminal would-be superman, a possessed rebel, a doomed demonic man, a complete sensualist, a tormented doubter, a divided soul.

FROM The House of the Dead

AKULKA'S HUSBAND

It was already late at night, past eleven o'clock. I had fallen asleep, but suddenly woke up. The tiny dim flame of the distant night lamp barely lit the ward. . . . Almost everyone was asleep. Even Ustyantzev slept, and in the stillness one could hear with what an effort he breathed and how he was wheezing with every breath from the phlegm in his throat. Far away in the entry there suddenly resounded the heavy footsteps of the sentinel coming to relieve the guard. The butt of a gun clanged against the floor. The door opened; the corporal, stepping cautiously, counted the patients. A minute later the ward was locked up, a new sentinel was posted, the guard took himself off, and there was again the same stillness. Only then did I notice that on the left, not far from me, two patients were awake and seemed to be whispering to each other. This used to happen in the wards: sometimes two men would lie side by side for days and months without saying a word to each other, and suddenly, encouraged by something provocative about the night hour, they would get to talking and each would begin to pour out his whole past to the other.

They had apparently been talking for some time. I had missed the beginning, and even now I could not make it all out, but little by little I grasped the thread of the conversation, and began to understand all of it. I could not sleep; what was there to do, then, but listen? One man was speaking heatedly, half reclining on the bed, his head raised, his neck craned toward his companion. He was seemingly flushed and excited; he was eager to talk. His hearer, sullen and perfectly indifferent, sat on his cot, his legs stretched out, and occasionally mumbled something in reply or in token of sympathy with the speaker, but, as it were, more for the sake of propriety than out of real feeling, and every moment stuffed his nose with snuff out of a box. He was Private Cherevin, from the disciplinary battalion, a man of about fifty, a morose pedant, a cold reasoner and a self-regarding fool. The speaker, Shishkov, was a young fellow of about thirty, a civilian convict, who worked in the tailoring shop. Until then I had taken little notice of him; and somehow I was not drawn to occupy myself with him during the rest of my time in prison. He was a shallow, unbalanced chap. Sometimes he was silent, sullen, behaved rudely and would not say a word to anyone for weeks on end. And sometimes he would get involved in some trouble, start bearing tales, would get excited over trifles, scurry from barrack to barrack, spreading gossip, slandering, flying into rages. He would be given a beating and relapse into silence. He was a cowardly, weak lad. Somehow everyone treated him with contempt. He was short and thin; his eyes were restless, but sometimes had a dully pensive look.

Occasionally in relating something he would begin excitedly, with ardor, even waving his arms—and suddenly break off, change the subject, carried away by new details and forgetting how he had begun. He often started quarrels, and when he did, and accused his opponent of wronging him, he spoke with feeling, almost in tears. . . . He played the balalaika fairly well and was fond of playing, and on holidays he even danced, and danced well when they got him to. It was easy to make him do things. Not that he was especially docile, but he loved to make friends, and so was eager to play up to people.

For a long time I could not grasp what he was talking about. At first I fancied that he was straying from his subject into irrelevant matters. He may have noticed that Cherevin took practically no interest in his story, but he semed eager to convince himself that his hearer was all ears, and it may be that it would have hurt him very much if he had become convinced of the contrary.

". . . Whenever he came to market," he went on, "folks bowed to him, paid him respect, in short—a rich man."

"He was in trade, you say?"

"Well, yes, in trade. We townsfolk lived from hand to mouth. A beggarly lot. Women carried water from the river ever so far up the steep bank to water the kitchen gardens; they worked themselves to the bone, and in the fall the pickin's wasn't enough for cabbage soup. Sheer ruination. Well, he had a lot of land, worked by hired men; he kept three of 'em; besides he had his own beehives, and traded in honey and in cattle, too, and in our parts, you know, he was greatly respected. He was an old bird, seventy; his bones got heavy, his hair gray, a great big man. He'd show up in the marketplace in his foxfur coat, and everybody would do him honor. 'Good mornin' to you, Ankudim Trofimych!' 'Good mornin' to you, too,' he'd say. He didn't hold no one beneath himself, you know. 'Long life to you, Ankudim Trofimych!' 'And how's business?' he'd ask. 'Why, with us business is bright as soot is white. How are you doin', father o' mine?' 'Not so bad, sinner that I am, idling my life away like the rest,' he'd say. 'Long life to you, Ankudim Trofimych!' Held no one beneath himself, that is, and when he spoke, every word of his was worth a ruble. Knew his Bible, could read, kept his nose in holy books. He'd seat his old woman before him, say: 'Now listen and mark, wife,' and he'd start expoundin'. And his wife wasn't so very old; she was his second, he married her for the sake of children; I mean—he had none with the first. Well, by Marya Stepanovna, the second, he had two sons, not grown up at the time. He was sixty when the younger one, Vasya, was born, and his daughter, Akulka, the eldest of the lot, I mean, was eighteen."

"Was that your wife?"

"Hold on, first Filka Morozov will be doin' some dirt here. 'You give me my share,' he says to Ankudim; 'give me all of the four hundred due me—am I your hired man, eh? I won't be in business with you and I don't want your Akulka. I'm goin' to have my fling now,' says he. 'My father and mother are dead now,' says he, 'so I'll spend my money on booze, and then sell myself as a substitute,* and in ten years I'll come back here a field marshal.' So Ankudim handed him the money, settled with him for good—because his father and the old man had been partners together. 'You're done for,' Ankudim says to him. 'Whether I'm done for or not,' Filka answers, 'all I could learn from you, graybeard, is to sup milk with an awl. You pinch a penny till it squeaks,' says he; 'you get all kinds of rubbish and stick it into the soup. I'd as lief spit on it all,' says he. 'You save and you save, and you end in the grave. I'm a man of character,' says he. 'All the same, I'm not gonna marry your Akulka. I've slept with her as it is. . . .' 'How dare you dishonor a respectable father, a respectable daughter?' says Ankudim. 'When did you sleep with her, you snake's fat, you pike's blood, you?' And he was all atremble. Them's Filka's words. 'What's more,' says he, 'I'll see to it that your Akulka won't get any husband; no one will have her, not even Mikita Grigorich, because now she's dishonored. Ever since fall we been livin' together. And now I won't agree for a hundred fish. You just try givin' me a hundred fish now—I won't agree. . . .'

"And didn't he run riot, the lad! The earth groaned under him; the town was ringin' with noise. He got a bunch of fellows together, had a barrel of money, made whoopee for three months on end, squandered everythin'. 'When I've run through the money,' says he, 'I'll sell the house and spend the money, spend everythin' and then I'll either sell myself as a substitute or turn hobo.' He'd be soused from morning till night and drive a team of horses with bells.

* A family required to supply a recruit was permitted to furnish a paid substitute.—A. Y.

And the way the wenches ran after him was terrible. He played the *torba* well."

"So he'd been carrying on with Akulka before that?"

"Hold on, wait. Just then I, too, buried my father; and my mother, she baked cakes, and we worked for Ankudim, that's how we made a living. It was hard goin'. Well, we had had a bit of land beyond the woods, sowed it to corn, but we lost everythin' after Father died, because I too went on a binge, brother. I'd get money out of my mother by beating her."

"That's not right—beatin'. A great sin."

"I used to be drunk from mornin' till night, brother. Our house was still so-so, not bad, rundown but our own, but it was bare as a bald head. We used to go hungry, gnawed a bone for a whole week. My mother'd nag and nag me, but I didn't care a bean. In those days I stuck closer than a burr to Filka Morozov, brother. I was with him day and night. 'Play the guitar and dance for me,' he'd say, 'and I'll be lyin' down and flingin' money at you, because now I'm the richest man in the world.' And what didn't he do! Only, he wouldn't receive stolen goods. 'I'm no thief,' he'd say; 'I'm an honest man.' Let's go and smear Akulka's gate with tar,* because I won't have Akulka married to Mikita Grigorich. I care more for that than for jelly,' says he. The old man meant to marry off his daughter to Mikita Grigorich before that. Mikita, too, was a graybeard, a widower in specs, a tradesman. When he got wind of the rumors about Akulka, he backed out. 'That would be a mighty disgrace for me, Ankudim Trofimych,' says he, 'and besides, I don't want to get married in my old age.'

"So we smeared Akulka's gate. And didn't they thrash her for it at home! Marya Stepanovna screamed, 'I'll finish you!' And the old man held forth: 'In olden days,' says he, 'in the days of the venerable patriarchs I'd have cut her to pieces at the stake,' says he, 'but nowadays the world is all darkness and corruption.' All along the street the neighbors would hear Akulka howling. They flogged her from mornin' till night. And Filka would shout for the whole market to hear: 'There's a fine wench and drinkin' companion, Akulka by name. You walk out in white so neat, who's the one you call your sweet? I've made a stink there,' says he; 'they won't forget me.'

* A way of dishonoring a girl.—A. Y.

136

"One day I met Akulka carrying pails, and I shouted: 'Good mornin' to you, Akulina Kudimovna! Greetings to Your Highness. You go walkin' out in white, say with who you spend the night.' That's what I said. And how she looked at me! She had such big eyes, and she had grown as thin as a lath. When she was lookin' at me, her mother thought that she was bandyin' words with me, and she shouted from the gateway, 'What are you chewin' the rag for, you shameless hussy?' And that day they gave her another thrashin'. They'd thrash her a good hour. 'I'll finish her,' the mother'd say, 'because she's no daughter of mine now.' "

"So she was a slut, eh?"

"You just listen, uncle. While Filka and me was boozin' together, my mother came up to me one day—I was lyin' down. 'Why are you lyin' down, you scoundrel?' says she. 'You bandit, you,' says she. She scolds, I mean. 'Get married,' says she; 'you marry Akulka. They'd be glad to marry her off even to you. They'd hand you three hundred rubles in cash alone!' 'But she's disgraced now,' says I, 'in the eyes of the whole world.' 'What a fool you are!' says she. 'The weddin' crown* covers all; it'll be the better for you if she's guilty before you her whole life. And with their money we'll be on our feet again. I talked it over with Marya Stepanovna already,' she says. 'She's all ears.' 'Twenty rubles down,' says I, 'and I'll marry her.' And, believe it or not, right up to the day of the weddin' I was dead drunk. And Filka Morozov was threatenin' me besides: 'I'll break every bone in your body, Akulka's husband,' says he, 'and I'll sleep with your wife every night, if I like.' 'You're lyin','' I says to him, 'you dog's meat!' Then he put me to shame before the whole street. I ran home. 'I won't get married,' says I, 'if they don't hand me fifty rubles more this minute!' "

"And did they let you marry her?"

"Me? Why not? We was respectable folk. My father was only ruined at the end by a fire; before that we'd been better off than them. 'You're down and out,' says Ankudim. 'There's been not a little tar smeared on your gate,' I answer. 'Don't bully us,' says he. 'There's no stoppin' people's mouths, but you prove that she's disgraced herself. Here's the icon and here's the door,' says he. 'Don't

---

* Crowns are placed on the heads of the bride and groom at a Russian church wedding.—A. Y.

marry her; only pay back the money you've taken.' So Filka and me made up our minds: I sent Mitry Bykov to tell him I'd dishonor him now before the whole world, and, right up to the day of the weddin' I was dead drunk. Only for the weddin' I sobered up. When we was brought back from the church and sat down, Mitrofan Stepanovich, my uncle, that is, says: 'Though the thing is done in dishonor, it's fully bindin' and it's finished.' Ankudim, too, was drunk, and he cried and he cried; he sat there and the tears run down his beard. And this is what I did then, brother: I put a whip in my pocket, I'd got it ready before the weddin', and I made up my mind that I'd have some fun with Akulka, to teach her, I mean, what it is to get a husband dishonorably and that folks might know I wasn't fooled when I married her. . . ."

"Right you was, too! To teach her a lesson for the future . . ."

"No, uncle, hold your tongue. In our part of the country, right after the weddin' they take you to the room one side of the entry, while the guests go on drinkin' in the other room. So they left Akulka and me in that room. She sat there white as a sheet, deathly pale. Scared, I mean. Her hair, too, was white as flax. And her eyes were big. And she was always silent; she didn't make a sound; she was like a dumb woman in the house. A strange girl altogether. And just imagine, brother—I got the whip ready, put it right there beside the bed, and, it turned out, brother, that she wasn't guilty before me at all."

"You don't say!"

"She was innocent, a respectable daughter of a respectable family. And what did she have to suffer all that torment for? Why did Filka Morozov disgrace her before the whole world?"

"Yes, why?"

"I got down on my knees before her right there, off the bed and put my hands together. 'Akulina Kudimovna, forgive me, fool that I am, for thinkin' ill of you, like the others. Forgive me, scoundrel that I am!' says I. She sat before me on the bed, looked at me, put both hands on my shoulders, laughin' while her tears was flowin'; she cried and she laughed. . . . When I went out to them all, I said, 'Well, if I meet Filka Morozov now, he's a goner!' And the old people, they didn't know who to pray to. The mother near threw herself at her

138

feet, howlin'. The old man says: 'If we'd known it, we'd have found another kind of husband for you, our beloved daughter.'

"When the two of us walked to church the first Sunday, me in my Astrakhan cap, a kaftan of fine cloth, and velveteen trousers, she with a new hareskin coat and a silk kerchief—we looked a well-matched pair, and that's how we walked! Folks was admirin' us. Let's say nothin' about me, but as for Akulina, she couldn't be praised above the rest, but then she couldn't be run down neither—she'd have held her own with any dozen. . . ."

"Very good, then."

"Well, you listen. The day after the weddin' I was drunk, and I ran away from the guests; I broke away and ran. 'Bring me that loafer, Filka Morozov,' says I, 'bring the scoundrel here!' I shouted all over the market. Well, I was good and drunk. So they caught me when I was near the Vlasovs', and three men brought me home by force. Meantime the town was ringin' with talk. The market wenches was sayin' to each other: 'Girls, dearies, have you heard? It turns out, Akulka's innocent.'

"Not long after Filka says to me before folks: 'Sell your wife—and you can stay drunk. Yashka the soldier got married just for that,' says he; 'he didn't sleep with his wife, but he was drunk for three years.' 'You're a scoundrel,' says I. 'And you're a fool,' says he. 'You was drunk when you got married, you know. How could you tell what was what then?' I came home and shouted, 'You married me when I was drunk,' says I. My mother landed into me. 'Your ears are stopped with gold, Mother,' says I. 'Let me have Akulka!' Well, I began to rough her up. I punched her and pommeled her, brother, I pommeled her near two hours, till I couldn't keep on my feet. She didn't get up from bed for three weeks."

"Of course," Cherevin observed phlegmatically, "if you don't beat them, they'll . . . But did you catch her with a lover?"

"No, catch her I didn't," Shishkov answered, after a pause and with an effort, as it were. "But I felt so bad, people teased me so, and Filka was back of it all. 'You've a wife: a model, for folks to ogle.' Filka invited me, along with some of his chums, and here's how he started off: 'His spouse,' says he, meanin' me, 'is a charitable soul, well-born, civil, mannerly, good in every way—that's what he believes now! And have you forgotten, my lad, how you yourself smeared her gate with tar?' I was sittin' there drunk, and now he grabbed me by the hair and pushed my head down. 'Dance,' says he, 'Akulka's husband, I'll hold you by the hair this way, and you dance: amuse me.' 'You're a scoundrel!' I shouted. 'I'll come to you with my crew and flog Akulka, your wife, before your eyes, as long as I please.' So, believe me or not, for a whole month I was afraid to leave the house: he'd come, I thought, and disgrace me. And just for that I began beatin' her. . . ."

"But why beat her? Hands can be tied, not the tongue. It ain't right to beat a wife too much. Punish her, teach her a lesson, but be good to her, too. She's your wife."

Shishkov was silent a while.

"I felt bad," he began anew; "then again I got into the habit of it. Some days I'd thrash her from mornin' till night: the way she got up, the way she walked, everythin' she did was wrong. If I didn't give her a beatin', I was bored. She'd sit without sayin' a word, lookin' out the window, cryin' . . . always cryin'. I'd feel sorry for her, and I'd beat her. My mother'd scold me and scold me on her account. 'You're a scoundrel, you bandit, you,' she'd say. 'I'll kill her,' I shouted, 'and no one dare say a word to me, because I was tricked into marryin'.' At first old Ankudim would stand up for her. He'd come himself and say: 'You're not such a big cheese yet; I'll have the law on you.' Then he gave it up. As for Marya Stepanovna, she knuckled under altogether. One day she came and said to me with tears in her eyes: 'Don't be sore, Ivan Semyonych, I come to ask a great favor of you. Bring light to my eyes, father o' mine,' and she bowed down, 'soften your heart, forgive her! Evil folk slandered our daughter; you know yourself you married an honorable maiden.' She bowed low and she cried. But I bullied her. 'I won't listen to you now!' says I. 'I do just what I want with the lot of you; I'm no longer master of myself. Filka Morozov is my chum and best friend. . . .' "

"So you were again whooping it up together?"

"Oh, no! There was no gettin' near him. He'd turned into a booze-hound. He'd drunk up all he owned and sold himself to a merchant to serve in the army instead of his eldest son. In our neck of the woods a man who does that, up to the very day he is taken away as a recruit, everythin' in the house is for him, and he's master over everythin'. He gets his pay in full when he goes, and until then he stays in the home of the man he's to replace, sometimes he lives there half a year, and the way he carries on there is a shame before the icons! 'I'm goin' to serve as a soldier in place of your son,' he'd say, 'so I'm your benefactor, and you all must pay me respect, or I'll back out.' So Filka helled around at the merchant's, slept with his daughter, pulled his beard every day after dinner—had the time of his life. A steam bath every day, and, to make steam, vodka had to be used instead of water, and the women had to carry him to the bathhouse. Coming home from a blowout, he'd stand in the street and declare: 'I won't go in at the gate; pull down the fence,' so they had to make an opening in the fence, and he'd march through.

"At last it was time for him to go; they sobered him up and drove off with him. Folks came out into the street in crowds: Filka Morozov was bein' taken away as a recruit! He bowed right and left. Just then Akulka was on her way from the kitchen garden. Soon as he caught sight of her at our gate, he cried, 'Stop!' jumped out of the cart, and bowed down to the ground before her. 'My darlin',' says he to her, 'my sweet one, I've loved you for two years, and now they're takin' me to be a soldier, with the band playin'. Forgive me,' says he, 'honorable daughter of an honorable father, because I'm a scoundrel before you, and it's all my fault!' And he bowed down to the ground before her again. Akulka stopped, scared-like at first; then she bowed to him from the waist, and said: 'You forgive me, too, goodly youth; I know of no wrongdoin' of yours.' I followed her into the house. 'What did you say to him, dog's meat?' And, believe me or not, she looked at me and she said, 'Why, I love him now more than all the world.' "

"How do you like that!"

"All that day I didn't say a word to her. Only toward evenin' I told her, 'Akulka, now I'll kill you.' At night I couldn't sleep; I went into the entry to have some kvass, and it was beginnin' to be day. I came back into the room. 'Akulka,' says I, 'get ready to drive to the field.' I'd been meanin' to go out there before, and when Mother heard that we was goin' she said: 'That's right, it's the height of the season, and I hear the hired man has been laid up with stomach trouble for three days now.' I got the cart ready without a word.

"As you drive out of our town you get into pine woods stretchin' for fifteen versts, and beyond the forest is our land. When we'd driven some three versts in the woods, I stopped the horse. 'Get up, Akulina,' says I; 'your end has come!' She looked at me; she got scared, stood up before me, without a word. 'I'm fed up with you,' says I; 'say your prayers!' Then I grabbed her by the hair—she had long thick braids—twisted them round my hand and squeezed her tight from behind between my knees; I took out my knife, pulled her head back and slid the knife across her throat. . . . She screamed, the blood spurted, I threw down the knife, turned and caught her in my arms, lay down on the ground, hugged her and cried, howled over her; she screamed and I screamed; she fluttered all over, struggled to get out of my arms, while the blood, the blood was pourin' out, pourin' over my face and my hands. I let go of her, fear came over me, I left the horse and myself started runnin', runnin'. I ran home along the backyards, and made for the bathhouse—we had an old bathhouse nobody used. I hid under the shelves and sat there. I sat there till nightfall."

"And Akulka?"

"It seems she got up after me and she walked toward the house, too. They found her afterward a hundred steps from that place "

"So you hadn't quite done her in."

"No . . ." Shishkov paused.

"There's a special vein," observed Cherevin; "if this vein ain't cut through right away, you'll go on strugglin' and won't die, no matter how much blood you lose."

"But she did die. They found her dead in the evenin'. The police was told; they started lookin' for me, and they found me at night, in the bathhouse. . . . And I've been here nigh on four years,' he added, after a pause.

"H'm . . . To be sure, if you don't beat them, no good will come of it," Cherevin observed coldbloodedly and sententiously, taking out his snuffbox again. He stuffed his nostrils slowly at intervals. "Then again, the way I see it, you're awful stupid, my lad. I, too, caught my wife with another man once. So I called her into the shed, took the bridle and doubled it. 'To who do you swear to be faithful?' says I. 'To who do you swear to be faithful?' And I thrashed her, I thrashed her, I mean with the bridle, I thrashed her for nigh on an hour and a half. So what do you think? 'I'll wash your feet and drink the water,' she cried. Ovdotya was her name."

NIKOLAY LESKOV
(1831–1895)

Leskov was the son of a civil servant who came of an ecclesiastical family. Orphaned at sixteen, he had to quit school to earn a living, so that he was largely a self-taught man. He was nearly thirty before he began writing. By then he had a wide knowledge of Russian life, gained through traffic with all manner of people, first as a minor official, later as an assistant to the manager of a nobleman's estates. It was as a contributor of miscellaneous articles to newspapers and periodicals that he broke into print. He never quite gave up journalism, but devoted himself chiefly to fiction. By 1870 he had published a number of stories and novellas, as well as two novels directed against the radical youth, which earned him the reputation of a reactionary. For some years he continued to champion Orthodoxy and monarchy, but in time he assumed a critical attitude toward Church and Throne. As a result, he lost his sinecure at the Ministry of Education. In 1889 the copies of a volume of his collected works were burned by official order.

The life of the clergy is the subject of many of his tales and of his best-known novel, *Minster Folk* (1872). His work reveals his intimate knowledge of other social groups. The story printed below—first published in 1887—is one of several narratives seeking to show that Russia does not lack righteous men like those for whose sake God was willing to spare Sodom. "The Sentry" is based on an actual occurrence. The ecclesiastical dignitary who figures in the final pages is patterned on Philaret, the Metropolitan of Moscow.

Leskov left behind a large body of writing, extremely varied in content and form, as well as in quality. Only posthumously has he come to be generally recognized as a major writer, a portrayer of Russian manners and morals possessed of a rare narrative gift, great imaginative power, a protean style all his own.

The Sentry

1

The event an account of which is here brought to the reader's notice is touching and terrible in its effect upon the protagonist of the piece, and its outcome is so singular that a thing of this sort could hardly have occurred in any country other than Russia.

It is partly a court anecdote, partly a bit of history that characterizes rather well the manners and spirit of a very curious yet little known period: the 1830's.

There is not a shred of invention in the following tale.

2

In the winter of 1839, just before Epiphany, there was a great thaw in Petersburg. It was so slushy that it seemed almost as if spring were on the way: the snow was melting, during the day water dripped from the roofs, and the ice in the rivers grew blue and swollen. On the Neva just in front of the Winter Palace, there was open water in several places. A warm but very strong wind was blowing from the west; the water was driven in from the bay and the signal guns boomed.

The guard at the Palace was made up of a company of the Izmailovski regiment, commanded by a brilliantly educated and socially prominent young officer, Nikolay Ivanovich Miller, who subsequently became a full general and a lyceum director. He was a man of so-called "humane" propensities, a trait that had early been noted in him and that, in the eyes of the highest authorities, somewhat impaired his prospects in the service.

In reality Miller was an efficient and reliable officer; and in those days mounting guard at the Palace involved no danger. It was a time of perfect peace and tranquillity. Nothing was required of the Palace guards except the scrupulous discharge of sentry duty. Nevertheless, it was precisely while Captain Miller was on guard that an extraordinary and alarming occurrence took place, doubtless scarcely remembered now by the few then living who are still in our midst.

3

At first all went well with the guard: the posts were distributed, the men took their places, and all was in perfect order. Emperor Nicholas Pavlovich was in good health; he had gone for a drive in the evening, had returned home, and retired. The whole Palace was wrapped in slumber. A night of utter tranquillity descended. Silence reigned in the guardroom. Captain Miller had pinned his white handkerchief over the traditional grease spot on the high, morocco-upholstered back of the officers' chair and settled down with a book to while away the time.

Captain Miller had always been a passionate reader, and so was never bored. He read on and did not notice that the night was passing. Suddenly, just before two o'clock, he was aroused by a most alarming occurrence: before him stood the sergeant on duty, pale, shaking with terror, and jabbering rapidly:

"There's trouble, Your Honor, trouble!"

"What's wrong?"

"A terrible disaster has occurred!"

Captain Miller jumped to his feet in indescribable alarm and only with difficulty ascertained the exact nature of the "terrible disaster."

4

This is what had happened: a sentry, a private of the Izmailovski regiment, named Postnikov, standing at what is now known as the "Jordan" entrance to the Palace, became aware that a man was drowning in the patch of open water in the ice of the Neva just in front of the Palace, and was desperately calling for help.

Private Postnikov, formerly a domestic serf, was a very high-strung and sensitive fellow. For a long time he listened to the distant cries and moans of the drowning man, and they turned him numb with horror. In anguish he scanned the visible expanse of the quay, but by the malice of Fate neither there nor on the Neva was a living soul to be seen.

There was no one to help the drowning man, and he was sure to go under. . . .

Meanwhile he continued to struggle stubbornly.

There seemed but one thing left to him: to go to the bottom without further expenditure of energy. But no! His feeble cries and calls for help now broke off and ceased, and then were heard again, always closer and closer to the Palace quay. Evidently the man had not lost his bearings, and was making straight for the light of the quay lanterns. But he hadn't the ghost of a chance, for he was heading for the "Jordan": the hole cut in the ice for the blessing of the waters at Epiphany. There he would be drawn under the ice and that would be the end of him. . . . Again he was quiet, but a minute later he was splashing and moaning: "Save me, save me!" He was now so close that the swishing of the water was heard distinctly. . . .

Private Postnikov reflected that it would be extremely easy to save the man. If he were to run out onto the ice, the man was sure to be within reach. One had merely to throw him a rope or pass him a pole or the gun, and he would be saved. He was so close that he could seize it with his hands and climb out. But Postnikov remembered the service regulations and his oath; he knew that he was a sentry, and that a sentry dare not leave his sentry box on any pretext or for any reason whatsoever.

On the other hand, Postnikov's heart was a rebellious one: it ached, it throbbed, it failed him. If only he could tear it out and trample on it: the groans and cries were so painful to hear. It was horrible to watch another man agonize and not come to his aid, when really it was quite possible to do so, for the sentry box would not run away, and no harm would be done to anybody.

"Shall I run down, eh? No one will see. . . . Oh, Lord, to get it over with! There he's groaning again."

By the end of the half-hour that this went on, Private Postnikov was completely worn out and began to experience "mental doubts." He was an intelligent and conscientious soldier with a good head on his shoulders, and he knew perfectly well that for a sentry to leave his post was a crime that meant court-martial, then a flogging and forced labor, or possibly even a firing squad. But from the swollen river came moans, sounding closer and closer, and he could hear gurgling and desperate floundering.

"I'm *drowning!* Help! I'm drowning!"

Now he was reaching the hole in the ice—and that would be the end!

Once more, and then again Postnikov glanced round. Not a soul to be seen; only the lamps shook and flickered in the gale, and on the wind was borne a faltering, broken cry, perhaps the last cry. . . .

There was another splash, a single outcry, and a gurgle.

The sentry could bear it no longer, and deserted his post.

5

Postnikov rushed to the stairs, ran out onto the ice, his heart beating violently, then waded through the water that had overflowed the ice hole, and, quickly locating the drowning man, held out to him the stock of his gun. The man clutched the butt end, and Postnikov holding onto the bayonet, pulled him out of the water.

Both rescued and rescuer were dripping wet, and as the former, in a state of exhaustion, was shaking and unable to keep on his feet, Private Postnikov had not the heart to leave him on the ice, but led him onto the quay and began looking about for someone to whom he could turn him over. While all this was going on, a sleigh had made its appearance on the embankment. It was carrying an officer of the now disbanded Palace Company of Invalids.

This gentleman, who arrived on the scene at a moment so inopportune for Postnikov, was apparently of a very frivolous disposition, and a rather scatterbrained, impudent fellow, to boot. He jumped out of the sleigh, and demanded:

"Who is this? Who are all these people?"

"He was sinking, drowning—" Postnikov began.

"What do you mean—drowning? Who was drowning? Was it you? Why at this spot?"

The man who had been pulled out of the water was merely gasping, and as for Postnikov, he had vanished: he had shouldered his musket and gone back to his sentry box.

Whether or not the officer guessed what had happened, he dropped his inquiries abruptly. He immediately bundled the rescued man into his sleigh and took him to the station house of the Admiralty District on Morskaya Street.

There the officer informed the police sergeant that the dripping man he had brought with him had been drowning in an ice hole opposite the Palace and that he had rescued him at the peril of his own life.

The man was still sopping wet, chilled, and spent. What with his fright and exhaustion, he was practically unconscious, and it was a matter of indifference to him who had rescued him.

A sleepy medical assistant on the police force was working on him, while in the office a report was being drawn up on the basis of the officer's oral deposition. The police, naturally given to suspicion, were wondering how he had managed to emerge from the water as dry as pepper. The officer, eager to get the medal "for the rescue of those in mortal peril," explained it by a happy concurrence of circumstances, but did so lamely and unconvincingly. Someone was dispatched to rouse the inspector, and others were sent to make further inquiries.

Meanwhile the incident had rapidly started another series of events in the Palace.

6

The developments that occurred after the officer of the Invalids had departed with the rescued man in his sleigh remained unknown in the Palace guardroom. There the soldiers and their officer knew only that Postnikov, a private of their regiment, had deserted his sentry box in order to save a man's life, that, this being a grave breach of military duty, Postnikov was certain to be court-martialed and flogged, and that all his superiors from the company commander up would have to face grave consequences, which they could neither avert nor mitigate.

The wet and shivering Postnikov was of course immediately relieved of his post, and when he was brought to the guardroom he candidly told Captain Miller all that we already know, mentioning every detail down to the point when the officer of the Invalids put the rescued man into his sleigh and ordered the driver to hurry to the Admiralty police station.

This last circumstance added to the danger of the situation. The officer was bound to give a full account to the police inspector, and the inspector would instantly lay the matter before the chief of police, Kokoshkin, who would report it to the Emperor in the morning, and then there would be the devil to pay!

There was no time for deliberation; the superior officer had to be called in.

Captain Miller at once dispatched a troubled note to his battalion commander, Lieutenant Colonel Svinin, asking him to come to the Palace guardroom as soon as he could and to give him all possible assistance in his terrible predicament.

It was already about 3 A.M., and Kokoshkin was accustomed to presenting his report to the Emperor rather early, so that there was little time left for thought and action.

7

Lieutenant-Colonel Svinin did not have the compassionate and kindly heart for which Captain Miller had always been distinguished. Svinin was not a heartless man, but first and foremost he was a careerist, a type which in our time is again remembered with regret. Svinin had a reputation for severity, and in fact he flaunted the strictness with which he disciplined his men. He was not cruel by nature, and never sought to cause anyone useless suffering, but if a man broke any of the rules of the service, he was inexorable. He considered it out of place to enter into a discussion of the motives of the culprit, but held to the rule that in the service a fault was a fault. And so everyone in the company knew that Private Postnikov was not going to escape the penalty for deserting his post and that Svinin was not going to break his heart over it.

Such was the character of this staff officer, as his comrades and superiors knew it. Among them there were some who did not sympathize with Svinin, for at that time "humaneness" and similar erroneous notions had not quite vanished. Svinin was quite indifferent as to whether the "humanitarians" blamed or praised him. To beg and entreat Svinin or to try to move him to pity was entirely useless. He had the thick skin that was usual with the careerists of the period.

Yet, like Achilles, he had a weak spot. His official career had begun well, and of course he zealously watched over it, careful that, as on a full-dress uniform, not a particle of dust should settle on it. And now this unfortunate step on the part of a member of the battalion entrusted to him was bound to cast a shadow on the reputation of the entire unit. Those on whom Svinin's well-launched and tenderly nurtured official career depended would not stop to inquire whether or not the battalion commander was to blame for what one of his men had done at the prompting of noble compassion. Indeed, many would be glad to place a log across his path to clear the way for a relative or to push forward some young protégé of highly stationed personages, especially if the Czar should be annoyed and remark to the regimental commander, as was sure to happen, that he had "poor officers" and that the men were "undisciplined." And who was to blame for it? Svinin, of course. And the word would go round that Svinin was "lax," and the reproach would remain a permanent blot on his reputation. Then he would never distinguish himself among his contemporaries, nor add his portrait to the gallery of notables of the Russian Empire.

Few studied history at the time, but people believed in history, and were particularly eager to take part in the making thereof.

8

It was nearly three in the morning when Svinin received Captain Miller's alarming note, and he at once leaped out of bed and put on his uniform, arriving at the guardroom of the Winter Palace frightened and angry. Here he forthwith questioned Private Postnikov and satisfied himself that the incredible incident had actually taken place. Private Postnikov again frankly recounted to his battalion commander all that had happened during his watch, just as he had previously related it to his company commander. The soldier admitted that he "was guilty before God and the Czar, and deserved no mercy." While on guard, he said, he had heard the groans of a man drowning in an ice hole; torn between duty and compassion, he had been tormented for a long time, and in the end, yielding to temptation, had given up the struggle: he had deserted the sentry box, jumped onto the ice, and pulled the drowning man out of the water, and then, as ill luck would have it, he had fallen under the eye of an officer of the Company of Invalids.

Lieutenant Colonel Svinin was in despair. He gave himself the only satisfaction possible under the circumstances: he wreaked his anger on Postnikov by immediately placing him under arrest and confining him to the regimental lockup. Then he made a few sharp remarks to Captain Miller, throwing up to him his "humanitarianism," which, he observed, was of no earthly use in the army. But all this could not mend matters. It was quite impossible to find an excuse, let alone a justification for such a transgression as a sentry's desertion of his post. And so there remained only one way out: to conceal the whole matter from the Emperor.

But was it possible to conceal such an occurrence?

Apparently not, since the man's rescue was known not only to all the soldiers on guard duty but also to that abominable officer of the Invalids who must have already reported the matter to General Kokoshkin.

Where was Svinin to rush now? To whom could he turn? Where was he to seek help and protection?

Svinin was on the point of dashing off to Grand Duke Michael Pavlovich and disclosing everything without reserve. Such a move was in those days not unusual. Let the hot-tempered Grand Duke fly

into a rage about it and shout himself hoarse. This was of no conse-
quence, for the more rudely he handled you at first, the more
insulting he was, the sooner he relented and himself took up the
cudgels in the culprit's defense. Such flare-ups were not infrequent,
and they were indeed sometimes solicited. *Names will never hurt
you*, and Svinin was anxious to bring the business to such a favorable
conclusion. But was it possible to gain admission to the Palace in
the dead of night and to disturb the Grand Duke? On the other
hand, to wait till morning and appear before Michael Pavlovich
after Kokoshkin had made his report to the Czar would be useless.
And while Svinin was thus floundering amidst all these perplexities,
he suddenly perceived another way out, which till then had been
hidden from him as by a fog.

9

One of the well-known rules of tactics is this: at the moment when
the greatest danger threatens from a beleaguered fortress, it is advis-
able not to retreat from its ramparts, but to come closer to them.
Svinin resolved not to do any of the things that had at first occurred
to him, but to go straight to Kokoshkin.

Many frightful stories, as well as absurd ones, were always being
repeated at that time in Petersburg about the chief of police, General
Kokoshkin. Among other things, it was stated that he was exceedingly
tactful and that, thanks to this trait, he was able to make a mountain
out of a molehill and, with equal ease, a molehill out of a mountain.

Kokoshkin was indeed very stern and terrible, and inspired great
fear in all. But he sometimes winked at the pranks of the gay young
blades among the military, and as there were not a few such scamps
in those days they found in him a powerful and zealous champion.
Generally speaking, he knew the ropes and was able to do a great
deal, if only he chose to. This side of his character was known to both
Svinin and Miller. In fact, Miller encouraged his battalion commander to take the risk of seeing Kokoshkin at once and to entrust
himself to the man's magnanimity and tactfulness. The general
would, no doubt, find a way of extricating all concerned from their
difficulties, without arousing the Czar's anger, which Kokoshkin, to
his honor be it said, always avoided doing.

Svinin donned his overcoat, raised his eyes to heaven, and exclaiming several times, "Lord, Lord!" drove off to Kokoshkin.

It was already past four o'clock in the morning.

10

Chief of Police Kokoshkin was roused from his sleep and informed that Lieutenant Colonel Svinin had arrived on business of great importance and urgency.

The General immediately got up and came out to receive Svinin in a dressing gown, rubbing his forehead, yawning, and stretching. He listened with keen attention, but quite calmly, to all Svinin had to relate. He broke in on the explanations and pleas for mercy only once.

"The soldier," he said, "deserted his sentry box and rescued a man?"

"Yes, sir," replied Svinin.

"And the sentry box?"

"It remained vacant in the meantime."

"H'm-'m . . . I know that it remained vacant. I am glad it wasn't stolen."

Svinin was confirmed in his conviction that the General had been apprised of everything, that he had already decided how he was to present the case to the Emperor at the morning audience, and that nothing would make him change his mind. Otherwise an incident such as the desertion of his post by a Palace sentry would no doubt have disturbed the energetic chief of police to a much greater degree.

As a matter of fact, Kokoshkin knew nothing about it. The police inspector to whom the officer had brought the rescued man did not think the incident of great importance. In his opinion, it was not a matter of sufficient gravity to warrant rousing the weary chief of police in the middle of the night. Besides, the whole affair appeared to the inspector to be rather suspicious, because the officer's clothes were entirely dry, which could not have been the case if he had really rescued the drowning man at the peril of his own life. The inspector thought that he was dealing with a vain, mendacious fellow who wanted another medal to wear on his chest, and for that reason, while his assistant was drawing up a report, he detained the officer and tried to get at the truth by dwelling on small details.

He was also rather annoyed that the incident had occurred in his district and that the drowning man had been rescued not by a policeman but by an army officer.

As for Kokoshkin's lack of excitement, it had a simple explanation: first, he was terribly tired after a grueling day and after having attended two fires during the night; and, second, Private Postnikov's breach of discipline did not directly concern him as chief of police.

Nevertheless, Kokoshkin instantly went into action. He sent for the inspector of the Admiralty District, ordering him to appear at once, together with the officer and the rescued man, and he asked Svinin to wait in the small reception room adjacent to his study. Then he retired to the study and, without closing the door, sat down at the desk and began to sign papers; but a moment later his head sank onto his arms, and he fell fast asleep right there at the desk.

11

In those days there were neither telegraphs nor telephones in the city, and in order to convey official orders speedily the "forty thousand couriers" who have been immortalized in Gogol's comedy* darted in every direction. They were not so fast as the telegraph or the telephone, of course, but they lent considerable animation to the city and testified to the ceaseless vigilance of the authorities.

By the time the inspector of the Admiralty police district had arrived, quite out of breath, and with him the rescuer and the rescued, the worn-out General had had a nap that thoroughly refreshed him. This was apparent both from the expression of his face and from the improvement in the functioning of his mental faculties.

Kokoshkin ordered the newcomers to enter his study and invited Svinin to step in, too.

"The report?" he demanded of the inspector in a voice that sounded refreshed.

The inspector silently handed him a folded sheet and then said in a whisper:

"I must beg permission to say a word to Your Excellency in private. . . ."

"Very well."

Kokoshkin stepped into a window recess, followed by the inspector.

* *The Inspector General.*—A. Y.

"What is it?"

The inspector's indistinct buzz was heard and the loud grunts of the General: "H'm-m . . . So! Well, what of it? It is possible. . . . They manage to come out dry. . . . Nothing else?"

"Nothing, sir."

The General left the recess, sat down at his desk, and began to read. He read the report in silence, betraying neither anxiety nor suspicion, and then, turning to the rescued man, spoke in a loud, firm voice:

"How is it, brother, that you found yourself in the water opposite the Palace?"

"My fault," replied the man.

"That's it. Were you drunk?"

"My fault; I wasn't drunk, but I'd had a drop."

"How did you get into the water?"

"I wanted to take a shortcut across the ice, lost my way, and got into an ice hole."

"You couldn't see where you were going?"

"It was pitch-dark all round, Your Excellency."

"So you didn't see who pulled you out?"

"Begging your pardon, I couldn't. It was this gentleman, I think." He pointed to the officer, and added: "I couldn't see. I was scared."

"That's it. You were prowling about, when you ought to have been asleep! Now, take a good look at this man and remember who it was that rescued you. A noble-hearted man risked his life to save you!"

"I shall remember it as long as I live."

And turning to the officer, he said, "What is your name, sir?"

The officer gave his name.

"Do you hear that?" Kokoshkin asked the rescued.

"I do, Your Excellency."

"Have a prayer said for his health."

"I will, Your Excellency."

"Pray to God for him, and now clear out: you are no longer wanted.

The man bowed to the ground and tumbled out, hugely pleased that he had been allowed to go.

Svinin stood there, amazed at the turn things had taken by the grace of God.

154

12

Then Kokoshkin turned to the officer of the Company of Invalids.
"You rescued this man at the risk of your own life?"

"Yes, Your Excellency."

"There were not witnesses of the occurrence, and, I suppose, there couldn't have been any, because of the lateness of the hour?"

"Yes, Your Excellency, it was dark, and there was no one on the quay except the sentries."

"The sentries needn't be mentioned: a sentry guards his post and must not let anything distract him. I credit this report completely. It is based on what you told them, isn't it?"

These words Kokoshkin spoke with particular emphasis, as though threatening or reprimanding someone. But the officer was not abashed. With bulging eyes and chest thrown out, he answered:

"Yes, it is perfectly true, Your Excellency."

"Your action merits a reward."

The officer started to bow gratefully.

"There's nothing to thank me for," continued Kokoshkin. "I shall report your valiant deed to our gracious Emperor, and perhaps this very day a medal will decorate your breast. And now you may go home, take a hot drink, and do not leave the house, as I may need you."

The officer beamed, bowed, and left.

Kokoshkin looked after him, and remarked:

"It is possible that the Emperor himself will wish to see him."

"Yes, sir," the inspector said brightly.

"You are free to go."

The police inspector withdrew and, having closed the door behind him, crossed himself out of pious habit.

The officer of the Company of Invalids was waiting for the inspector downstairs, and they went off together better friends than when they had arrived.

Svinin alone remained in the study of the chief of police. Kokoshkin first stared hard at him for a considerable length of time and then said:

"You haven't been to see the Grand Duke?"

In those days when "the Grand Duke" was mentioned, everyone knew that Grand Duke Michael Pavlovich was meant.

"I came straight to you," was Svinin's reply.

"Who was the officer on duty?"

"Captain Miller."

Kokoshkin again scrutinized Svinin, and then said:

"I think you told me something different before."

Svinin failed to grasp the meaning of this, and said nothing, while Kokoshkin added:

"Well, it doesn't matter. Have a good sleep."

The audience was over.

13

At one o'clock in the afternoon the officer of the Company of Invalids was indeed again summoned by Kokoshkin, who very amiably informed him that the Emperor was highly gratified to know that among the officers of the Company of Invalids attached to his Palace there were such vigilant and valiant men and that he bestowed upon him the medal "For the rescue of those in mortal peril." And with these words Kokoshkin handed the medal to the hero, and the officer departed to show it off.

The incident might therefore have been considered closed, but Lieutenant Colonel Svinin felt that the business was somehow unfinished and thought himself called upon to dot the *i*.

The affair upset him to such an extent that he was ill for three days. On the fourth day he quit his bed, drove out to the House of Peter the Great,* had a thankgiving mass said before the icon of our Savior; and, returning home with his spirit calmed, sent for Captain Miller.

"Well, Nikolay Ivanovich," he said to Miller, "the storm that was threatening us has blown over, thank God, and the unfortunate affair with the sentry has been satisfactorily settled. Now, I think, we can breathe quietly again. Doubtless we owe this, first, to God's mercy, and second, to General Kokoshkin. People may say that he is harsh and heartless, but I am filled with gratitude for his magnanimity and with respect for his tact and resourcefulness. It was wonderful the way he masterfully took advantage of the vanity of that fraud from the

* The little wooden house built for the Emperor in 1703; it has been preserved as a museum.—A. Y.

Invalids, who, truth to tell, deserved a good flogging in the stable for his impudence, instead of a medal. But there was no alternative: he had to be made use of for the salvation of the others, and Kokoshkin handled the affair so cleverly that there wasn't the slightest unpleasantness; on the contrary, everybody is content and very well pleased. Between you and me, I have learned from an unimpeachable source that Kokoshkin himself is *very pleased* with me. He was flattered that I went directly to him and that I refrained from arguing with the rascal who got the medal. In a word, no one has suffered and everything was done with so much tact that there is nothing to fear in the future; but yet there is a trifle that we still have to settle. We must tactfully follow Kokoshkin's example and conclude the business on our part in such a way as to ensure ourselves against any future charges. There is still one person whose position remains unregulated. I mean Private Postnikov. He is still behind bars, and he is no doubt racked by the thought of what is in store for him. We must put an end to his misery."

"Yes, it's high time," Miller urged, delighted.

"Yes, indeed. And you are the best man to do it. Please go to the barracks at once, assemble your company, and release Postnikov from jail, and see that he receives two hundred strokes before the ranks."

14

Miller was dumbfounded, and made an attempt to persuade Svinin, in view of the happy conclusion of the affair, to extend a complete pardon to Private Postnikov, especially since he had already endured so much suffering while in prison, awaiting his fate. But Svinin lost his temper and did not even allow Miller to proceed.

"No," he interrupted, "none of that: just now I spoke of tact, and you are at once ready to commit a tactless act. Quit it."

Then he shifted to a drier and more official tone, and added firmly:

"And since you personally are not without blame in this matter and indeed are much at fault, for there is a softness in your character which does not befit an army man and which results in a lack of discipline on the part of the men under you, I hereby order you to be present at the flogging and to see to it that it is carried out seriously, indeed with the utmost severity. To that end, please issue orders that the punishment be carried out by young soldiers newly arrived from the ranks of the regular army, because the old-timers are all infected in this respect with the liberalism of the Guard: they don't flog a comrade properly, but only scare the fleas on his back. I will look in to see for myself whether the culprit is properly tanned."

It was out of the question, of course, to evade an official order issued by a superior officer, and tenderhearted Captain Miller was obliged to carry out with the utmost precision the instructions given him by his battalion commander.

The company was drawn up in the courtyard of the regiment's barracks, the rods were fetched in sufficient quantity from the stores, and Private Postnikov, brought from the lockup, was "properly tanned" with the zealous aid of young comrades recently arrived from the army ranks. These men, uninfected by the liberalism of the Guard, thoroughly dressed their comrade's hide, as ordered by the battalion commander. Thereupon, Postnikov, having received his punishment, was lifted up on the very overcoat on which he had been flogged, and carried to the regimental hospital.

15

Battalion Commander Svinin, having been informed that the punishment had been carried out, with fatherly solicitude at once visited Postnikov in the hospital and, to his satisfaction, convinced himself by direct examination that his orders had been carried out to the letter. The high-strung and tenderhearted man had been "properly tanned." Svinin was pleased, and issued an order that the patient be given, as a present from him, a pound of sugar and a quarter of a pound of tea, with which he might regale himself while he convalesced. Postnikov, on his cot, heard the instruction concerning tea and sugar, and said:

"I am much pleased, Your Honor, and thank you for your fatherly kindness."

And "pleased" he really was, for, in the three days which he had spent in the lockup, he had prepared himself for a much worse eventuality. Two hundred strokes with the rods in those stern days was nothing compared to the punishments that men endured by order of the military courts; and such a punishment would indeed have been meted out to Postnikov, were it not that, by good luck, the bold and strategic moves, described above, had been made.

But the number of those pleased by the incident related above was not confined to the persons mentioned thus far.

16

Private Postnikov's exploit was quietly bruited about in various circles of the capital, which in those days, when the press was mute, lived in an atmosphere of endless gossip. As the story was transmitted orally, the name of the hero, Private Postnikov, was lost, but on the other hand the tale grew in size and assumed an intriguing, romantic character.

It was rumored that some mysterious swimmer was making for the Palace from the direction of the Fortress of Saints Peter and Paul, that one of the sentries posted at the Palace fired a shot and wounded the swimmer, that an officer of the Company of Invalids who was passing by jumped into the water and rescued him, for which the officer received a just reward, while the sentry got the punishment he deserved. This absurd rumor even reached the abbey inhabited at the time by an ecclesiastical dignitary, who was discreet, yet not indifferent to mundane matters, and who was furthermore favorably disposed toward the devout Svinin family of Moscow of which the battalion commander was a member.

The story of the shot seemed dubious to the astute ecclesiastic. Who was this nocturnal swimmer? If he was an escaped prisoner, why then punish the sentry who had only done his duty in firing at him when he was swimming across the Neva from the fortress? And if he was not a prisoner, but some important personage who had to be saved, how could the sentry know about it? In that case, too, things could not have happened as was frivolously rumored. The laity is very careless and given to idle talk, but those who dwell in monasteries and abbeys take a more prudent attitude, and get the gist of worldly matters.

17

One day when Svinin happened to be visiting His Reverence to receive a blessing from him, his distinguished host broached the subject of "the shot." Svinin told him the whole truth, which, as we know, had nothing in common with the rumor.

His Reverence heard the true story in silence, gently fingering his white rosary and without taking his eyes off the narrator. And when Svinin had finished, His Reverence spoke in a voice that was like the rippling of gentle waters:

"Hence one may conclude that in this matter not everything has been set forth *everywhere* in accordance with the whole truth?"

Svinin became confused and answered evasively that the report had been made not by him, but by General Kokoshkin.

His Reverence again passed the beads through his waxen fingers several times and dropped the remark:

"A distinction must be made between what is false and what is not wholly true."

Again fingering of the rosary, again silence, and at last words sounding like the rippling of gentle waters:

"A half-truth is not falsehood. But concerning this let the least be said."

"It is really so," said Svinin, encouraged. "What disturbs me most, of course, is that I was obliged to punish this soldier, who, though he failed in his duty—"

Again fingering of the rosary, and the ecclesiastic's mild voice broke in:

"One must never fail to perform one's official duty."

"Yes, but he did it out of magnanimity, out of compassion, and besides, after such an inner struggle and at such a risk: he knew that, while saving another man's life, he was endangering his own. . . . It was a sublime, sacred sentiment."

"What is sacred is known to God alone, and bodily punishment administered to a man of the people is not pernicious, nor is it in conflict either with the customs of nations or with the spirit of Holy Writ. It is easier for the coarse body to bear the rod than for the soul to endure more subtle chastisement. In this matter, you have in no wise violated justice."

"But he is even deprived of the reward for the rescue of those in mortal peril."

"To rescue those in peril is no merit, but indeed a duty. He who could save a life and does not is subject to punishment by law; he who does has but performed his duty."

A pause, the rosary, and rippling words:

"It perhaps profiteth a warrior more to suffer humiliation and wounds for his noble exploit than to be distinguished by a decoration. But the most important thing in this matter is that it be treated with the utmost discretion and that what actually happened should never be mentioned anywhere."

Obviously His Reverence, too, was pleased.

18

Had I the boldness of Heaven's fortunate favorites, to whom, because of their great faith, it is given to penetrate the mysteries of God's designs, I should perhaps dare allow myself the conjecture that God Himself was probably pleased with the conduct of Postnikov, this meek soul that He had created. But my faith is small; it does not enable me to comprehend things supernal: I am of the earth, earthy. I think of those mortals who love goodness for its own sake and expect no rewards for it whatsoever. These upright, steadfast men, too, should be, I think, sincerely pleased with the holy impulse toward selfless love and the no less holy patience of the humble hero of my accurate and artless tale.

LEO TOLSTOY
(1828–1910)

The son of a count and a princess, both of ancient lineage, Tolstoy grew up in the manorial atmosphere common to the family's Moscow residence and to his birthplace, the ancestral estate of Yasnaya Polyana, situated in the heart of European Russia. His formal education was scanty: as a boy he was tutored privately, and in his late teens he studied Oriental languages and law at a provincial university, acquiring a distaste for academic life and taking no degree. For a time he led a rather giddy existence in Moscow. Apparently out of boredom, he enlisted in the army at the age of twenty-three.

While his unit was stationed in the Caucasus, where border warfare was in progress, he finished the first part of the semiautobiographic tale *Childhood, Boyhood, and Youth*, with which he made his bow before the public in 1852. With the outbreak of the Crimean campaign he was shifted to besieged Sevastopol. Here he saw serious action, yet found time and composure to write his *Sevastopol Tales* (published in 1855–1856), in which he described war with unprecedented candor. Returning to civilian life shortly after the end of hostilities, he moved for a while in literary circles, but the strong-minded young aristocrat found them uncongenial. Several trips abroad strengthened his dislike of Western civilization, which he condemned as materialistic. He continued to write, completing the narrative mentioned above and publishing several short stories, but in these years his heart was in teaching. He taught the children of his serfs (he had inherited hundreds of them together with thousands of acres) at Yasnaya Polyana, and edited an educational review advocating extremely libertarian principles. Before long he gave up his classes, and the review was short-lived, but his interest in elementary education persisted. In the seventies, when he was already a celebrated novelist, he compiled a primer, a graded reader, and an arithmetic, which had enormous circulation.

In 1862 he married a girl nearly half his age and settled down to the life of a country squire who combined writing with farming. Aside from *The Cossacks* (1863), he now produced the two magisterial works which give his fullest measure as a writer of fiction: *War and Peace* (1865–1869), a historical novel, and *Anna Karenina* (1875–1877), a novel of contemporary manners.

From the first, Tolstoy was preoccupied with the meaning of life and had a craving for a rule of right conduct, but for a long time these tendencies did not interfere with the man's delight in mere living or with the artist's proper business. When he had completed *Anna Karenina*, however, he experienced an inner crisis, recorded in his *Confession* (1879), which, after bringing him to the verge of suicide, made a religious convert of him. With all the fervor of which his passionate nature was capable, he embraced a rationalistic Christianity stripped of dogma and ritual and devoted to the proposition that men should love one another and refrain from resisting evil by force. He repudiated not only the established Church, but also the State and all its works, as relying on coercion. Naturally, he opposed war, as well as revolution, though he poured water on the mill-wheel of the radicals by his sharp criticism of the existing order. He also rejected many of the achievements of civilization, including science, and much of what was admired as art and literature, on the ground that it failed to unite men in true fellowship. This condemnation included his own writings. He pictured the good life as a simple, preferably rural, existence based on manual labor, innocent of exploitation, and free from artificially cultivated needs and appetites. He was excommunicated in 1901 by the Synod of the Russian Church. In his reply he pointed out, among other things, that he could no more renounce his convictions than "a flying bird can re-enter the eggshell from which it has emerged."

After his conversion his chief concern was to elaborate his doctrine and propagate his newly found faith. He wrote theological treatises, essays, pamphlets, thousands of private letters, and narratives that were frankly tales of moral edification. He did not abandon the practice of fiction, producing several stories and novels, namely, "The Death of Ivan Ilyich" (1886), *Kreutzer Sonata* (1890), *Resurrection* (1899), but in these writings the artist rarely triumphs over the doctrinaire and preacher. Nor could he forego the temptation to use the medium of the theater to drive home his views. He composed half a dozen pieces, including two temperance plays, *The Power of Darkness* (1886), a stark and effective drama of crime, and *The Living Corpse*, which, published posthumously, achieved great success on the stage both in Russia and abroad.

Russian censorship barred many of Tolstoy's nonfictional writings, and these appeared abroad, but the authorities dared not molest a man whose fame as novelist and spiritual leader ringed the world. At home the sage of Yasnaya Polyana acquired a following which was in the nature of a lay sect, and even those who did not share his views acclaimed him as the country's greatest writer and "living conscience."

Tolstoy's private circumstances in his last years were far from happy. His wife, who had borne him thirteen children and had long been a devoted helpmate, was out of sympathy with his beliefs and insisted on conventional domestic arrangements that were at variance with his professed views. Furthermore, she had become unbalanced. Finding life at Yasnaya

Polyana unbearable, he secretly left home on November 10, 1910 (N.S.), with the intention of going into seclusion. He did not travel far, and ten days later died at a railway station.

FROM War and Peace

(PLATON KARATAYEV)

The Pierre in this episode is Count Bezukhov, one of the leading figures in the novel. Having remained in Moscow after it was invaded by the French, with the quixotic idea of assassinating Napoleon, he is arrested as an incendiary. He witnesses the execution of five men, an experience that has a shattering effect upon him, and is placed in a shed for prisoners of war.

Beside him in a stooping position sat a small man of whose presence he was first made aware by a strong smell of perspiration which came from him every time he moved. This man was doing something to his legs in the darkness, and though Pierre could not see his face he felt that the man continually glanced at him. On growing used to the darkness Pierre saw that the man was taking off his leg bands, and the way he did it aroused Pierre's interest.

Having unwound the string that tied the band on one leg, he carefully coiled it up and immediately set to work on the other leg, glancing up at Pierre. While one hand hung up the first string, the other was already unwinding the band on the second leg. In this way, having carefully removed the leg bands by deft circular motions of his arm following one another uninterruptedly, the man hung the leg bands up on some pegs fixed above his head. Then he took out a knife, cut something, closed the knife, placed it under the head of his bed, and seating himself comfortably, clasped his arms round his lifted knees and fixed his eyes on Pierre. The latter was conscious of something pleasant, comforting, and well rounded in these deft movements, in the man's well-ordered arrangements in his corner, and even in his very smell, and he looked at the man without taking his eyes from him.

"You've seen a lot of trouble, sir, eh?" the little man suddenly said.

And there was so much kindliness and simplicity in his singsong voice that Pierre tried to reply, but his jaw trembled and he felt tears rising to his eyes. The little fellow, giving Pierre no time to betray his confusion, instantly continued in the same pleasant tones:

"Eh, lad, don't fret!" said he, in the tender singsong caressing voice old Russian peasant women employ. "Don't fret, friend—'Suffer an hour, live for an age!' that's how it is, my dear fellow. And we live here, thank heaven, without being molested. Among these folk, too, there are good men as well as bad," said he, and still speaking, he turned on his knees with a supple movement, got up, coughed, and went off to another part of the shed.

"Eh, you rascal!" Pierre heard the same kind voice saying at the other end of the shed. "So you've come, you rascal? She remembers. ... Now, now, that'll do!"

And the soldier, pushing away a little dog that was jumping at him, returned to his place and sat down. In his hands he had something wrapped in a rag.

"Here, eat a bit, sir," said he, resuming his former respectful tone as he unwrapped and offered Pierre some baked potatoes. "We had soup for dinner and the potatoes are grand!"

Pierre had not eaten all day, and the smell of the potatoes seemed extremely pleasant to him. He thanked the soldier and began to eat.

"Well, are they all right?" said the soldier with a smile. "You should do like this."

He took a potato, drew out his clasp knife, cut the potato into two equal halves on the palm of his hand, sprinkled some salt on it from the rag, and handed it to Pierre.

"The potatoes are grand!" he said once more. "Eat some like that!"

Pierre thought he had never eaten anything that tasted better.

"Oh, I'm all right," said he, "but why did they shoot those poor fellows? The last one was hardly twenty."

"Tss, tt . . . !" said the little man. "Ah, what is a sin . . . what a sin!" he added quickly, and as if his words were always waiting ready in his mouth and flew out involuntarily, he went on: "How was it, sir, that you stayed in Moscow?"

"I didn't think they would come so soon. I stayed accidentally," replied Pierre.

"And how did they arrest you, dear lad? At your house?"

"No, I went to look at the fire, and they arrested me there, and tried me as an incendiary."

"Where there's a trial there's injustice," put in the little man.

"And have you been here long?" Pierre asked as he munched the last of the potato.

"I? It was last Sunday they took me, out of a hospital in Moscow."

"Why, are you a soldier then?"

"Yes, we are soldiers of the Apsheron Regiment. I was dying of fever. We weren't told anything. There were some twenty of us lying there. We had no idea, never guessed at all."

"And do you feel unhappy here?" Pierre inquired.

"How can one help it, lad? My name is Platon, and the surname is Karatayev," he added, evidently wishing to make it easier for Pierre to address him. "They call me 'little falcon' in the regiment. How is one to help feeling unhappy? Moscow—she's the mother of cities. How can one see all this and not feel unhappy? But 'The maggot gnaws the cabbage, yet dies first'; that's what the old folks used to say," he added rapidly.

"What? What did you say?" asked Pierre.

"Who? I?" said Karatayev. "I say things happen not as we plan but as God judges," he replied, thinking that he was repeating what he had said before, and immediately continued:

"Well, and you, have you a family estate, sir? And a house? So you have abundance, then? And a housewife? And your old parents, are they still living?" he asked.

And though it was too dark for Pierre to see, he felt that a suppressed smile of kindliness puckered the soldier's lips as he put these questions. He seemed grieved that Pierre had no parents, especially that he had no mother.

"A wife for counsel, a mother-in-law for welcome, but there's none as dear as one's own mother!" said he. "Well, and have you little ones?" he went on asking.

Again Pierre's negative answer seemed to distress him, and he hastened to add:

"Never mind! You're young yet, and, please God, may still have some. The great thing is to live in harmony. . . ."

"But it's all the same now," Pierre could not help saying.

"Ah, my dear fellow!" rejoined Karatayev, "never decline a prison or a beggar's sack!"

He seated himself more comfortably and coughed, evidently preparing to tell a long story.

"Well, my dear fellow, I was still living at home," he began. "We had a well-to-do homestead, pleanty of land; we peasants lived well and our house was one to thank God for. When Father and we went out mowing there were seven of us. We lived well. We were real peasants. It so happened . . ."

And Platon Karatayev told a long story of how he had gone into someone's copse to take wood, how he had been caught by the keeper, had been tried, flogged, and sent to serve as a soldier.

"Well, lad," and a smile changed the tone of his voice, "we thought it was a misfortune but it turned out a blessing! If it had not been for my sin, my brother would have had to go as a soldier. But he, my younger brother, had five little ones, while I, you see, left only a wife behind. We had a little girl, but God took her before I went as a soldier. I come home on leave and I'll tell you how it was; I look and see that they are living better than before. The yard full of cattle, the women at home, two brothers away earning wages, and only Michael, the youngest, at home. Father, he says, 'All my children are the same to me: it hurts the same whichever finger gets bitten. But if Platon hadn't been shaved for a soldier, Michael would have had to go.' He called us all to him and, will you believe it, placed us in front of the icons. 'Michael,' he says, 'come here and bow down to his feet; and you, young woman, you bow down too; and you, grandchildren, also bow down before him! Do you understand?' he says. That's how it is, dear fellow. Fate looks for a head. But we are always judging, 'That's not well—that's not right!' Our luck is like water in a dragnet: you pull at it and it bulges, but when you've drawn it out it's empty! That's how it is."

And Platon shifted his seat on the straw.

After a short silence he rose.

"Well, I think you must be sleepy," said he, and began rapidly crossing himself and repeating:

"Lord Jesus Christ, holy Saint Nicholas, Frola and Lavra!* Lord Jesus Christ, holy Saint Nicholas, Frola and Lavra! Lord Jesus Christ, have mercy on us and save us!" he concluded, then bowed to the ground, got up, sighed, and sat down again on his heap of straw.

* Florus and Laurus, martyrs, venerated as patron saints of horses.—A. Y.

"That's the way. Lay me down like a stone, O God, and raise me up like a loaf," he muttered as he lay down, pulling his coat over him.

"What prayer was that you were saying?" asked Pierre.

"Eh?" murmured Platon, who had almost fallen asleep. "What was I saying? I was praying. Don't you pray?"

"Yes, I do," said Pierre. "But what was that you said: 'Frola and Lavra'?"

"Well, of course," replied Platon quickly, "the horses' saints. One must pity the animals too. Eh, the rascal! Now you've curled up and got warm, you daughter of a bitch!" said Karatayev, touching the dog that lay at his feet, and again turning over he fell asleep immediately.

Sounds of crying and screaming came from somewhere in the distance outside, and flames were visible through the cracks of the shed, but inside, it was quiet and dark. For a long time Pierre did not sleep, but lay with eyes open in the darkness, listening to the regular snoring of Platon who lay beside him, and he felt that the world that had been shattered was once more stirring in his soul with a new beauty and on new and unshakable foundations.

Twenty-three soldiers, three officers, and two officials were confined in the shed in which Pierre had been placed and where he remained for four weeks.

When Pierre remembered them afterward they all seemed misty figures to him except Platon Karatayev, who always remained in his mind a most vivid and precious memory and the personification of everything Russian, kindly, and round. When Pierre saw his neighbor next morning at dawn, the first impression of him, as of something round, was fully confirmed: Platon's whole figure—in a French overcoat girdled with a cord, a soldier's cap, and bast shoes—was round. His head was quite round; his back, chest, shoulders, and even his arms, which he held as if ever ready to embrace something, were rounded; his pleasant smile and his large, gentle brown eyes were also round.

Platon Karatayev must have been fifty, judging by his stories of campaigns he had been in, told as by an old soldier. He did not himself know his age and was quite unable to determine it. But his brilliantly white, strong teeth, which showed in two unbroken semicircles when he laughed—as he often did—were all sound and good; there was not a gray hair in his beard or on his head, and his whole body gave an impression of suppleness and especially of firmness and endurance.

His face, despite its fine, rounded wrinkles, had an expression of innocence and youth; his voice was pleasant and musical. But the chief peculiarity of his speech was its directness and appositeness. It was evident that he never considered what he had said or was going to say, and consequently the rapidity and justice of his intonation had an irresistible persuasiveness.

His physical strength and agility during the first days of his imprisonment were such that he seemed not to know what fatigue and sickness meant. Every night before lying down, he said: "Lord, lay me down as a stone and raise me up as a loaf!" and every morning on getting up, he said: "I lay down and curled up; I got up and shook myself." And indeed he had only to lie down, to fall asleep like a stone, and he had only to shake himself, to be ready without a moment's delay for some work, just as children are ready to play directly they awake. He could do everything, not very well but not badly. He baked, cooked, sewed, planed, and mended boots. He was always busy, and only at night allowed himself conversation—of which he was fond—and songs. He did not sing like a trained singer who knows he is listened to, but like the birds, evidently giving vent to the sounds in the same way that one stretches oneself or walks about to get rid of stiffness, and the sounds were always high-pitched, mournful, delicate, and almost feminine, and his face at such times was very serious.

Having been taken prisoner and allowed his beard to grow, he seemed to have thrown off all that had been forced upon him—everything military and alien to himself—and had returned to his former peasant habits.

"A soldier on leave—a shirt outside breeches,"* he would say.

He did not like talking about his life as a soldier, though he did not complain, and often mentioned that he had not been flogged once during the whole of his army service. When he related anything it was generally some old and evidently precious memory of his "Christian"† life, as he called his peasant existence. The proverbs, of which

* A peasant wears his shirt hanging loose outside his breeches; a soldier's shirt is tucked inside.—A. Y.

† In Russian the words *Christian* and *peasant* are very similar, and Karatayev's pronunciation identified them.—Translator

his talk was full, were for the most part not the coarse and indecent saws soldiers employ, but those folk sayings which taken without a context seem so insignificant, but when used appositely suddenly acquire the significance of profound wisdom.

He would often say the exact opposite of what he had said on a previous occasion, yet both would be right. He liked to talk and he talked well, adorning his speech with terms of endearment and with folk sayings which Pierre thought he invented himself, but the chief charm of his talk lay in the fact that the commonest events—sometimes just such as Pierre had witnessed without taking notice of them —assumed in Karatayev's speech a character of solemn fitness. He liked to hear the folktales one of the soldiers used to tell of an evening (they were always the same), but most of all he liked to hear stories of real life. He would smile joyfully when listening to such stories, now and then putting in a word or asking a question to make the comeliness of what he was told clear to himself. Karatayev had no attachments, friendships, or love, as Pierre understood them, but loved and lived affectionately with everything life brought him in contact with, particularly with man—not any particular man, but those with whom he happened to be. He loved his dog, his comrades, the French, and Pierre who was his neighbor, but Pierre felt that in spite of Karatayev's affectionate tenderness for him (by which he unconsciously gave Pierre's spiritual life its due) he would not have grieved for a moment at parting from him. And Pierre began to feel the same way toward Karatayev.

To all the other prisoners Platon Karatayev seemed a most ordinary soldier. They called him "little falcon" or "Platosha," chaffed him good-naturedly, and sent him on errands. But to Pierre he always remained what he had seemed that first night: an unfathomable, rounded, eternal personification of the spirit of simplicity and truth.

Platon Karatayev knew nothing by heart except his prayer. When he began to speak he seemed not to know how he would conclude.

Sometimes Pierre, struck by the meaning of his words, would ask him to repeat them, but Platon could never recall what he had said a moment before, just as he never could repeat to Pierre the words of his favorite song: *darling* and *birch tree* and *my heart is sick* occurred in it, but when spoken and not sung, no meaning could be got out of it. He did not, and could not, understand the meaning of words apart from their context. Every word and action of his was the manifestation of an activity unknown to him, which was his life. But his life, as he regarded it, had no meaning as a separate thing. It had meaning only as part of a whole of which he was always conscious. His words and actions flowed from him as evenly, inevitably, and spontaneously as fragrance exhales from a flower. He could not understand the value or significance of any word or deed taken separately.

FROM *Anna Karenina*

(HAYING)

Konstantin Levin, one of the central characters of the novel, is a bachelor in his early thirties. An aristocrat by birth, and the owner of thousands of broad acres, he is a gentleman farmer deeply attached to country life. Summering with him on his estate is his half-brother, Sergey Koznyshev, a well-known author. In the course of a conversation between the two, Levin is chided by his brother for failing to take an interest in the *zemstvo* (local self-government) institutions. He vainly tries to defend himself, and this upsets him. Feeling that physical exercise would enable him to regain his balance, he decides to spend a whole day haying with the peasants.

Toward evening Levin went to the office, gave orders about the farm work, and sent word to the villages summoning men for the following day to mow the Kalinov meadow, his biggest and best.

"And please send my scythe to Tit so he can set it and take it to the meadow tomorrow; I myself may be mowing, too," he said, trying not to feel embarrassed.

The steward smiled and said, "Yes, sir."

That evening, at tea, Levin said to his brother:

"The weather looks settled; tomorrow I begin mowing."

"I am very fond of that work," said Sergey.

"I like it awfully. I have mown with the peasants now and then, and tomorrow I want to be mowing all day long."

Sergey lifted his head and looked at his brother with interest.

"How do you mean? Just like the peasants, all day long?"

"Yes, it's very enjoyable," said Levin.

"It's splendid physical exercise, but you'll hardly be able to stand it," remarked Sergey, without a hint of sarcasm.

"I've tried it. At first it's hard; then you get drawn into it. I think I'll hold out. . . ."

"Well, well! But tell me, how do the peasants take it? They probably smirk at the master for behaving so queerly."

"No, I don't think so; but it's such jolly work and strenuous, too, that there's no time for thinking."

"But how can you have your dinner with them? It would be awkward to send you a bottle of Lafitte and roast turkey out there."

"No, I'll just come home when they take their rest."

Next morning Levin got up earlier than usual, but giving instructions about the work on the estate delayed him, and when he reached the meadow the men were already on the second swath.

Even from the top of the hill he could see below in the shadow the part of the meadow that had already been mown, with the gray rows of cut grass and the dark piles of the caftans the mowers had removed at the spot where they had started their first swath.

As he drew nearer, the peasants came into view. They formed a straggling line, some wearing caftans, others in their shirts, each swinging his scythe in his own way. He counted forty-two men.

They were moving slowly over the uneven bottom of the meadow, where an old dam had once been. Levin recognized some of his own men. Here was old Yermil, in a very long white smock, swinging his scythe, with his back bent; here was young Vaska, Levin's coachman, swinging his scythe wide. Here was also Tit, who had taught Levin to mow, a short, thin little peasant. He walked erect, toying with his scythe, as it were, and cutting a wide swath.

Levin dismounted and, having tethered his horse by the roadside, went over to Tit, who got another scythe from a bush and handed it to him.

"It's ready, master; sharp as a razor, it mows by itself," said Tit, taking off his cap with a smile and handing the scythe to Levin.

Levin took it and started trying it out. As they finished their strips, the mowers, sweating and in high spirits, came out onto the road one after another and, grinning, exchanged greetings with the master. They all stared at him, but no one said anything until a tall old man in a sheepskin jacket with a wrinkled, beardless face, who had stepped onto the road, spoke up.

"Watch out, master, once you've begun, you can't back out!" he said, and Levin heard repressed laughter among the mowers.

"I'll try not to back out," he said, taking his place behind Tit and waiting for the sign to start.

"Watch out," the old man repeated.

Tit made room, and Levin followed him. They were close to the road, where the grass was short and coarse, and Levin, who had not done any mowing for a long time and was embarrassed by the many eyes upon him, mowed badly at first, although he swung his scythe vigorously. Voices sounded behind him:

"The handle ain't right; too high, look how he has to stoop," said one.

"Press harder on the heel," said another.

"Never mind, it's all right, he'll get into it," said the old man. "See, there he goes. . . . You swing too wide, you'll be done up. . . . He's the master, no stopping him, he's working for himself. But look at the edge of the swath! The likes of us used to catch it for leaving it like that."

They were coming to softer grass, and Levin, who was listening without answering back and who tried to mow the best he could, followed Tit. They had gone about a hundred paces. Tit kept on going ahead, without showing the slightest sign of fatigue. But Levin was already beginning to fear that he would not be able to keep it up: he was dog-tired.

He felt that he was swinging his scythe with the last ounce of his strength, and decided to ask Tit to stop. But just then Tit halted of his own accord, and, stooping, picked up some grass, wiped his scythe, and began sharpening it. Levin straightened up and, catching his breath, looked round. The peasant behind him was still mowing, but he too was obviously tired, for he stopped before catching up with Levin and started sharpening his scythe. Tit whetted his own and Levin's, and they moved on.

The same thing happened once more. Tit kept swinging his scythe without a pause and without getting tired. Levin followed him, trying not to fall behind, but he found the going harder and harder. The moment came when he felt he had no strength left, but just then Tit stopped and began sharpening his scythe.

Thus they finished the first strip. It was long, and to Levin it seemed a particularly hard one, but when they reached the end, and Tit, shouldering his scythe, turned about and slowly retraced his steps, placing his feet in the tracks left by his own boots on the swath, while Levin walked back on his swath in the same way—then in spite of the large drops of sweat that poured down his face and dripped from his nose, and though his back was sopping wet, he felt a profound satisfaction. What delighted him particularly was the knowledge that he would be able to keep up with the men.

The only thing that spoiled his pleasure was the fact that his strip was poorly mown. "I'll swing my arms less and my whole body more," he reflected, comparing Tit's swath, cut perfectly straight, with his own, which was messy and uneven.

Levin noticed that on the first swath Tit's pace was particularly brisk, probably to test his master's endurance, and the strip chanced to be a long one. The next swaths were easier, but still Levin had to strain every nerve not to fall behind the peasants.

He thought of nothing, desired nothing except to keep up with the men and do his own work to the best of his ability. He heard nothing except the swish of the scythes and saw ahead of him only Tit's receding erect figure, the convex semicircle of the swath, the grass and the stems of flowers falling in slow waves about the blade of his scythe, and up ahead the end of the strip, which meant rest.

Suddenly, while immersed in his toil, he felt a pleasant sensation of coolness on his sweating shoulders, without knowing what it was and where it came from. He looked up at the sky while his scythe was being sharpened. A dark cloud was hanging low overhead and spilling heavy drops of rain. Some of the peasants put on their caftans; others, like Levin, merely twitched their shoulders delightedly under the pleasant coolness.

They finished another swath and yet another. There were long strips and short ones, good grass and bad grass. Levin lost all sense of time and had absolutely no idea whether it was early or late. His work was now undergoing a change which gave him immense pleasure. In the midst of his labors there were moments when he forgot what he was doing, was perfectly at ease, and during that time his swath was nearly as even and straight as Tit's. But no sooner did he recall what he was doing and try to improve his work, than he immediately became aware of how hard the toil was, and he mowed badly.

Having finished yet another swath, he was about to start one more when Tit stopped and, going up to the old man, spoke to him in a low voice. Both of them looked at the sun. "What are they talking about and why aren't they starting another swath?" Levin wondered. It did not occur to him that the peasants had been mowing for four hours on end and that it was time for breakfast.

"Time for breakfast, master," said the old man.

"Is it time? Very well, then."

Levin handed his scythe back to Tit, and with the peasants who went to their caftans to fetch their bread, made his way to his house, crossing the swaths of the oblong mown area, which were slightly sprinkled with rain. Only then it dawned on him that he had been wrong about the weather and that the rain was wetting his hay.

"The hay will be ruined," he said.

"Oh, no, master, mow when it rains, rake when it shines!" said the old man.

Levin untied his horse and rode home to have his coffee.

Sergey had only just got up. Levin had his coffee before his brother dressed and came to the dining room.

After breakfast Levin did not get his former place, but found himself between an old man, who was something of a wag and who invited him to be his neighbor, and a young peasant who had been married in the autumn and this summer was mowing for the first time.

The old man, holding himself erect, walked ahead with long, even strides, turning out his toes, and playfully, as it were, laid the grass in level ridges with a precise, smooth motion that seemed to cost him no more effort than swinging his arms in walking. It was as though not he but the sharp scythe, of its own accord, swished through the juicy grass.

Behind Levin walked young Mishka. His whole face, handsome and boyish, a plait of fresh grass tied round his hair, worked with his effort, but whenever anyone glanced at him he smiled. Obviously, he would rather have died than own up that he found the going hard.

Levin walked between them. Now, in the heat of the day the mowing did not seem so hard to him. The sweat with which he was drenched cooled him, and the sun which burned his back, his head, and his arms, bare to the elbow, added to his vigor and perseverance;

and the periods of automatism when it was possible not to think of what you were doing came more and more often now. Those were happy moments. Even more delightful were the moments when, on reaching the river at the end of the strips, the old man would wipe his scythe with wet grass, rinse the blade in the fresh water of the stream and, scooping up some with his whetstone box, treat Levin to a drink.

"Have a little of my kvass! Good, eh?" he would say with a wink.

And, in fact, Levin had never had such a delicious drink as this tepid water with bits of green stuff floating in it and a rusty taste from the tin box. And immediately there came the blissful slow walk, one hand on the scythe, during which you could wipe off the sweat, fill your lungs with air, look over the entire file of mowers, see what was going on all around in field and forest.

The longer Levin mowed, the oftener he knew those periods of oblivion when not his arms swung the scythe, but the scythe itself was in control of the whole body conscious of itself and vibrant with life, and, as if by magic, with no thought given it, the work did itself of its own accord properly and neatly. Those were the most blissful moments.

Mowing became a hardship only when he had to bring the automatic motion to a halt and think—for instance, when it was necessary to mow around a hillock or a cluster of sorrel stalks. The old man did this with ease. When he came to a hillock, he changed his motion and mowed on both sides of it with short strokes, using now the tip, now the heel of the scythe. And while doing so, he took notice of everything he came to; now he would pluck a stalk and chew it or treat Levin to it; now he would toss a branch out of the way with the tip of the scythe, or examine a quail's nest, from which the female bird had flown up right under the scythe, or again he would catch a snake that crossed his path, and, lifting it with the point of the scythe as with a fork, show it to Levin and fling it aside.

These changes of motion were hard on both Levin and the young peasant behind him. Having adjusted to one tense movement, they worked feverishly and were unable to alter the movement and at the same time observe what was before them.

Levin did not notice how time was passing. If he had been asked how long he had been mowing, he would have said: "Half an hour," but it was nearly dinnertime. As they walked back over the cut grass of their last swaths, the old man called Levin's attention to the little girls and boys who were heading toward the mowers from various directions along the road and across the tall grass, above which they were hardly visible. They were carrying hunks of bread tied up in bundles and jugs of kvass plugged with rags, which weighed down the children's arms.

"Look, the wee ones are toddling along!" he said, pointing to the children; and shading his eyes with his hand, glanced at the sun. After they had done two more swaths the old man halted.

"Well, master, time for dinner!" he said resolutely. On reaching the river the mowers walked over the cut grass to the caftans, where the children who had brought their dinners sat waiting for them. The peasants who had driven from a distance gathered near their carts; those who lived nearby hung tufts of grass on a willow for shade.

Levin sat down beside the men; he did not want to leave.

All restraint in the presence of the master had long disappeared. The peasants began preparing for dinner. Some washed; the younger men bathed in the river; others arranged places for rest after their dinner, untied the bundles of bread, removed the plugging from the jugs of kvass.

The old man broke some bread into a bowl, mashed it with the handle of a spoon, poured some water from the whetstone box over it, broke some more bread, salted it and, turning to the east, stood up to say a prayer.

"Come, master, have some of my mush," he said, squatting on his knees before the bowl.

The mush was so delicious that Levin gave up the idea of going home to dine. He shared the old peasant's meal and got to talking with him about his domestic affairs, taking the liveliest interest in them, and told him about his own, mentioning all the particulars that could interest the old man. He felt much closer to him than to his half-brother, and involuntarily smiled with pleasure at his affection for the man. When the old peasant stood up again, said a prayer, and then lay down under the willow, putting some grass beneath his head, Levin did the same and, in spite of the clinging flies so persistent in the sunshine, and insects that tickled his sweaty face and body, he immediately fell asleep and only woke up when the sun reached him, having moved to the other side of the tree. The old man had been awake for quite some time and sat sharpening the scythes of the younger peasants.

Levin looked about him and scarcely recognized the place: everything was so changed. The vast expanse of the meadow was mown, and the hay already giving off a fragrance; it shone with a peculiar new glitter in the slanting rays of the sun. The bushes on the bank of the river near which the grass had been cut, the winding river itself, previously invisible and now glittering like steel, the men getting up and moving about, the steep wall of the still uncut grass, the hawks hovering over the bare meadow—all that was completely new. When Levin was fully awake he started figuring how much grass had been cut and how much more could be mown that day.

The forty-two men had accomplished an extraordinary amount of work. The great meadow, which under serfdom it had taken thirty men two days to mow, was all finished except for some small patches at the corners. But Levin wanted to have as much done that day as possible, and he was annoyed with the sun for sinking so fast. He did not feel tired in the least and was only eager to resume work and do as much as possible.

"Could we do Mashkin Heights too today, do you think?" he asked the old man.

"God willing, we might. The sun is low, though. Would there be a nip of vodka for the boys?"

At the afternoon break when the men sat down again and the smokers lighted their pipes or rolled cigarettes, the old man announced to the peasants that if they mowed Mashkin Heights there would be vodka.

"What, not mow that? Get going, Tit! We'll do it in a jiffy! We can eat after dark. Let's get busy!" voices were heard, and, chewing the last of their bread, the mowers went back to work.

"Well, men, hold fast!" said Tit, and was off almost at a trot.

"Get on, get on!" the old man repeated, hurrying after him and easily overtaking him. "I'll mow you down! Watch out!"

Young and old mowed, racing each other, as it were. But no matter how much they hurried they did not spoil the grass, but cut the swaths as neatly and as accurately as before. The little corner patch was cleared in a matter of five minutes. The last mowers were still finishing their swaths when others, their caftans slung over their shoulders, were crossing the road on their way to Mashkin Heights.

The sun was already sinking into the trees when, rattling their whetstone boxes, they entered the wooded ravine of Mashkin Heights. The grass at the bottom of the hollow was waist-high, tender, soft, broad-bladed, speckled here and there with wild pansies.

After a brief conference on whether to cut the swaths lengthwise or across the ravine, a famous mower, Prokhor Yermilin, a swarthy giant of a peasant, took the lead. He mowed a swath, turned round and moved aside, and all fell into line behind him, moving downhill along the hollow and uphill right to the edge of the forest. The sun set behind the trees, and the dew had already fallen The mowers were in the sun only on the hilltop; down below where the mist was rising, and on the opposite side, they mowed in cool, dewy shade. The work was in full swing.

Cut with a juicy swish, the grass, which exhaled a heady fragrance, formed high ridges as it fell. On short swaths the mowers crowded together, their whetstone boxes rattling, their scythes ringing when they happened to touch, the whetstones whirring against the blades, their gay outcries resounding as they urged each other on.

Levin's place was again between the young peasant and the old man. The latter had his sheepskin jacket on and was just as merry, jovial, and easy in his movements as before. In the woods amid the juicy grass they often came upon plump mushrooms their scythes had cut down. Each time the old man stooped, picked up the mushroom and put it in his bosom, saying, "Another present for the old woman."

While it was easy to cut the wet, limp grass, it was very hard to climb up and down the steep slopes of the ravine. This did not daunt the old man. Swinging his scythe as usual and taking short, firm steps with feet shod in large bast sandals, he slowly climbed up the steep slope; though his whole body and the breeches below his smock shook with the exertion, he did not not let a single blade of grass, a single mushroom escape him on his way, and he joked with the peasants and Levin as usual. Levin followed him, and often thought that he would surely drop as he toiled up a knoll so steep that he would have found it difficult to climb even unencumbered by a scythe in his hand. But he managed to clamber up and he did what was necessary. He felt that some external force kept him going.

The men mowed Mashkin Heights, finished the last swaths, put on their caftans, and headed for home in high spirits. Levin, having regretfully taken leave of the peasants, mounted his horse and rode home too. From the top of the hill he looked back. The men could not be seen in the mist rising below, but he heard their rough merry voices, bursts of laughter, and the ring of clashing scythes.

ANDREY BELYI
(1880–1934)

"Once more I pray"

Once more I pray, as doubt torments me and appals;
The saints with a dry finger threaten from the walls.

Stern faces like black spots upon the icons show,
And, dark with centuries, the gilt has lost its glow.

But now the window is aflood with streaming rays,
And in the molten sun all is alive, ablaze.

"Thou gentle light," the choir is chanting, and behold,
The saints' dark faces gleam with a puce-colored gold.

And, incense-wreathed, the priest moves altarward as one
Who as a nimbus wears this ecstasy of sun.

[1903]

ANTON CHEKHOV
(1860–1904)

Born at Taganrog, a wretched market town on the sea of Azov, Chekhov was the grandson of a serf and the son of a grocer. As a boy he had to wait on customers in the store, and what with the harsh, mean circumstances at home, his childhood was an unhappy one. The family was sufficiently well-to-do to provide schooling for all five sons, and Anton was sent to the local Gymnasium (secondary school). He was sixteen when his father failed in business and, to avoid debtors' prison, absconded, going to Moscow, where two of his sons were studying. He was soon followed by the rest of the family except Anton, who was left behind to shift for himself. He managed to complete his schooling, rejoining the family after his graduation in 1879.

In Moscow the young man entered the medical school. His student years were difficult ones: he had to earn his own living and contribute to the support of the family, of which he was practically the head. The year 1884, in which he took his degree, was marked by another event: the appearance of his first book, a thin volume of stories. Ever since his arrival in the old capital he had been contributing skits and sketches to the humorous weeklies to keep the pot boiling. For some years he combined doctoring with writing. He referred to medicine as his "lawful wife" and to literature as his "mistress." Eventually the latter completely supplanted the former, but he always valued his medical training and experience, which, he felt, had exercised a profound and happy influence on his writing.

Chekhov had great facility with the pen, and a ready, if rather commonplace, sense of humor; and at first he took advantage of these gifts to toss off a succession of amusing trifles, chiefly for the sake of turning an honest penny. Before long, however, a change came over his writing. He began to treat his material with care, and his work took on a serious tone. The short narrative continued to be his chosen form, but it was now employed in the interests of a realistic art, avoiding contrived effects, an art sensitive, compassionate, humane, giving a sense of the pathos of trivial, frustrated lives. At thirty he was an established author, esteemed by the critics and immensely popular with the public. The lean years were behind him. In 1892 he bought a small estate near Moscow and settled there with his parents. The half-dozen years he lived there were very productive. Toward the end of the century Chekhov was, next to Tolstoy, the foremost literary figure in Russia.

He wrote some six hundred short stories, about as many as O. Henry, but he did not confine himself to fiction. Early in his career he developed an interest in the theater. He began by composing entertaining skits, some of which were dramatizations of his own stories. In later years he wrote half a dozen full-sized pieces, most of which were first produced with consummate effectiveness by the newly formed Moscow Art Theater. The best-known of them is *The Cherry Orchard*, his last play. Like the others, it is a drama which, though written in prose, is full of lyrical overtones and is suffused with emotion that seldom finds vent in action. It presents the breakup of a single family of gentlefolk as a transparent symbol of the decline of a social class, and it is noteworthy that it should have been first produced on the eve of the Revolution of 1905.

In his last years Chekhov wintered in the Crimea, occupying a villa near Yalta with his wife, the actress Olga Knipper, whom he married in 1901. He was chained to this uncongenial if balmy spot by tuberculosis, the symptoms of which had first shown themselves in his early twenties and which was now making rapid progress. On the opening night of *The Cherry Orchard*, on January 30, 1904 (N.S.), his forty-fourth birthday, he was barely able to stand up to receive the ovation tendered him. Less than six months later he died in a German health resort.

As a student Chekhov remained untouched by the radicalism that attracted young intellectuals. For years he moved in conservative circles, and he did not scruple to contribute to an influential reactionary daily. At the same time he was keenly aware of the existence of social evils and of his personal responsibility for them. In 1890 he spent three months in Sakhalin making a thorough study of the penal colony there for the purpose of bringing to light the bitter lot of the convicts. He set down his findings in an impressive, if badly organized, book, which failed, however, to effect a prison reform. Later his civic-mindedness expressed itself in other ways.

Soon after his return from the Far East his stories began to appear in organs of liberal and radical opinion, but he did not ally himself with any ideological group. The least doctrinaire and dogmatic of men, he put his trust in individuals of goodwill and right instincts. He counted among his friends Tolstoy and Maxim Gorky. Not that he shared the former's creed or the latter's socialist faith and revolutionary zeal. He believed in science, in the power of the mind, in the civilizing effect of material progress, and he hated coercion and violence. "My holy of holies," he wrote to a friend, "is the human body, health, intelligence, talent, inspiration, love, and perfect freedom—freedom from force and falsehood, no matter what form they may take."

A writer's whole duty, Chekhov held, is to tell the truth about life as he sees it, to the best of his ability. A jotting in his notebook reads: "Man will become better when you show him what he is."

Sergeant Prishibeyev*

"Sergeant Prishibeyev, the charge against you is that on the third of September you committed assault and battery on Constable Zhigin, the village elder Alyapov, Policeman Yefimov, special deputies Ivanov and Gavrilov, and on six other peasants, the three first named having been attacked by you while they were performing their official duties. Do you plead guilty?"

Prishibeyev, a wrinkled noncom with a face that seemed to bristle, comes to attention and replies in a hoarse, choked voice, emphasizing each word, as though he were issuing a command:

"Your Honor, Mr. Justice of the Peace! It follows, according to all the articles of the law, there is cause to attest every circumstance mutually. It's not me that's guilty, but all them others. This whole trouble started on account of this dead corpse, the Kingdom of Heaven be his! On the third day instant my wife, Anfisa, and me was walking quiet and proper. Suddenly I look and what do I see but a crowd of all sorts of people standing on the riverbank. By what rights, I ask, have people assembled there? What for? Is there a law that says people should go about in droves? Break it up, I holler. And I start shoving people, telling them to go on home, and I order the policeman to chase 'em and give it 'em in the neck. . . ."

"Allow me, but you are not a constable, not a village elder—is it your business to break up crowds?"

"It ain't! It ain't!" Voices are heard from various parts of the courtroom. "There's no standing him, Your Honor! It's fifteen years he's been plaguing us! Since the day he came back from the army, there's no living in the village. He's done nothing but badger us."

"Just so, Your Honor," says the elder. "The whole village is complaining. There's no standing him! No matter whether we carry the icons in a church procession or have a wedding or some accident happens, there he is, shouting, making a racket, setting things straight. He pulls the children's ears; he spies on the womenfolk, afraid some-

* An approximate English equivalent of the name would be Squelch.—A. Y.

184

thing might go wrong, like he was their father-in-law. The other day he made the round of the huts, ordering everybody not to sing songs, not to burn lights. 'There ain't no law,' he tells 'em, 'as says people should sing songs.' "

"Hold on; you'll have a chance to testify," says the justice of the peace; "and now let Prishibeyev continue. Go on, Prishibeyev."

"Yes, sir!" crows the sergeant. "Your Honor, you're pleased to say that it ain't my business to break up crowds. . . . Very well, sir. But what if there's breach of the peace? You can't allow folks to carry on disgracefully. Where is the law that says people should do as they please? I won't have it, sir! If I don't chase 'em and call 'em to account, who will? Nobody here knows the rights of things; I'm the only one, Your Honor, I'm the only one in the whole village, you might say, who knows how to deal with the common people. And I know what's what, Your Honor. I'm no hick, I'm a noncommissioned officer, a retired quartermaster sergeant. I served in Warsaw; I was attached to headquarters, sir; and after, when I got my honorable discharge, I was on duty as a fireman, and then on account of ill health I retired from the Fire Department, and for two years I held the post of doorman in a junior high school for boys of good family. I know all the rules and regulations, sir. But the peasant, he's ignorant, he don't understand the first thing; and he's got to do as I say, seeing as how it's for his own good. Take this affair, for instance. Here I was, breaking up the crowd, and right there on the shore, on the sand, lies the drowned corpse of a dead man. What right has he got to lie there? I asks. Is that proper? What's the constable thinking of? How come, Constable, says I, that you didn't notify the authorities? Maybe this drowned corpse drowned himself or maybe this smells of Siberia? Maybe it's a case of criminal homicide. But Zhigin, the constable, he don't take no notice, but just puffs away at a cigarette. 'Who is this,' says he, 'as is laying down the law to you fellows? Where does he come from?' says he. 'Don't we know what's what without him putting in his oar?' says he. 'It looks as if *you* don't know what's what, you fool, you,' says I, 'if you stand there and don't take no notice.' 'I notified the district police officer yesterday,' says he. 'Why the district police officer?' says I. 'According to what article of the Code of Laws? In cases like drowning and hanging and matters of a similar kind, is there anything the district police officer can do about them?

Here's a corpse,' says I; 'this is a criminal case, plainly a civil suit. The thing to do,' says I, sir, 'is to send a dispatch right away to His Honor the examining magistrate and Their Honors the judges. And first off,' says I, 'you ought to draw up a report and send it to His Honor the Justice of the Peace.' But the constable, he just listens to it all, and laughs. And the peasants, too. They all laughed, Your Honor. I can testify to it under oath. This one here laughed, and that one there, and Zhigin, he laughed too. 'What's the joke?' says I. And the constable, he says, 'Such cases ain't within the jurisdiction of the justice of the peace.' I got hot under the collar when I heard them words. You did say them words, didn't you, Constable?" The sergeant turned to Zhigin.

"I did."

"Everybody heard you say them very words in front of the common people: 'Such cases ain't within the jurisdiction of the justice of the peace.' Everybody heard you say them words. I got hot under the collar, Your Honor. Honest, it took away my breath. 'Repeat,' says I, 'repeat, you blankety blank, what you just said.' And he did. 'How can you say them words,' says I, 'about His Honor the Justice of the Peace? You, a police officer, and you're agin the government! What? Do you know,' says I, 'that if he takes it into his head, His Honor the Justice of the Peace can ship you off to the provincial office of the Gendarmerie on account of your unreliable conduct? Do you know,' says I, 'where His Honor the Justice of the Peace can send you for such political words?' And the village elder, he says: 'The Justice of the Peace can't do nothing,' he says, 'beyond his limits. Only minor cases comes within his jurisdiction.' Them's his exact words; everybody heard him. 'How dare you belittle the authorities?' says I. 'Don't you get gay with me,' says I, 'or you'll come to grief, brother.' When I was serving in Warsaw and when I was doorman at the junior high school for boys of good family, if I heard something as shouldn't be said, I'd look up and down the street for a gendarme. 'Come here, Officer,' I'd say, and I'd make a report of the whole affair to him. But here in the village, who can you report to? This made me sore. It got under my skin to see folks indulge in license and insubordination, and I gave the elder a crack. . . . Of course, not much of a one, just easy-like, so he'd know better than to say such words about Your Honor. The constable stuck up for the elder. So, naturally, I went for the constable, too. . . . And then there was a rumpus. I forgot myself, Your Honor. But how'll you get along if you don't punch 'em sometimes? If you don't thrash a fool, you take a sin on your soul. And all the more if he deserves it, if there's breach of the peace."

"Allow me, but there are proper authorities to keep order. There is the constable, the village elder, the policeman."

"The constable can't keep an eye on everything, and besides, he don't understand things like I do. . . ."

"But get it into your head: this is none of your business!"

"How's that, sir? What do you mean—'none of my business'? That's queer, sir. People carry on disgracefully, and it's none of my business! Should I pat 'em on the back for it? Here they kick because I don't let 'em sing. What's the good of singing? Instead of doing something useful, they sing. And now they've got into the way of sitting up evenings and burning lights. They should go to bed, and instead they gab and cackle. I've got it all wrote down!"

"What have you written down?"

"About them as sit up and burns lights."

Prishibeyev takes a greasy sheet of paper out of his pocket, puts on his spectacles, and reads:

" 'Peasants what burn lights: Ivan Prokhorov, Savva Mikiforov, Pyotr Petrov, Shustrova, soldier's widow, lives in sin with Semyon Kislov. Ignat Sverchok practices witchcraft, and his wife Mavra is a witch: she milks other folks' cows at night.' "

"That will do," says the judge, and starts to question the witnesses.

Sergeant Prishibeyev shoves his spectacles up on his forehead and stares in astonishment at the judge who appears not to side with him. His protruding eyes glitter; his nose turns bright red. He gazes at the justice of the peace and at the witnesses, and cannot grasp why the judge is so agitated or why now a murmur, now subdued laughter is heard from all the corners of the courtroom. The sentence, too, is incomprehensible to him: a month in jail!

"What for?" says he, throwing up his arms in bewilderment. "By what law?"

And it is clear to him that the world has changed and that it is utterly impossible to go on living. He falls prey to gloomy, despondent thoughts. But when he leaves the courtroom and catches sight of a crowd of peasants milling about and talking, a habit that he can no longer control makes him come to attention and shout in a hoarse, angry voice:

"Break it up, folks! Move along! Go on home!"

1885

Anna on the Neck

After the ceremony not even light refreshments were served; the bride and groom each drank a glass of wine, changed their clothes, and drove to the station. Instead of having a gay ball and supper, instead of music and dancing, they traveled a hundred and fifty miles to perform their devotions at a shrine. Many people commended this, saying that Modest Alexeich had already reached a high rank in the service and was no longer young and that a noisy wedding might not have seemed quite proper; and besides, music is likely to sound dreary when a fifty-two-year-old official marries a girl who has just turned eighteen. It was also said that Modest Alexeich, being a man of principle, had really arranged this visit to the monastery in order to make it clear to his young bride that in marriage, too, he gave the first place to religion and morality.

The couple were seen off by relatives and the groom's colleagues. The crowd stood, with the glasses in their hands, waiting to shout "Hurrah" as soon as the train should start; and the bride's father, Pyotr Leontich, in a top hat and the dress coat of a schoolmaster, already drunk and very pale, kept craning toward the window, glass in hand and saying imploringly, "Anyuta! Anya, Anya! Just one word!"

Anya leaned out of the window toward him and he whispered something to her, enveloping her in a smell of alcohol and blowing into her ear—she could understand nothing—and made the sign of the cross over her face, her bosom, her arms. His breathing came in gasps, and tears shone in his eyes. And Anya's brothers, Petya and Andryusha, schoolboys, pulled at his coattails from behind, whispering embarrassedly, "Papa dear, enough . . . Papa dear, don't. . . ."

When the train started, Anya saw her father run a little way after the coach, staggering and spilling his wine; and what a pitiful, kindly, guilty face he had! "Hurrah!" he shouted.

The couple were left alone. Modest Alexeich looked about the compartment, arranged their things on the shelves, and sat down opposite his young wife, smiling. He was an official of medium height, rather stout, who looked bloated and very well fed and wore Dundreary whiskers. His clean-shaven, round, sharply outlined chin looked like a heel. The most characteristic thing about his face was the absence of a moustache, this bare, freshly shaven spot which gradually passed into fat cheeks that quivered like jelly. His demeanor was dignified; his movements were unhurried, his manners suave.

"At the moment I cannot help recalling one circumstance," he said smiling. "When, five years ago, Kosorotov received the order of St. Anna of the second class, and came to thank His Excellency for the honor, His Excellency expressed himself thus: 'So now you have three Annas: one in your buttonhole and two on your neck.' I must tell you that at that time Kosorotov's wife, a quarrelsome person of a giddy disposition, had just returned to him and that her name was Anna. I trust that when I receive the Anna of the second class, His Excellency will have no cause to say the same thing to me."

He smiled with his small eyes. And she, too, smiled, troubled by the thought that at any moment this man might kiss her with his full, moist lips and that she no longer had the right to prevent him from doing so. The soft movements of his bloated body frightened her; she felt both terrified and disgusted. He got up without haste, took an order off his neck, took off his dress coat and vest, and put on his dressing gown. "That's better," he said, sitting down beside Anya.

She remembered what agony the marriage ceremony had been when it had seemed to her that the priest, the guests, and everyone in the church had looked at her sadly: Why was she, such a sweet, nice girl, marrying an elderly, uninteresting man? Only that morning she had been in raptures over the fact that everything had been satisfactorily arranged, but during the ceremony and now in the railway carriage, she felt guilty, cheated, and ridiculous. Here she had married a rich man, and yet she had no money. Her wedding dress had been bought on credit, and just now when her father and brothers had been saying goodbye, she could see from their faces that they had not a kopeck to their name. Would they have any supper tonight? And tomorrow? And for some reason it seemed to her that her father and the boys without her were suffering from hunger and feeling as miserable as they did the day after their mother's funeral. "Oh, how unhappy I am!" she thought. "Why am I so unhappy?"

189

With the awkwardness of a man of dignified habits who is un-accustomed to dealing with women, Modest Alexeich touched her on the waist and patted her on the shoulder while she thought of money, of her mother and her mother's death. When her mother died, her father, a high-school teacher of penmanship and drawing, had taken to drink and they had begun to feel the pinch of poverty; the boys had no shoes or galoshes. Time and again her father was hauled before the justice of the peace, the process server came and made an inventory of the furniture. . . . What a disgrace! Anya had to look after her drunken father, darn her brothers' socks, do the marketing, and when she was complimented on her beauty, her youth, and her elegant manner, it seemed to her that the whole world was looking at her cheap hat and the holes in her shoes that were inked over. And at night there were tears and the disturbing, per-sistent thought that soon, very soon her father would be dismissed from the school for his failing and that he would not be able to endure it and would die like their mother. But then some ladies they knew had bestirred themselves and started looking about for a good match for Anya. This Modest Alexeich, who was neither young nor good-looking but had money, was soon found. He had about a hundred thousand in the bank and an ancestral estate which he rented to a tenant. He was a man of principle and stood well with His Excel-lency; it would be very easy for him, Anya was told, to get a note from His Excellency to the high-school principal or even to the trustee, and Pyotr Leontich would not be dismissed. . . .

While she was recalling these details, strains of music together with a sound of voices suddenly burst in at the window. The train had stopped at a small station. On the other side of the platform in the crowd an accordion and a cheap squeaky fiddle were being played briskly, and from beyond the tall birches and poplars and the small cottages that were flooded with moonlight came the sound of a mili-tary band: there must have been a dance in the place. Summer visitors and townspeople who came here by train in fine weather for a breath of fresh air were promenading on the platform. Among them was the owner of all the cottages, Artynov, a man of wealth. Tall, stout, black-haired, with prominent eyes, he looked like an Armenian. He wore a strange costume: an unbuttoned shirt that left his chest bare, high boots with spurs, and a black cloak that hung from his shoulders and trailed on the ground. Two borzois followed him with their sharp muzzles to the ground.

Tears were still glistening in Anya's eyes, but she was now no longer thinking of her mother or money or her marriage. She was shaking hands with high-school boys and officers of her acquaintance, laughing gayly and saying quickly, "How do you do? How are you?"

She went out into the moonlight and stood so that they could all see her in her new splendid costume and hat.

"Why are we stopping here?" she asked.

"This is a siding. They are waiting for the mail train to pass."

Noticing that Artynov was looking at her, she screwed up her face coquettishly and began talking aloud in French; and because her voice sounded so well and because music was heard and the moon was reflected in the pond, and because Artynov, the notorious Don Juan and rake, was looking at her greedily and inquisitively, and because everyone was gay, she suddenly felt happy, and when the train started and her friends, the officers, saluted her, she was humming a polka, the strains of which reached her from the military band that was blaring somewhere beyond the trees; and she returned to her compartment feeling as if she had been persuaded at the station that she would certainly be happy in spite of everything.

The couple spent two days at the monastery, then returned to town. They lived in an apartment supplied by the government. When Modest Alexeich left for the office, Anya would play the piano or cry out of sheer boredom or lie down on a couch and read novels or look through fashion journals. At dinner Modest Alexeich ate a great deal, talked about politics, new appointments, transfers and bonuses, and declared that one should work hard, that family life was not a pleasure but a duty, that if you took care of the kopecks, the rubles would take care of themselves, and that he put religion and morality above everything else in the world. And holding the knife in his fist like a sword, he would say:

"Everyone must have his duties!"

And Anya listened to him, was frightened and could not eat, so that she usually rose from the table hungry. After dinner her husband took a nap and snored loudly while she went to see her own people. Her father and the boys looked at her in a peculiar way, as if just before she came they had been blaming her for having married for money a tedious, tiresome man whom she did not love. Her rustling skirts, her bracelets, and her general ladylike air made them uncomfortable, offended them. In her presence they felt a little embarrassed, and did not know what to talk to her about; but they still loved her as before and were not used to having dinner without her. She sat down with them to cabbage soup, thick porridge, and potatoes fried in mutton fat that smelled of tallow candle. With a trembling hand Pyotr Leontich filled his glass from a decanter and drank it off quickly, greedily, with disgust, then drank a second glass, then a third. Petya and Andryusha, thin, pale boys with big eyes, would take the decanter and say with embarrassment:

"You mustn't, Papa dear. . . . Enough, Papa dear."

Anya, too, was troubled, and would beg him to drink no more; and he would suddenly fly into a rage and strike the table with his fist. "I will not be dictated to!" he would shout. "Wretched boys! Wretched girl! I will turn you all out!"

But there was a note of weakness, of kindness in his voice, and no one was afraid of him. After dinner he usually spruced up. Pale, with cuts on his chin from shaving, he would stand for half an hour before the mirror, craning his thin neck, preening himself, combing his hair, twisting his black moustache, sprinkling himself with scent, tying his cravat in a bow; then he would put on his gloves and his top hat and would go off to give private lessons. If there was a holiday, he would stay at home and paint or play the harmonium, which hissed and growled; he would wrest melodious tones from it and would storm at the boys: "Scamps! Wretches! They've spoiled the instrument!"

Evenings Anya's husband played cards with his colleagues who lived under the same roof in the government quarters. During these parties the wives of the functionaries would also assemble—homely, tastelessly dressed women, as coarse as cooks; and gossip, as ugly and insipid as the women themselves, would start in the apartment. Sometimes Modest Alexeich would take Anya to the theater. During the intermissions he would not let her go a step from his side, but walked about arm in arm with her through the corridors and the foyer. When he bowed to anyone, he immediately whispered to Anya, "A councilor of state . . . received by His Excellency," or, "A man of means . . . has a house of his own." When they passed the buffet Anya had a great longing for sweets; she was fond of chocolate and apple tarts, but she had no money and she did not like to ask her husband. He would take a pear, feel it with his fingers and ask uncertainly, "How much?"

"Twenty-five kopecks."

"I say!" he would exclaim, and put the pear back, but as it was awkward to leave the buffet without buying anything, he would order a bottle of soda water and drink it all himself, and tears would come into his eyes. At such times Anya hated him.

Or suddenly turning quite red, he would say to her hurriedly, "Bow to that old lady!"

"But I am not acquainted with her. . . ."

"No matter. That is the wife of the director of the local treasury office! Bow to her, I mean you," he said grumbling insistently. "Your head won't fall off."

Anya bowed, and her head really didn't fall off but it was very painful. She did everything her husband told her to do and was very angry with herself that she had let herself be deceived like the silliest little fool. She had married him only for his money, and yet she had less money now than before her marriage. Formerly her father would sometimes give her a twenty-kopeck piece, but now she never had a groat. She couldn't take money on the quiet, or ask for it; she was afraid of her husband. She trembled before him. It seemed to her as though she had been afraid of him for a long time. In her childhood the high-school principal had always seemed to her the most imposing and terrible power in the world, moving along like a thundercloud or a steam locomotive ready to crush everything in its way. Another such power of which they often talked at home, and which for some reason they feared, was His Excellency. Then, there were a dozen other, less formidable powers, and among them were the high-school teachers, strict and implacable, with shaven upper lips. And now, finally, it was Modest Alexeich, a man of principle, who resembled the head of the school in every particular, including his face. And in Anya's imagination all these powers combined into one, and in the shape of a terrible, huge white bear, bore down upon the weak and guilty, such as her father. And she was afraid to contradict her husband, and with a forced smile and a show of pleasure, submitted to his coarse caresses and defiling embraces, which terrified her.

Only once did Pyotr Leontich make bold to ask for a loan of

fifty rubles in order to pay a very unpleasant debt, but what agony it was!

"Very well, I'll give you the money," said Modest Alexeich after a moment's thought. "But I warn you, I won't help you again until you stop drinking. Such a weakness is disgraceful in a man holding a government post! I cannot refrain from calling your attention to the well-known fact that many able people have been ruined by that passion, though temperance might perhaps have permitted them to attain a very high rank."

Followed long-winded sentences with such phrases as, "in proportion to," "whereas," "in view of the aforesaid," while poor Pyotr Leontich was in an agony of humiliation and felt an intense craving for alcohol.

And when the boys came to visit Anya, generally in worn shoes and threadbare trousers, they too had to listen to lectures.

"Everyone must have his duties!" Modest Alexeich would say to them. But he would not give them money. To Anya, he would give rings, bracelets, brooches, saying that these things would come in handy on a rainy day. And he often unlocked her chest of drawers to see if they were all safe.

II

Meanwhile the cold season had arrived. Before Christmas it was announced in the local newspaper that the usual winter ball would take place on December 29th in the Hall of the Nobility. Every evening after the card playing, Modest Alexeich was excitedly conferring in whispers with his colleagues' wives and glancing anxiously at Anya, and afterward he paced the room from corner to corner for a long time, thinking. At last, late one evening he stood still before Anya and said: "You must have a ball dress made for yourself. Do you understand? Only, please consult Marya Grigoryevna and Natalya Kuzminishna."

And he gave her one hundred rubles. Though she took the money, she didn't consult anyone when she ordered the gown. She spoke to no one but her father, and tried to imagine how her mother would have dressed for the ball. Her mother had always dressed in the latest fashion and had always taken great pains with Anya, fitting her out elegantly like a doll, and had taught her to speak French and dance the mazurka magnificently. (She had been a governess for five years prior to her marriage.) Like her mother, Anya could make a new dress out of an old one, clean gloves with benzine, hire jewelry and, like her mother, she knew how to screw up her eyes, speak with a burr, strike pretty poses, fly into ecstasies when necessary, and assume a sad and enigmatic air. And from her father she inherited dark hair and eyes, sensitive nerves, and the habit of always trying to look her best.

When, half an hour before they had to start for the ball, Modest Alexeich came into her room coatless to put his order round his neck in front of her mirror, he was so struck by her beauty and the splendor of her crisp, gauzy attire, that he combed his side whiskers complacently and said: "So that's how my wife can look. . . . So that's how you can look!" And he went on, suddenly assuming a tone of solemnity: "Anyuta, I have made you happy, and tonight you can make me happy. I beg you to introduce yourself to His Excellency's spouse, for God's sake! Through her I may get the post of senior reporting secretary."

They drove to the ball. There it was, the Hall of the Nobility, the lobby with the stately doorman. The vestibule was full of hangers, fur coats, footmen scurrying about, and décolleté ladies putting up their fans to protect themselves from the draft; the placed smelled of illuminating gas and soldiers.

When Anya, walking up the stairs on her husband's arm, heard the music and saw herself full-length in the huge pier glass glowing with numberless lights, her heart leaped with joy and with that presentiment of happiness she had experienced in the moonlight at the station. She walked in proudly, confidently, for the first time feeling herself not a little girl but a lady, and unwittingly imitating her late mother's gait and manners. And for the first time in her life, she felt rich and free. Even her husband's presence did not embarrass her, for as she crossed the threshold of the hall she had guessed instinctively that the proximity of her elderly husband did not humiliate her in the least, but on the contrary, gave her that touch of piquant mystery that is so attractive to men.

In the ballroom the orchestra was already thundering, and dancing had already begun. After their apartment, Anya, overwhelmed by the lights, the bright colors, the music, the din, looked round the hall, and thought, "Oh, how lovely!" and instantly spotted in the crowd all her acquaintances, everyone she had met before at parties or at picnics, all these officers, teachers, lawyers, officials, landowners. His Excellency, too, was there, and Artynov, and society ladies in low-neck dresses, the pretty ones and the ugly. These were already taking up positions in the booths and pavilions of the charity bazaar, ready to begin selling things for the benefit of the poor. A huge officer with shoulder straps—she had been introduced to him when she was a schoolgirl and now could not remember his name—loomed up before her, as though he had sprung out of the ground, and asked her for a waltz, and she flew away from her husband. She felt as though she were sailing in a boat during a violent storm, while her husband remained far away on the shore. . . . She danced passionately, eagerly— waltzes, polkas, quadrilles—passing from one pair of arms to another, dizzy with the music and the hubbub, mixing Russian and French, speaking with a burr, laughing, and not giving a thought to her husband or anybody or anything. She scored a success with the men—that was clear, and it couldn't have been otherwise. She was breathless with excitement, she squeezed her fan in her hand convulsively, and felt thirsty. Her father in a crumpled coat that smelled of benzine came up to her offering her a saucer of pink ice cream.

"You are ravishing tonight," he said, looking at her enraptured, "and I have never so regretted that you were in such a hurry to get married. . . . Why? I know you did it for our sake, but . . ." With a shaking hand, he drew out a roll of notes and said: "I got the money for lessons today, and can pay my debt to your husband."

She thrust the saucer back into his hand and, snatched by someone, was carried off far away. Over her partner's shoulder she caught a glimpse of her father gliding across the parquet, putting his arm round a lady and whirling her down the hall.

"How charming he is when he is sober!" she thought.

She danced the mazurka with the same huge officer. He moved gravely and heavily, like a lifeless carcass in uniform, twitching his shoulders and his chest, stamping his feet almost imperceptibly—he was loath to dance—while she fluttered round him, teasing him with her beauty, her bare neck. Her eyes glowed provokingly, her movements were passionate, while he grew more and more indifferent, and held out his hands to her graciously like a king.

"Bravo! Bravo!" people were exclaiming in the crowd.

But little by little the huge officer, too, lost his composure; he came to life, grew excited, and yielding to her fascination, was carried away and danced lightly, youthfully, while she merely moved her shoulders and looked slyly at him as though she were now the queen and he were her slave. At that moment it seemed to her that the whole ballroom was looking at them and that everyone was thrilled and envious of them.

The huge officer had hardly had time to thank her for the dance when the crowd suddenly parted and the men drew themselves up queerly and let their arms drop. It was His Excellency, with two stars on his dress coat, walking toward her. Yes, His Excellency was really walking toward her, for he was looking directly at her with a sugary smile and was chewing his lips as he always did when he saw pretty women.

"Delighted, delighted . . ." he began. "I shall have your husband put under arrest for keeping such a treasure hidden from us till now. I have come to you with a commission from my wife," he went on, offering her his arm. "You must help us. . . . M-m-yes . . . we ought to award you a prize for beauty as they do in America. . . . M-m-yes . . . the Americans. My wife is waiting for you impatiently." He led her to a booth and presented her to an elderly lady, the lower part of whose face was disproportionately large, so that she looked as though she had a big stone in her mouth.

"You must help us," she said through her nose in a singsong voice. "All the pretty women are working for our charity bazaar, and for some reason you alone are doing nothing. Why won't you help us?"

She went away, and Anya took her place beside the silver samovar and the cups. She was soon doing a rushing business. Anya charged no less than a ruble for a cup of tea, and forced the huge officer to empty three cups. Artynov, the rich man with the bulging eyes, who suffered from asthma, came up too; he no longer wore the strange costume in which Anya had seen him in the summer at the station, but was in evening clothes like everyone else. Without taking his eyes off Anya, he drank a glass of champagne and paid one hundred rubles for it, then had a cup of tea and gave another hundred, all this without saying a word, and wheezing with asthma. Anya solicited customers and got money out of them, firmly convinced by now that her smiles and glances could afford these people nothing but great pleasure. It had dawned upon her that she was made exclusively for this noisy, brilliant life, with laughter, music, dances, admirers; and her old dread of a power that was bearing down upon her and threatened to crush her now seemed ridiculous to her. She was afraid of no one, and only regretted that her mother was not there to rejoice with her at her success. Her father, pale by this time, but still steady on his legs, came up to the booth and asked for a glass of cognac. Anya turned crimson, expecting him to say something inappropriate (she was already ashamed of having such a poor, ordinary father), but he emptied his glass, took a ten-ruble note from his roll, threw it down, and walked away with silent dignity. A little later she saw him dancing in the *grand rond*, and by now he was staggering and kept calling out something, to his partner's great embarrassment. And Anya remembered how, at a ball three years before, he had staggered and called out in the same way, and it had ended by a police officer taking him home to bed, and the next day the principal had threatened to dismiss him from his post. What an inappropriate recollection it was!

When the samovars had been allowed to cool in the booths and the weary charity workers had handed over their takings to the middle-aged lady with the stone in her mouth, Artynov led Anya on his arm to the hall where supper was being served for all who had helped at the bazaar. There were some twenty people at supper, not more, but it was very noisy. His Excellency proposed this toast: "This luxurious dining room is the appropriate place in which to drink to the success of the soup kitchens for which the bazaar was held."

The brigadier general proposed a toast "to the power to which even the artillery must bow," and all the men proceeded to clink glasses with the ladies. It was very, very jolly!

When Anya was escorted home, it was daylight and the cooks were going to market. Elated, intoxicated, full of new sensations, exhausted, she undressed, sank into bed, and instantly fell asleep.

It was past one in the afternoon when the maid waked her and announced that Mr. Artynov had come to call on her. She dressed quickly and went into the drawing room. Soon after Artynov left, His Excellency called to thank her for her part in the bazaar. Eying her with a sugary smile and chewing his lips, he kissed her hand, asked her permission to come again, and took his leave, while she remained standing in the middle of the drawing room, amazed, entranced, unable to believe that a change in her life, a marvelous change, had occurred so quickly. And just then her husband walked in. He stood before her now with that ingratiating, saccharine, cringingly respectful expression that she was accustomed to seeing on his face in the presence of the illustrious and the powerful, and with rapture, with indignation, with contempt, confident now that she could do it with impunity, she said, articulating each word distinctly,

"Get out, you blockhead!"

After that, Anya never had a single free day, as she was constantly taking part in picnics, excursions, private theatricals. Each day she returned home in the early hours of the morning and lay down on the floor in the drawing room, and afterwards told everyone touchingly that she slept under flowers. She needed a great deal of money, but she was no longer afraid of Modest Alexeich, and spent his money as though it were her own; and she did not ask or demand it, but simply sent him the bills or brief notes like these: "Give the bearer two hundred rubles," or "Pay one hundred rubles at once."

At Easter, Modest Alexeich received the order of St. Anna of the second class. When he went to offer his thanks, His Excellency put aside the newspaper he was reading and sank deeper into his armchair: "So now you have three Annas," he said, examining his white hands with their pink nails, "one in your buttonhole and two on your neck."

Modest Alexeich put two fingers to his lips as a precaution against laughing out loud, and said: "Now I have only to look forward to the arrival of a little Vladimir. I make bold to beg Your Excellency to stand godfather."

He was alluding to the Vladimir of the fourth class, and was already imagining how he would repeat everywhere this joke of his, so felicitous in its aptness and audacity, and he was making ready to say something equally good, but His Excellency was again absorbed in his newspaper, and merely nodded to him.

And Anya went on driving about in troikas, hunting with Artynov, playing in one-acters, going out to supper parties; and she saw less and less of her own people. They dined alone now. Her father was drinking more heavily than ever; there was no money, and the harmonium had long since been sold for debt. The boys did not let him go out alone in the street now, but followed him for fear he might fall; and whenever they met Anya driving down Old Kiev Street in a smart carriage drawn by a team of two horses abreast and an outrunner, with Artynov on the box instead of a coachman, Pyotr Leontich would take off his top hat, and would be about to shout something at her, but Petya and Andryusha would take him by the arms and say imploringly: "Don't Papa dear. . . . Enough, Papa dear . . ."

1895

At Christmastime

I

"What'll I write?" asked Yegor, and dipped his pen in the ink.

Vasilisa had not seen her daughter for four years. After the wedding her daughter Yefimya had gone to Petersburg with her husband, sent two letters home, and then disappeared without leaving a trace. She was neither seen nor heard from. And whether the old woman was milking the cow at dawn or lighting the stove or dozing at night, she was always thinking of one thing: How was Yefimya getting on out there? Was she alive? A letter should have gone off, but the old man did not know how to write, and there was no one to turn to.

But now it was Christmastime, and Vasilisa could bear it no longer, and went to the teahouse to see Yegor, the proprietor's brother-in-law, who had been staying there, doing nothing, ever since he came back from the army; it was said that he could write a fine letter if he were properly paid. At the teahouse Vasilisa had a talk with the cook, then with the proprietress, and then with Yegor himself. Fifteen kopecks was the price agreed on.

And now—this took place in the teahouse kitchen on the second day of the holidays—Yegor was sitting at the table, pen in hand. Vasilisa was standing before him, thoughtful, an expression of care and grief on her face. Pyotr, her husband, a tall, gaunt old man with a brown bald spot, had come with her; he stood staring fixedly ahead of him like a blind man. On the range a piece of pork was being fried in a saucepan; it sizzled and hissed, and seemed actually to be saying, "Flu-flu-flu." It was stifling.

"What'll I write?" Yegor asked again.

"What?" asked Vasilisa, looking at him angrily and suspiciously. "Don't rush me! You're not writing for nothing; you'll get money for it. Well, write: 'To our dear son-in-law, Andrey Khrisanfych, and to our only beloved daughter, Yefimya Petrovna, our love, a low bow, and our parental blessing enduring forever and ever.'"

"Done; keep going."

"'And we also send wishes for a merry Christmas; we are alive and well, hoping you are the same, please God, the heavenly King.'"

Vasilisa thought for a moment and exchanged glances with the old man.

"'Hoping you are the same, please God, the heavenly King,'" she repeated, and burst into tears.

She could say nothing further. And yet before, when she had lain awake at night thinking of it, it had seemed to her that she could not get all she had to say into ten letters. Since the time when her daughter had gone away with her husband, much water had flowed under the bridge; the old people had lived like orphans, and sighed heavily at night, as though they had buried their daughter. And during all that time how many events had occurred in the village, how many weddings and funerals! What long winters! What long nights!

"It's hot," said Yegor, unbuttoning his vest. "Must be 150 degrees. What else?" he asked.

The old couple were silent.

"What does your son-in-law do there?" asked Yegor.

"He used to be a soldier, son, you know," the old man answered in a weak voice. "He came back from the service the same time you did. He used to be a soldier, and now, to be sure, he is in Petersburg at a hyderpathic establishment. The doctor treats sick people with water. So, he works as a doorman, to be sure, at the doctor's."

"It's written down here," said the old woman, taking a letter out of a kerchief. "We got it from Yefimya, goodness knows when. Maybe they're no longer in this world."

Yegor thought a little, and then began writing rapidly:

"At the present time"—he wrote—"as your fate has of itself assined you to a Militery Carere, we advise you to look into the Statutes on Disiplinery Fines and Criminal Laws of the War Department and you will discover in that Law the Sivelisation of the Officials of the War Department."

201

He was writing and reading aloud what he had written, while Vasilisa kept thinking that the letter should tell about how needy they had been the previous year, how the flour had not lasted even till Christmas, and they had had to sell the cow. She ought to ask for money, ought to say that the old man was often ailing and would soon no doubt give up his soul to God. . . . But how to put it in words? What should be said first and what next?

"Observe," Yegor went on writing, "in volume five of Militery Regulashuns. Soldier is a common name and an honorable one. The Topmost General and the lowest Private is both called soldier. . . ."

The old man moved his lips and said quietly, "To have a look at the grandchildren, that wouldn't be bad."

"What grandchildren?" asked the old woman, and she gave him a cross look. "Maybe there ain't any."

"Grandchildren? Maybe there are some. Who knows?"

"And thereby you can judge," Yegor hurried on, "what a foreign enemy is and what an Internal enemy. Our foremost Internal Enemy is Bacchus."

The pen creaked, forming flourishes on the paper that looked like fishhooks. Yegor wrote hurriedly, reading every line over several times. He sat on a stool, his feet spread wide apart under the table, a well-fed, lusty fellow, with a coarse snout and a red nape. He was vulgarity itself: coarse, arrogant, invincible, proud of having been born and bred in a teahouse; and Vasilisa knew perfectly well that here was vulgarity but she could not put it into words, and only looked at Yegor angrily and suspiciously. The sound of his voice and the incomprehensible words, the heat and the stuffiness, made her head ache and threw her thoughts into confusion, and she said nothing further, stopped thinking, and simply waited for him to cease scratching away. But the old man looked on with full confidence. He had faith in his old woman, who had brought him there, and in Yegor; and when he had mentioned the hydropathic establishment earlier, it was clear from his expression that he had faith in the establishment and in the healing virtues of water.

Having finished writing, Yegor got up, and read the entire letter from the beginning. The old man did not understand it, but he nodded his head trustfully.

"That's all right; it's smooth. . . ." he said. "God give you health. That's all right. . . ."

They laid three five-kopeck pieces on the table and went out of the teahouse; the old man stared fixedly before him as though he were blind, and his countenance showed perfect trustfulness; but as Vasilisa went out of the teahouse, she made an angry pass at the dog, and said crossly, "Ugh, the pest!"

The old woman, disturbed by her thoughts, did not sleep all night, and at daybreak she got up, said her prayers, and went to the station to send off the letter.

It was some seven miles to the station.

II

Dr. B. O. Moselweiser's hydropathic establishment was open on New Year's Day just as on ordinary days; but the doorman, Andrey Khrisanfych, wore a uniform with new braid, his boots had an extra polish, and he greeted every visitor with a "Happy New Year!"

Andrey Khrisanfych was standing at the door in the morning, reading a newspaper. Precisely at ten o'clock a general arrived, one of the regular patients, and directly after him came the postman.

Andrey Khrisanfych helped the general off with his overcoat, and said, "Happy New Year, Your Excellency!"

"Thank you, my good man; the same to you."

And as he walked upstairs the general asked, nodding toward a door (he asked the same question every day and always forgot the answer), "And what's in that room?"

"That's the massage room. Your Excellency."

When the general's steps had died away, Andrey Khrisanfych looked over the mail and found one letter addressed to himself. He opened it, read several lines; then, glancing at the newspaper, he walked unhurriedly to his own quarters, which were on the same floor at the end of the corridor. His wife, Yefimya, was sitting on the bed, nursing her baby; another child, the eldest, was standing close by, his curly head resting on her lap; a third was asleep on the bed.

Entering the room, Andrey handed his wife the letter, and said, "Must be from the village."

Then he walked out again without removing his eyes from the paper, and stopped in the corridor, not far from his door. He could hear Yefimya reading the first lines in a trembling voice. She read them and could read no more; these lines were enough for her. She burst into tears, and hugging and kissing her eldest child, she began to speak—and it was impossible to tell whether she were laughing or crying.

"It's from Granny, from Grandpa," she said. "From the country . . . Queen of Heaven, saints and martyrs! The snow is piled up to the roofs there now. . . . The trees are white as white can be. Children are out on tiny little sleds. . . . And darling bald old Grandpa is up on the stove. . . . And there is a little yellow puppy. . . . My precious lambs!"

Hearing this, Andrey Khrisanfych recalled that three or four times his wife had given him letters and asked him to send them to the village, but some important business had always intervened; he had not sent the letters, and somehow they were mislaid.

"And little hares hop about in the fields," Yefimya continued mournfully, bathed in tears, and kissing her boy. "Grandpa is gentle and good; Granny is good, too, and kindhearted. In the village folks are friendly; they fear God. . . . And there is a little church in the village; the peasants sing in the choir. If only the Queen of Heaven, the Mother of God, would take us away from here!"

Andrey Khrisanfych returned to his room to have a smoke before another patient arrived, and Yefimya suddenly stopped speaking, grew quiet, and wiped her eyes, and only her lips quivered. She was very much afraid of him—oh, how afraid of him she was! She trembled and was terrorized at the sound of his steps, his look; she dared not say a word in his presence.

Andrey Khrisanfych lighted a cigarette, but at that very moment there was a ring from upstairs. He put out his cigarette, and, assuming a very grave face, hastened to the front door.

The general was coming downstairs, fresh and rosy from his bath.

"And what's in that room?" he asked, pointing to a door.

Andrey Khrisanych came to attention, and announced loudly:

"Charcot douche, Your Excellency!"

1900

ALEXANDER BLOK
(1880–1921)

"To sin, unshamed"

To sin, unshamed, to lose, unthinking,
The count of careless nights and days,
And then, while the head aches with drinking,
Steal to God's house, with eyes that glaze;

Thrice to bow down to earth, and seven
Times cross oneself, and then once more
With the hot brow, in hope of heaven,
To touch the spittle-covered floor;

With a brass penny's gift dismissing
The offering, the holy Name
To mutter with loose lips, in kissing
The ancient, kiss-worn icon frame;

And to come home, then, and be tricking
Some wretch out of the same small coin,
And with a hiccough to be kicking
A trembling cur in his lean groin;

And where the icon's flame is quaking
Drink tea, and reckon loss and gain,
From the fat chest of drawers taking
The coupons marked with spittle stain;

And sunk in feather beds to smother
In slumber such as bears may know—
Dearer to me than every other
Are you, my Russia, even so.

1914

205

IVAN BUNIN
(1870–1953)

A descendant of an old line of impoverished landed gentry, Bunin is the author of a body of sharply etched imagist verse, but is better known as a writer of fiction, chiefly short stories. Not a few of them have been translated into English. He is a master of a highly evocative realistic prose, abounding in lyrical overtones. From the first he ranged himself against the Bolshevik seizure of power. In 1920, with the defeat of the White forces in the civil war, he crossed the frontier, settling in France, and to the end of his long life his anti-Soviet attitude remained unchanged. The expatriate's literary gift suffered no impairment, but his work took on a wholly reminiscent, nostalgic character. He was the first Russian author to be awarded the Nobel Prize (in 1933). Not long after Stalin's death he was posthumously repatriated, as it were. In 1955 the leading Moscow monthly printed several of his stories written abroad, and in 1956 the Moscow State Publishing House issued a five-volume edition of his collected works, provided with a generous appreciation of his writings, as well as a one-volume selection, which includes the story printed below, first published in 1911.

Cricket

This little story was told by a harness maker nicknamed Cricket, who, with another harness maker, Vasily, had worked all through November for Remer, a landowner.

November was murky and muddy; winter was slow setting in. Remer and his young wife, who had recently settled on their ancestral estate, were bored, and so, of evenings, took to leaving their still boarded-up mansion, where there was only one decent, habitable room downstairs, under the colonnade, and dropping into the old wing of the house, formerly the office, which was now the winter quarters of the poultry, the harness makers, the hired man, and the cook.

On the eve of the Presentation of the Holy Virgin in the Temple [November 21st] a thick wet snowstorm was raging. It was very warm and damp in the spacious, low-ceiled office, which had once upon a time been whitewashed, and there was a heavy stench from the small tin lamp burning on the workbench, mixed with the smell of shag, cobbler's wax, varnish, and the sour minty odor of leather. Pieces and scraps of it were piled on the workbench and on the littered, trampled floor together with tools, new and old harness, rolls for horse collars, felt, waxed thread, and brass harness decorations. There was also the stench of poultry from the dark room adjacent; but Cricket and Vasily, who slept in this stench, and day after day sat in it with bent backs for some ten hours, were, as always, very much pleased with their quarters, especially by the fact that Remer did not spare firewood.

The narrow windowsills were dripping; wet, sticky snow sparkled on the black panes. The harness makers were working diligently, and the cook, a small woman in a sheepskin coat and peasant boots, who had got thoroughly chilled during the day, was resting on a chair with a torn seat near the hot stove. She was toasting her back and, without taking her eyes off the lamp, listened to the noise of the wind, which sometimes shook the whole building, to the tapping of Vasily's hammer on the horse collar he was making, to the breathing, like that of a child or an old man, of bald-headed Cricket, who was busy with a breech band and wagging the red tip of his tongue when he was in a quandary.

The small lamp, wet with kerosene, stood on the very edge of the workbench and just midway between the two workers, so as to provide them with an equal amount of light, but Vasily, whose arm was bare to the elbow, kept shoving it toward himself with his strong, sinewy dark hand. Strength and the assurance of strength were felt in the whole bearing of this dark-haired man who looked like a Malay; they were felt in every bulge of his muscular body, which was clearly defined under his thin shirt of faded red; and it always seemed as if tiny Cricket, decrepit in spite of his apparent sprightliness, were somewhat afraid of Vasily, who had never feared anyone. It seemed so to Vasily himself; jestingly, for the amusement of those around him, he had acquired a way of shouting at Cricket, who indeed encouraged the jest.

Holding a new horse collar between his knees, which were covered with a greasy apron, Vasily was upholstering it with thick, dark-violet leather. With one hand he seized it firmly and pulled it tight over the wood with pliers, with the other hand taking from between his pursed lips brass-headed nails, sticking them into holes previously made with an awl, and then at a single stroke of the hammer deftly and vigorously driving each nail into the wood. He bent low his large head with its black, moist curls bound by a narrow strap, and worked with that pleasing, smooth intensity that is vouchsafed by well-developed strength, by talent. Cricket, too, worked intensely, but his intensity was of a different kind. He was stitching a new, flesh-pink breech band, holding it, as Vasily did, between his knees, and he found it hard to make the cuts and get the bristles into the holes. He wagged the tip of his tongue and tried to keep his bald head from cutting off his light. But he managed to pull the ends of the bristles apart and to tie them securely with the swagger of an old, experienced craftsman.

Bent over the horse collar, Vasily's broad, scowling face, its bones prominent under the oily tan skin and with scanty coarse black hairs above the corners of his lips, had a severe, self-important look. But from the expression of Cricket's face, bent over the breech band, it was clear only that he found the light poor and the work hard. He was exactly twice Vasily's age and nearly half his height. It made no great difference whether he sat or stood up—so short were his legs, in their worn boots soft with age. Because of his own age and his rupture, he walked awkwardly, so badly stooped that his apron hung away from his body, and you could see his caved-in belly, loosely belted, like a child's. Dark like a child's, too, were his black little eyes, resembling small ripe olives, and his face wore a slightly arch, mocking expression; his lower jaw protruded; his upper lip, darkened by thin whiskers, always moist, was sunk in. He omitted his *r*'s, pronounced *l* like *v*, and frequently sniffled, wiping with the forefinger of his large, cold hand his little drooping nose, at the tip of which a transparent tiny drop was always hanging. He smelled of shag and leather, and gave off the pungent odor common to old men.

Above the howling of the snowstorm sounded the stamping of feet shaking off the snow, the slamming of doors, and, bringing with them a fresh odor, the master and mistress came in, plastered with white flakes, their faces wet and drops shining on their hair and clothes. Remer's auburn beard and bushy eyebrows overhanging his serious, vivacious eyes, the glossy Persian-lamb collar of his shaggy overcoat, and his Persian-lamb cap were rendered even more magnificent by the drops; and his wife's gentle, charming face, her soft, long eyelashes, blue-gray eyes and downy kerchief seemed even more gentle and charming. The cook offered her the battered chair, but the lady thanked her sweetly, made her keep her seat, and sat down on a bench in another corner, having carefully removed from it a bridle with a broken bit. Then she yawned faintly, twitched her shoulders, smiled, and in her turn fixed her wide-open eyes on the flame. Remer lighted a cigarette and began to pace the room, without taking off his overcoat and cap. As always, the master and mistress had dropped in for just a minute—the air at the harness makers' was so very close and warm— but then, as always, they forgot themselves and became used to the smell. It was at this point that Cricket, unexpectedly, told his tale.

"You're a smart one, though, brother," he lisped, when Vasily, after greeting the master and mistress with a nod of his head, had again moved the little lamp toward himself. "You're a smart one, brother. I'm a bit older than you, you know," he said, sniffling and wiping his nose.

"What?" Vasily shouted with feigned sternness, frowning. "Maybe you'd have us light a gas burner for you? If you've gone blind, to the poorhouse with you!"

Everyone smiled—even the lady, who found this banter somewhat unpleasant—and thought that Cricket would, as always, manage to get off something funny. But this time he merely jerked his head and, with a sigh, fixed his gaze on the black windowpanes, plastered with snowflakes. Then, picking up an awl in his big, large-veined hand the thumb and forefinger of which were far apart, he stuck the tool into the pink rawhide awkwardly and with difficulty. The cook, noticing that he stared at the windows, said she was afraid that her man, who had gone to Chicherino to fetch a vet, would lose his way and freeze to death, when Cricket, making believe that he was absorbed in his work, suddenly spoke up in a tone of good-natured sadness:

"Yes, brother, gone blind . . . A man will go blind, willy-nilly! You just get to be my age and feel what I've felt! But no, you couldn't! I've been the way I am since time out of memory; it's a marvel I keep body and soul together; yet I've pegged away, I've lived, and I'd live as long again if there were anything to live for. I wanted to live, brother, and very much, as long as it was interestin', and I did live and I didn't knuckle under to death. And how tough *you* are—we don't know yet. You're green; what have you seen?"

Vasily looked at him intently, and so did the master, the mistress, and the cook, all of whom were astonished at his unusual tone. For a moment, what with the stillness, the howling of the wind became particularly noticeable. Then Vasily asked him seriously:

"What are you kicking up a fuss about, now?"

"Me?" said Cricket, raising his head. "No, brother, I ain't kickin' up no fuss. It's just I was reminded of my son. You must have heard what a fine lad he was. Maybe a cut above you, and yet he couldn't stand what I did."

"He froze to death, I believe?" asked Remer.

"I knew him," said Vasily, and, without embarrassment, as people speak of a child in its presence, he added: "Why, they say he wasn't a son of his, Cricket's, that is. Not like his mom nor his dad, but like some wayfaring lad."

"That's somethin' else," said Cricket just as simply. "That may be so, but he honored me just like I was his father—God grant your sons honor you as much. Besides, I didn't try to find out if he was my own son or not, my own blood or another's. . . . We all have the same blood, I guess. Here's the point: he was maybe dearer to me than ten sons of my own woulda been. Now you, master, and you, ma'am," said Cricket, turning his head to the visitors and pronouncing "ma'am" with particular tenderness, "you listen to how it all came about, how he froze to death. I lugged him all night long on my back, you know!"

"Was it a bad blizzard?" asked the cook.

"Not at all," said Cricket. "Fog."

"Fog?" asked the mistress. "But can you freeze to death in a fog? And why did you lug him?"

Cricket smiled gently.

"H'm!" he brought out. "But you, ma'am, you couldn't even imagine how this kind of fog can torment a man to death! And I was luggin' him because I was so terrible sorry for him, ma'am; I kept thinkin' that I could save him from it . . . from death, that is. It all came about," he began, addressing neither Vasily nor the master, but the mistress alone, "it all came about on the eve of the Feast of St. Nicholas." [December 6th, O.S.]

"Was this long ago?" asked Remer.

"Five or six years back," Vasily answered for Cricket, listening gravely and rolling a cigarette.

Cricket glanced at him with an old man's sternness.

"Leave a butt for me to have a drag," he said, and went on. "We was workin', ma'am, for Master Savich at Ognyovka. He—my son, that is—always paired off with me, always stuck by me. Well, we worked there, and we rented a lodging in the village; after Mother's death we lived like two chums. At last, St. Nicholas' Feast came along. It was time we were leaving for home, we thought, time we were putting ourselves to rights a bit, because, honest, we needed quite a little cleaning up. We was getting ready to take off toward evening and didn't notice that it had turned awful cold and the fog so heavy that you couldn't see the village beyond the little meadow, to say nothin' of that whole neck of the woods bein' very lonely. We dawdled, putting away our tools, and we had to do it in the dark, because the master was so stingy that he begrudged us a candle end. We had a feeling that it was gettin' late, and, would you believe me? suddenly I was seized with such anguish that I said: 'Listen, my dear boy, Maxim Ilyich, shouldn't we stay on here and set out in the morning?' "

"Why, is your name Ilya?" asked the mistress, suddenly realizing that she did not know Cricket's first name.

"Ilya it is, ma'am," said Cricket gently, with a sniffle, and wiped his nose. "Ilya Kapitonov is my name. But my son, too, used to call me Cricket and nothin' more; just like His Royal Highness Vasily Stepanych, he made fun of me, sassed me. Well, of course, he'd have his laugh this time too, and he shouted at me: 'What's this you say? Cut out the gab!' He pulls my cap over my ears, puts on his own, tightens his belt—a handsome lad he was, ma'am, it's God's truth I'm tellin' you!—picks up his stick and with no more talk steps out on the porch. I follow him. . . . I see the fog is somethin' frightful; and by now it's quite dark, and the master's orchard is all covered over with bluish caps, seems, of hoarfrost, and looks like a cloud, kind of, in this fog. But there's nothing to be done; I don't want to hurt the young man's feelin's, so I keep mum.

"We crossed the little meadows, went up a hill, and looked back, but the master's windows couldn't be seen any longer. I turned my back to the wind: it took my breath away in a minute; this murk, this fog was comin' in puffs—I hadn't taken more than two steps when I felt chilled to the bone, and, mind you, our boots were thin and our coats were nothin' to brag about. So I said again: 'Listen, Maxim, let's go back; don't try to show off!' He did fall to thinkin' for a while. . . . But you know how young folks are, you can tell, ma'am, from your own experience, I guess: how can you miss a chance to cut a figure? He frowned right away and was off again. We came to the village, and of course things looked up a bit. Even though the lights in the huts were blurred, still it showed people was livin' there. So he mutters: 'Well, you see? What was you scared of? It's so much warmer when you're walkin'. It's only at first it seemed so raw. . . . Don't you fall back, don't you fall back, or else I'll have to be pushin' you. . . .' But how could you talk of warmth, ma'am? All the water carts were coated thick with hoarfrost, all the osiers were bent to the ground, and there wasn't a roof to be seen for the fog and the frost. Of course, there were livin' quarters, but the lights just made the fog worse, and my eyelashes were as heavy with rime as a horse's, and there was not a trace of the lights in the master's windows. In short, it was a fierce night, a wolfish night."

Vasily scowled, blew the smoke out of both nostrils and, handing the butt to Cricket, interrupted him:

"Oh, you and your wolves; at this rate you won't get through till Second Advent. Make it short."

And, in a businesslike fashion, he turned over the horse collar between his knees, intending to go on with his work. Taking the butt with the tips of his smoke-stained fingers, Cricket inhaled deeply and for a moment grew sadly pensive, as if listening to his own childish breathing and the howling of the wind behind the walls. Then he said timidly:

"Very well, God bless you, I'll make it shorter. All I wanted to say is we simply lost our way after takin' two steps. Yes, ma'am," he went on with more assurance, glancing at the lady, catching sympathy in her eyes, and feeling his grief, which had long become habitual, more keenly, "and so we lost our way, I mean. As soon as we left the village and found ourselves in this darkness, this murk, this cold, and walked on for a verst or so, we lost our way. There is a big ravine there, an enormous meadow and gulleys all the way to the village where we lodged. There is a road above them, so we kept to it, thinking all the time that we was keeping a true course. But instead we bore to the left, followin' somebody's tracks—that is, to the Bibikov ravines, and then, as ill luck would have it, we lost this track too, and after that started wadin' through the snow in the wind, helter-skelter.

"But all this is an old story, ma'am—who hasn't lost his way? Everybody has. What I wanted to say, ma'am, is what tortures I went through that night! Truth to tell, I got so scared, so frightened after we'd been circlin' for two or three hours and got all pooped out, winded, frozen, driven to the wall, done for—I got so scared, I say, that needles of fire went through my hands and feet: of course, everybody prizes his life. Only, it never entered my head what was in store for me, how the Lord would punish me! Naturally, I thought *my* end would come first: you can see for yourself what vigor there's in me. But when I saw that I was still alive, standin' up, while he had sat down in the snow, when I saw him—"

Cricket uttered a low cry with the last words, glanced at the cook, who was already in tears, and blinking his eyes started looking for his tobacco pouch, his eyebrows and lips contorted, his jaw trembling. Vasily crossly shoved his own into his hand, and Cricket, rolling a cigarette with his shaky hands and dropping tears into the tobacco, spoke again, but his tone was different, higher, and markedly firmer.

"My dear ma'am, we once had a master, Ilyin by name; in the whole province there wasn't a more brutal man, that is, when it came to our kind, house serfs, I mean. Well, he too froze to death. They found him near town, lying in his carriage, all snowed under, frozen stiff with ice inside his mouth. And right near him a live hound, his favorite setter, crouched shivering under a raccoon coat. That fiend took his own coat off his back and covered the hound, while he himself froze to death, and so did his driver and his troika—the horses leaned their weight against the shafts, and croaked. And here was not a hound, but my own son, my dearest mate! Yes, ma'am! What could I take off? This coat of mine? It was as old as me; his was twice as warm. But here even a fur coat wouldn't have helped. Even if I was to take off my shirt, I couldn't have saved him; if I was to shout over the whole wide world, not a soul would hear me. In a little while he grew even more frightened than me, and for that very reason we were done for. As soon as we lost the tracks, he got restless. At first he kept callin' out; his teeth chattered and he panted—the wind and frost had pierced us to the bone. Then he started goin' off his head, sort of.

" 'Stop!' I shout. 'For Christ's sake, stop; let's sit down and put our heads together!' He don't say nothin'. I grab him by the sleeve and shout again. He keeps mum and that's all. Either he don't understand nothin' or he don't hear. It's pitch-dark; we no longer feel our hands or feet; our faces are frozen; our lips don't seem to be there, nothin' left but a bare jaw. And you can't see nothin', understand nothin'! The wind howls in your ears, blows the murk about, and he keeps circlin' and tossin', and don't listen to me. I run, swallow the fog, sink in the snow up to my waist. At any moment, I think, I'll lose sight of him. . . . All at once we tumble, start rollin' down, choke in the snow. . . . It comes over me we're at the bottom of a ravine. We keep quiet awhile, catch our breath; and suddenly he says: 'What's this, Father? The Bibikov ravines? Well, sit still, sit still; let's take a rest. We'll climb out and go back, and we'll make it without the road. Now I understand it all. And don't you be scared, don't be scared—I'll get you there safely.' But it's not like his own voice, not natural, sort of. . . . Right then and there it came to me that we was done for. We climbed out, started walkin' again, lost our heads again. . . . We went on wadin' in the snow another two hours, and stumbled into some shrubbery; young oaks it was. And when we'd run into them, we knew that we was all of ten versts away from Ognyovka, in the open steppe. It was then he suddenly slumped down and said, 'Goodbye, Cricket.' 'Hold on, what do you mean, "Goodbye"? Pull yourself together, Maxim!' But no, he sat down, and was still.

"It's a long story, ma'am," Cricket's voice rang out again and he twisted his eyebrows awry. "Just then I lost all fear. Soon as he slumped down, it hit me like a blow on the head. So, I think to myself, that's what it is; this ain't the time for me to be dyin'! I began to kiss his hands, to beg him, sayin': 'Hold out for even a little while longer; don't sit there; don't give in to this sleep of death; let's cut across the field, road or no road; lean on me!' But no—he don't keep on his feet, and that's that! Me, I'd have died in this fix, but I just couldn't, was in no position. . . . And when he'd already met his end, got all quiet, turned heavy and frozen, I loaded him on my shoulders, big man that he was, got hold of him by his legs, and tramped off, without looking for path or road. 'No,' I think to myself, 'halt, no; don't you believe it; I ain't giving him up—I'll drag him around, dead as he is, a hundred nights!'

"I run, I get stuck in the snow, I can't hardly catch my breath because of my load; my hair stands on end with terror when his icy head—his cap had fallen off long ago—knocks against my shoulder, touches my ear. I keep runnin' and shoutin': 'Halt, no! I'm not givin' him up; this ain't the time for me to be dyin'!' You see, ma'am, I kept thinkin'," Cricket said in a voice that suddenly dropped—he burst into tears, and wiped his eyes with his sleeve, picking out the least dirty spot nearer the shoulder—"I kept thinkin' that I'd bring him to the village . . . maybe he'd thaw out, maybe he could be brought back by rubbin'. . . ."

After a long pause, when Cricket had already calmed down and was staring at a point in front of him with red-rimmed eyes, and when both the lady and the cook had wiped their tears and drawn a sigh of relief, Vasily said seriously:

"I shouldn't have cut you short. You tell a story well. I didn't expect such spirit from you."

"That's just it," Cricket observed, also seriously and simply. "I could go on tellin' this story all night long, brother, and not tell it all, even so."

"And how old was he?" asked Remer, now and then glancing askance at his wife, who was smiling gently after her tears. He was wondering uneasily if the tale might not affect her adversely in her delicate condition.

"He was going on twenty-five, master," Cricket answered.

"And you had no other children?" asked the mistress timidly.

"No, ma'am, we didn't."

"But me, I've all of seven," said Vasily, frowning. "The cottage is but two paces wide, and there's a whole pile of 'em. Children—they're no great pleasure. Plainly, the sooner we die, the better for us."

Cricket reflected awhile.

"Well, this matter is over our heads," he brought out, even more simply, seriously, and sadly, and picked up his awl again. "If he hadn't frozen to death, brother, no kind of death would take me before I was a hundred."

The master and mistress exchanged glances and, buttoning up, rose to go. But for a long time they remained standing there and listening to Cricket while he answered the cook's questions as to whether he had brought his son all the way to the village and how it all ended. Cricket explained that he had managed to carry his son, not to the village but as far as the railroad, and there he had fallen down, stumbling against the rails. His hands and feet were frostbitten and he was about to lose consciousness. Dawn had come; there was a snowstorm; everything around him was white, and he sat on the open plain and watched the snow drifting over his dead son, covering his sparse moustaches and filling his white ears. They had been picked up by the crew of a freight train coming from Balashov.

"It's a wonder of the world," said the cook when he had finished. "What I can't understand is how you yourself weren't froze in such terrible weather."

"My mind was on other matters, mother," Cricket answered absent-mindedly, looking for something on the workbench among the scraps of leather. "On other matters."

Russian Spring

In the valley the birches are bored.
On the meadows, a dingy fog.
Sodden, with horse dung floored,
The highroad is bleak as a bog.

From the village asleep on the plains
Comes the odor of fresh-baked bread.
Two tramps with their packs are at pains
To limp on till they come to a bed.

Spring mud is thick on the streets
Where puddles gleam in the sun.
Steam drifts from damp earthen seats;
The fumes from the oven stun.

216

The sheep dog, dragging his chain,
Yawns on the barn-door sill.
Indoors there is reek and stain.
The haze-wrapped steppe is still.

The carefree cocks perform
For spring, till the day is spent.
The meadow is drowsy and warm,
The glad heart indolent.

[1905]

OSIP MANDELSTAMM
(1891–1940?)

"On every still suburban street"

On every still suburban street
The gatekeepers are shoveling snow;
A passerby, I do not know
The bearded peasants whom I meet.

The kerchiefed women come and go,
There's yelping from some crazy tike,
In teahouse and in home alike
The samovars' red roses glow.

[1913]

"The air strikes chill"

The air strikes chill. Although transparent spring
Has clothed Petropolis in pale green down,
The Neva's waves are faintly sickening
As if they were Medusa's coiling crown.
On the embankment of our northern stream
The fireflies of hurrying motors gleam.
Steel dragonflies and beetles flit and whirr,
And stars are pins of gold whose glitter pricks,
But stars can never mortally transfix
The heavy emerald of the sea water.

[1916]

MAXIM GORKY
(1868–1936)

An upholsterer's son, Alexey Peshkov, who achieved world fame under the pseudonym of Maxim Gorky (the Bitter), was born in the age-old trading and shipping center on the Volga, Nizhny Novgorod, renamed Gorky to honor the "Father of Soviet Literature." He spent his early years in a wretched environment, of which more presently. His formal education was limited to several months in an elementary school, but as he moved from one odd job to another the boy managed to read avidly and to pick up scraps of book learning. Eventually the self-taught man achieved considerable culture. In his youth he had tramped all over the southern section of the country, earning his bread by occasional work as a day laborer or stevedore, and accumulating impressions of Russian life in the raw. He had, too, some contacts with the Populists and Marxists, which stimulated his rebellion against the established order and led to his being placed under police surveillance.

Gorky made his triumphal entry into the literary world in his middle twenties with sketches and short narratives centering largely on the unskilled workers, vagrants, derelicts, underworld figures he had come to know in his wanderings. These stories owed their appeal to the novelty of the subject matter, as well as to the undercurrent of social protest that was sensed in them. In later years more short fiction on similar subjects came from his pen, as well as a score of plays. Of these, *The Lower Depths* alone, which belongs thematically with his stories, was a popular success at home and abroad. Both in his writings for the stage and in his novels, largely *romans à thèse*, he exalted the proletariat and inveighed against the Establishment, singling out for attack the middle-class intelligentsia. A somewhat heterodox left-wing socialist, he had a hand in the political upheavals of 1905–1906 and, as a result, expatriated himself, returning to Russia shortly before the World War. At the start of the Revolution he opposed the Bolshevik dictatorship, but before long he made his peace with it and eventually became a pillar of the Stalinist regime. It is noteworthy that while in his forensic writings and public addresses he spoke for the new order, the Soviet scene is practically absent from his imaginative work.

Gorky had no great interest in man's inner world; his gaze was turned outward. Invention was not his forte, but he had a gift for storing up in his memory what his senses seized upon. His best pages are those that are plotless, factual, documentary, free from the fanciful imagery, the rhetoric, the obtrusive sermonizing, for which he had a weakness. Such are his recollections of his childhood and early youth (three volumes, 1913–1923), set down in middle age. This trilogy evokes life in the lower strata of pre-revolutionary Russian society with extraordinary vividness and candor— chiefly the darkness in which it moved, but also the light that broke through.

As Volume One, entitled *Childhood*, opens, the three-year-old boy, usually addressed as Alyosha, is taken by his mother from Astrakhan to Nizhny Novgorod, to stay with her family, the Kashirins. She has just lost her husband and newborn baby. Old Kashirin, the owner of a dyeing shop, is a domestic tyrant, and the atmosphere in the household, which includes two sons with their families, is heavy with "leaden abominations," as the memoirist puts it. The two brothers brutally slug each other in a dispute over property. Together they had tried to drown their brother-in-law in an ice hole. One of them, when drunk, goes berserk, threatens to murder his father, and nearly breaks his mother's arm with a stick; the other had beaten his wife to death. Saturday is set aside by the master of the house for whipping the children—on one occasion the old man flogs little Alyosha till he loses consciousness. Sometimes the boy feels that he lives in "a deep, dark pit." Gross superstitions, loathsome coarseness, greed, viciousness, wanton cruelty are largely the stuff of his memories, and the man setting them down is at pains to inform the reader that these horrors have not disappeared from Russian life.

Not that the picture is without bright spots. Kindness, contrition, momentary tenderness are not unknown in the household. A Kashirin workman—a bold thief by avocation, who practices his skill at the risk of his life—dances to the accompaniment of a guitar played by a son of the house, bringing tears of joy to the onlookers. The boy comes to know some good people. Above all, he is afforded relief from the oppressive gloom by the affection of his grandmother, by the rich store of songs and stories in which the old woman delights. She gives him courage, and teaches him patient endurance—a lesson he will eventually repudiate. Unforgettable is the picture of this hunched crone, with her spongy, red-tipped nose, who has borne eighteen children to her husband and does not resent the savage beatings he gives her—one Easter Day he thrashed her from early Mass till sundown, taking time out to rest. She cooks, sews, gardens, nurses the sick, acts as a midwife. It is on her, the peacemaker, the pillar of strength, that the household depends in a crisis. Possessed of an unshakable faith in a just and merciful Providence, she is the embodiment of compassion and wisdom, a rugged and tender soul, with a rare capacity for loving life and rejoicing in it.

A glimpse of this woman, in whom the poet, Alexander Blok, saw a symbol of Mother Russia, is offered by the pages from the Autobiography given below:

FROM # Childhood

(GRANDMOTHER AT PRAYER)

I lie in a wide bed, a heavy blanket wrapped round me four times, and listen to Grandmother praying on her knees, one hand pressed to her breast, the other making the sign of the cross, unhurriedly, infrequently.

Outside, the ground is snapping with the frost; greenish moonlight filters in through the ice patterns on the windowpanes, outlining clearly the kindly face with its prominent nose and kindling a phosphorescent light in her dark eyes. The silk kerchief that covers her hair gleams like hammered steel; her dark dress falls in ripples from her shoulders, spreads about her on the floor.

Her prayers over, Grandmother undresses in silence, carefully lays her clothes on the chest in the corner, and approaches the bed, while I pretend to be fast asleep.

"You're not asleep, you rascal; you're fibbing, aren't you?" she says quietly. "You're not asleep, my darling, are you? Now, let me have the blanket!"

Anticipating what will follow, I cannot help smiling; then she growls:

"So you're playing tricks on your old grandmother, eh!"

And grasping the edge of the blanket, she pulls it toward her with so strong and deft a jerk that I bounce up in the air and, turning over several times, tumble onto the soft featherbed, and with a burst of laughter she exclaims:

"Well, you son of a radish? You didn't fool me!"

But sometimes her prayers last so long that I really fall asleep and do not hear her come to bed.

Long prayers always conclude a day of vexation, quarrels, fights. It is very interesting to listen to them. Grandmother, looking massive on her knees, gives God a detailed account of everything that has happened in the house; at first she whispers indistinctly, rapidly, and then mutters thickly:

221

"Lord, you know yourself—everybody seeks what is better for him. Mikhailo, the elder, wants to stay in town; he'd rather not set up shop beyond the river: it's a new neighborhood, no knowing how you'll make out there. And Yakov, he's his father's pet. Is it right—to love one child better than another? The old codger is stubborn—I wish you'd teach him good sense, Lord."

Gazing at the dark icons with her big, luminous eyes, she counsels her God:

"Send him a good dream, Lord, so he will understand that the children must be given their share of the property."

She makes the sign of the cross, prostrates herself, striking her large forehead against the floor and, straightening up, says forcefully:

"And how about smiling on Varvara [the boy's mother], sending her a bit of joy? How has she angered you? In what way is she more sinful than others? A young woman in good health, and so unhappy. And, Lord, have a thought for Grigory [a workman in the Kashirin shop]—his eyes are getting worse every day. If he goes blind, he'll have to beg his bread; that's not right! He's used up all his strength for the old man, but will *he* help Grigory? Oh, Lord, Lord!"

She lapses into a long silence, her head bowed meekly and her arms hanging at her sides, as if she had fallen fast asleep or were frozen stiff.

"What else is there?" she asks herself, thinking aloud, her forehead wrinkled. "Lord, save, have mercy on all the Orthodox folk, and forgive me, accursed fool that I am—you know, I sin not because of an evil heart, but because of a foolish mind." And with a deep sigh she says tenderly and contentedly: "You know everything, dear Lord; nothing is hidden from you, Father."

I was very fond of Grandmother's God, with whom she was so familiar, and would often ask her:

"Tell me about God!"

She would speak of him in a special manner, very quietly, drawing out her words strangely, and shading her eyes. Invariably she would sit down, cover her head with a kerchief, and then talk until I fell asleep:

"The Lord sits on a hill in the midst of the meadow of Paradise, on a throne of blue sapphire, under silver lindens, and those lindens blossom all the year round; in Paradise there's no winter, no autumn, and the flowers never wither, never stop blossoming, for the joy of God's saints. And round about the Lord ever so many angels hover, like snowflakes or swarming bees; other angels, like white doves, fly from Heaven to earth and back again, and they tell God everything about us, about folks. You, and me, and Grandfather—each one has his own angel; the Lord treats everybody alike. Here, now, your angel comes and reports to the Lord: 'Alyosha stuck his tongue out at Grandfather.' Well, then the Lord orders: 'Let the old man give him a whipping!' And that's the way it goes with all of us; everybody gets from the Lord what's coming to him—some get grief, others joy. And all his doings are so right that the angels rejoice, wave their wings, and sing without stopping: 'Glory unto thee, Lord, glory unto thee!' And he, the darling, just smiles at them, meaning: All right!"

She herself smiles, shaking her head.

"Have you seen all that?" I ask.

"I haven't, but I know!" she answers, pensively.

When she spoke of God, of Paradise, of angels, she would turn small and meek; her face grew younger, her moist eyes radiated a particularly warm light. I would take her heavy, satiny braids in my hands, wind them around my neck and, sitting quite still, I would listen to her endless stories, of which I never had my fill.

"It isn't given to a human being to see God—you'd go blind; only saints look at him without screwing up their eyes. But angels I've seen; they show themselves when your soul is pure. I was standing in church one day at early Mass, and right there, at the altar, two of them were walking about, like thin clouds. You could see everything through them, and they were bright as bright, and the wings, all lace and muslin, reached to the floor. They were walking around the communion table and helping old Father Ilya: he'd lift his poor old arms in prayer and they'd hold up his little elbows. He was very, very old, and blind, bumped against everything, and soon afterward he died. When I saw them I nearly fainted with joy; my heart was so full, tears rolled down my cheeks—oh, what a delight it was! Oh, Alyosha, dear heart, how well God orders everything in Heaven and on earth, how well!"

"But does all go well in our house?" I asked.

Crossing herself, Grandmother answered: "Glory be to the most holy Mother of God—yes, all goes well!"

A description of Grandmother saying her morning prayers, after perfunctory ablutions, follows. The Kashirins have given up the shop, and
now live in a tenement house that they own, Grandmother and Alyosha
occupying the attic. The two sons have received their share of the property
and gone off. The child's mother, too, is away, apparently having an illicit
affair.

Straightening her humped back, raising her head, gazing tenderly at
the rotund face of the Kazan Mother of God, she would cross herself
fervently with sweeping movements, and whisper ardently and loudly:

"Most glorious Mother of God, grant me your mercy for the
coming day!"

She would bow down to the ground, then slowly straighten up and
again whisper more and more ardently and rapturously:

"Wellspring of Joy, Stainless Beauty, Apple Tree in Bloom!"

Nearly every morning she found new words of praise, and this
made me listen to her prayer with keen attention.

"My Darling Heart, Pure and Heavenly! My Protection and my
Cloak, Golden Sun, Mother of God, guard me from evil witchcraft;
keep me from harming anyone and from being harmed for nothing!"

With a smile in her dark eyes, and looking less than her age, she
would cross herself again with slow motions of her heavy arm, saying:

"Jesus Christ, Son of God, be merciful to me, sinner that I am,
for thy Mother's sake."

Always her prayer was a song of sincere, simple-hearted praise.

In the morning her prayers were brief: she had to heat the samovar
—Grandfather no longer kept a servant—and if the tea was not ready
on time he swore at her long and furiously.

Occasionally, waking up before Grandmother did, he would come
up to the attic, where we slept. Finding her at prayer, he would
listen to her whisper, curling his thin dark lips contemptuously, and
over his tea he would growl:

"How many times have I taught you how to pray properly, you
blockhead? But you keep mumbling your own nonsense, you heretic,
you damn heathen! It's a wonder God puts up with you!"

"He understands," Grandmother would retort confidently. "No
matter what you say to him, he makes it out."

Her God was with her all day long; she spoke about him even to
animals. It was clear to me that all and sundry: people, dogs, birds,

bees, and grass, willingly and gladly submitted to him; he was equally kind, equally close to everything on earth.

One day the saloonkeeper's pampered tomcat, a cunning toady with a sweet tooth, cloudlike fur, and golden eyes, the favorite of the entire yard, brought a starling from the garden. Grandmother took away the maimed bird from the cat and began to upbraid it:

"Have you no fear of God, you vicious brute?"

The saloonkeeper's wife and janitor laughed at these words, but Grandmother shouted at them furiously:

"You think animals have no knowledge of God? They know more about him than you, you heartless creatures."

Harnessing Sharap, the horse, who had grown obese and was melancholy, she would converse with him:

"Why are you down in the mouth, God's worker that you are? Old age, my dear, I suppose."

The horse would sigh, wagging his head.

Alyosha's mother returns, eventually marries a young man above her station, and for a while the boy stays with the couple. One day he sees his pregnant mother kneeling on the floor before his stepfather, who, stretching his long leg, kicks her in the breast with the tip of his boot, and the boy goes for him with a kitchen knife; the would-be avenger is shipped back to his grandparents. They are living in two dark basement rooms, and the old man no longer supports his wife—an arrangement to which she has assented with complete equanimity. To provide for herself and the child she makes lace, a craft she had learned from her mother. Alyosha, too, helps out by joining a gang of boys who sell rags, bones, and pilfered lumber—Alyosha is rather proud of his prowess in stealing planks. Eventually his mother, whose husband has left her, joins the household with her sickly baby, Kolya. Before long she dies. Alyosha, now eleven years old, is sent out into the world to earn his keep. Therewith *Childhood* comes to an end.

FROM **Apprenticeship**

(GRANDMOTHER'S SECRET ALMS)

The second volume of the Autobiography, entitled *Apprenticeship* (literally, *In the World*), begins with an account of Alyosha's first job: that of a "boy" in a shoe store. So horrible is this experience that he decides to run away. Before he can do so he scalds his hands with boiling water from a samovar and is placed in a hospital. Grandmother calls for him there and takes him home.

Grandfather met me in the yard—he was on his knees, trimming a wedge with an ax. He raised the ax, as if getting ready to hurl it at my head, and, removing his cap, said mockingly:

"How do you do, Your Reverence? How do you do, Your Honor? Your service is over? Well, now you can look out for yourself—yes! Oh, you . . ."

"We know, we know," Grandmother spoke hastily, brushing him aside. She went into the room and, as she heated the samovar, she talked to me:

"Grandfather's down and out now; what money there was he had lent at interest to his godson Nikolay and, it seems, got no receipts for it—so, I don't know how it happened, but he's ruined now; the money's gone. And all because we didn't help the poor, took no pity on the unfortunate; so the Lord thought to himself, 'Why did I give the Kashirins property?' He thought it over and has taken it all away."

Glancing round, she continued: "I'm doing my best to mollify the Lord a bit, so he isn't too hard on the old man. I've started giving secret alms: at night, out of what I earn. Why, we'll go out tonight, if you like—I've got some money."

Grandfather came in, screwed up his eyes, and asked, "Aiming to guzzle?"

"Nothing of yours," said Grandmother. "If you want, sit down with us; there's enough for you too."

"Pour it out."

Everything in the room was unchanged, except for the sad emptiness of the corner that Mother used to occupy, and on the wall, above Grandfather's bed, hung a sheet of paper with an inscription in large printed letters: "Jesus the Savior, Ever Living! May thy holy name be with me all the days and hours of my life."

"Who wrote that?" I asked.

Grandfather did not answer. After a pause, Grandmother said with a smile, "That piece of paper cost a hundred rubles!"

"None of your business!" Grandfather shouted. "I'll give everything away to strangers."

"There's nothing to give away, and when there was, you held on to it," Grandmother said calmly.

"Shut up!" screamed Grandfather.

Everything was as it used to be.

Kolya, lying in a washbasket on a chest in the corner, woke up and peered out. His eyes were blue slits, hardly visible under his lids. He was more sallow, flabby, frail than ever. He did not recognize me, turned away in silence, and closed his eyes. [The baby was to die shortly].

The boy goes out into the street, where sad news awaits him: one of his former chums had died and another had been taken ill. He also hears that two of his playmates have fallen in love with a lame girl by the name of Lyudmila whose family had moved into the neighborhood. He sees her later in the evening, and she tells him that she had been ailing for a long time because a neighbor, having quarreled with her mother, had cast a spell over her. He returns to the house. The narrative resumes.

It must have been about midnight when Grandmother woke me up gently.

"Let's go, shall we? You'll do something for people, and your hands will heal more quickly."

She took me by the hand and led me in the dark as if I were blind. It was a black, humid night; a steady wind was blowing like a fast-flowing river, the cold sand was gripping my feet. Cautiously going up to the dark windows of the hovels, Grandmother would cross herself three times, lay a five-kopeck coin and three cracknels on each windowsill, and cross herself again. Looking up at the starless sky, she whispered: "Most holy Queen of Heaven, help the people! We're all sinners in thy sight, Mother!"

The farther from home we went, the more desolate and lifeless everything around us became. The night sky, a fathomless pit of darkness, seemed to have hidden the moon and stars forever. Suddenly emerging from God knows where, a dog halted in front of us and growled, its eyes glittering in the darkness. I pressed close to Grandmother timidly.

"Don't be afraid," she said; "it's only a dog; it's too late for the Devil: the cocks have crowed already!"

She called the dog, patted it, and admonished it: "Mind, doggy, don't you go scaring my grandson."

The dog rubbed itself against my legs, and the three of us walked on. Twelve times did Grandmother go up to windows, leaving "secret alms" on the sills. It began to dawn; gray houses emerged from the darkness; the belfry of Napolnaya Church, white as sugar, loomed up; the brick wall of the graveyard thinned out like a worn bast mat.

"The old woman is tired," said Grandmother, "time to go home! The housewives will wake up tomorrow and find that the Mother of God has provided a little something for the children. When there isn't enough of anything, even a scrap comes in handy. Oh, Alyosha, folks live in such poverty, and nobody takes thought for them!

> The rich man never thinks of the Lord.
> He has no thought of Judgment Day.
> To him the poor man is neither friend nor brother.
> All he is after is piling up gold.
> But that gold will turn to coal in hell!

That's how it is! We ought to live one for another, while God lives for all! And I'm glad you're with me again."

I too was quietly happy, and had a vague feeling that I had taken part in something that I would never forget. At my side, shivering, trotted the fawn-colored dog, with its foxy muzzle and kind, guilty eyes.

"Will he live with us?" I asked.

"Why not? Let him, if he likes. Here, I'll give him a cracknel, I've two left. Let's sit down on this bench; I'm tired somehow."

We sat down on a bench beside a gate; the dog lay down at our feet, crunching the dry cracknels, and Grandmother went on talking to me:

"There's a Jewish woman lives here; she has nine children, one smaller than the other. I ask her: 'How do you live, Mosevna?' And she says: 'I live with my God—how else would I live?'"

I leaned against Grandmother's warm side, and fell asleep.

In the weeks that followed, lame Lyudmila and Alyosha struck up a friendship. The grandmother approved of it, but warned them against "carrying on." Although in explaining what she meant she did not mince words, the way she spoke to them about sex was in sharp contrast to the coarseness and obscenity with which the subject was usually treated by those around them. The boy was able to take sugar candy to Lyudmila because he and his grandmother were eking out what she earned as a lace-maker by selling the berries and mushrooms they picked, the medicinal herbs and nuts they gathered—they trespassed to do so—in a neighboring forest. Whenever she had a bit of money she would give away some of it as "secret alms," herself going around in rags. The trips to the woods were delightful occasions. Grandmother was at home among the trees and grasses. Nothing escaped her attention. Ambling like a she-bear, she would mumble a prayer to the Holy Virgin, talk to the plants, the frogs, to a wolf she mistook for a dog, to God, upbraiding him gently for failing to provide the poor with an ampler crop of mushrooms. She radiated warmth and gentle joy, and the boy noted with particular pleasure that the moss she pressed down when she stepped on it readily sprang up behind her as she moved on.

The happy interval did not last beyond the summer. In the fall Alyosha was apprenticed to a draftsman, who made the boy run errands, clean the rooms, wash dishes, mind the baby. He ran away from his employer, and was taken on as a scullion on a river steamboat. By autumn he was back in the hovel that was shared by the old couple. The boy hit on a new way of earning money. He snared songbirds, which the grandmother sold. The occupation proved rather lucrative, but she disliked it. She thought it wrong to keep birds in cages. With the first snow the boy was again out in the world, the draftsman having agreed to reemploy him.

Alyosha saw his grandmother rarely during the half-dozen years left her. He caught his last glimpse of her as he stood in the stern of the steamer that was to take him to Kazan—he dreamed of entering the university there. As she bade him farewell, her final admonition to him was: "Remember one thing: it isn't God who judges people; that's the Devil's pleasure."

She continued to work tirelessly to provide for her husband, who had become senile, and to help two of her grandchildren. One was a rather shiftless youth employed from time to time as a dyer, the other a girl married to a drunkard who beat her and kept chasing her out of the house. Eventually the old couple were reduced to mendicancy. Begging "for Christ's sake," the Russian formula, the grandmother did not consider wrong. The daughter of a widowed (or unmarried?) peasant lacemaker, who, having lost the use of her right arm, was forced to beg from door to door, in her childhood she had accompanied her mother on foraging ex-peditions, which in the fair season took them far afield, and she remem-bered those years as an exceptionally happy time. Furthermore, she con-ceived the idea that at one time Christ himself had begged his bread. She shared the alms that she received with her semidependents. One day, while begging on the porch of a church, she fell and broke a leg. No one thought of calling a doctor; gangrene set in, and she died. Her husband did not long survive her.

The news reached Alexey weeks after the funeral. The nineteen-year-old youth was then working as a baker's assistant in Kazan. (He had not been admitted to the university.) His grandmother had not tried to communicate with him, nor had she asked him for help. For his part, he did not offer any. "I did not cry," Gorky writes in *My Universities*, the third volume of his Autobiography, "only, I remember, it was as though an icy wind had enveloped me. At night, sitting in the yard on a pile of wood, I felt an urgent desire to tell someone about Grandmother, about how she had the wisdom of the heart and was a mother to all around her. For a long time I carried this painful longing within me, but there was no one to talk to, and so the desire, unfulfilled, burned itself out. I recalled those days many years afterward, when I read Chekhov's marvelous story about a coachman who spoke to his horse about his son's death. I was sorry that in those days of acute misery there was neither a horse nor a dog near me and that it had not occurred to me to share my grief with the rats—there were many of them in the bakery, and I was on friendly terms with them."

MAXIMILIAN VOLOSHIN
(1877–1932)

Crimean Twilight

The evening light has soaked with ancient gold
And gall the hills. Like strips of tawny fur,
The tuffs of shaggy grass glow ruddier;
Past fiery bushes metal waves unfold;
Piled boulders, naked cliffs the sea has holed
Show enigmatic fronts that lour and blur.
In the winged twilight figures seem to stir:
A huge paw looms, a jowl grins stark and bold,
Like swelling ribs the dubious hillocks show;
On what bent back, like wool, does savory grow?
What brute, what titan, to this region cleaves?
The dark is strange . . . and yonder, space is clean
And there the weary ocean, panting, heaves,
And rotting grasses breathe of iodine.

SERGEY YESENIN
(1895–1925)

Autumn

How still it is among the junipers!
Autumn—a bay mare—cleans her mane of burrs.

Her hoofs' blue clatter sounds above the bank
Of the still river where the reeds are rank.

The monkish wind steps gingerly; his tread
Kneads the heaped leaves with which the road is spread,

And at the rowan clusters he will lean
To kiss the red wounds of the Christ unseen.

1914

II: Under The Hammer and Sickle

ISAAK BABEL
(1894–1941)

The son of a small Jewish merchant, Babel grew up in Odessa, receiving a high-school education in that teeming, cosmopolitan Black Sea port. Two short stories by him were printed in 1916, but half a dozen years passed before more of them began to appear. Some had to do with Odessa's Jewish gangsters, others with episodes in the civil war and in the Soviet-Polish war of 1920—Babel had served under General Budyonny in the Cossack Cavalry Corps, which fought the Poles. The publication of these miniature stories and vignettes in book form confirmed the impression that here was a new writer of gifts that were sadly rare: the instinct of workmanship, a keen sense of form, a strict economy of means in description and narration, a mastery of language resulting in an immensely expressive style.

An art like Babel's, ironical, sophisticated, candid, vehemently individual and stubbornly, if implicitly, humane, scarcely fitted into the Soviet scheme of things. In the years that followed the issuance, in 1926, of the slim volume entitled *The Cavalry Corps*, little came from his pen: a few short stories, some of them autobiographical; a scenario, two plays, only one of which was produced. Of a novel of his, in which he took a dim view of rural collectivization, only a fragment is available. A few pages of recollections of Maxim Gorky, who had been the first to recognize his talent, were printed in 1938. This was Babel's last appearance in print. Arrested in June, 1939, he vanished from the scene, becoming, as was usual in such cases, an Orwellian "unperson." The presumption is that he was confined to a concentration camp. In 1956 his decease was publicly admitted. The following year, by way of posthumous rehabilitation, his selected works were reprinted in Moscow. A Soviet bibliography published in 1959 gave the date of his death as March 17, 1941. Where and under what circumstances he met his end is uncertain.

The piece that follows first appeared in a Moscow monthly in 1924, and was included in *The Cavalry Corps*:

A Letter

Here is a letter home dictated to me by Kurdyukov, a boy in our dispatch office. It deserves to be remembered. I have copied it out without touching it up, and I give it word for word, just as it came to me.

Dear *Mom, Yevdokia Fyodorovna*. In the first lines of this letter I hasten to inform you that thanks be to the Lord I am alive and well wishing to hear the same from you. . . (Follows a list of relatives and friends. Let us omit it and pass on to the second paragraph.)

Dear Mom, Yevdokia Fyodorovna Kurdyukova. I hasten to write to you that I am in Comrade Budyonny's Red Cavalry and here is my godfather Nikon Vasilich too, who is now a Red Hero. He did me the honor of taking me into the dispatch office of the Political Section,* where our job is to carry literature and newspapers to the front line: the Moscow *Izvestia*, the Moscow *Pravda*, and our own merciless paper, *The Red Cavalryman*, which every fighter on the forward positions wants to read and after that he slashes the filthy Polish gentry to bits like a hero and I'm having a grand time living here with Nikon Vasilich.

Dear Mom, Yevdokia Fyodorovna. Do be sending me something, as much as lies in your power. I beg you to slaughter the little speckled boar and make a parcel for me in care of Comrade Budyonny's Political Section, to be given into the hands of Vasily Kurdyukov. Every night I lay down to rest without a bite to eat and without a rag to cover me so that I am mighty cold. Write me a letter about my Styopka, is he alive or not, do be looking after him I beg you, and write me about him is he still knock-kneed or has he got over that, and what about the scabs on his forelegs, has he been shod or not? I beg you, dear Mom Yevdokia Fyodorovna, do be sure to wash his forelegs with the soap that I left behind the ikons, and if Pop has used up the soap, buy some more at Krasnodar and God will not forsake you. I can also write to you that the country hereabouts is mighty poor, the peasants with their horses hide from our Red eagles in the woods. There isn't much wheat and it's awfully stunted, it makes us laugh. The farmers

* The propaganda department of the Corps.—A. Y.

234

here sow rye and oats too. Hops grow on sticks hereabouts so it's all very neat; they make homebrew out of it.

In the next lines of my letter I hasten to tell you about Pop, that he did in brother Fyodor something like a year ago. Our Red brigade under Comrade Pavlichenko was moving on the city of Rostov when treason broke out in our ranks. And at that time Pop was with Denikin* as company commander. Them as saw him said that he wore medals on him like under the old regime. And on account of that treason we were all taken prisoners and brother Fyodor came under Pop's eye. And Pop began to slash at Fedya and call him names: rat, red cur, son of a bitch, and such, and that went on till dark and by then it was all up with brother Fyodor. I wrote you a letter at the time how your Fedya lays without a cross over him, but Pop caught me with the letter and says: you are your mother's sons, you stem from that slut, I used to give your mother a big belly and I'll do it again, my life's finished, for the sake of what's right I'll stamp out my own seed, and such talk. I took it from Pop; I suffered at his hands like our Savior, Jesus Christ. Only soon I ran away from Pop, and got to my unit under Comrade Pavlichenko. And our brigade was ordered to go to the city of Voronezh to fill up our ranks, and there we did get some more men and horses too and knapsacks and revolvers, and whatever was coming to us. As for Voronezh, dear Mom Yevdokia Fyodorovna, I can tell you about it that it is a mighty handsome little town, it's a bit bigger than Krasnodar and the folks there are good-looking and the river you go swimming in. They gave us two pounds of bread a day, half a pound of meat, and sugar to match, so that when we got up we drank sweetened tea and supper the same, and we forgot what it meant to go hungry, and dinner I used to eat with brother Semyon, and we had pancakes or roast goose, and afterward I would lay down and rest. That was the time when the whole regiment wanted to have Semyon for commander, because he was such a daredevil and Comrade Budyonny gave the order for it and he was given two horses, a uniform in good condition, a cart all to himself for his stuff, and the Order of the Red Flag, and me right there his brother! Now listen, if a neighbor starts giving you trouble, Semyon can just cut his throat proper, then we began to chase General Denikin, we cut them down by the thousand and drove them into

* General Denikin, a leader of the White forces in the civil war.—A. Y.

the Black Sea, only Pop was nowhere to be seen, and Semyon was on the lookout for him wherever we went, because he missed brother Fedya bad. Only, dear Mom, you know Pop and his pigheaded character, so listen what he did. He went and had the cheek to dye his red beard a raven-black, and he stayed in the city of Maikop wearing civilian clothes, so nobody living there knew that he was the one as was village constable under the old regime. But truth will out, my godfather Nikon Vasilich happened to light on him in a cottage there and he wrote a letter to brother Semyon. We jumped on our horses and rode a hundred and fifty miles, me, brother Senka,* and boys from our village as wanted to come along.

And what did we see in the city of Maikop? We saw that the rear was at odds with the front and the whole place was full of treason and swarming with Sheenies, like under the old regime. And brother Semyon had a terrible row with the Sheenies in the city of Maikop, because they wouldn't let Pop out of their hands, and they put him in jail under lock and key and said there was an order had come through from Comrade Trotsky not to kill prisoners, we'll try him ourselves, says they, don't be sore, he'll get what's coming to him. Only brother Semyon had his way, and proved that he was a commander of a regiment and had all the Orders of the Red Flag from Comrade Budyonny, and he threatened to do them in, the lot of them who were quarreling over Pop's person and refusing to hand it over, and the boys from the village made threats too. Only brother Semyon did get Pop and began to baste him and he lined up the fighters in the courtyard in proper military style. And then Senka dashed water over Pop's beard and the dye began to run. And Senka asked Father:

"Do you feel good, Pop, now you're in my hands?"

"No," says Pop, "I don't."

Then Senka asked:

"And Fedya, when you were slashing at him, did he feel good when he was in your hands?"

"No," says Pop, "he didn't."

Then Senka asked:

"And did you think, Pop, that it would go badly with you too?"

"No," says Pop, "I didn't."

And Senka turns right round to the men, and then he says to Pop:

* A familiar form of Semyon.—A. Y.

"And I think that if your side gets hold of me, it'll be the finish of me. And now, Pop, we're going to finish you."

And then Father had the cheek to swear at Senka, laying it on strong, and to punch Senka in the face, and brother Semyon sent me out of the courtyard, so that, dear Mom Yevdokia Fyodorovna, I can't tell you exactly how they did Pop in because I was sent out of the courtyard.

After that we were stationed in the city of Novorossiysk. About this place you can say that on the other side of it there's no dry land any more, but only water, the Black Sea, and we stayed there until May came round, when we marched off to the Polish front, and we're pounding the gentry here to a jelly.

I remain your own dear son, Vasily Timofeich Kurdyukov. Mom, do be sure to look after Styopka and God will not forsake you.

That is Kurdyukov's letter, not a single word of which has been changed. When I had finished it, he took the sheet covered with writing and tucked it under his shirt next to his skin.

"Kurdyukov," I asked the boy, "was your father a mean fellow?"

"Father was a cur," he answered sullenly.

"And your mother, was she different?"

"Mother is all right. If you'd like to see, here's our family."

He handed me a broken photograph. It showed Timofey Kurdyukov, wearing the cap of a village constable, sitting there rigidly, a man with the shoulders of an ox, high cheekbones, a well-combed beard, and a hard, bright stare in his stupid, colorless eyes. Glimmering beside him, in a small bamboo chair and wearing a loose blouse, was a tiny peasant woman with a bashful look on her luminous, worn face. And behind this pair, against the wretched backdrop of flowers and doves provided by a provincial photographer, towered two stalwarts, monstrously huge, loutish, broad-faced, goggled-eyed, and stiff as at drill, the two elder Kurdyukov brothers, Fyodor and Semyon.

YEVGENY ZAMYATIN
(1884–1937)

At the outbreak of the Revolution, Zamyatin, a naval architect by profession, was a noted writer of satirical fiction in an expressionistic style. As a student he had been a left-wing socialist, and not unacquainted with prison and exile. Life under the Soviet regime quickly disillusioned him with the theory and practice of Bolshevism. He ceased to be a Bolshevik, he declared publicly in 1926, but he did not follow the example of the many of his fellow intellectuals who expatriated themselves. Settled in Leningrad, he devoted himself entirely to writing. Some of his pieces, like that presented here, are couched in the vernacular of the untutored, of which he was a past master.

For some years he was able not only to exemplify a writer's integrity but also to advocate that virtue in print without mincing words. In several vigorous short essays he lashed out at the debasement of literature by the dictatorship. Furthermore, he had a following in the shape of a confraternity of budding authors who stood up for freedom in art as an absolute value. Before long, however, they submitted to regimentation. As time went on, it was more and more difficult for Zamyatin to have his work printed or staged. He was becoming a proscribed author, denounced as "an internal émigré." His novel We, composed in 1920, which he himself truly described, in English, as "the funniest and most earnest thing I have ever written," has not been published in the Soviet Union. It is a satire on totalitarian communism, laid in the twenty-sixth century, anticipating George Orwell's 1984. Like Pasternak's Doctor Zhivago, We has appeared abroad both in the original and in translation—first into English (New York, 1924), later into eight other languages.

In a letter addressed to Stalin in 1931, Zamyatin said that the measures taken against him by the authorities sentenced him to death as a man of letters. He asked that he be deported from the country or allowed to stay abroad until it became possible for a writer in Russia "to serve great ideas without fawning on little men." He added that if he was not permitted to be a Russian writer, he might become an English one, like Joseph Conrad. Surprisingly enough, he was permitted to cross the frontier. Half a dozen years later he died in Paris, one of the casualties of Stalinism.

Comrade Churygin Has the Floor

Dear citizens—and likewise the little citizenesses amongst you who are laughing way back there, disregardful of this moment which is entitled an Evening of Revolutionary Recollections. I'm putting this question to you, citizens—are you wishful to include my recollections, too, together with yours? Well, if such be the case, I would request you to sit there without none of this here business of laughing, and not to be heckling the speaker, and allow me to precede.

First and foremost, maybe I'm apologizing, on account of my recollections, as stacked up against all the others, are the actual bitter fact; for to hear you tell it everything would seem to have gone off as slick as butter with you, somehow, whilst what I have to tell you isn't slick at all, but just the way it naturally come about in our village of Kuymani, in the district of Izbishchensk, which same is my own dear birthplace.

All nature in our parts is disposed amongst nothing but woods, so that there's nothing more or less resembling a town of any size on the horizon, and the life going on there is very benighted, like amongst gorillas or suchlike tribes. And, amongst the others, there was I, too, naturally, a socially unconscious element of sixteen, and I even believed in religion—well, nowadays that sort of thing is all over and done with, of course. As for my brother Styopka—may the Kingdom of Heaven be his!—he was twenty-five or so, and besides that he sure ran to height; however, he was literate, to some extent. And, in addition to Styopka, we had another hero, you might say, and that was our cooper's son Yegor, who had also been shedding his life at the front.

But since all this existed at the moment of capitalism, there was also on hand a contrary class just a couple of versts away—well, to be exact, it was an ex-leech, a squire by the name of Tarantayev who, of course, had been sucking our blood and who kept bringing back with him from his trips abroad all sorts of objects in the form of naked statues, and these statues were placed about in his garden without much order, especially one of them that toted a spear and was a kind of a god —not our own Orthodox God, of course, but just a fair-to-middling sort of god. And they also used to put on parties in that garden, and there would be songs and lanterns, and our womenfolk used to stand and peek through the fence, and Styopka would be right there too.

239

Styopka, now, he wasn't a loafer, exactly, or anything like that, but he was sort of odd; and then again something had gone wrong with his insides, so they wouldn't take him as a soldier, even, and he wound up an unemployed member of the household. Everybody was envying him all over the lot, but all he did was sit there, sighing, and read books. And, you might ask, what books did we have at that Czarist moment? They weren't books even, you might say, but the refuse of society—or, to cut it short, just plain manure. And the whole public library, if you could call it that, consisted of Agafya, a nun of forty-three, who used to recite the Psalter over the dead.

Well, naturally, Styopka lapped up all them books and started in horsing around. Happen you woke up at night, you'd look down from your bunk, and there he'd be, standing all white in front of a holy image and hiss-hissing away through clenched teeth: "Dossst Thou hear me? Dossst hear me?" And so one time I ups and tells him: "I dossst." That's just what I told him. So then he gets the shakes and leaps up; but me, I couldn't hold in anymore—I was just snorting from laughter. Well, that's when he gave me such a lambasting that my liver and things got mixed up with my lights—it was all I could do to recover.

As for Styopka, come morning he throws himself at our dear papa's feet: "Let me go into a monastery," says he, "I can't live just each day, the way you do," he says, "because there's an unknown dream lodged in my breast." But Papa dear he says to him: "You, Styopka," he says, "are practically a fool, and no later than tomorrow I'm packing you off to town, to go to work with your uncle Artamon." At first Styopka started bringing up all sorts of scriptural stuff against Papa dear, but Papa dear was a long ways off from being at all foolish, and on top of that he was somewhat on the foxy side. So he says to Styopka: "Well, now, and what does it say in them Scriptures of yours? It says that every son of a bitch has a bounden duty to honor his mother and father. Now them there words really is holy words." So the way things turned out, he got the better of Styopka with the help of the Scriptures, so that Styopka gave in and, soon as it was daylight, rode off to Uncle Artamon, who was working in a factory as a retired janitor.

And so, as folks say, we have a bird's-eye picture taken from life: here, for instance, we have a factory spinning around under a full head of steam, whilst somewheres off on an African frontier there's impossible crags of mountains, and there's a fearsome battle going on, but we in the midst of our woods don't see a thing, and the womenfolk without their men are bawling like heifers, and to round it all out it's mighty cold.

In due course of time the cooper's daughter-in-law got a letter from her husband Yegor at the front, that he had been promoted to a hero of the first rank with a St. George medal, and expect me back in a short while. At that, the woman was overcome with joy, naturally, and put on clean stockings. On the eve of St. Nicholas' Day Papa dear and me, we stepped out of the house; we looked, and what did we see but the cooper's son Yegorka racing along in a low-slung country sledge, waving his hand and saying something or other, but just what it was we couldn't make out; there was only the vapor billowing out of his mouth, on account of the cold frost.

Of course, I was ever so excited, being wishful to take a look at the hero, but Papa dear he says to me, "We ought to bide a while until he puts through a connection with his woman." But no sooner did he say this than Yegor's woman herself burst into our house. Her eyes were all whites, frightful to look at, her hands shaking, and she spoke in a gloomy voice: "Help me get Yegor in hand, for Christ's sake!" Well, we were thinking he must have given her a beating—we had to step in to help a female creature. We rinsed our hands, and went.

We stepped in and looked around: the samovar was boiling, there was a bench made up as a bed, everything all proper and fitting, actually, and Yegor himself standing quiet-like close to a trunk. But then, how was he standing? He was leaning up against the trunk like he was a sack of oats or something, and the head on him was level with the lid of the trunk, but as for legs there was none left to mention—they was cut off right close to his belly.

We were dumbfoundered—just standing there and nothing whatsoever happening. After a time Yegor gave a laugh—but it weren't good laughter at all; it actually put my teeth on edge—and he says to us: "What about it? A fine hero of the first rank? Seen enough? Well, now you can lay me down on my woman with your help." And the woman lay down on the bed, you understand, whilst we lifted Yegor off of the floor and placed him properly. After which we left. I slammed the door to and mashed this finger here in the door; only, I actually didn't feel even a bit of pain; I walked along, and all the while there was the image before my eyes of Yegor, the way he was standing by that trunk.

Naturally, the folks gathered that evening in Yegor's hut, all present and accounted for. Yegor was on a bench, under the icons, but whether he were standing up or leaning against the wall, or whether he were sitting—well, I don't rightly know how you would describe it. And them that had gathered there, they was all staring at him in horror and not saying a word, and he don't say a word neither, just smoking, and as for me, I'm standing near the oven and actually hear the cockroaches come crawling out and go swishing along the wall.

At this point, luckily, the cooper came, Yegor's father, that is, and he took a spirited object out of his pocket. Yegor, naturally, tossed off a noggin, and he had just refilled it when somebody's little boy tumbled in off the street and called out right heartily, "The squire! The squire!" We looked, and there he was, for a fact: Squire Tarantayev himself, standing in the doorway. All clean-shaven, and with ever so elegant a smell about him: you could see he was a delicate feeder. He nodded to us, sort of, and then made a beeline for Yegor: "Well, Yegor," says he, "congratulations, congratulations!" But Yegor, he twisted his face to one side in a mean smile, and managed to say; "But if I may make so bold—what are you congratulating me about?" So the squire told him, with an important air, "On account of you are our pride, and a hero who has suffered for his fatherland." And he lifted up the piece of sacking that covered Egor's lower parts, and bent over, nose and all, taking a good look.

At this Yegor's face got all twisted; he gnashed his teeth—and then what a sock he gave him right in the neck, and then another! In the heat of the excitement Squire Tarantayev shoved Yegor, who slumped over on his side like a sack and couldn't right himself, but kept shouting: "Let him have it! Let him have it!" Me, together with a couple of others, went for the squire; my heart was quivering within me like the scut of a rabbit, and right then there weren't a thing I wanted excepting to get my hands around his throat—well, to cut it short, there was a class struggle on. Squire Tarantayev was all red; he had his yap wide open to say something to us, but he was brought up short by our hate-filled eyes, like as if he had stepped into a bed of nettles, and he legged it out of the door.

Under the pressure of this victory the fellows quieted down, and they told Yegor, "You, now, are a hero of the first rank, sure enough." Yegor, naturally, downed another noggin, and little by little delivered a speech that, after all, what sort of a hero was he, seeing as how, whilst he was at the front, he had merely squatted down in a hole in the ground for to answer a crude call of nature, and that's when he was smacked in the legs from above. "But," said he, "we will shortly put an end to this trick of pulling the wool over the peoples' eye in the shape of war. Because," said he, "we know beyond any dispute that right now there's a certain peasant, who's one of us, by the name of Grigory Yefimych Rasputin, and he's right next to the Czar, and he's head of all the ministers, and he'll give them all holy hell." Now, when our fellows heard that, they sure went soft and started yelling right heartily that now, of course, it was curtains and a final reckoning both to the war and the masters, and that all of us were relying to the utmost on this Grigory Yefimych, seeing as how he was in power, and a peasant who was one of us. Well, fellow citizens, I naturally have quite a thorough understanding of this Grigory Yefimych now, but at that time the news actually gave me palpitation of the pulse.

Well, now, let's get on with the story. To be precise, then: when Yegor insulted the squire by socking him in the neck, the result was that we had a strained breaking-off of relations with this leech, and there was actually a full-blooded Circassian with a dagger stationed at the Tarantayev gate to bar anybody from entering. Up to then we used to go up to the manor house for newspapers and the like, but now we were living in a thick forest, the same as gorillas and knew nary a thing as to what events was taking place on the remote territorial globe, like in Petersburg, for instance.

And so, in due time, the former holiday of Christmas come around, and then it was Shrovetide, with variable frosts. And at Shrovetide Papa dear got a sudden letter from Styopka, who was living in town. And since at that time we had no liquidation of literacy whatsoever and Yegor was, you might say, the only man amongst us who could read, it follows that a slew of folks gathered in his hut to listen to the reading of that letter of Styopka's. And Styopka wrote that it was now known at their factory, beyond any dispute, that as far as God was concerned the whole business was just a superstitious fact, but to off-set that there was a book, called Marx, and that a certain significant killing had taken place in the capital city of Petersburg, and therefore you just wait, for shortly even bigger things nor that will be happening. And as for our wages—they're as miserable as can be, nine rubles and a half per month, and I'm leaving here to see you personal.

Yegor was up on a bench, propped against the windowsill, and he added, waving his hands: "Well, now," he shouted, "what was I telling you about Grigory Yefimych, eh? All this here is his work; you can sure rest assured of that!"

Even though it weren't clear in the letter about the killing, and about God, in view of certain prejudices, the information weren't complete neither, we felt just the same that all this weren't going on just for nothing, and we was expectant, for a fact. What we was expecting we didn't know, but it was like with an animal dog, if you'll excuse the expression, feeling all jumpy before there's a fire—that's just the state we were in. And besides that, there was the dreadful frost, a great stillness, and a woodpecker tap-tapping away in the forest. And all of us, like that woodpecker, kept tapping away at one thing— and that was Grigory Yefimych.

In due course of time a day or two passes like that, and then twilight is coming on, and that's when we see a horseman galloping on a black horse, heading straight for the Tarantayev manor house, and over that manor house the sun is setting, and it's all bloated from the frost, is that sun, and all red. Yegor, of course, is commander in chief over us, and he says: "There, it's starting. Now keep your eyes on that manor house and don't go a step from it, and keep reporting to me."

By way of sentries they posted me and also another fellow, a hunch-back from our village—Mitka, they called him. There we were, sitting behind some bushes, breathing on our fingers to warm them, and on top of all that we heard all the nervous excitement going on in the yard of the manor house, and then there were the dogs, too, and we sure had the shakes. A little while later we give a look: without any warning, the gate opens and a fierce troika pops out; sitting in the sleigh is the squire's wife with a little girl, and she's crying, and by then that horseman, the one on the black horse, comes dashing out of the gate too, and he's plain yelling at her, like it were to a dog: "Alley!"— which is French for "Get going!" And so the sleigh goes off one way, whilst this horseman wheels around and rides off the other way— heading straight for us, that is. Mitka the hunchback is pulling at me to get in the bushes, but my breath is plain cut off and me—really, like I was under the influence of alcohol—I don't myself know what I'm doing; I'm threshing my arms about and running to cut off this horseman. He naturally pulls up and asks me, "What's up?" and makes that horse snort right in my face. But I let him have it straight: "Nothing's up with us," I told him, "but what's up with you?" "That," says he, "is no concern of yours. *Alley!*" But me, I stare him right in the eye, and I ask him mighty impressive: "Well, now," I say, "How's about Grigory Yefimych—does that concern you?" And he comes right back at me, laughing, sort of: "Your Gregory Yefimych has kicked the bucket—he was shot long since, glory be to God!" and with that he's off at a gallop.

That's when I started running for all I was worth to get to Yegor. Our men were there in his hut, all present and accounted for, and all of them on edge from waiting. When I started in on my report, why, my innocent sixteen-year-old heart come right up in my throat and stuck there, and I was weeping on account of my perished dream in the form of Grigory Yefimych, and I saw that all those sitting there were also sighing, like all the fight had been knocked out of them. And at the conclusion of this most lamentable intermission Yegor issued his orders: to go our ways to our homes until morning, for the carrying out of various natural needs, such as food and rest-giving slumber.

Then that significant morning gradually dawned when you folks in Petersburg was having your celebration and jubilee of the Revolution with banners, whereas what was going on in our midst bore no resemblance to nothing whatsoever, and yet, of course, it amounted to remote yet fully connected echoes of all that, and into the bargain there was a dreadful frost. And we all gathered near Yegor's hut in our felt boots, whilst as for Yegor, we put him in a sort of basket lined with hay and then placed him on a low-slung country sledge. Then, a little later, Yegor announced from his basket that now the hour had struck and that things couldn't go on like they had been any longer, and that now we was going to march abreast against the Tarantayev manor house, and let the squire give us a full account of how that peasant Grigory Yefimych, who had stood up for us, had been killed—and maybe, God grant, he's still amongst the living. Of course, all of us strode off over the snow unanimously, and the snow was that blue in the sun that it brought tears to your eyes, whilst everything within us was in a ferment, like in a dog that's been chained up for ten years and suddenly he's broke loose and is off, running and rampaging.

Tarantayev's full-blooded Circassian, soon as he caught sight of us in our quantity, lost no time in locking the wicket, and started yelling on the inside and raising all sorts of commotion, including in which we also caught the voice of Squire Tarantayev, addressed to us, saying that now was an unusual day in the capital city, and you'd better disperse without no deplorable consequences, in order to await something in the near future. But Yegor yells to him from his basket that we've been waiting long enough and have run out of patience and that right now we was bound to find out the fact, and let him open the gate right off, for otherwise we would break it down anyway.

At that point we heard silence with whispering; then the gate creaked and there was a pleasant view of a piny alley, and in plain sight a spear-toting statue, which same will prove useful in playing rôles in other events. We was, of course, marching in orderly ranks—to be precise, Yegor in his basket was out front, with us milling in a pile behind him any old way, whilst the squire, showing us his hindback, was running for all he was worth, aiming to reach the house. Suddenly we see Yegor holding a revolver which he produced out of thin air, and pointing it at the squire and yelling at him to stop. And as soon as that outcast of society caught sight of the revolver, he come to a halt with nary a peep out of him, close to that same spear-toting god, and you could have took him for a statue too, sort of; but just the same he says to us: "You're downright mistaken; I myself belong to the Party of the People's Freedom." But Yegor puts it to him straight, in a menacing voice: "That means you're with Grigory Yefimych? Speak up!" To which the squire answers like he meant it, and every word of his has the shakes: "Come, now," says he, "we all of us are ever so glad that that scoundrel Grishka was killed." That's when Yegor turns ferocious and shouts so's to be heard on all sides: "You hear that, fellows? He's ever so glad, he says! Oh, you so-and-so!" and the like—that is, all sorts of remarks about his mother. "And," says he, "we're going to pick you off right now with this here revolver."

Naturally Yegor, seeing as how he was a specialist, had mastered every kind of military killing, and that sort of thing meant no more to him than spitting; but as for us, at that time we still had an inward inkling that it was somehow awkward to do in a man that was totally

246

alive. And whilst all this exchange of notions, as they say, was going on, Squire Tarantayev kept standing there without any indications of life, like a total corpse, and the only thing he did, I remember, was to wipe his runny nose, just once.

At this point a new fact bobbed up beyond the gate, out on the road, in the form of a man who was legging it toward us for all he was worth, and waving his arms about. And gradually we looked to see what this might betoken, and it turned out to be our Styopka on his way from town, in accordance with the letter he'd sent at the time aforesaid. The mug on him was blissful; there was tears running down over it, and he was going with his arms just like this, like they was wings—well, really, as if he was all set to take off under airpower, like a certain bird. And at the same time he was yelling: "Brothers, brothers dear, there's been an overthrow and a revolution, and my heart's going to bust this very minute from the impossible liberty, hip, hip, hurrah!"

We don't know just what's what; we can only sense that the pressure of the soul, as they say, is simply spurting out of Styopka, and it sends ants crawling down your spine just to hear him yelling, and at that point there's hurrahing and a general alemental gladness like at the Easter superstition. As for Styopka, he gradually gets up on a bench close to the statue and, wiping his tears with a mitten, adds to what he has said, telling us that the Czar, in the person of Nicholas, has been removed, and that all the foul palaces must be liquidated to the foundations of the face of the earth, so's there shouldn't be no more Moneybags, but all of us will be living as poor proletariat, in keeping with the former Gospel; but all this is now taking place, however, in accordance with the teachings of our dear Marx. And all of us confirm this as one, in the form of a hip, hip, hurrah, whilst Yegor in his basket is shouting at the top of his lungs: "Thanks to Styopka, Styopka our hero, from the bottom of an Orthodox heart! Wreck all their luxurious budget, and God be with you!"

That's when Styopka snatched an ax from one of our men, skipped over to the statue—the one with the spear—and, putting all his heart into it, swung at it to liquidate it. But at that moment Squire Tarantayev seemed to stir out of his corpse, and he says: "This here is a precious statue which ain't no way to blame for anything, and maybe I carted it over dry land all the way from Rome, since this is none other than him who is called Mars, of unnumbered value."

And all of us see how Styopka's arm drops without any consequences, and he says with expression: "Fellows! No sooner did I utter that beloved name to you than we suddenly have his actual image in the guise of a statue. And this I consider in the nature of an omen, and I propose that we bare our hats."

Citizens, I ask you again to consider that at that time we were wholly benighted folk; we were, you might say, so many Hindus. And owing consequently to the same we all of us unanimously took off our hats and thus, without our hats, we grabbed this beloved image by its behind and placed it on the sledge alongside of the basket in which Yegor had his existence. As for Styopka, he adopted a resolution, that we should let Squire Tarantayev go unharmed, on account of the service he done us by making this image known to us, but at the same time, by way of a lesson against riches, let him look on whilst we're liquidating his entire budget. All of us again ratified this with pleasure, in the form of a hip, hip, hurrah, because a program was shaping up without shedding a single live person but, nevertheless, there came about a grievous fate that ran counter to our expectations.

Well, to be precise, there we were, advancing against the house, and we had a vanguard in the form of the low-slung sledge with the statue and with Yegor in his basket on it, whilst walking alongside the sledge were our Styopka and Squire Tarantayev, he tied up. And we were greeted by the windowpanes, glittering like they were suspicious eyes, sort of, and there was one in particular, I remember, a dormer window right up under the roof, and there was a pleasant pigeon perched on it. As for Styopka, he slewed his beautiful smile of happiness at us and called out with all his heart and soul: "Fellows, I just can't hold out— that's how extraordinary this present first and last day of the new life is!"

No sooner did he utter this than what do we see but that same pigeon fluttering upward and, coming out of the attic window, a paltry puff of smoke. And, following that, after another tenth instant of a second, there come a dreadful sound in the form of a shot—and our Styopka, with that smile of his, falls nose first into a snowdrift.

We were all standing there like stricken posts and we haven't had a chance to come to ourselves when right then there's another shot, which knocks the little fingers off of the statue, and then Yegor with dreadful cursing expressions lets go with two bullets out of his revolver into the attic window and, turning round, sends another into Squire

Tarantayev, who lies down in his dead state alongside of Styopka. And Yegor in his emotion of hatred fires three more shots at him, following them up with the words: "Take that for Styopka! And take that for Grigory Yefimych! And that for everything!"

Here, of course, a general hullabaloo takes place and the last merciless stage of events or, to cut it short, total extermination. And thereupon you could see on that same innocent snow splinters of window glass and other dishes, and a divan that had sort of pegged out with its legs up in the air, and also the shattered corpse of Tarantayev's full-blooded Circassian, because, of course, it was him had sniped from the attic, and been drilled by a bullet from Yegor's military hand. And I also remember a gilded cage hanging high up on a bough, and there was some unknown aristocratic bird hopping up and down in it and squawking its head off.

In due course of time and in accord with nature, night and the generally accepted system of stars took place, making believe like nothing whatsoever had happened, excepting that a premature red dawn was rising out of the darkness or, to cut it short, the rest of the former manor house was burning out. At the same time there was complete quiet in our village and the dogs howling, whilst in the communal hut Styopka was lying under the icons, by way of a victim, with a smile on him, and right there, too, was the statue, and Agafya, the nun, age forty-three, reciting away at the Psalter, and the folks shedding sundry tears.

So this is the end of our somber events of every sort, like they had all took place in a dream, and then came a fully socially conscious day. Well, to be exact, a real orator come to our village, and in due order we got to know about the whole current moment, and that Grigory Yefimych—or, to cut it short, Grishka—was no hero but actually the other way around altogether, and that that same statue of ours owed its origin to a mistaken sound.

And, in conclusion, I see that those citizenesses who had at first been sitting there and looking like they was laughing—well, now they have the opposite look, and I fully endorse it, seeing as how all this was the bitter fact of our benighted culture, which nowadays, glory be to God, exists against the background of the past. And at this point I place a dot, in the form of a period, and withdraw, citizens, into your nameless ranks.   1927

SERGEY YESENIN
(1895–1925)

Transfiguration

Ho, Russians,
Fishers of the universe,
You who scooped heaven with the net of dawn,
Blow your trumpets!

Beneath the plow of storm
The earth roars.
Golden-tusked, the colter breaks
The cliffs.

A new sower roams the fields;
New seeds
He casts into the furrows.

A radiant guest drives toward you
In a coach.
Across the clouds
A mare races.

The breeching on the mare:
The blue;
The bells on the breeching:
The stars.

1918

VLADISLAV KHODASEVICH
(1886–1939)

"It scarcely seems worthwhile"

It scarcely seems worthwhile to sing, to live:
Uncouth, unsafe, the days through which we crawl.
The tailor sews, the builder rears his beams;
The seams will come apart, the house will fall.

But then through this corruption suddenly
I hear sometimes, how moved to feel it true,
Astir and throbbing in that rotten frame,
A different life, one altogether new.

Just so, enduring her routine dull days,
A woman restlessly will lift and press
Her hand against her belly's swelling weight
With what a swift astonished tenderness.

1922

ANNA AKHMATOVA
(b. 1888)

Lot's Wife

And he who was righteous loomed radiant, striding
Behind the Lord's messenger up the black hill.
But she walked reluctant—alarm spoke within her:
"It is not too late, you may look on it still,

Upon the vermilion-stained towers of Sodom;
You spun in that court, and you sang on that square;
That house whose tall windows confront you with blankness
Once knew you, a bride; you bore your sons there."

She turned to behold it, and pain was her master;
Her eyes yearning toward it could no longer see;
Salt-white grew her body, the blood in it withered;
Firm earth held her feet that would never go free.

And is there not one who would weep for this woman,
Or one who would find her loss bitter to brook?
Alone in my heart, uneclipsed, unforgotten,
Is she who gave over her life for one look.

1924

LEON (LEV) TROTSKY
(1879–1940)

Born into a middle-class Jewish family by the name of Bronstein, Trotsky became a professional revolutionary at an early age. Twice he was deported to Siberia and twice managed to escape, crossing the frontier to find refuge in western Europe. The news of the Czar's abdication (in March, 1917) reached him in New York, where he had been staying for several weeks. He returned to Russia and joined the Bolsheviks. (He had previously been aligned with the Menshevik faction of the Social Democratic Workers' Party, occasionally taking an independent position.) With Lenin, he was largely responsible for the success of the Revolution. After Lenin's death, in January, 1924, a struggle for power ensued between Trotsky and Stalin, in which the latter was victor. In 1929 Trotsky was banished from the USSR. He stayed in one country after another, finally settling in Mexico, where he was assassinated by a Soviet agent. To the end he continued to denounce Stalin as a traitor to the cause of communism.

The pages by Trotsky given below come from his book on Lenin, which appeared in Moscow several months after that leader's death. A vignette by a writer with a sharp eye and the knowledge of an intimate, the excerpt offers an authentic view of a man who has long been a figure of legend.

Lenin on the Platform

After the October Revolution Lenin was photographed more than once, and moving pictures were also taken of him. His voice can be heard on phonograph records. His speeches were taken down in shorthand, and printed. Thus all the components of Vladimir Ilyich are available to us. But only components. Only their always dynamic union, never to be repeated, gives an idea of the living personality.

When mentally I try to see and hear Lenin on the platform with a fresh eye and a fresh ear, as if for the first time, I see a robust figure, inwardly pliant, a figure of medium height, and hear a steady, smooth, unbroken, very rapid voice with a slight burr, having no characteristic intonation at the start, and running on without pause.

The first phrases are usually generalities; the tone is tentative; he has not found his equilibrium, as it were; the gestures are uncertain; the gaze is turned inward; the expression is sullen, even showing vexation—he is seeking an approach to the audience. The preliminaries take more or less time—depending upon the audience, the subject, the mood of the speaker. But now he has hit on it. The subject begins to come into focus. The speaker leans forward, sticking his thumbs into the armholes of his vest. The two movements make his head and hands stand out. On this rather short yet sturdy, well-built, well-proportioned body the head does not seem large in itself. But the forehead and the naked knobs on the skull look enormous. His hands are very active, but not fidgety or nervous. It is a "plebian" hand, broad, strong, with short fingers. It suggests the same features of reliability and virile good nature as does the whole figure. You perceive this most clearly when the speaker glows inwardly as he manages to puzzle out an opponent's stratagem, or when he has succeeded in trapping him. Then from under his powerful beetling brow Lenin's eyes protrude—a successful photograph taken in 1919 has caught that look. Even the indifferent listener, catching this look for the first time, pricks up his ears, impatient for what is to follow. At such moments Lenin's angular cheekbones glow, giving his face a softened look of intelligent lenience, behind which you sense a keen knowledge of people, relationships, situations—down to what is hidden deepest. The lower part of hs face with its reddish hairy growth remains in the shade, as it were. His voice loses its harshness, becomes more flexible, and at moments slyly ingratiating.

But now the speaker cites a supposed objection on his opponent's part or a malicious quotation from an enemy's article. Before he has had time to grasp the opponent's thought fully, he makes it clear to you that the objection is unfounded, superficial, or false. He removes his thumbs from the armholes of his vest, throws his body back slightly, takes a few short steps backward as if to get a running start, and now ironically, now with feigned despair, shrugs his heavy shoulders and spreads out his arms, his thumbs sticking up expressively. Invariably he either condemns or ridicules or defames his adversary—depending on the occasion and on who the adversary is—before refuting him. The listener is warned in advance, as it were, what kind of proofs to expect and in which direction he should turn his own

thoughts. Therewith the logical attack is mounted. The left hand is
again thrust into the armhole of the vest, or—more frequently—
into the trouser pocket. The right hand follows the logic of his
thought and marks its rhythm. When needed, the left lends assistance.
The speaker strides toward his audience, moves to the edge of the
platform, leans forward, and with rounded gestures works over his
own verbal material. This means that he has reached the heart of
the matter, the point of the whole speech.

If there are opponents in the audience, from time to time critical
or hostile remarks are flung at the speaker. In nine cases out of ten
they remain unanswered. The speaker says what he thinks needs to
be said, to whom he thinks it needs to be said, in the way he thinks
it needs to be said. He does not like to break the thread of the argument in order to make casual retorts. His concentration does not
allow for ready repartee. What happens after hostile exclamations is
that his voice becomes harsher, his speech more compact and ag-
gressive, his thinking keener, his gestures more abrupt. He takes notice
of a hostile remark from the floor only if it fits the general trend
of his thought and helps him to reach the necessary conclusion more
quickly. Then his replies are apt to be completely unexpected—in
their devastating simplicity. He bares the situation completely, where
he is expected to mask it. The Mensheviks learned this by personal
experience during the first period of the Revolution, when charges of
violating democratic principles were still a novelty.

"Our newspapers have been suppressed!" they would shout.

"Of course, but unfortunately, not yet all of them. Soon they will
all be suppressed." (Stormy applause). "The dictatorship of the
proletariat will wipe out this disgraceful sale of bourgeois opium."
(Stormy applause).

The speaker draws himself up. Both hands are in his pockets. Not
a trace of pose, no oratorical modulations in the voice. But adamantine
assurance that he is right and that truth is on his side shows in his
whole bearing, in the way he holds his head, his tightened lips, in his
cheekbones, and in the slight huskiness of his voice. "If you want to
fight, come on!"

When the speaker hits out at people in his own camp, and not
at an adversary, this is sensed both in his tone and in his gestures.
Then the most savage attack on these people is still in the nature of

an effort to bring them to reason. Sometimes the speaker's voice breaks on a high note. This happens when he impetuously upbraids a man, puts him to shame, proves that this opponent hasn't the slightest understanding of the subject and has cited nothing, but nothing at all, in support of his objections. It is while he is harping on these nothings that his voice rises to a falsetto and breaks, so that a furious tirade is unexpectedly tinged with good nature.

The speaker has worked out his thought to the last detail, to its practical conclusion—the thought, but not the wording, the form, except perhaps for the tersest, most pointed, most felicitous phrases and *mots*; these subsequently become political bywords of the Party and part and parcel of the language of the man in the street. The phraseology is usually cumbersome: one sentence is tacked on to another or, on the contrary, lodges inside it. Such a style is a heavy affliction for stenographers, and later for editors. But through these cumbersome phrases a taut, powerful thought makes its way.

Is it true, however, that you are listening to an erudite Marxist, an economist, a man of great learning? There are at least moments when it seems that the speaker is some self-taught fellow who has reached all these conclusions on his own, who has thought it all out in his own way, without any scholarly apparatus or technical terminology, and now presents it, again in his own simple way. What has happened is this: in turning the matter over in his mind, he took into consideration not only his own experiences but also those of the masses, and in presenting the argument he discarded altogether the theoretical scaffolding that he had erected when he first tackled the problem.

Sometimes, however, the speaker in his presentation moves up the ladder of his thought too rapidly, skipping two or three rungs at a jump. This happens when the conclusion seems obvious to him and from a practical point of view too urgent, and when he feels that it is necessary to have his hearers reach it as quickly as possible. But now he senses that his audience is lagging behind him, that he has lost contact with it. Then he takes himself in hand at once, jumps down a rung and begins his ascent anew, but in a slower and measured fashion. Even his voice changes, grows less tense, acquires an enveloping persuasiveness. The structure of the address naturally suffers from this backward leap. But does the speech exist for the sake of the structure? Is any logic of value in a speech except that which compels to action?

And when the speaker reaches his conclusion the second time, having seen to it that his hearers have reached it too, without having lost any of them on the way, you sense physically in the hall that grateful joy which arises when the tension of collective thinking is relaxed. Now all that remains is to hammer the conclusion two or three times so that it holds fast, to give it a simple, striking, graphic expression that will make it stick in the memory, and then one can give oneself and others a respite; one can crack a joke, have a laugh, so that during this interval the collective mind may better take in the new acquisition.

Lenin's oratorical humor is as simple as his other devices, if you can speak of devices here. Wit, let alone piquancy, is absent from Lenin's speeches, but he can crack a joke, a pungent one, accessible to simple folk, a truly popular one. If the political situation is not too alarming, if the majority of the listeners are "his own people," he doesn't mind having a bit of fun. The audience welcomes a sly remark, ostensibly simple-minded, a characterization at once good-natured and pitiless. It feels that the banter is indulged in not casually, not just for effect, but for the same purpose as the address itself.

When the speaker, who can laugh contagiously, resorts to a joke, the lower part of his face becomes more prominent, especially the mouth. The lines of his forehead and skull soften, as it were; the eyes, no longer piercing, gleam cheerfully; his burr gets more pronounced; the tension of his virile mind is relieved by animal spirits and fellow feeling.

The main features of Lenin's speeches, as of his activities generally, are clarity and firmness of purpose. The speaker does not build an address, but aims at a definite result in terms of action. He approaches his hearers in various ways: he explains, persuades, shames, jests, explains again, persuades again. What holds his speech together is not a formed plan but a clearly defined, practical goal that it is the need of the moment to reach and that must lodge in the consciousness of his audience like a splinter. His humor, too, is subordinated to this. His joking is utilitarian. The catchword has a practical purpose: to urge some on, to check others. He coined dozens of winged words which have gained currency.* Before he finds such a word, the speaker describes several circles, as if in search of the appropriate place for it. Having formed it, he takes the word as though it were a nail he was holding in position, and hits it on the head with the hammer again and again, until it is properly driven in, so that it will be extremely hard to pull it out when there is no more need for it. Then Lenin himself will have to hit it on the right and on the left in order to loosen it, and pulling it out, throw it onto the archivist's heap of scrap metal—to the utter dismay of those who have grown used to the nail.

And now the speech approaches its end. The summing up is over; the conclusions have been firmly established. The speaker looks like a workman who is dog-tired but has finished his job. From time to time he passes his hand over his naked skull dotted with drops of sweat. The voice has lost its tension; it is like a dying fire. It could be the end. But do not wait for the rising finale that crowns a speech, without which, it would seem, one cannot leave the platform. Others cannot, but Lenin can. There is no oratorical peroration with him: he finishes the job and puts a period to it. Not seldom the concluding sentence is: "If we grasp this, if we act thus, then surely victory will be ours." Or else: "That is what we must strive for, not in words, but in deeds." And sometimes, and ever more simply: "That's all I wanted to say." And such an end, fully in keeping with the nature of Lenin's eloquence and the nature of Lenin himself by no means dampens the ardor of the audience. On the contrary, after such a banal, dull conclusion the audience by an effort of the mind grasps anew all that Lenin gave it in his address and bursts into stormy, grateful, ecstatic applause.

But, having somehow gathered up his notes, Lenin hastily leaves the platform to escape the inevitable. His shoulders are slightly hunched so that his head seems retracted; his chin is down, his eyes are hidden under his brows, his upper lip is raised in annoyance, and his moustache bristles almost angrily. The thunder of hand clapping grows, billow on tossing billow. "Long live . . . Lenin . . . leader . . . Ilyich . . ." In the glare of the electric bulbs a man's unique pate flickers, as the crowd surges round him in indomitable waves. And

* Here the author cites several of Lenin's neologisms, such as *smychka* (adjustment of conflicting interests, as of city and country).—A. Y.

when, it seems, the hurricane of ecstasy has reached the height of frenzy—all at once, rising through the hubbub, the boom, the roar, a young, tense, blissful, passionate voice, like a siren rips through the storm: "Long live Ilyich!" And from the inmost quivering depths of solidarity, enthusiasm, love, rises in response like an awesome cyclone, a general massive shout, at once a howl and a clarion call, that shakes the vaulted ceiling: "Long live Lenin!" ·

MIKHAIL ZOSHCHENKO
(1895–1958)

Awell-born southerner, Zoshchenko was wounded and gassed in the First World War. For a short time he also served in the Red Army. Moving from city to city, he tried a variety of occupations, from a shoemaker's to an actor's, before, in 1921, he settled in Petrograd and turned to writing. He had a genuine gift for caricature and comedy, and mastered a Damon-Runyonesque style based on the vernacular of the man in the street. No wonder that his many skits and sketches—some of them are available in English—enjoyed immense popularity.

Not always does his humor, which is not generally of a high order, carry a sting, as it does in the piece offered below, but he dwelt too much on the seamy side of Soviet life and Soviet mentality to be persona grata with the authorities. In 1943 a monthly printed two installments of a curious autobiographical work of his which promised to be an autoanalysis. It was attacked in the journal of the Central Committee of the Party, and publication was stopped. His stories continued to appear, however, and in April, 1946, he received a medal for "valiant work during the Great Fatherland War." Then came a bolt from the blue. A Party ruling, dated August 14, 1946, denounced the two Leningrad periodicals for having printed Zoshchenko, especially his story "The Adventures of a Monkey," described as "a cheap lampoon on Soviet everyday life and the Soviet people." As a matter of fact, "The Adventures of a Monkey" is a children's tale devoid of satirical intent—indeed, rather flattering to the Soviet public. So completely innocent had it looked to the censors that immediately on its publication in the issue of a Leningrad monthly for May–June, 1946, it was reprinted in two of Zoshchenko's books, one of them an edition of 100,000 copies for mass circulation.

The Party edict was elaborated at great length in a vituperative address delivered by a member of the Politbureau. He declared the moral of the tale to be that "in a cage you breathe more freely than among Soviet people." Such an interpretation suggests that at the time the Party hierarchy was suffering from a paranoidal derangement. Be that as it may, Zoshchenko's career as a writer came to an abrupt end. The critics ganged up on him; he was expelled from the Writers' Union; his books ceased to be reprinted. He made a feeble attempt to toe the line by writing some patriotic and anti-American pieces, and then lapsed into silence. A selection from his more innocuous writings appeared posthumously.

The Cap

It's only now that you begin to see what we've done in the past ten years, what headway we've made! Why, look at our life from any angle you like—everywhere there's progress, we're on the make, we're going places!

I used to be a transport worker, and I can tell you chaps I know what a lotta improvement there's been on this front, and believe you me, it's a kinda important front. Trains keep moving. Rotten sleepers have been replaced. Semaphores are back where they belong. Whistles really whistle. It's perfectly safe to travel. Why, man, it's a pleasure.

But only a few years ago! Take 1918. You'd ride and ride—and all of a sudden: stop! The engineer would stick his head out and shout: "Hey, folks! Come up here." Well, the passengers would troop up to the front of the train. The engineer would make a little speech. "I can't go any farther, comrades," he'd say, "on account there's no fuel. If any of you have a yen to get to the next station I suggest you climb out of the coaches, go into the forest, and cut some wood." So the passengers would do a little swearing, and they'd bawl out the new way of doing things, but all the same they'd get to work sawing and chopping. They'd manage to pile up half a cord of wood, and the train would get going again. And of course the wood was green, it would hiss like the devil, and you couldn't exactly brag about the speed we'd make.

I can tell you about something that happened to me. It was back in 1919. We was making a routine run to Leningrad. All of a sudden between stations the train jerks to a stop. Then she backs up and stops again. The passengers want to know: "What are we stopping for? Why are we backing up? God help us, do we have to go get firewood again? Is the engineer trying to find a birch grove for us? What the devil, can it be bandits?"

The fireman explains: "It's this way. There's been an accident. The engineer's cap blew off and he's gone to look for it." The passengers get out of the coaches and stand around on the embankment. All at once they see the engineer coming out of the woods. He's pale, he looks down in the mouth, he shrugs his shoulders. "Hell no," he says, "I can't find it. The deuce knows where it blew to." He backs her up again another five hundred feet. The passengers break up into searching parties and start beating the woods for the cap.

Twenty minutes later some bagman* calls out: "Hey, you! There it is!"

We look, and sure enough, there's the engineer's cap hanging on a bush.

He puts on his cap, ties it to a button with a string so it won't blow off again, and begins to get up steam. Half an hour later we're on our way.

That's what I mean. Our transportation used to be in bad shape. But these days, if a passenger's blown off, let alone a cap, there'll be a minute's stop and no more. Time's precious. We must keep going.

1927

* So called because during the famine in the early years of the Revolution city people went out into the country with sacks in search of provisions.—A. Y.

YURY OLESHA
(1899–1961)

Like Babel, Olesha (who came of Polish stock), grew up in Odessa, worked at his craft with the fervor of a perfectionist, and was out of step with the age. A popular purveyor of newspaper verse, he achieved fame overnight with the publication, in 1927, of his novel *Envy*, a work showing his mastery of a graphic style. It is a covert lament for the humanity and the idealism that found a place in the old world, and a stifled outcry against the dehumanizing temper of Bolshevism with its worship of the machine. In the next ten years he produced a whimsical tale for the young about a revolution in an imaginary country, reflections on writing techniques, and some fragmentary reminiscences, as well as a score of short stories. Two of them, "Love" and "Liompa," dated 1929 and 1928 respectively, represent him here. Both illustrate the extent to which Olesha's performance deviates in manner and matter from the Soviet literary canon. The heroine of a play of his, which was printed in 1931, and subsequently staged, is torn between intellectual acceptance of the Revolution and emotional rejection of it. In arguing with herself, she draws up a list of its benefits, but also of its crimes. A trip to Paris brings about her conversion to Bolshevism. The playwright himself was still far from orthodoxy. The principal character in a piece of his printed the following year is a Soviet author who declares art to be "the chief thing in life," and insists that self-scrutiny, introspection, are essential to his profession. This brought Olesha a critic's counsel "to merge with the life of the masses," and an open letter from a workers' literary circle, in which he was urged to stop standing before the mirror and instead concern himself with the problems of the proletariat. In reply he admitted that the need for "making himself over" was clear to him, but that he could do it solely "in his own way."

Apparently in fulfillment of this task he wrote a play directed against Western decadence, but only one scene was printed and it was never staged. He also composed a script for a motion picture, which was made but not exhibited, on the grounds of being "ideologically and artistically defective." Strangely enough, not a line of his seems to have appeared in print for the decade prior to 1947, and this has led to the conjecture that he was in a concentration camp during those years. After that hiatus he reentered literature with a few sketches and entries from his notebooks.

A miscellany of jottings, mostly autobiographical, has been printed posthumously. His collected works are in preparation.

Love

Shuvalov was waiting for Lelya in the park. It was midday and hot. A lizard showed up on a stone. Shuvalov thought: on the stone the lizard is quite defenseless; it can be detected at once. "Mimicry," he reflected, and that made him think of the chameleon. "Hello," he said, "that's all that was needed: a chameleon!"

The lizard slipped away.

Annoyed, Shuvalov got up from the bench and walked rapidly along the path. He was vexed. Suddenly he felt like opposing something. He stood still and said rather loudly: "Oh, to hell with it! Why should I be thinking about mimicry and a chameleon? I haven't any use for such notions."

He came to an open space and sat down on a stump. Insects were darting about. Stalks were quivering. The architecture of the flight of birds, flies, and bugs was spectral, but one could discern the faint outlines of arches, bridges, towers, terraces—a shifting city that changed its shape from moment to moment. "I'm beginning to lose my grip," he thought; the field of my attention is getting messy. I'm becoming an eclectic. What's got hold of me, anyway? I'm beginning to see things that don't exist."

There was no sign of Lelya. He had not meant to stay in the park so long. He resumed his stroll. He became aware of the existence of many species of insects. A gnat was climbing up a grass-blade. He took it off and placed it on the palm of his hand. Suddenly its tiny belly flashed in the sun. Shuvalov grew angry. "Damn it, if this keeps up, in half an hour I'll become a naturalist!"

The tree trunks were of many kinds, and so were the stems and leaves; he saw grass jointed like bamboo; he was struck by the many colors of the greensward; the varied colors of the soil itself were a complete surprise to him. "I don't want to be a naturalist," he pleaded. "I have no use for these chance observations."

But there was no sign of Lelya. He had already made some statistical deductions, done some classifying. He could assert that the greater number of trees in this park had broad trunks and leaves shaped like the ace of clubs. He distinguished the noises of the various insects. Against his will, his attention was fastened upon matters of absolutely no interest to him.

Still there was no sign of Lelya. He was filled with longing and irritation. Coming toward him, instead of Lelya, was a citizen in a black hat whom he had never seen before. The citizen sat down on the green bench beside Shuvalov. There was a despondent air about him as he sat there with hanging head, a white hand on each knee. He was young and quiet. It appeared later that the young man was suffering from color blindness. The two fell to talking.

"I envy you," said the young man. "They say that leaves are green. I've never seen green leaves. I have to eat blue pears."

"Blue," said Shuvalov, "is not edible. A blue pear would turn my stomach."

"I eat blue pears," repeated the color-blind youth gloomily.

Shuvalov shuddered.

"Tell me," said he, "have you noticed that when birds fly around you, the result is a city, imaginary lines . . . ?"

"Can't say I have," answered the color-blind one.

"So you perceive the world as it actually is?"

"Yes, except for some details of color."

The color-blind young man turned a pale face to Shuvalov.

"Are you in love?" he asked.

"Yes, I am," answered Shuvalov candidly.

"Aside from a slight confusion in the matter of color, everything's as it should be," said the color-blind youth more cheerfully, and he made a patronizing gesture in the direction of his neighbor.

"But blue pears, that's no trifle!" Shuvalov grinned.

Lelya appeared in the distance. Shuvalov jumped up. The color-blind youth arose and, lifting his black hat, started to walk away.

"You're not a violinist?" Shuvalov called after him.

"You see things that don't exist," answered the young man.

"You look like a violinist!" Shuvalov shouted heatedly.

The color-blind one, continuing on his way, made a reply that Shuvalov did not catch, but he thought he heard him say, "You're in a bad way."

Lelya was walking rapidly. He got up and took a few steps toward her. The branches with club-shaped leaves were waving. Shuvalov stood in the middle of the path. The branches were making a noise. As she approached, the foliage gave her an ovation. The color-blind youth, turning off the path, thought, "It's getting windy," and looked up at the leaves. They were behaving like any leaves agitated by the wind. He saw blue treetops swaying. Shuvalov saw green treetops. But Shuvalov drew an unnatural conclusion. He thought that the trees were giving Lelya an ovation. The color-blind young man was mistaken, but Shuvalov was even more seriously mistaken.

"I see things that don't exist," Shuvalov repeated.

Lelya came up to him. In one hand she had a bag of apricots. The other hand she held out to him. The world changed precipitously.

"Why are you making such a face?" she asked.

"I feel as if I were wearing glasses."

Lelya took an apricot out of the bag, tore its tiny buttocks and threw away the pit. It fell into the grass. Shuvalov looked around frightened. He looked around and saw that where the pit had fallen, a tree had sprung up, a slim radiant sapling, a miraculous parasol. At that he said to Lelya:

"Something absurd is going on. I'm beginning to think in images. The laws of nature don't exist for me any more. In five years there will be an apricot tree on this spot. It may well be so. It's perfectly possible, scientifically. But in defiance of all that's natural, I've just seen this tree five years in advance. How ridiculous! I'm becoming an idealist."

"It's because you're in love," she said, shedding apricot juice.

She was sitting on pillows, waiting for him. The bed had been moved into the corner. The garlands on the wallpaper had a golden gleam. He came up to her, and she put her arms about him. She was so young and so slight that when she was wearing nothing but her chemise, her nakedness appeared preternatural. The first embrace was tempestuous. The childish locket flew from her throat and was caught in her hair like a golden almond. Shuvalov bent over her face, which sank into the pillows as slowly as the face of one dying.

The lamp was burning.

"I'll blow it out," said Lelya.

Shuvalov lay next to the wall. The corner moved down upon him. He traced the design on the wallpaper with his finger. It dawned upon him that the portion of the wallpaper pattern near which he was falling asleep had a double existence: one, its ordinary daytime existence with nothing remarkable about it, simply garlands; the other, nocturnal, perceived five minutes before falling asleep. Suddenly looming up close to him, the elements of the design grew larger, more detailed, and strange. Upon the verge of falling asleep, his perceptions grown childlike, he made no protest against the transformation of familiar and proper shapes—all the more so, since this transformation had something touching about it: instead of circles and curlicues, he saw a goat, a chef's cap . . .

"And here is a treble clef," said Lelya, catching on.

"And a chameleon," he lisped, falling asleep.

He woke up early in the morning. Very early. He woke up, looked about him, and uttered a cry. A beatific sound issued from his throat. During the night just past, the transformation of the world which had begun with their first meeting had been completed. He woke up on a new earth. The radiance of morning filled the room. He noticed the window ledge and on it pots of varicolored flowers. Lelya was asleep, with her back turned toward him. She lay curled up, her back curved, and under her skin her spine showed like a slender reed. "A fishing rod," thought Shivalov, "a bamboo cane." On this new earth everything was absurd and touching. Voices reached him through the open window. People were talking about the flowerpots ranged on her window ledge.

He got up and dressed, keeping a hold on the earth with an effort. Terrestrial gravitation had ceased to exist. He hadn't yet grasped the laws of this new world, and therefore acted cautiously, timidly, fearing that some rash movement might have a devastating effect. Even just to think, merely to perceive objects, was a risky business. And what if suddenly, during the night, he had been gifted with the ability to materialize thoughts? There was some basis for such a supposition. Thus, for instance, his buttons just buttoned themselves. Again, as soon as he thought of wetting his brush in order to plaster down his hair, he heard water dripping from the tap. He looked around. Hanging against the sun-bright wall a heap of Lelya's dresses was blazing with all the colors of a Montgolfier balloon.

"I'm here," the voice of the tap sounded from the heap.

Under the heap he discovered the tap and the washbasin. A piece of pink soap lay nearby. Now Shivalov was afraid that he might think of something terrible. "A tiger entered the room," he almost thought against his will. But somehow he managed to escape the thought. . . . He looked at the door, however, in terror. The materialization took place, but since the thought had not been fully formed, the effect of the materialization was approximate and remote: a wasp flew in through the window. . . . It was striped and bloodthirsty.

"Lelya, a tiger!" shouted Shivalov.

Lelya woke up. The wasp hung on the edge of a plate. It buzzed gyroscopically. Lelya jumped out of bed and the wasp flew at her. Lelya waved it away. The wasp and the locket circled about her. Shuvalov swatted the locket with his palm. The pair of them pursued the wasp determinedly. Lelya covered it with her creaky straw hat.

Shuvalov had to leave. They said goodbye standing in a draft, which in this new world proved amazingly active and many-voiced. . . . It blew open a door belowstairs. It sang like a washerwoman. It whirled the flowers on the window ledge. It lifted Lelya's hat, freeing the wasp, and hurled the hat into the salad bowl. It made Lelya's hair stand on end. It whistled. It puffed up Lelya's chemise.

They parted. And Shuvalov, too happy to feel the steps underfoot, walked downstairs and out into the courtyard. No, he didn't feel the steps, or the porch, or the pavement. It was then that he discovered that all this was not a mirage but reality: his feet were suspended in the air; he was flying.

"He is flying on the wings of love," he heard as he passed a window.

He shot up, his long, belted blouse turned into a crinoline; there was fever on his lips; he flew, snapping his fingers.

At two o'clock he arrived in the park. Fatigued with love and happiness, he fell asleep on a green bench. He slept on. The sweat on his face boiled in the sun. He slept, his collarbone sticking out of his open blouse.

A stranger, wearing something like a cassock, a black hat, and heavy blue spectacles, was walking slowly along the path with the gait of a priest, his hands clasped behind his back and his head bobbing up and down. He approached Shuvalov and sat down beside him.

"I am Isaac Newton," said the stranger, lifting his hat. Through his spectacles he saw his blue, photographic world.

"How do you do?" murmured Shuvalov.

The great scientist was sitting up straight, alert, on pins and needles. He listened intently, his ears twitching, and the forefinger of his left hand raised as though he were calling to order an invisible choir, ready to burst into song any moment at his signal. All nature held its breath. Shuvalov quietly hid behind a bench. Once the gravel screeched under his heel. The celebrated physicist hearkened to the vast silence of nature. Far off, under a clump of greenery, a star shone, as during an eclipse, and it became cool.

"There!" Newton exclaimed suddenly. "You hear?"

Without looking, he stretched out his hand, seized Shuvalov by his blouse, and, getting up, pulled him out of his hiding place. They walked on the lawn. The scientist's roomy shoes trod softly and left white imprints on the grass. A lizard darted ahead of them, glancing back at them every now and then. They passed through a thicket, which decorated the steel frame of the scientist's spectacles with fluff and ladybugs. They came to a clearing. Shuvalov recognized the sapling that had sprung up the previous day.

"Apricots?" he asked.

"No," snapped the scientist with irritation. "It's an apple tree."

The skeleton of the apple tree, the cagelike framework of its crown, light and fragile as the framework of a Montgolfier balloon, was visible through the scanty cover of foliage. Everything was still and motionless.

"Here," said the scientist, stooping, and because of his bent back his voice sounded like a growl. "Here!" He had an apple in his hand. "What does this mean?"

It was obvious that he did not often have occasion to stoop. Having straightened out, he threw back his shoulders several times, humoring his spine, the old bamboo cane of the spine. The apple rested on three fingers.

"What does this mean?" he repeated, with a wheeze that muffled his speech. "Will you tell me why the apple fell down?"

Shuvalov looked at the apple as Wilhelm Tell once did.

"It's the law of gravitation," he lisped.

Then after a pause the great physicist asked:

"Do I understand that you were flying this morning, young man?"

He spoke like a professor examining a student. His eyebrows soared above his spectacles.

"Do I understand that you were flying this morning, my young Marxist?"

A ladybug crawled from his finger onto the apple. Isaac Newton eyed it. The ladybug appeared dazzlingly blue to him. He frowned. It rose from the highest point on the apple and flew away with the aid of wings which it had produced from behind somewhere, like a man in a frock coat pulling a handkerchief from a back pocket.

"Do I understand that you were flying this morning?"

Shuvalov was silent.

"Pig!" said Isaac Newton.

Shuvalov woke up.

"Pig!" said Lelya, standing over him. "You're waiting for me and you fall asleep! Pig!"

She took a ladybug from his forehead and smiled at the metallic sheen of its little belly.

"Damn it!" he swore. "I hate you. There was a time when I knew that this was a ladybug and that was all I knew about it. Well, perhaps I might have concluded too that there was something antireligious about its name.* But ever since we met, something's happened to my eyesight. I see blue pears and I take a fly agaric for a ladybug."

She wanted to hug him.

"Leave me, leave me!" he cried. "I'm fed up with you. I'm ashamed."

Shouting, he ran off like a deer. He ran, snorting and leaping wildly, shying away from his own shadow and squinting his eyes. Finally he stopped, out of breath. Lelya vanished. He decided that he must forget everything. He must find once more the world he had lost. "Goodbye," he sighed, "we shall never see each other again."

He sat down above a slope on a ledge overlooking a wide landscape dotted with summer homes. He sat on the apex of a prism, his legs dangling over the incline. Below him the huge parasol of an ice-cream vendor was circling about, and the man's whole outfit somehow gave the impression of an African village.

"I am living in paradise," said the young Marxist in a crushed voice.

* The Russian for "ladybug" is, literally, "God's little cow."—A. Y.

"Are you a Marxist?" he heard himself addressed.

A young man in a black hat, the color-blind youth whose acquaintance Shuvalov had already made, was sitting close beside him.

"Yes, I'm a Marxist," answered Shuvalov.

"Then you mayn't live in paradise."

The color-blind youth was playing with a twig. Shuvalov kept sighing.

But what can I do? Earth has turned into paradise."

The color-blind young man whistled, scratching his ear with the twig.

"Do you know," Shuvalov continued in a whimper, "to what lengths I've gone? This morning I was flying."

A kite hung in the sky like a postage stamp pasted askew.

"If you like, I'll show you. I'll fly over there," and Shuvalov stretched out his hand.

"No, thanks. I don't want to be a witness to your disgrace."

"Yes, it's terrible," Shuvalov let fall, after a pause. "I know it's terrible. I envy you," he continued.

"Really?"

"Honest. It's wonderful to perceive everything correctly and to be confused only about some details of color, like you. You don't have to live in paradise. The world hasn't been blotted out for you. Everything's in proper order. And me—just think of it! I'm perfectly well, I'm a materialist. And suddenly, a criminal, antiscientific distortion of substances, of matter takes place before my very eyes!"

"Yes, it's terrible," the color-blind young man agreed, "and all because of love!"

Shuvalov suddenly seized his neighbor's hand.

"Listen!" he exclaimed heatedly. "I agree. Give me your retina and take my love."

The color-blind young man started climbing down the slope.

"Excuse me," he said. "I have no time. Goodbye. Go on living in your paradise."

It was difficult for him to make his way down the incline. He was climbing with legs wide apart, and looking less like a man than like the reflection of one in water. Finally he reached level ground and trudged off gaily. Then, throwing the twig into the air, he blew Shuvalov a kiss, and shouted:

"Remember me to Eve!"

Meanwhile Lelya was sleeping. An hour after his meeting with the color-blind youth Shuvalov found her in the depths of the park, in the very heart of it. He was no naturalist; he could not identify the vegetation surrounding him: hazelnut, hawthorn, elderberry, or eglantine. Branches, shrubbery, pressed upon him from every side. He walked like a peddler loaded with baskets of interwoven twigs knotted thickly at the center. He kept throwing away the baskets that poured over him leaves, petals, thorns, berries, birds.

Lelya lay on her back in a pink dress open at the throat. She was asleep. He could hear a faint crackling in her nose, congested in sleep. He sat down near her.

Then he laid his head on her breast, fingering the cotton print she wore. His head lay on her breast damp with perspiration; he could see the pink nipple, faintly wrinkled like the skin on milk. He was deaf to the sounds of leaves rustling, twigs crackling, of breathing.

Suddenly the color-blind young man loomed up behind the bars of a bush. The bush did not let him pass.

"Listen," said the color-blind youth.

Shuvalov lifted his head, sweetness clinging to his cheek.

"Don't follow me around like a dog," said Shuvalov.

"Listen: I agree. You take my retina and give me your love."

"Go and eat blue pears," answered Shuvalov.

Liompa

The boy Alexander was whittling strips in the kitchen. The cuts on his fingers were getting covered with golden edible scabs.

The kitchen opened onto the courtyard; it was spring, the doors were not closed, grass grew at the threshold, water spilled on a stone gleamed. Now and then a rat showed up in the trash box. Potatoes, sliced fine, were frying in the kitchen. A kerosene burner was being lighted. The life of the kerosene burner began sumptuously; the flame shot up to the ceiling like a torch. It was dying as a meek blue flame. Eggs were bouncing about in boiling water. A tenant was cooking crawfish. He would pick up a live crawfish by its waist with two fingers. The crawfish were of a greenish tap-water color. All of a sudden two or three drops would spurt spontaneously out of the faucet. The faucet would blow its nose gently. Afterward the water pipes upstairs would start talking in several voices. Then promptly dusk would take shape. A single drinking glass continued to shine on the windowsill. It was receiving the last rays of the sun through a wicket. The faucet was talking. Manifold stirrings and cracklings started up around the stove.

The twilight was beautiful. People were cracking sunflower seeds, there was the sound of singing, the yellow light from indoors fell on the sidewalk, the food store was brightly lighted.

Ponomaryov, critically ill, was lying in a room adjacent to the kitchen. He was lying in the room alone; a candle was burning, above his head was a bottle of medicine trailing a prescription tag.

When acquaintances came to see Ponomaryov, he would say, "Congratulate me, I'm dying."

Toward evening he would become delirious. The bottle of medicine looked at him. The prescription tag trailed like the train of a dress. The medicine bottle was a duchess being married. The name of the bottle was Her Highness' Name Day. The sick man was delirious. He wanted to write a treatise. He was conversing with the blanket.

"Now, aren't you ashamed?" he whispered.

The blanket would sit beside him, lie down beside him, leave the room, tell him the news.

The things around the sick man were not many: medicine, a spoon, the light, the wallpaper. The other things had gone. When he realized that he had become seriously ill and was indeed dying, he also understood how great and various the world of things was and how few of them remained in his power. With every day the number of such things shrank. A thing as near as a railroad ticket had already become irrevocably distant. At first the number of things shrank on the periphery, far away from him; then, and with increasing rapidity, the shrinking began to come closer to the center, to him, to the heart—into the courtyard, into the house, into the corridor, into the room.

At first the disappearance of things did not distress the sick man.

Countries vanished, America, the possibility of being handsome or rich, of having a family (he was a bachelor). His illness had no relation whatever to the disappearance of these things: they slipped away from him as he got older. The real pain came when it grew clear to him that even those things that constantly kept pace with him were also beginning to recede from him. Thus in the course of one day he was deserted by the street, the office, mail, horses. And then in a rush things began to vanish right alongside him: the corridor had already escaped from his control, and in the room itself, before his very eyes, the overcoat, the door latch, the shoes ceased to have meaning. He knew: death, on its way to him, was annihilating things. Out of all their enormous and idle number death left him only a few, and those were things which, if he could have helped it, he would never have admitted to his household. He received a bedpan. He received dreadful visits and looks from his acquaintances. He realized that he lacked the strength to defend himself against the invasion of these unbidden and, as he had always felt, unnecessary things. But now they were the only ones remaining, and indisputable. He had lost the right to choose things.

The boy Alexander was making a model airplane.

He was more complex and serious than the others thought him to be. He cut his fingers, bled; he littered the place with shavings, made a mess with glue, got silk by begging, cried, was slapped. The grown-ups considered themselves absolutely justified. Yet the boy was acting in a perfectly grown-up way. Moreover, he acted as only a certain number of adults can act: he worked in complete accord with science. The model was being built from a drawing, calculations had been made— the boy knew the laws. He could have parried the attacks of the grown-ups by explaining the laws, performing experiments, but he said and did nothing, because he did not consider himself entitled to appear more serious than the adults.

Ranged around the boy were rubber bands, wire, strips, silk, the gossamer teaey fabric of silk, the smell of glue. The sky sparkled. Insects walked on a stone. Inside the stone a shell had petrified.

Another boy, very tiny, naked, except for blue shorts, kept coming over to the boy who was at work. He kept touching things and was in the way. Alexander kept shooing him off. The naked India-rubber boy wandered about the house, about the corridor, where a bicycle was standing. (The bicycle was leaning against the wall. The pedal scratched the wallpaper. By this scratch the bicycle held on, as it were, to the wall.)

The little boy would drop in on Ponomaryov. The tot's head appeared vaguely above the side of the bed. The sick man's temples were pale like those of the blind. The boy would come close to the head and examine it. He thought that it was always like this in the world and that it always had been thus: a bearded man lies abed in a room. The boy had only just entered into the knowledge of things. He was not as yet able to distinguish the stages of existence in time.

He would turn around and walk about the room. He saw the parquetry, the dust under the baseboard, the cracks in the plaster. About him lines were composing and distributing themselves, bodies lived. Light would focus suddenly—the boy would hurry toward it, but he hardly moved a step when the change of distance would destroy the spot of light, and the boy would look about him, look up and down, look behind the stove and spread out his arms in perplexity, failing to find what he was seeking. Every instant created a new thing for him. The spider was amazing. The spider flew away at the boy's mere thought of touching it with his hand.

The departing things left the dying man only their names.

There was an apple in the world. It shone in the foliage, revolving gently; it caught and turned with it bits of the day, the azure of the garden, the window sash. The law of gravitation lay in wait for it under the tree, on the black earth, on mounds. Beady ants scurried among the mounds. Newton sat in the garden. Concealed in the apple was a multitude of causes, capable of having a still greater multitude of effects. Not a single one of these causes was earmarked for Ponomaryov. The apple had become an abstraction for him. And the fact that the body of the thing vanished for him, but the abstraction remained—tormented him.

"I thought the external world did not exist," he reflected. "I thought that my eye and ear ruled things. I thought that the world would cease to exist when I ceased to exist. But now . . . I see that everything turns away from me while I am still alive. I do still exist! Why, then, do things no longer exist? I thought that my brain gave them form, weight, and color, but now they have gone away from me and only their names—useless names that have lost their masters —swarm in my brain. What good are these names to me?"

Ponomaryov looked at the child despondently. The little boy was walking about. Things rushed to meet him. He smiled at them, not knowing a single name. He would leave the room, and a luxuriant train of things would be tossing after him.

"Listen," the sick man called the child, "listen. . . . You know, when I die nothing will remain. Neither the courtyard nor the trees, nor Papa nor Mama. I'll take everything with me."

The rat made its way into the kitchen.

Ponomaryov listened: the rat was playing the housewife, clattering plates, opening the faucet, rustling in the pail.

"Aha—she's a dishwasher," Ponomaryov decided.

Just then a disturbing thought entered his head: the rat might have a proper name that people did not know. He started devising such a name. He was delirious. The more he tried to do this, the more strongly he was gripped by fear. He understood that at all costs he must stop thinking of what the rat's name was, and yet he continued to do so, knowing that at the very instant when this unique, senseless, and frightening name came to him—he would die!

"Liompa!" he shouted suddenly in a terrifying voice.

The house slept. It was early morning, a few minutes past five. The boy Alexander was not asleep. The kitchen door leading into the courtyard was open. The sun was still somewhere down below.

The dying man was walking about the kitchen, doubled up, his arms extended, his hands hanging loosely. He was bent on taking things away with him.

The boy Alexander was running through the courtyard. The model airplane was flying ahead of him. It was the last thing Ponomaryov saw.

He did not take it with him. It flew away.

In the afternoon a pale-blue coffin with yellow ornaments appeared in the kitchen. The India-rubber boy watched from the corridor, his hands clasped behind his back. It took a lot of time and much maneuvering to get the coffin through the door. It caught against a shelf, a saucepan; crumbled plaster came down. The boy Alexander climbed onto the stove and helped, supporting the box from below. When finally the coffin worked its way into the corridor, immediately turning black, the India-rubber boy, flapping his sandals, ran on ahead.

"Grandfather, grandfather," he cried, "they've brought you a coffin."

VLADIMIR MAYAKOVSKY
(1893–1930)

FROM **At the Top of My Voice**

1.

My voice will reach you
                across the range of ages
and over the heads
                of poets and premiers.
My verse will reach you,
                but not in this wise:
not like an arrow
                in lyrical venery,
not the way a worn coin
                reaches a numismatist,
not like the light from a dead star.
My verse
        by its labor
                will pierce the mountain of years,
and appear
        visible,
            tangible,
                hefty,
as an aqueduct
        built by Roman slaves
enters
      our days.
Finding by chance,
            in barrows of books
where verse lies buried,
the iron lines,

277

touch them
> with respect
like old,
> but terrible weapons.

2.

Let fame,
> like a comfortless
>> widow,
Walk behind geniuses
> in funeral processions;
You, my verse, die,
> die like a common soldier,
As in an attack our men
> died their anonymous deaths.
I spit
> on tons of bronze,
I spit
> on marble slime.
As for fame,
> we'll square accounts amicably—
Sharing one monument:
Socialism
> built
>> in battle.

1930

MIKHAIL SHOLOKHOV
(b. 1905)

Though not of Cossack stock, Sholo-
khov opened his eyes in a Don *stanitza* (Cossack village), where he is
making his home to this day. As a writer he has virtually limited his
horizon to the Don steppes. His imagination has been busy chiefly with
the impact of the Revolution on the *stanitzas* of the Don Region, the
Russian Vendée. From the first, his pen was at the service of the new
order. His heart belonged to the Party even before he formally joined it,
in 1932. Nevertheless, *The Quiet Don*, his four-volume novel, which
came out piecemeal in 1928–1940, flouts the cardinal principle of Communist aesthetics by treating the subject matter with a large measure of
balance and impartiality. It is a turbulent, full-blooded, powerfully evocative narrative centering on the civil war, with its searing passions and
savage brutalities.

Sholokhov did not scruple to alter certain passages in later editions of
the novel to keep up with the changes in the Party line. Yet he disregarded
the official canon by portraying his protagonist sympathetically, though
he is poles removed from a model Soviet man. Grigory Melekhov, the
central figure in *The Quiet Don*, a tough-bodied, strong-minded Cossack
of humble parentage who became an officer during the World War, several
times shifts sides in the fratricidal struggle. In the end he cries a plague
on both revolution and counterrevolution, deciding that Red fanatics and
White zealots are birds of a feather. He wants nothing better than to
cultivate his cabbages in peace. His wife dies, his mistress is killed, and
when he gets home at last, leaving a hideout that shelters a group of
men who are evading mobilization, he finds that one of his two small
children has been carried off, apparently by diphtheria. As the massive
tale comes to a close, his surviving little son is all that binds him to life.
It is reported that this tragic finale was kept in spite of Stalin's demand
that the novel—it was immensely popular—should end happily with
Melekhov embracing the Red cause.

Sholokhov interrupted his work on *The Quiet Don* to write his only
other novel, *Virgin Soil Upturned* (known in English also as *Seeds of
Tomorrow*). The scene is once more the Don countryside with its Cossack
population, and the villages are again in the throes of a crisis: rural collectivization, a burning issue in the late twenties and early thirties. But

the drama is presented without the comparative objectivity that marks *The Quiet Don*. Its unmistakable objective is to promote the official policy. The active enemies of the Soviet state are pictured in the blackest colors. Davydov, the hero, is a paragon of Communist virtues. A metalworker who had been a sailor in the Red Navy, he is one of the twenty-five thousand activists deputized by the Party to help local Communists fully socialize the farms in certain key areas, including the Don Region, at a forced tempo. The setting up of kolkhozes (collective farms) was accompanied by the ruthless "liquidation" of the well-to-do farmers (kulaks). These measures resulted in grave damage to agriculture, and in 1932–1933 caused a famine that carried off untold thousands of lives in southern Russia. Years later Stalin told Churchill that this policy had meant "a terrible struggle" that had been harder on him personally than "the stresses" of the World War.

It is January, 1930. Davydov arrives in Gremyachy Log, a Cossack village, and is received by Makar Nagulnov, secretary of the local Party cell, and Andrey Razmyotnov, chairman of the village Soviet. They call the poorer peasants together, and these agree to start a kolkhoz. The assembly also decides to evict the kulaks and confiscate their property, turning it over to the collective farm. This decision is being carried out as the following scene opens:

FROM **Virgin Soil Upturned**

(1. THE KULAKS ARE EXPROPRIATED)

Andrey Razmyotnov arrived at Frol Damaskov's cottage when he and his family were having their midday meal. At the table sat Frol himself, a little, puny old man with a small wedge-shaped beard and a torn left nostril (when still a child, he had disfigured his face, falling from an apple tree, whence his nickname "Torn"); his wife, a corpulent and stately old woman; his son Timofey, a young man of about twenty-two; and a daughter of marriageable age.

Timofey, a handsome, well-built youth who resembled his mother, rose from the table. With a rag he wiped his red lips under his youthful fluffy moustache, screwed up his insolent protruding eyes, and with the pertness of the best accordion player in the village and a favorite with the girls, beckoned:

"Step in, sit down, our dear officials!"

"We've no time to sit down," said Andrey, taking a paper out of his briefcase. "The assembly of poor peasants has resolved to evict you from your house, Citizen Frol Damaskov, and to confiscate all your property and livestock. So finish your meal and get yourself out of the house. We'll make an inventory of the property at once."

"Why is this?" said Frol, flinging down his spoon, and rose.

"We're destroying you as a kulak class," Dyomka Ushakov enlightened him.

His sturdy, leather-soled boots creaking, Frol went into the best room and brought back a paper.

"Here's the certificate; you signed it yourself, Razmyotnov."

"What certificate?"

"Saying that I delivered my grain tax in full."

"Grain has nothing to do with it."

"Then what am I being driven out of my house for, and why is my property being confiscated?"

"That's what the poor peasants have resolved; I've already explained it to you."

"There are no such laws!" Timofey cried sharply. "This is daylight robbery! Dad, I'll ride over to the District Executive Committee right away. Where's the saddle?"

"You'll go to the Committee on foot, if you want to. I won't let you have a horse."

Andrey sat down at the edge of the table and produced a pencil and paper.

Frol's torn nose turned blue; his head began to shake. He sank to the floor right where he stood, with difficulty moving his swollen tongue, which had grown black.

"S-s-sons! Sons of bitches! Rob! Cut our throats!"

"Dad, get up, for Christ's sake!" The girl burst into tears, grabbing her father under his armpits.

Frol recovered, got up, lay down on a bench, and now listened apathetically to Dyomka Ushakov and tall, shy Mikhail Ignatyonok dictating to Razmyotnov:

"One iron bedstead with white knobs, a feather bed, three pillows, and three wooden beds . . ."

"A cupboard with china! Am I to go through all the dishes? Ah, the hell with it!"

281

"Twelve chairs, one long chair with a back. An accordion with three rows of keys."

"I won't let you have my accordion!" Timofey shouted, snatching it out of Dyomka's hands. "Hands off, squint-eye, or I'll bust your nose!"

"I'll bust yours so that even your mother won't wash you clean."

"Hand over the keys to the chests, mistress of the house."

"Don't give 'em to him, Ma. Let 'em break 'em open, if they've got the right."

"Do we have the right to break 'em open?" asked Demid the Silent, coming to life. He was known to speak only when it was absolutely necessary. The rest of the time he worked silently, smoked silently with the other Cossacks who gathered in the lane on holidays, sat silently at meetings, and on the rare occasions when he did answer a question he would smile guiltily and pitifully.

For Demid the wide world was full of unnecessarily loud noises. They filled life to the brim; even at night they did not die down, and prevented him from listening to the stillness and shattered the wise silence with which steppe and forest overflow in autumn. Demid disliked the hubbub people made. He lived apart at the edge of the village, and was a hard worker and the strongest man in the whole neighborhood. But somehow fate had wronged him, treating him like a stepson. . . . For five years he had lived at Frol Damaskov's as a laborer; then had married and started his own farm. Before he had finished his farm buildings, a fire destroyed them. The next year a second fire left him nothing but his plows reeking with smoke in the yard. And soon his wife left him, declaring: "Two years I've lived with you and haven't heard you say two words. Enough, live alone! It'll be more cheerful for me to live in the woods with a wolf. Staying here with you a woman can go off her head. I've already started talking to myself. . . ."

But in fact she had got used to Demid. True, during the first months she would cry, and badger her husband: "Demid, honey, do talk to me a little. Say one little word at least!" Demid only smiled his quiet, childlike smile, scratching his hairy chest. And when he could no longer stand his wife's nagging, he would say in his deep bass voice, "You're a regular magpie!"—and would be off. For some reason Demid had the reputation of a proud and crafty man. Perhaps it was because all his life he had shunned garrulous people and loud noises.

That is why Andrey raised his head when he heard the muffled thunder of Demid's voice above him.

"Right?" he repeated, staring at Demid as if he was seeing him for the first time. "We've got the right!"

Demid, walking clumsily and dirtying the floor with his wet, broken-down shoes, went into the best room. Smiling, and as easily as pushing aside a twig, with his hand he shoved Timofey out of the way where he was standing, and, passing the cupboard with a heavy tread that made the china tinkle plaintively, walked up to the chest. Squatting down, he turned the heavy padlock over in his fingers. The next moment the lock, its hasp broken, lay on the chest, and Arkhashka Menok, eyeing Demid with unconcealed amazement, exclaimed admiringly:

"I'd like to swap my strength for his!"

There wasn't time for Andrey to write down the items. From the best room came the voices of Dyomka Ushakov, Arkashka, Aunt Vasilisa—the only woman in Andrey's group—vying with each other:

"A woman's fur coat!"

"A man's fur coat!"

"Three pairs of new boots with galoshes!"

"Four lengths of cloth!"

"Andrey! Razmyotnov! There is more than a cartful of goods here, lad! There's cotton cloth, black satin, and all sorts of things. . . ."

On the way to the best room Andrey heard the girl's wails, her mother's cries, and Ignatyonok's placating voice coming from the entry. Andrey threw open the door.

"What's going on here?"

The snub-nosed daughter of the house, her face swollen with tears, was leaning against the door and yelling bloody murder. Her mother was fussing and cackling around her, while Ignatyonok, red in the face and smiling with embarrassment, was pulling at the hem of the girl's skirt.

"What are you up to?" Andrey, failing to make out what was going on, choked with rage and gave Ignatyonok a violent push. Ignatyonok fell on his back, his long legs in ragged felt boots shooting up in the air. "We're busy with a political matter," roared Andrey;

"we're attacking the enemy, and you're pawing girls in corners? I'll have you tried for—"

"Hold on! Wait!" Ignatyonok jumped up from the floor, frightened. "Pawing her! Take a look; she's pulling on the ninth skirt! I was trying to stop her, and then you fly off the handle and start pushing people."

Only then did Andrey become aware that the girl, taking advantage of the general commotion, had dragged a bundle of finery from the best room, and had in fact already succeeded in pulling on several woolen dresses. Huddled in a corner, she kept pulling down her top skirt, which was too short because of the abundance of clothes that hampered her movements. Her wet eyes, red like a rabbit's, aroused Andrey's disgust and pity. He slammed the door and said to Ignatyonok:

"Don't try to undress her! What she has managed to put on—the hell with it, but take away the bundle."

The making of the inventory of the goods found in the house was coming to an end.

"The keys to the barn!" Andrey demanded.

Frol, black as a charred stump, waved his hand. "There are no keys!"

"Go and break the lock," Andrey ordered Demid.

Demid went to the barn, pulling a bolt out of a cart on his way.

The five-pound padlock was broken with an ax, but not without difficulty.

"Don't cut into the doorpost! The barn is ours now, so take care. Easy! Easy!" Dyomka admonished the puffing Demid.

They started to measure out the grain.

"Maybe we ought to sift it at once? There's a sieve lying in the bin," proposed Ignatyonok, who had got drunk with joy.

They laughed at him, and for a long time kept cracking jokes as they poured the heavy wheat into the measures.

"There's another couple of hundred poods here for the grain collection," observed Dyomka Ushakov, wading up to his knees in grain. With a shovel he threw the wheat toward the opening of the bin, caught some up in his hand and let it run through his fingers.

"It's bound to show a good weight on the scales."

"Sure enough! The wheat is pure gold, but it must have been buried in the earth: see, it's gone a bit moldy."

Arkashka Menok and another young fellow from the group were bossing it in the yard. Stroking his small flaxen beard, Arkashka pointed to ox dung with undigested grains of maize sticking out of it.

"Why shouldn't the beast have worked well? They ate grain, while in our association* they had even hay only in handfuls."

From the farm came animated voices, laughter, the scent of fragrant grain dust, and now and then a salty oath. Andrey returned to the house. The mistress and her daughter had collected a sackful of dishes and iron pots. Frol, his fingers crossed over his chest like a dead man's, was lying on a bench in his stocking feet. Timofey, who had quieted down, looked at Andrey with hatred in his eyes, and turned to the window.

In the best room Andrey found Demid crouching on his haunches. He wore Frol's new leather-soled felt boots. Not seeing Andrey, he was scooping honey with a tablespoon from a tin bucket and eating it, delightedly screwing up his eyes, smacking his lips, letting sticky yellow drops trickle down into his beard.

Toward evening Andrey Razmyotnov dismissed his group of poor peasants, sent off the last carload of confiscated goods from the yard of the dispossessed kulak Gayev to Titok's house [Titok was the first kulak to be expropriated], where all the kulak possessions were being collected, and went to the village Soviet. In the morning he had agreed to meet Davydov there an hour before the general meeting, which was to begin at nightfall.

From the entry he saw a light in the corner room of the Soviet, and walked in, throwing the door wide open. At the sound Davydov raised his bandaged head from a notebook, and smiled.

"And here's Razmyotnov," he called out. "Sit down; we're figuring out how much grain has been found in the kulaks' hands. Well, how did things go with you?"

"All right . . . Why is your head bandaged?"

Nagulnov, who was making a lampshade from a newspaper sheet, said reluctantly:

"Titok did it. With a yoke pin. I've sent him off to Zakharchenko at the GPU."

* The producers' cooperative that had existed before the formation of the collective farm.—A. Y.

"Wait, we'll tell you about it in a minute," said Davydov, giving a shove to the abacus on the table. "Add a hundred and fifteen. Got that? A hundred and eight . . ."

"Easy! Easy!" Nagulnov muttered anxiously, as he carefully pushed the abacus beads with one finger.

Andrey looked at them and, his lips trembling, said thickly, "I don't work anymore."

"Don't work? Where?" Nagulnov pushed the abacus aside.

"I'm not going to dispossess kulaks anymore. Well, why are you staring? Are you going to work yourself into a fit, or what?"

"Are you drunk?" Davydov anxiously scrutinized Andrey's face, which wore an expression of angry determination. "What's the matter with you? What d'you mean?"

His calm tenor infuriated Andrey and, stammering, he shouted excitedly:

"I haven't been trained! I—I—I haven't been trained to make war on children! At the front it's another matter! There I could strike anyone with a saber or whatever came to hand. . . . And you can all go to the devil! I won't do it!"

His voice rose higher and higher, like the notes of a string that is being tightened, and it seemed about to break. But, sighing hoarsely, he unexpectedly lowered his voice to a whisper:

"Can it be that this is right? Who am I? An executioner? Is my heart made of stone? I had my fill in the war. . . ." And his voice rose to a shout again: "Gayev has eleven children. When we arrived —how they yowled! Made my hair stand on end! We started turning them out of the house. . . . Well, at that point I screwed up my eyes, stopped up my ears, and ran into the courtyard! The women were wailing as for the dead; water was poured on the daughter-in-law . . . the children . . . to bring them round. The hell with you!"

"Have a cry! It'll ease you," Nagulnov advised, with his hand pressing hard the twitching muscle in his cheek, his burning eyes fixed on Andrey.

"And I will cry! Maybe my own little boy . . ." Andrey stopped short, baring his teeth and abruptly turned his back on the table.

Silence fell.

Davydov slowly rose from his chair. . . . And just as slowly did his unbandaged cheek turn blue and his ear go white. He went up to

Andrey, took him by the shoulders and gently turned him round. Choking, his widened eyes fixed on Andrey's face, he spoke:

"You're sorry for them. . . . You pity them. Did they pity us? Did our children's tears make our enemies cry? Did they weep for the orphans of the killed? Did they? After a strike at his factory my father was fired and sent to Siberia. . . . Mother had four of us—I, the eldest, was then nine. . . . There was nothing to eat, so Mother . . . Look at me! Mother walked the streets to keep us from croaking with hunger! She'd bring a guest into our small room—we lived in a basement. . . . There was only one bed left . . . so we'd lie behind a curtain . . . on the floor. . . . And I was nine years old. . . . Drunken men would come to her . . . and I'd stop my little sisters' mouths to keep them from bawling. Who wiped our tears? Do you hear? In the morning I'd take the accursed ruble"—Davydov lifted his leathery palm to Andrey's face and ground his teeth in torment—"the ruble earned by mother, and go to buy bread. . . ." Suddenly he flung his black fist down on the table like a leaden weight, and shouted: "You! How can you pity them?!"

And again there was silence. Nagulnov dug his nails into the table-top and clung to it like a kite to its prey. Andrey kept quiet. His breath coming in labored gasps, Davydov paced the room for a while, then threw his arms about Andrey's shoulders and sat down with him on a bench. In a cracked voice he said:

"You're a blockhead! You come in and start yelling: 'I won't work . . . children . . . pity. . . .' What's all that babble? Get hold of yourself! Let's talk it over. You're sorry that the kulak families are being evicted? The idea! We're evicting them so that they won't prevent us from building a life without all this. . . . So it won't happen again in the future . . . You're the Soviet power at Gremyachy, and do I have to try and win you over?" He gave a forced smile. "Well, we'll deport the kulaks; the hell with them, we'll settle them on the Solovetzky Islands. They won't peg out, will they? If they work, we'll feed them. And when we've built the new life, these children won't be kulak children any more. The working class will re-educate them." He took out a package of cigarettes, and for a long time could not pick one with his trembling fingers.

All the while Andrey kept watching Nagulnov's face, which was being pervaded by a ghastly pallor. To Davydov's surprise, Nagulnov quickly rose to his feet and immediately jumped up as if tossed by a springboard.

"Skunk!" he gasped out, clenching his fists. "How do you serve the Revolution? You pity? Why, I . . . Now line up thousands of old men, children, women—and tell me that they must all be reduced to dust. . . . For the sake of the Revolution . . . I'd do them in . . . all of them!" he suddenly shouted wildly; his large, dilated pupils glittered with frenzy, and foam boiled up at the corners of his lips.

"Stop shouting, man! Sit down!" Davydov took alarm.

Knocking over a chair, Andrey hurriedly stepped toward Nagulnov, but the latter, leaning against the wall, his head thrown back and his eyes rolling, shouted piercingly, lingeringly:

"I'll fi-i-inish 'em off!"

But he was already collapsing sideways, his left hand catching at the air in search of a sheath, his right convulsively groping for an invisible sword hilt.

As Andrey managed to catch him in his arms, he felt how terribly all the muscles in Nagulnov's heavy body stiffened and how his legs straightened out like a steel spring.

"A fit! Hold his legs!" Andrey had time to shout to Davydov.

(2. KONDRAT JOINS THE KOLKHOZ)

After nightfall a stormy general meeting of the villagers takes place. It has been called to persuade the farmers who are neither as destitute as the poor Cossacks nor as well-to-do as the kulaks to join the collective. One of the few such householders is Kondrat Maydannikov.

Kondrat was walking from the meeting. High above him the Pleiades glowed like a smoldering bonfire. It was so quiet that from a distance you could hear the crackling of the earth splitting with the frost and the rustle of a freezing branch. When he reached his house he went into the stable and put a meager armful of hay in the manger for his oxen; but recalling that tomorrow he would be driving them to the communal farmyard, he gathered a great load of hay and said aloud:

"Well, the time has come when we must part. . . . Move over, baldhead! Four years we've worked, the Cossack for the ox and the ox for the Cossack. And nothing good has come of it. You're half starved, and I'm far from well off. That's why I'm giving you up for communal life. Hey, what are you stirring for, as if you really understood what I'm saying?"

He kicked the wrinkled ox automatically, pushed aside its chewing, driveling jaws and, his gaze meeting the animal's lilac eye, he suddenly recalled how he had waited for this ox to come into the world about five years before. The old cow had taken the bull so secretly that neither the herdsman nor Kondrat had seen it. In the autumn for a long time she showed no sign of being with young. "She's gone dry, damn her!" Kondrat had thought, turning cold as he looked at her. But, like all old cows, she began to show signs a month before calving, late in November. How many times on cold nights by the end of Advent would he wake up, as if someone had nudged him, and, thrusting his feet into felt boots, and wearing only his drawers, run into the warm stable to see if she had calved. The frosts were severe that year, and the calf could freeze as soon as the mother had licked it clean. Toward the end of the fast Kondrat had hardly slept. One morning Anna, his wife, came in and said joyously, indeed solemnly:

"The old one has already emptied her veins. It'll be tonight, as like as not."

In the evening Kondrat lay down without undressing and without putting out the lantern. Seven times he went out to the cow! And only the eighth time, at daybreak, even before he opened the stable door, he heard a deep and painful moan. Coming in, he saw the cow expelling the afterbirth, while a tiny, shaggy, white-nostriled calf, already licked clean, and trembling pitifully, was seeking the mother's udder with chilled lips. Kondrat grabbed the afterbirth to keep the cow from eating it.* Then he lifted the calf in his arms, and warming it with his breath and wrapping it in the skirt of his coat, he ran with it into the house.

"A bull!" he shouted joyously.

Anna crossed herself.

"Glory be to God! The Merciful one has seen our need!" she said.

And sure enough, with one wretched nag Kondrat was in sore need. And then the bull had grown up, and toiled well for Kondrat,

---

* There was a widespread popular belief in the Upper Don Region that if the cow ate the afterbirth its milk should not be used for twelve days.—Author's note.

summer and winter, setting down its cloven hoofs on road and field, pulling the cart or the plow.

As he looked at the ox, Kondrat suddenly felt a sharp lump in the throat, a smarting in the eyes. He wept, and left the yard, as if the tears had relieved him. The rest of the night he did not sleep, but lay smoking.

"How will it be at the collective farm? Will everyone feel and think, as I do, that this is the only way, that this is unavoidable? No matter how distressing it is to hand over to strangers the cattle that have grown up together with the children on the earthen floor of the hut, it has to be done. And this vile attachment to your own possessions must be crushed, must not be allowed to find its way to your heart. . . ." Thus Kondrat reflected as he lay beside his snoring wife, and stared with unseeing, blind eyes into the black abysses of the darkness. And he also thought: "And where shall we take the lambs and kids? They need warm quarters and much looking after. How can you tell the difference between these imps when they're almost all alike? Their mothers will mix them up, and so will people. And the cows? How's their food to be supplied? We'll lose a lot of them! What if the people clear out after a week, scared by the difficulties? Then it's the coal pits for me, and goodbye to Gremyachy for good and all. There'll be nothing to live on."

Just before daybreak he dozed off. Sleep gave him no relief. The collective farm did not come easy to Kondrat. With tears and blood, he was cutting the umbilical cord that connected him with his property, his oxen, his parcel of land.

In the morning after breakfast he sat a long time composing the application, his sunburned brows knitted. It read:

TO COMRADE MAKAR NAGULNOV, THE GREMYACHY COMMUNIST PARTY CELL.

Application.

I, Kondrat Khristoforov Maydannikov, a middling Cossack, beg to be admitted to the collective farm with my spouse and children, and my possessions and all livestock. I beg you to allow me into the new life, seeing that I fully agree with it.

K. MAYDANNIKOV

"Have you joined?" his wife asked.

"I have."

"Will you take the livestock along?"

"I'm taking it at once. . . . Now, why are you crying, you dunder-head? Haven't I spent enough breath on you trying to persuade you; but you haven't changed. And you'd agreed yourself!"

"I'm only sorry for the cow, Kondrat dear. . . . I do agree. Only, my heart aches so," she said, smiling and wiping the tears with her apron.

Seeing her mother cry, their youngest child, the four-year-old Khris-tishka, also burst into tears.

Kondrat let the cow and the oxen out of the farmyard and, having bridled the horse, drove them to the stream to water. Having drunk their fill, the oxen turned to go home, but Kondrat, with anger boiling up in his heart, rode the horse at them, barred their way, and forced them along in the direction of the village Soviet.

The women kept staring out of the windows; the Cossacks watched from behind the fences, without showing themselves in the street. Kondrat became distraught. But turning the corner, he saw near the Soviet a large herd of oxen, sheep, horses, as at a fair. From a neigh-boring lane Lyubishkin emerged dragging a cow by a strap tied to its horns; behind it hurried a calf with a rope dangling from its neck.

"Let's tie their tails together and drive them side by side," Lyubish-kin tried to joke, but he looked pensive and stern. He had had great difficulty in taking away the cow, as a fresh scratch on his cheek witnessed.

"Who's been clawing you?"

"I won't hide the sin: it's the wife. The devil of a woman set upon me on account of the cow." Lyubishkin tucked the tip of his whisker into his mouth and spoke resentfully through clenched teeth: "She went into attack like a tank. There was such bloodletting in the yard that I was ashamed before the neighbors. She came at me with a knife, will you believe it? 'Ah, says I, 'you'd strike a Red Partisan? We've jabbed even into generals,' says I—and I pulled her hair for her. Who-ever was watching us must have enjoyed the show. . . ."

From the Soviet Office they set out for Titok's place. [His large house with its outbuildings became the headquarters of the collective farm.] During the morning twelve more middling Cossacks, who had changed their minds overnight, made out applications and drove in their livestock. With two carpenters Nagulnov was trimming elders for mangers, the first communal mangers at Gremyachy Log.

(3. THE CONFISCATED CLOTHING AND SHOES ARE DISTRIBUTED)

The members of the collective farm elect a board of directors. It includes Yakov Ostrovnov, a substantial and competent husbandman, who is appointed manager of the farm, while Davydov becomes its chairman. Though Ostrovnov professes devotion to the government and the kolkhoz, he is hiding in his house two former White officers who are plotting an anti-Soviet uprising, and is active in an underground "union" of dispossessed kulaks engaged in sabotage. He takes part in killing a member of the group suspected of having turned informer, as well as the man's wife, both of them wholly innocent. Meanwhile the expropriation of the kulaks has been completed under the guidance of Andrey Razmyotnov, who has overcome his scruples. In the scene that follows, Ostrovnov supervises the distribution of confiscated clothing and shoes at kolkhoz headquarters.

In Titok's farmyard there was a ceaseless hubbub till dark. Right then and there in the snow near the barn people took off their shoes and tried on sturdy kulak boots and also pulled on overcoats, jackets, sheepskin coats. The lucky ones to whom the commission had allotted clothes or footwear on account of future work undressed right in the storeroom attached to the barn and, grunting with satisfaction, their eyes shining, their dark faces brightening with trembling, niggardly smiles, hastily crumpled their old patched and repatched rags and put on their new garments, through which their bodies no longer showed. But before anything was taken, what talk there was, what advice offered, what doubts voiced, how much swearing went on! Davydov ordered that a jacket, trousers, and boots be issued to Lyubishkin. Sullen Yakov Ostrovnov pulled out a pile of clothes from a chest and tossed it at Lyubishkin's feet, saying:

"Choose in all conscience."

The former guardsman's whiskers trembled, his hands shook. He took a long time choosing a jacket, sweating blood over it! He tested the garment with his teeth, held it up to the light to see if there were any moth holes in it, crumpled it in his black fingers for ten minutes or so. And around him people breathed hotly and urged aloud:

"Take it; your children will be wearing it after you."

"Where are your eyes, man? Can't you see it's been turned?"

"You're lying!"

"Take it, Pavlo!"

"Don't, try another!"

Lyubishkin's face was the color of a red brick; he chewed his black moustache, looked round like an animal brought to bay, and reached out for another jacket. He chose one. A fine jacket in every respect. He put his long arms into the sleeves; they came up to his elbows, and the seams burst at the shoulders. And again, smiling in embarrassment and agitation, he rummaged in the pile of clothing. He was dazzled like a little child before a profusion of toys at a fair; there was such a serene, childlike smile on his lips that you expected someone to give this giant of a man a fatherly pat on the head. Half a day was gone, and he hadn't yet made his choice. He put on the trousers and boots and, swallowing a sigh, said to gloomy Ostrovnov:

"I'll come back tomorrow to try 'em on again."

Lyubishkin left the farmyard in new trousers with a stripe down the side and squeaking boots, looking some ten years younger. He purposely walked down the main street, although it was out of his way, and frequently stopped to smoke or to chat with passersby. It took him nearly three hours to get home, and by evening the rumor spread all through the village: "They've dressed up Lyubishkin fit for a recruit! He was a-choosing clothes all day long. Went home in new things, in Sunday trousers. Strutted like a crane, must have walked on air . . ."

Dyomka Ushakov's better half nearly fainted before a chest, and was only with difficulty pushed away. She put on a gathered woolen skirt that had once belonged to Titok's woman, got her feet into new slippers, wrapped herself in a flowered shawl, and only then did it dawn on people that she was by no means homely, and had a fine figure. And how could the poor thing help being stunned at the sight of the kolkhoz wealth if in all her bitter life she had never tasted a morsel of good food, never worn a new blouse on her shoulders? How could her lips, faded from constant penury and semistarvation, help going white when Yakov Ostrovnov pulled out of a chest a whole sheaf of women's finery? Year after year she had borne children, wrapping the sucklings in rotted rags and strips of worn sheepskin. Grief and constant need had robbed her of her former beauty, freshness, and health; all summer long she wore one skirt, as full of holes as a sieve, and in winter, having washed her one and only smock that crawled with lice, she would sit with her children on the stove naked, because she had nothing else to change into.

"Dearies! Darlings! Wait a minute; maybe I won't take this skirt. I'll change it. Maybe I can get something for the children, for Mishatka, Dunyashka. . . ." she whispered frantically, gripping the lid of the chest, her blazing eyes glued to the many-colored pile of clothing.

Davydov's heart—he happened to be present at this scene—was wrung. He elbowed his way to the chest and asked, "How many children have you, my dear?"

"Seven," Dyomka's wife answered in a whisper, afraid to raise her eyes in sweet anticipation.

"Have you any children's things here?" Davydov asked Ostrovnov quietly.

"We have some."

"Give this woman everything she wants for her children."

"That'll be too much for her."

"What's that? Eh?" Davydov bared his teeth with gaps between them, and Yakov hastily bent over the chest.

Dyomka Ushakov, usually talkative and sharp-tongued, stood behind his wife, silently licking his dry lips and holding his breath. But at Davydov's last words, he glanced at him. Suddenly tears spurted from his squinting eyes, like juice from a ripe fruit. He dashed to the exit, pushing people aside with his left hand, covering his eyes with the right. Jumping off the steps, he strode from the yard, trying to hide his tears in shame. . . . But they flowed from under the black shield of his palm and down his cheeks, chasing each other, bright and sparkling like dewdrops.

The uncertain beginnings of the kolkhoz, which is named for Stalin, the mistakes made because of inexperience or excessive zeal, are related in some detail. Nagulnov is expelled from the Party for rejecting a directive of Stalin's, but is soon reinstated. At one time many of the members withdraw from the farm. Aroused by false rumors, a mob of Cossack women severely maul Davydov. But the renegades return to the fold, the women are pacified, the requisite amount of seed grain is collected in time, and by spring a bumper crop is in prospect. Therewith the tale comes to a close.

Virgin Soil Upturned appeared in 1932 and proved a great popular success. It was dramatized, and furnished the libretto for an opera. Three years later the Moscow monthly in which the novel had been serialized announced that it would print the second part that very year. Actually, a quarter of a century passed before the publication of the sequel (translated into English as *Harvest on the Don*). It traces the fortunes of the kolkhoz as it gains strength during its first summer. The author manages to instill plenty of comedy into his account, which is also enlivened by an episode in which the village blacksmith plays the detective with considerable skill. Ostrovnov continues to manage the farm. The two anti-Soviet conspirators are still using his house as a hideout, and he starves to death his mother, who lives with him, for fear that the garrulous old woman will reveal the presence of the officers to neighbors. A new figure is the secretary of the District Party Committee, pictured as a pattern of Communist leadership. Davydov's reputation is somewhat tarnished by his affair with the wholly unpolitically-minded village Jezebel, but this is only a temporary aberration on his part. He gives up the seductive wanton and arranges to marry an innocent young girl who works as a driver of oxen and who is in love with him. But the book does not end with a wedding: Davydov and Nagulnov die at the hand of one of the plotters sheltered under Ostrovnov's roof, the protagonist of the novel thus achieving martyrdom in the Communist cause.

MIKHAIL KOLTZOV
(1898–1942)

This author, known under the pen name above, was born in Kiev of Jewish parents. A dedicated Bolshevik since his youth, he engaged in political propaganda and muckraking journalism, wielding a caustic pen. As is clear from the piece printed here —it was first published in 1933—his sarcasm was not always directed against the "bourgeois" world that he despised and hated. From 1922 to the mysterious end of his career, he was a regular contributor to *Pravda*, the principal newspaper of the Party. Collections of his *feuilletons* appeared from time to time in book form. He collaborated with Maxim Gorky on a bizarre enterprise: a record of the events of a single day throughout the world. Koltzov covered the early phase of the Spanish civil war for *Pravda*, returning home in 1937. The following year his *Spanish Diary* came out, he was elected to the Supreme Soviet of RSFSR and named corresponding member of the Academy of Sciences. That December he was arrested, and disappeared without a trace.

Shortly after Stalin's death Koltzov was posthumously rehabilitated. A selection from his writings, in three volumes, appeared under a Moscow imprint in 1957. The highly laudatory introduction to this edition says nothing about his arrest except that "in 1938 he became a victim of hostile slander." A biography of Koltzov, published in 1959, is equally close-mouthed on the subject, but gives the date of his death, presumably in prison or in a labor camp. Under what circumstances it occurred is not known.

Ivan Vadimovich, a Man in the Swim

IVAN VADIMOVICH BURIES A COMRADE

Let's slow down. I have tight shoes, and we have a long way to go. Yes, it's a sad business. As recently as the first we served together on the Costs Commission. He was nervous before the report, and how glad he was that it went off smoothly! He didn't know, the poor devil, what awaited him two weeks later. Who is there up front, at the coffin? Ah, it's Kondakov! Is he from the presidium or on his own account? I've spoken to him on the phone; I've never met him. Young, though . . . A member of the presidium at such an age, not bad. Lately new people have been coming in. Unknown people. They say many are being transferred from the Party apparatus to industrial jobs. These people have great ambitions. . . . Perhaps he died in time. They were beginning to make it hot for him on the Board. Friction, with me? That's a barefaced lie. He never got in my way. I was truly shaken by his death. What a lie! I know who told it to you. It's Kruglyakovsky. No, don't deny it—clearly it was Kruglyakovsky. I don't understand why he's spreading such rumors. You're the third person I hear it from. I'll have to talk to him. . . . In a crematorium? No, this makes the third time. The first time when one of our workers died, then at Boris Grigoryevich's funeral. Weren't you there? It was a beautiful funeral. Lots of people, wreaths, music, a representative of the presidium, banners. It didn't matter to him, of course, he couldn't see it. . . . At my funeral there won't be so many people. Although, it's all a matter of organization. Much depends on the attitude of the comrades. Yes, it was beautiful! Particularly the moment when the coffin was smoothly lowered. And did you go down to the furnaces in the basement, to look in the little window? Neither did I. What kind of a spectacle is it? I don't understand. They say the corpse writhes. I have recently heard that some fools persuaded the wife of a responsible worker to look in. To feast her eyes, so to speak, on her husband. Well, of course, a fit. The idiots! On principle I don't take my wife to funerals. All the more so that her father is getting on in years. . . . Yes, that's how it is: you live, work, struggle desperately to make both ends meet, and then—please, get into a box, and they take you away. Each in his turn. Only in my case I hope it will be quick. A train wreck, for instance—one, two, three, and it's done. That's his sister-in-law. A beautiful dame, isn't she? Her husband is in a Trade Delegation or something; that's why she's so dressed up. Remind me to tell you a joke about two Jews who came to Kalinin. Counterrevolutionary, but very funny. It's interesting to know who thinks up all those stories. No, now it's awkward, it will attract attention. Better on our way back . . . They say he had had an enlarged heart for a long time. He didn't take care of himself, and here you are. I understand him very well. The same thing will happen to me. No, I have no particular ailments, but, for instance, at the height of an evening my hands will begin to itch terribly. Something incredible! Not long ago it started when I was in the theater. I was ready to leave in the middle of the act. Then suddenly it stopped. . . . Doctors—you can't get any sense out of them! Professor Segalovich says: "Try not to scratch, it's just nerves!" "Just nerves"—what does that mean? I must know what it leads to, what it threatens. Personally my health is of no importance to me, but I am a part of something, there is a big institution on my shoulders! I ask him what my diet should be, what I should, what I shouldn't eat. He says: "It's of no importance." Nothing is of any importance to them! Two absurd professions: doctors and investigators. Doctors should insure you against illness; instead they use it to torture us. It's a good thing that I myself follow a certain regimen. I take my days off, I have a warm bath after work. And here is what I advise you: on principle I don't smoke before eating. This is very important! I think I'll take my vacation early this year. Where do you expect to go? No, I'll go South again. Remind me to tell you the joke about three ladies on the beach. Yes, it's sad, sad. . . . The main thing is, he was such a good fellow. He never hurt anybody. There was nothing of the schemer in him, no desire to take advantage of others. His successor? I don't know. Officially, I don't know, but in strict secrecy I can tell you—Sventzyansky. It's settled. In fact, I put my foot in it. I congratulated Myatnikov on his new appointment. And Myatnikov, mind you, didn't deny it. He kept mum and smiled. . . . At the last moment everything was turned upside down. It is said that they demanded a strong, active man for prompt practical guidance. But it was possible to have an assistant good at practical work, and still have Myatnikov. Myatnikov, say what you may, is a figure. . . . What are you doing the day after tomorrow? Be sure to come to see us. Just so, nothing special, comrades will come in and visit awhile. We had no housewarming, so this will be something like a semidemi housewarming. We'd planned to have it this evening, but postponed it on account of the funeral. It would have been awkward, all the same. Somebody would just mention it, and they'd say: "They chose that evening to throw a party." You may come late. There will be only our own crowd. Sergey Solomonovich promised to drive in. . . . Many people are being sent off to political departments. . . . I myself would be happy to go, but they won't have me on account of my health. As soon as I unfolded the paper from the doctor, as soon as they glanced at it, they stopped talking about the matter. I was even sorry that I brought them the paper. . . . My shoes are killing me! Let's slow down, let's fall behind a little. There's my car behind us. We'll rest a bit, and just before we get to the crematorium we'll march briskly again.

IVAN VADIMOVICH ON THE FIRING LINE

Comrades, I have listened with keen attention to your discussions. If only they may be called discussions . . . I listened and almost fell asleep. Yes, comrades, almost fell asleep! I ask: why these endless arguments all over again about raw materials, fuel, labor, tariffs? Only one thing is clear from these arguments: the Lazarev factory has not fulfilled the Plan. Not fulfilled, that's all. Not fulfilled to the tune of 46 per cent. That's the fundamental fact! What is the meaning of this fact? Our Board is composed of grown-up people. I shan't indulge in demagogy with you, comrades. I shan't kick up a row, shouting that the workers are deprived of our output. That the village stores look at us reproachfully with their empty shelves. That the orders of the Red Army, our valiant fighters, have not been filled, and so on. You're grown-up people, there's no need wasting time on these well-known facts. But I will say something else. Forty-six per cent nonfulfillment —do you know what that means? You don't read the newspapers! Your minds have become cluttered with the slime of everyday hum-drum existence, comrades! But I keep up with politics! I read the papers, and let me tell you: the Central Administration of Construc-tion Supplies received four severe reprimands for 11 per cent non-fulfillment. Eleven per cent, and we have what? The entire Silicate Committee was disbanded for 20 per cent nonfulfillment. The All-Union Administration for the Marketing of Calico received a severe reprimand, the chairman was dismissed, the production manager and his deputy were expelled from the Party! In the RSFSR Administra-tion of the Clay and Faience Industries the entire Board was deprived of vacations on account of 3 per cent! In the Hard Metals Association one man was expelled, four dismissed, two forbidden to hold respon-sible positions. What? Right! Anton Fridrikhovich supplements what I said: in the same institution the Cell Bureau was disbanded and an extraordinary purge of the staff prescribed. An extraordinary purge, comrades! Ex-tra-ord-in-ary purge. In the Dairy Industries Trust three members of the Board were discharged and brought to trial, the deputy chairman was removed, the chairman transferred to another post. . . . But why mention the Dairy Industries Trust? Entire Commissariats get it in the teeth—read the papers. Well, you think they will stand on ceremony with us? They won't stand on ceremony! They won't. And what are we being offered here? Replace our representative at the factory? Obtain supplies of raw material faster? Increase the bonuses? Appoint a new director? Install a red-and-black board? Naïve, comrades! Ridiculous! Infinitely naïve and ridiculous! Why shut our eyes? Let anyone present guarantee that the factory will climb up even halfway by the end of the quarter! Not one of us can give such a guarantee. The situation is difficult. Half-measures would be nearsighted, doubly dangerous. We must act boldly, resolutely, and also farsightedly. What do I offer? We transform, rename the Lazarev factory—in a word, turn it into a group of enterprises. Yes, a combine, a trust, if you please. What? Why not? There are even smaller, local trusts. We transform it into a regional trust. Olga Maximovna, look in the files, there must be a paper from the Ivanovo Regional Committee. Dating from some time early last year, I believe. They requested us to transfer the Lazarev plant to the jurisdiction of the Region. At the time we refused categorically. And now, now we agree categorically. What? I didn't interrupt you, so be good enough to hear out your chairman and not interrupt. We turn it into a regional trust. We immediately recall our representative, so as not to prevent the local administration from taking over. We leave it to the Regional Committee to appoint a new director or keep the old. That's their business, let them be answerable! But the main thing is that we immediately remove the Lazarev establishment from our centralized financial plan. And thus, as is not hard to see, we at once change our fulfillment percentage! To separate the sick from the well—that's the meaning of the measure! Let the healthy answer for the healthy, and the sick for the sick! We amputate the rotten part of the organism and give it a chance to die or recover under conditions of timely isolation. Let the Regional Committee manage the factory, let them direct the enterprise by all the means at their disposal. Let them expel people from the Party, let them cut them to pieces. How do we come in? The factory isn't in Moscow, you know! We must do it now, immediately, instantly! We must have maximal action. There are five weeks left to the end of the quarter. When they start examining the quarter totals, let them see that we've had nothing to do with that enterprise for a long time. What? Not tricky, but wise, dear comrades! One must have brains! Brains! The pot on our shoulders must boil. Without it you and I would have been lost long ago!

IVAN VADIMOVICH LOVES LITERATURE

Sholokhov? Of course I've read him. Not everything, but I've read him. Exactly what I don't remember, but I've read him. *The Quiet Don*—is that his? Sure, I've read it. Properly speaking, I've dipped into it. I looked through it. . . . You don't have time, you know, to read every line. And, in my opinion, it isn't necessary. Personally, I only have to glance at a page and I grasp the gist. I've developed that ability by reading reports. But, generally speaking, how poor the writing is! No vigor, you know. No depth. I don't know what's the matter with them. Consider the conditions they enjoy, if you only knew! Honorariums, passes, creative leaves, traveling grants. Moreover, no responsibilities, no industrial-financial plan. Give me such conditions for six months, and what wouldn't I write! Do I have the makings? What makings do you need? If the Party assigns you to a definite sector, say literature, if you're given a chance to do your job without the Workers' and Peasants' Inspection, without investigations, without any strain on the nerves—then say thank you, and write a novel. Of course, a non-Party man must have talent. But even he is helped by the Party. Fadeyev? Is that the one from Leningrad? There's only one? I thought there were two of them. . . . Generally speaking, they are a rather eccentric lot. Completely unorganized. When Mayakovsky was still around I decided to order a poem to mark the anniversary of the merger of the Main Administration of the Faience and Chinaware Industries with the All-Union Trust for the Marketing of Pottery. I ring up and ask for Mayakovsky. "Left for six weeks." I ask who takes his place. No one, they say. How come "no one"? A man goes away for six weeks, and leaves no substitute. Does he think he's irreplaceable? With us there are no irreplaceables! I called up again once or twice—the telephone doesn't answer. In broad daylight!

Well, in a word, he shot himself. They're the type of people with an eye on the main chance. The other day I was at the Moscow Soviet— imagine, one of them requested a *dacha*.* And the way they talked to him! "We regret to say that no *dachas* are available at the moment. We regret to say that you will have to apply to the *Dacha* Trust." When he left I asked why all this "regretting." Can't he buy a *dacha* through the Foreign Trade Syndicate? They rake in the money, you know. The Academia editions? I collect them all—how cultural! They all have sateen binding with gilt edges. They say there are special numbered copies—in kid or shagreen bindings, something like that. Wonderful books! Apuleius' *Golden Goat,* or something like that. How nice! Or take Boccaccio. What a master of the word! Those people knew how to serve up smut, and how refined, cultural, fault- less . . . *The Iron Torrent?*† Of course! I read it even before the Revolution, in high school. It's one of those books I owe my political education to. . . .

IVAN VADIMOVICH ENTERTAINS

What's the matter with you, boys, I don't understand! What's the hurry? Stay a while longer? Pyotr Ilyich, it's your fault: "I have to get up early, I have to get up early." And everybody has followed you. After all, we can send Pyotr Ilyich to bed, and the rest of us can stay on. We can heat the samovar again. There are still some hors d'oeuvres left, vodka, two bottles of Durseau. Only the ashberry brandy is all gone. That's Nikita's work. There's a fine fellow for you! At the office he is so stern, but here how tenderly he began to woo the brandy. That's where Young Communist League spirit shows up! Don't you be abashed, Nikita, you funny fellow! That's the right way to act— resolutely, stopping at nothing! It's a pity Sergey Solomonovich left early, we would have asked him to establish a brandy department. And of course appoint Nikita head! Allow me, I'll find your over- coat. . . . Anyuta! Don't you hear? Ilya Grigoryevich is saying goodbye to you. She—pooped out? Who, Anyuta? Oh no, what are you saying! My Anna Nikolayevna is an amazon, a peach of a wife. You can't wear her out so easily. What? Let's have a bet: come every day. We've

* A summer house in the country.—A. Y.

† *The Iron Torrent,* a novel by Serafimovich, came out seven years after the Revolu- tion.—A. Y.

a simple household, but Anna Nikolayevna will give you food, drink, fondle you. . . . But no, Anyutka, I mean it figuratively. Your virtue is beyond suspicion. Although—what did Zhertunov keep whispering to you in a corner? Asked for vodka? Fiddlesticks! Zhertunov, speak openly, what did you demand of my lawful spouse?! Just think! He comes to see you, takes advantage of the husband's trustfulness and, in a manner of speaking, seduces the wife. . . . No comrades, I am serious: do come oftener. You know the way now. For Nikitushka we'll always have a supply of ashberry brandy. So long, Anton Fridrik-hovich! Come again, Ilya Grigoryevich! If downstairs the door is locked, knock at our Cerberus' door on the left. So long, so long! Come without fail! And oftener! So long! . . . Faugh! I'm tired. How they stayed on! What time is it? Half past three? It's a good thing Pyotr Ilyich had the good sense to take the whole gang with him. They would have stayed till eight. Neighbors from downstairs came up twice, threatened to complain to the super. How do people fail to understand that it is time to leave? Let's go to bed—to spite them all I want to come to work tomorrow early. . . . Well, how was it? In my opinion, it was quite all right. Sventzyansky was very pleased. He told Anton Fridrikhovich that he'd have stayed longer if he didn't have to prepare the report. Of course, he left to show off, really. . . . It turns out that we could have easily invited his wife too. Generally speaking, she has her own crowd, but she would have gladly come here. They say she's a sinister dame. The grub, generally speaking, turned out satisfactory. You were right, but I was afraid all the time that it would not be enough. The Piramovs were very clever. For his fortieth an-niversary the missus bought just pigs' feet, heads, all kinds of trash in the market, prepared ordinary jellied meat in washbasins—every-body liked it very much. No, do I say it was badly organized? It turned out very, very decent. Particularly the salad, it was very welcome. Let them see that we serve a homey meal, not like the Morfeyevs. They had a catered affair, could have taken everybody to a restaurant with equal success. Well, now there's an end to it all. Until May we don't invite anyone. It was impossible not to throw this party. All winter long we went visiting, gorged ourselves, guzzled—we had to recipro-cate somehow. We have reciprocated and—period. If we entertain oftener, they will start saying: "Where does he get the money to do it on?" Well, how do you like that puppy, Nikita? He threw up all over

the hall, the son of a bitch. Isn't used to the stuff. Why did we have
to invite him? Because it was necessary. Anyutka, you haven't any
political flair. Understand, Nikita is the secretary of the Young Communist League Cell. Until now he blabbed about nepotism and friendship. Now let him try and say a single word! I was guided by the same
consideration in inviting Zhertunov and Karasevich. . . . That swine,
Karasevich! He came, as though doing us a favor. But when he saw
that Sventzyansky was here, that Sventzyansky was drinking—he
melted at once! A sly chap. And Salomeya Markovna—how she
looked at her records! "Careful, don't break them, don't break them,
there are none like them left in Moscow." Just like a snake. I bet,
when she borrowed our dishes, she wasn't afraid of breaking them.
Let Dunyasha clear the table. Incidentally, what is this way she has
of snatching the plates of food from the guests' hands! A man hasn't
finished, and she snatches! And then what did your mama jabber
about to Zhertunov? A thousand times I pleaded—don't let her talk
to the guests! Let her hold her peace, or spend the night at Nadya's.
She must have bothered his head again about how she used to entertain guests. You ought to realize that people put the worst interpretation on things! He will nod assent and smile, and afterward he will
gossip maliciously about our bourgeois environment. Very well, don't
let's argue, it's as old as the hills. Did you notice how Pyotr Ilyich
shoved tangerines into his pocket? I just found it funny. But afterwards Sventzyansky wanted very much to have some tangerines, but
there were none left, and Pyotr Ilyich sat right there. I got really sore,
I could hardly control myself. You invite people, you invite them
cordially, you invite them in a comradely fashion, and they pinch
tangerines, as in some co-op.

IVAN VADIMOVICH ENGAGES IN DISTRIBUTION

No, be good enough not to interrupt me. I repeat: there must be the
right approach to everything. You can't approach anything without
the right approach. You have received the first forty majolica tea
services from the Kudryashev factory? Good. They are specimens of a
new manufactured article? Very good. Beautiful work? Excellent. You
want to distribute them? Wonderful. You have drawn up a plan of
distribution? Thanks. We have examined the plan. It is no good at

all. Not at all! Ten services to the All-Union Administration of Public Nutrition, five to the All-Union Nutrition Cooperatives, eight for RSFSR, four for the Ukraine, three each for White Russia and Transcaucasia, one for Uzbekistan . . . Two services to each Central Committee of the Trade Unions as bonuses for shock workers and the best dining rooms. There's routine for you! What a bore! What rot! How can you make such a mess of things? Which dining rooms and shock workers will you award these services to, I ask you. I just ask you! You say yourselves that each service has twelve cups, twelve saucers, a teapot, a milk jug, a sugar bowl, and a slop basin. What dining room will find twelve cups sufficient? And what shock worker will seat twelve people at his table? You don't know the working class, I tell you plainly. For an institution your service is too small, for an individual worker, too big. Such articles are not distributed in this way. All the same I'm amazed: for three years you've been under my guidance, and you haven't grown in your work! Everything must be done with maximum efficiency. You ought to realize that distribution is stocktaking. Distribution is the calculation of all the factors that must be calculated in the process. That is, in the process of distribution. Is that clear? Now let's look at it concretely: what is majolica? First of all, it's kaolin. So. Who is the chairman of the Kaolin Procurement and Marketing Trust? Petukhov. Correct. So write: five services for Comrade Petukhov, to be disposed of at his discretion. So that he knows, he feels why he gives us kaolin, what for . . . Better still, not five but eight. Let's say, six. Have you written six? How many are left? Thirty-four. Good. What else does majolica mean? Fuel. Write: eight services to the directors of the fuel establishments personally, according to Pyotr Ilyich's instructions. Then there is the Committee of Ceramic Paste. Put it down for four services. One each to the deputy chairman, the two members of the presidium, and the office manager, so that our papers don't get stuck there. The chairman? But he never looks in there, it isn't his main post. . . . Very well, let the Committee have five services. Now let's go on. What? Zhertunov always has practical ideas: let's put down two services for the Silicate Bank. What? Which publicity agencies? Oh, the press? Correct. Sensible. Note down: to the editorial office of the newspaper *Chinaware* two, no, three services. One for the staff, another personally to Pleshakov, the third personally to Okachuryan. And we must have something engraved on the services: "To the fighters for self-criticism on the glazed earthenware front," or something like that. *The Red Potter?* They won't croak without a service. A trade-union sheet, nothing more! Very well, let'em have one! Now, how many are left? Only fifteen services? What has become of all of them? They've slipped between the fingers! . . . To whom, me? A service for me personally?! You're crazy! Where do I come in? What the devil do I need this trash for? No, give it up. . . . And why just me? Anton Fridrikhovich has a large family, he needs it more than I do. And that goes for the other members of the Board. Well then, let's assign six to the Board. And put down the seventh for yourself, Olga Maximovna. You're a working member of our collective; you answer for too much through your secretarial work to be considered a mere technician. How many are left? Eight? Yes, not many. Wouldn't it be better, comrades, wouldn't it be better to avoid all this squabbling about self-provisioning? Wouldn't it be better to sacrifice two more? For the Cell and the local Party Committee. Olga Maximovna, write down two. Give them services with the same design, so they don't quarrel. So. And keep six services in reserve. Something may come up. An investigating commission may arrive, somebody may have an anniversary, or we may take some institution under our patronage. . . . Let them lie around. It's wrong to squander valuable goods!

IVAN VADIMOVICH FACES POSTERITY

Why do you put the entire polynomial in parentheses? X^2 plus $2ax$ minus $8a^2$ . . . What? I say: you divide the highest term of the dividend by the highest term of the divisor. . . . Why, yes . . . You multiply the first term of the quotient by the divisor and . . . wait . . . and you subtract the dividend from the product. That is, the other way round: you subtract the product from the dividend. What did I say? Correct: from the dividend. In this case the highest term of the remainder is not divisible by the highest term of the divisor. . . . Hm . . . So. What's the answer? An integer? Without a fraction? No, there's some error here. Perhaps a misprint in the book. Try and divide once more, Petya. I would do it for you if I had a free moment. In a minute the car will be honking downstairs, they'll be calling for me to attend a conference. In general, Petya, you don't know how good you have it. Nowadays school is a cinch. You should have tasted schooling in our time, under the czar! What a nightmare it was, what a horror! Nowadays you all but spit at your teachers. In our time we were in terror of teachers! They were simply tyrants, Petya! We called them Chaldeans. Well, who is your math teacher, for instance? Some fellow in a belted blouse, shabby and dirty, gets a hundred rubles a month, spends half a day standing in line . . . But imagine, we had Nikolay Aristarkhovich Shmigelsky—a Councilor of State, blue uniform, gold spectacles, the beard smells of eau de cologne! On holidays the scoundrel wore a sword. We boys were simply in raptures. With a teacher like that, you go to the board to explain Newton's theorem and you feel that you're in government service! Or Father Oleandrov, who taught religion . . . Another vile character! A violet cassock, rustles pleasantly, well-cared-for beard, velvety voice . . . With this son of a bitch I was always the first in catechism! No, that's a book, written by Metropolitan Philaret. The dogma and morality of Christianity in concise form, admitting of no doubt and needing no interpretation. Terrible rubbish, I still remember it all by heart! In spite of the hardships of czarist schooling, Petya, I was always at the head of my class, and I graduated from high school with a gold medal. This gave me cultural baggage for the Revolution and now for constructive work. You too must study hard. Buick? What do you mean, Buick? Why don't I have a Buick? How you jump from one thing to another! What do I need a Buick for? Do I ride in a poor car? Vitka? What if he did brag? Vitka's papa is a member of the presidium; they received four new Buicks for the presidium. Why am I not a member of the presidium? There are all kinds of reasons. This is nothing you can understand. The time will come—I too will be a member of the presidium. He asked you to go for a drive with him in the Buick? Don't you dare, you hear? I forbid you! Don't thrust yourself on them, Vitka's papa will get huffy, and I don't want to quarrel with him on account of you. Was it his papa who invited you to go for a drive? You mumble so, nobody can understand you! Who invited you— Vitka or Vitka's papa? Take your finger out of your nose. I talk to him, and he sticks half his hand into his nostril! Did he actually say: "Come, let me take both of you for a ride"? Go, by all means! What else did he say? Didn't ask about me? Not at all? Well, that's good, though. And what did you say to him? Nothing at all? Are you dumb?

Your father's comrade speaks to you, and you keep mum like a block-head. Think hard, perhaps you did say something? About what apart-ment? That's just what you said: "Your apartment is lousy, ours is much better." Idiot! Who asked you? Why do you gab, create the wrong impression about me? Anyuta, do you hear the way our darling son talks to people? No, it concerns you very much! The child is grow-ing up a degenerate, tells people the devil knows what to their faces—that must concern you! All day long I'm in the devil of a rush, I work feverishly, I don't sleep nights, I keep thinking how to better things, and here in my own home my own children stab me in the back! I insist: sit down with Petya for an hour, explain to him in an elemen-tary way what he must and what he mustn't say, if he loves his father and values his family. No, I'll sit down with him myself; you aren't any brighter than Petya. When is he going to take you for a ride? Well, the day before, you and I will have a serious talk. You're no baby any more, you are obliged to help your father in some things.

IVAN VADIMOVICH RELATES AN INCIDENT

Who, me? You dreamed it. In Kamerny Theater? I never go there. I don't know where it is! When was it? At the end of March I couldn't have had a single free evening. I lead a circle, we were winding things up. And in connection with my job there was the annual report. Physi-cally I simply couldn't have been there. Two steps away? You were either mistaken or you're pulling my leg. Yes, we know those tricks! ... In the buffet, in front of you? I was sitting? A petite? Generally speaking, if I do ... it's only with tall ones. My voice? You must have been tight. I said: "Test my strength." Is it like me to have said such a vulgar thing? All right, pull somebody else's leg. Perhaps I have a double. Well—all right, I'll tell you about it. But I beg you most earnestly: keep it a deep secret. Don't breathe a syllable of it to a soul! A dark secret. For you it's a joke; for me it may turn out far from funny. ... I wanted to confide in you myself. But I implore you: be as silent as the grave. She herself? Never in her life will she blab. In that respect she's an awfully nice dame. It simply isn't in her interest. ... Yes, at an open meeting of the Cell. It turned out that she'd been working for two years, but in the planning section—that's on an-other street. Some fool came forward to ask why Kovzyukhov, unlike the other chauffeurs, gets extra vacation and uses notes to obtain provisions. And the speaker insinuated that it was because he chauffeured me. I waited for someone to rebuff such demagogy. No one spoke up; they were all busy with other matters. I was on the point of making a factual statement when this very girl steps forward. . . . Well, in a word, Galya. She speaks sensibly, very quietly. "I am not in the Party myself," she says, "but I am surprised that in discussing such a grave question as food supply the comrades drag in various chauffeurs, various provisions, and notes. Why do they allow themselves irresponsible attacks on our leading workers?" she asks. She didn't speak quite to the point, it is true, but well enough, about obliteration of personal responsibility and about wage leveling. "He of whom much is demanded," she observed, "must be given much. Since Kovzyukhov," she said, "had the responsible job of chauffeuring Ivan Vadimovich, therefore . . ." and so on. After the meeting I leave on foot, and accidentally overtake her. We start talking—not a word about the incident, but just like that, about the epoch in general, about how interesting it is to work. I accompanied her, but not all the way to the house, so that she wouldn't get ideas into her head. Then we met again a few times. . . . Well, you know, in my institution I don't even look at anyone. I have a principle: where you feed you don't . . . Nevertheless, I see the girl is chasing me. . . . I'm not made of stone either, you know. I asked for the file on her. But I don't do such things clumsily, so as to rouse suspicion. As if by way of checking on our personal, I marked fourteen names on our list of workers and called for their papers. Hers were among them. I see by her application that everything is in order: for a number of years she worked in a children's home, then in transport; with us she's a planning instructor. Well, the wife went off to visit her relatives, and we met. She's registered as married, but doesn't live with her husband. What's remarkable about her is that she has a room with a private entrance! The door opens into a corridor right at the exit. Reads much—Zweig, Sofia Tolstoy's letters to her husband, Kogan in the original. Subscribes to the Lesser Soviet Encyclopedia. Besides—fine lingerie. That too plays a certain part, you know. Well, I didn't disgrace myself, either. She said to me . . . But, of course, this is silly—I'm simply giving you the picture—she said to me that there was much primitive strength in me. . . . But, please, not a word to anybody! It's a deep secret! And we were in Kamerny before that. A week after the Cell meeting . . . She wanted to go to the Bolshoi Theater, but I refused, politely and firmly. At the Bolshoi any dog could see us. Another important consideration: I was afraid of catching something. After all, I'm a family man. I even took measures. It turned out to be foolish. There were no grounds for apprehension. She told me that for the four months before my coming absolutely no one had been to see her. I readily believe her. What's pleasing about her: she makes no demands. "I am aware," she says, "of the distance between us, and," she says, "let it always remain so." Only one thing—she has been made secretary of the section; in the common room, where she had been working, the noise gave her a headache. . . . Well, a couple of times Kovzyukhov took her some provisions. And I promised her a little firewood—a person has to have heat. "I want nothing from you, darling," she says, "except what I cannot get by myself." Say what you may, but such an attitude is pleasant. . . . I beg you, don't get it into your head to say a word in Anna Nikolayevna's presence, even in jest! She understands no jokes, she takes everything seriously. Her approach to all such questions is extremely primitive!

IVAN VADIMOVICH CANNOT SLEEP

What time can it be now? Anyuta didn't believe that we had mice. Shall I wake her up and have her listen? No, it isn't worth it, she'll start gabbing; then I surely won't fall asleep. How wretchedly these cooperative houses are built! You can hear literally everything. A gramophone . . . That must be at Bodarchuk's—it's a sendoff, since he's assigned to work in an outlying province. Last spring I too was almost dispatched to a district like that. I barely crawled out of it! Although . . . In those regions people live too. I would be coming to Moscow to attend conferences. Out there I would ride horseback. I should go horseback riding—I'd lose weight. Piramov is stouter than me. He has a regular corporation; with me it's just starting. And I used to be so slim. How I used to dive into the river from the float! Now I couldn't dive like that. Although, perhaps I could. What was the name of the river? Serebryanka . . . I ought to answer Serebryakov's query tomorrow—the paper has been lying about for two weeks. Serebryakov. There is also a Serebrovsky. He's in the Central Administration of Gold Mining. Strange: Serebrovsky* in the Central Administration of Gold Mining. And the other way round: Zolotovsky† in the Central Administration of Silver Mining. Not very funny. The devil knows what gets into your head at night! I must go to sleep! Petya moans in his sleep. I wasn't able to solve his problem for him, was I? I lied saying I had no time. He guessed it, I think, but said nothing. Funny—Petya is a little fellow, but he already protects me, tries not to offend me. I'm getting old. His handwriting is already like mine. It's interesting to think what Petya will be like at my age. By then there's sure to be a classless society already. Damn it, how I've neglected the Marxist circle! I cut the fourth meeting. I must prepare, read something. There'll be a purge soon. . . . No, that isn't worth thinking about. Although, no, it's better to prepare for the worst. Karasevich is sure to speak against me. What if I was to transfer him to the Rostov office? He'll guess, the swine! He'll come to Moscow on purpose to be present when I'm purged! How vile it is to feel that somewhere nearby an enemy lives and breathes! It's like a thorn in your flesh. I have many of them. If I could get a leave for a year. No, that's not long enough. For ten. Even for five years . . . The way they do it in the West: "He announced that he was withdrawing from politics." It's interesting—how would I have lived if there'd been no Revolution? I would have graduated from law school and become an attorney. I would have stayed on in Penza, perhaps. How strange it was last year when I found myself in the park where Olga and I used to neck! Where is she now? During the war she was a nurse. Had a good time with officers . . . Me she almost stopped to greet. Then she must have made off for foreign parts. Beautiful, damn it! If she hadn't run away I'd have married her. There was no one else in Penza she could have married; I was the only one to make good. Yashka Kiparisov behaves decently now. Yet only recently he was taking liberties with me—on the ground that we used to fly pigeons together. There are lots of people I did things with! It was smart of me to have cold-shouldered him. . . . I have let the winter slip by again, skated only twice. And I promised myself: twice a week! How many broken resolutions! To skate, stop smoking, read *Capital*, break with Galya, study English, fire Kovzyukhov . . . To drive out of town with

* *Serebro* means silver.—A. Y.
† *Zoloto* means gold.—A. Y.

Petya—well, that's a trifle. To master technics. To control myself when Anyuta irritates me. Isn't she ashamed to be so nasty to me! If I should die, then she'd learn how bitter life could be! This very Anton Fridrikhovich, who sticks to her like a wet shirt, wouldn't want to place her even as a typist. They're all fair-weather friends! Well, I'm no better. When Yanushkevich was expelled, I cut him in the reception room. He must be sore! I'll have to invite him to tea. Only alone, so there should be no talk. . . . They're sure to rehabilitate him soon. . . . What if I were to be expelled? I'd shoot myself. No, perhaps not. What would I do with myself? Nowadays wherever you go you must have technical knowledge. What could I be? Perhaps a consultant . . . But on what problems? No, they won't expel me. It couldn't be. And what if they do all of a sudden? People are being expelled. Can they all be worse than me? If you count to a thousand, they say, you fall asleep. . . . One, two, three, four, five, six, seven . . . No, it's disgusting. . . . Dunyashka hasn't come home yet. She lives with a Young Communist Leaguer, the cow! I must tell her not to bring him here. Stupid—a member of the Young Communist League in my kitchen! But I can't very well have him in the dining room! Maybe I should read a book? No, Anyuta will wake up—it'll be worse.

BORIS AGAPOV
(b. 1899)

In his youth a member of a literary coterie that went by the name of Constructivists, this author has engaged in journalism and written literary criticism. He was an editor of the monthly *Novyi mir* at the time when it rejected Pasternak's novel *Doctor Zhivago*. The automobile plant that figures in the piece below, published in 1934, was built in 1930–1932 (and named for Vyacheslav Molotov) in the city of Gorky, formerly Nizhny Novgorod, situated at the confluence of the Oka and the Volga.

Let's Raise Our Glasses

The talk lasted late into the night. The best-trained mind could not hold all that was recounted. My cubicle, full of tobacco smoke, sailed the Volga night, steered by dozens of topics.

Devotees of bodies came, fanatics about carburetors, champions of springs, doctors of driving. Blueprints rustled on my desk, foreign catalogs were slammed, pencils broke. "De luxe!" an enthusiast would exclaim. "Look at the mudguard, darling!"

Yes, it was a mudguard!

How it rolled under the radiator! How, flowing back from the headlight, it skirted the front wheel, barely covering it, then extended, turning into a step, then formed a wave over the rear tire and recoiled ever so slightly, as if leaving a trace of its flight in the air. It did fly, by God! It rushed forward and hummed gently.

"Here! Look at this automobile!"

Oh, it was an automobile! I swear, I heard the swish of its tires on the highway; it was like the sound of water spurting from a pump. How it differed from its ancestors, which rose perpendicularly over the plane of the road, which emerged from their garages to fight space, thrusting out their chests with the naïve directness of youth. Now it squatted, crouched as though preparing to leap, exposed itself to the pressure of air currents, and they molded it for a speed of 120 miles an hour, these transparent, raging sculptors: the headwinds. She moved on the glossy paper of the catalogs, sinuous, resilient, surrounded by blossoming turbulences, ready to ride into the letterpress, roll off onto the desk and go through the wall.

"Look at our buses! Look at our bodies, our casting shops, our grinding, stamping, forging. . . ."

"De luxe! Special!" Hell, my head swelled, my eyes blinked; I had no time to design bodies, while devising fuel mixtures, taking part in races, calculating cutting speeds. These people were tireless; they discussed automobile shapes with the ardor of voluptuaries; they argued about speed with the passion of gamblers. Their wives and mothers were miserable:

"Semyon, not another word about the plant!"

"Moisey, you're killing me with the crankshaft."

The dream of the automobile, of millions of automobiles, already half realized, suffused the entire grandiose plant and animated everyone I met.

From my window I saw in the distance the huge, beloved plant, which had been built before my eyes. When a snowstorm whistled overhead and hares crouched in their burrows, afraid to crawl out into the slashing blizzard, I would step under the glass sky of the shops, into a world, organized, functioning, purged of arbitrariness; my throat tightened with a most sentimental, most schoolboyish emotion —the kind you feel when you suddenly come upon good lines of verse or when you return to camp after a difficult march and find yourself at home, among your own. Like a Utopian vision, rectangular prisms of luminous ice, which four years ago did not exist, rise in the darkness. They look lusterless because the glass on the walls is misted, and they ring with noise. About us Nature has not changed: the complex of winds, frosts, forests is as chaotic and absurd as before, but a certain amount of brute matter has been gathered together, cast into new shapes, organized at man's will, and now lives a life as different from the former one as the existence of an organism differs from that of stones and of fire. This new, luminous excrescence on the desert rests on a concrete foundation, extends upward in the steel of machines and, further, in the convolutions of the brain and the nerves that blossom like flowers near the metallic branches, and pulsate in thousands of men.

Oh, these men! How I love to watch them from a corner of a shop. On our day off, I might have a ski race with them, or a glass of wine, or we would dance till we dropped. Now they are at work. Their manner of walking, of holding themselves, of talking, is the same and yet different. Their biographies may be read in it. Rolled-up sleeves, overalls stiff as tarpaulin and furnished with brass buckles, a pipe or a cigar in the mouth—these are our Americans, boys who had been to Detroit. They brought from there a swinging gait, the habit of chewing gum and of doing everything with their own hands. Tousled hair over the forehead, an irate face, fierce wrinkles between the brows, a cheap cigarette but between the teeth. But this is Mitya! Hello, Mitya! Hello, old man, long time no see!

Above the tents lanterns suspended from posts pressed the camp against the earth with their light. The tarpaulin of the tents flapped, and so did the wash hung out to dry; the field kitchens smoked.

Mitya, do you remember the year '30?

What a windy autumn it was! The water of the Oka kept rising; it stole up to the sand that had been piled up on the shore, threatened to carry off the logs and planks. The port rang with the whistles of tugboats; a star blazed on a tall elevator; hundreds of lanterns screwed the red-hot drills of their reflections into the water. Kaisers were unloading cement; Brown hoists were unloading lumber; the piles of gravel and sand were growing. During the day the sun was fierce, and in the holds the heat was unbearable. Blue cement smoke was choking you. You'd tear off the respirator—it only made things worse, and heave up a sack and lay it on Petka's back and slap his backside with a wet palm: get going! Then Vera and Katya would lay a sack on your back, and burst into tears!

"What's wrong, girls?"

"Tired."

A solution of cement and tears flowed down their cheeks, and Vera lifted her skirt to wipe her mug, and her knees looked so childish that you could find no words.

At night you made a speech and said: "Fellows, the girls are really unable to work."

"And what about the plant?" you were asked. Of course, the plant demanded lumber and cement.

"We aren't tired," the girls said; "we can still go on working."

"Replace the girls," the secretary ordered. And everyone's load was increased one-third.

The sun would rise. It would kindle the yellow sashes of the wooden towers, reach the copper parts of pumps, and finally plunge into the river in a torrent of scaly flame. And without enough sleep, you would put the cushion on your round shoulders again, make for the harbor, and walk the gangplank between the bank and the barge, keeping your balance under the weight of the log. One arm embraced it, the other was stretched out like a blind man's. And it is good that your dad passed on to you this square chest, the short legs with the heavy calves, your whole stout frame, inherited from generations of longshoremen and tillers of the soil. With high cheekbones, lowbrowed, broad-footed, rotund, tough: there you were, the whole of you covered with the sunny vaseline of sweat, and there was a red beard under your nipples. You were not yet much of a hand at reading, but even then you were a grand dancer. After a mad tap dance you would suddenly stop as though astonished by the big toe of your right foot; you would freeze and, your face assuming an unctuous expression, you would dance without budging from the spot: your body motionless, the balls of the muscles on your back, your arms, your chest under the silken skin would boil up in time with the whisper of the accordion. One was tempted to slap you between the shoulder blades, to make the tent ring with the sound. Yes, Mitya, that was a fierce autumn! Our minds weren't on dancing!

What had brought you to the harbor? Bread didn't come easy here; there was no soft bed, and the ruble didn't go far. "Mobilization of the Komsomol!" was your answer. True. And what else? And a dream: it was rumored that cars were going to be made in Gorky. An automobile plant was going to be built, new, huge, marvelous. To work in this plant. To make automobiles. To take your stand with a shining tool at a bench: now I am not a longshoreman, not a shepherd; I am a trained worker. Thus boys dreamed of running away to America to become Indian chiefs. Simultaneously, moved by a like dream, hundreds of boys your age came from Kursk and Cheboksary, from the Ukraine and northern Caucasus. They left their local Komsomol organizations, came to Gorky, and found themselves in another Komsomol organization. Here they met Grisha Perekhodnikov.

Small, swarthy, puny, nervous, he was the head of the commune. Common paybook, common kitchen—everything the same for all, the *kasha* [gruel] and the blanket, hunger and cold. Cots on the earthen floor, here too the chairman's desk. Overhead, under the roof of the tent, bunches of tin teakettles and mugs rang in the wind. Bright kerchiefs of Ukranian girls, skirts of Chuvash girls with unbelievable flounces, talk in ten languages. "Hello, comrades, where shall I put you?" and Grisha made out papers: some he assigned to barges, others to freight cars, a hundred men to unload gravel. Himself still a boy, he was in charge of the lives of a thousand youths—their beds, their pants, their training, discipline, morals. The commune soon became indispensable to the construction project. Its crews appeared in the sectors where the work went badly. Longshoremen swore at you for exceeding their production quotas; laborers threatened to beat the daylights out of you for working with such ardor. Mr. Miter, an American, drove in to marvel at you. And you stopped with a sack on your shoulders and stared at his Buick. The tires hissing on the sand, he applied the brake sharply; smoke issued from under the rear wheels, the horn blared, the windows and the mudguard glistened. An automobile! A car, a dream on rubber tires.

I'll make one!

But first it was necessary to haul logs, and planks as well, and no end of other things, heavy, awkward, rough. Then it was necessary to dig foundation pits, to cut and knock together wooden forms for the concrete, to lay bricks. How little this resembled the dream of the automobile! And plastering. There were no plasterers, and they were essential. The instructor from the Central Institute of Labor lined up the boys as for gymnastics. On a volley-ball field they stood in single file, each with a bucket and a trowel. Bend right—scoop; bend left—spread. Scoop, spread. One, two. At first they practiced on plain clay. People took offense: automobile workers, and they had to mess about with muck. Then a quota: 2½ meters a day per man. Those were the walls of the houses in which you were to live. The walls of the shop where you were to work. The rate of 6½ meters was attained—that of an experienced plasterer. In the same way carpenters and masons were

317

trained. "The Perekhodnikov Commune on the construction job"—that sounded as "the Kotovsky Division"* used to sound at the front.

In essence, it was a battlefront. The muddy foundation pits, dug in the cold, were your trenches; the concrete mixers your fieldpieces; the pneumatic hammers your machine guns. You lived like a division: at the crack of dawn—reveille, roll call. Then you took up your positions by company and squad. Tents, army songs, fatigue, no sentiments. The second generation of the revolution was going into battle through cement smoke, amidst the crash of explosions, the screeching of machines. Happy are those who had the courage not to hide in the rear, who threw themselves into the thick of the difficult struggle that the country faced. They will always carry in their hearts the badge of battle memories, which will never let them slip, turn tail. They will always be abreast of the age, for which they bled and sweated. Mitya, everything was still before you, but how much you already had done in your twenty-two years!

Here comes an excursus on the metallurgy of pig iron and steel. This is followed by an account of a visit to a wing of the automobile plant in which malleable cast-iron parts are manufactured. The machinery is described in detail, and its working is explained to the visitors by an engineer, who turns out to be none other than the Mitya who worked as a stevedore when the plant was under construction.

The glorious Perekhodnikov commune celebrates its third anniversary. The malleable-cast-iron shop celebrates its overfulfillment of the plan.

A conveyor is loaded with the good Volga beer and the good Volga fish. Eh, wake up; fill the glasses with beer, put the fish on the plates.

Who is the toastmaster?

Gay Shamirgon, irate Shamirgon, the engineer who heads the shop, is toastmaster. Let's raise our glasses to Bolshevik youth, to our own indomitable automobile plant, to the malleable-cast-iron shop! At first one of the most backward sections, it is now one of the foremost. Tomorrow its entire staff gets a month's leave of absence. So many holidays at once! So let's have songs, an accordion player. Girls, come out of the kitchen, bring the kids, if you got any—we'll have dancing.

"No, wait! First we must have speeches."

* The cavalry division commanded by Grigory Kotovsky, a Red hero of the civil war, from 1920 to the end of his life—he was assassinated in 1925.—A.Y.

The chairman rises and reminisces about the days when you worked as stevedores, plasterers, and carpenters. Then he speaks of how the automobile dream has come true and how the plasterers and carpenters have mastered the technique of casting. The Perekhodnikov boys would go off to take courses on the quiet, for no one wanted to lose an experienced construction worker. They returned openly as casting specialists. The staff of the shop was made up of members of the commune. We lacked equipment; instead of American steam shovels, spades were used; parts were carted all over the plant in search of cutting and cleaning machines. And now . . .

"And where's Grisha?"

Grisha has moved to a construction site in the Urals. There he is in his element again.

"Shamirgon has the floor!"

"Speak, Semyon Agarych!"

In his speech the engineer expatiates on the mistakes he and the workers under him had made in building the shop, on the difficulties they had overcome by dint of hard work, and because they were not handicapped by old buildings and old equipment, and because, too, they took advantage of American experience. ("We took from America the best it has.") He winds up thus:

"Now the quality of our production approximates that of what the best American plants turn out. We've won out, boys. So let's raise our glasses to the commune, to the shop, to the rest you've earned!

"Long live the shop!

Long live the commune!

Long live dances!"

And now came dancing. And accordion playing and clapping. The floor creaked, singing rang out. Then Mitya stepped forward. He took off his jacket, froze to the spot, spread his hands; his face took on an unctuous expression, and he stared in amazement at the dandyish tip of his polished shoe. And then he flung into a dance and went on dancing, so that the girls screamed with delight. The walls were decorated with glossy pictures. They showed views of the automobile that the plant would produce shortly—an "extra special, de luxe" model, a dream on rubber tires. Black, lacquered, it flew over the smooth highway, and at the wheel sat Mitya with the most beautiful girl in the country.

VASILY GROSSMAN
(b. 1908)

An alumnus of the University of Moscow, this author has published short stories as well as a novel about the activities of the prerevolutionary Bolshevik underground. But the central theme of his writings is the Soviet-German war, especially the Stalingrad campaign, which is the subject of *For a Just Cause*, his most substantial work of fiction, as well of another novel, which is in preparation.

Here are two of a group of sketches on the defense of Stalingrad (now Volgograd), written by Grossman while he was on the spot from September, 1942, to January, 1943, as a war correspondent. A month later a German rout brought the Battle of Stalingrad to an end. The text has been somewhat abridged to eliminate repetitions and certain details.

FROM Stalingrad

1. THE LINE OF THE MAIN ATTACK

At night the regiments of Colonel Gurtyev's Siberian Division moved into position. There has always been something grim and severe about the factory called "The Barricades" that they were defending, but nowhere in the world could a grimmer sight have been seen than that which met the men's eyes on that October morning of 1942: the dark bulk of the shops, the wet glistening rails already touched with rust in spots, the jumble of shattered freight cars, the piles of steel pillars scattered in confusion over a yard as spacious as the chief plaza of a capital, the heaps of coal and slag, the mighty smokestacks pierced in many places by German shells. Craters dug up by aerial bombs yawned dark in the asphalted ground and, wherever you looked, were fragments of steel rent by the force of the explosions as though they were so many thin strips of calico.

The division was to take its stand in front of this plant and to remain there to the death. Behind it were the dark, icy waters of the

Volga. Two regiments defended the plant itself. A command post was set up in the concrete canal under the building of the main shops. A third regiment defended the deep ravine that runs through the workers' settlements as far as the Volga. "Death Valley" the men and the commanders called it. Yes, behind them flowed the dark, icy waters of the Volga; behind them was the fate of their country.

What in the First World War was divided between two fronts, what last year pressed with all its weight on Russia only along a front of 3,000 kilometers, this summer and this autumn was brought down with sledgehammer force on Stalingrad and the Caucasus. Moreover, here in Stalingrad the Germans further narrowed down the area of their assault. They refrained from pressing forward in the southern and central sections of the city. The full weight of their numberless batteries of mortars, their thousands of guns, and their air armadas was brought to bear on the northern section of the city, on "The Barricades" situated in the heart of the industrial district. The Germans assumed that human nature could not stand such a strain, that there were no hearts or nerves on earth that would not break in the inferno of fire, shrieking metal, shaken earth, and frenzied air. Here was assembled the entire diabolical arsenal of German militarism: heavy and flame-throwing tanks, six-barreled mortars, armadas of dive bombers with howling sirens, splinter and demolition bombs. Here submachine gunners were provided with explosive bullets, artillerymen and mortar men with thermite projectiles. Here was assembled German artillery from small-caliber antitank submachine guns to heavy long-range fieldpieces. Here were fired shells looking like harmless green and red little balls and aerial torpedoes that dug craters the size of two-story houses. Here night was bright from the glare of conflagrations and flares, and day dark with the smoke of burning buildings and German smoke screens. Here the din was as dense as earth and the rare moments of quiet seemed more terrible and sinister than the roar of battle. . . .

"The line of the main attack"—no words are more terrible to a military man than these. War has no more frightful words, and it was not for nothing that on that gloomy autumn night it was Colonel Gurtyev's Siberian Division that took up the defense position in the factory region. Siberians are sturdy folk, stern, inured to cold and hardships, taciturn, fond of order and discipline, blunt of speech.

Siberians are dependable, rugged folk. In grim silence they dug into the stony earth with their picks, cut embrasures in the walls of the factory buildings, made dugouts, bunkers, and communication trenches, preparing for a stand to the death. . . .

Scarcely had the division dug itself into the rocky Stalingrad soil, scarcely had the division staff installed itself in the deep shelter hollowed out in a sandstone cliff rising above the Volga, scarcely had the telephone wires been laid and the keys of the wireless transmitters connecting the command posts with the artillery firing points across the Volga begun to tap, scarcely had the darkness of night given way to the light of dawn, when the Germans opened fire. For eight hours on end Junker-87's dive-bombed the division's defenses; for eight hours on end, without a minute's respite, German aircraft kept coming over wave after wave; for eight hours on end sirens howled, bombs whistled, the earth shook, the remains of brick buildings crashed; for eight hours on end the air was filled with clouds of smoke and dust, and deadly splinters shrilled. Whoever has heard the wail of air made white-hot by aerial bombs, whoever has lived through a harrowing ten-minute raid of German aircraft, will have some idea of what eight hours of intense dive-bombing mean.

For eight hours on end the Siberians used all their weapons against the German aircraft, and something akin to despair must have seized the Germans when from the burning earth of this factory region, wrapped in a dark pall of dust and smoke, rifle volleys stubbornly continued to crack, bursts of machine-gun fire to come, antitank rifles to yelp and antiaircraft guns to discharge evenly, viciously. It seemed as though everything alive must be crushed, destroyed; but the Siberian Division, having dug itself in, did not bend, did not break, and continued to fire—stubborn, deathless. The Germans brought heavy regimental mortars and artillery into action. The monotonous hissing of mortar bombs and the scream of shells joined the howl of sirens and roar of bursting aerial bombs. This lasted until nightfall. In mournful, grim silence the Red Army men buried their dead. That was the first day—the housewarming. Never for a moment throughout the night did the German artillery and mortar batteries fall silent, and hardly anyone slept.

That night, at the command post, Colonel Gurtyev met two old friends whom he had not seen for over twenty years. They had parted as young, unmarried men, and now they met again—their hair already gray and their faces wrinkled. Two of them commanded divisions, and the third, a tank brigade. They embraced, and the men standing around—the chiefs of staff, adjutants and majors—saw tears in the eyes of these gray-headed men. "It's fate! it's fate!" they exclaimed. And indeed, there was something majestic and moving in the meeting of these men who had been friends in their youth, at this grim hour, amid the burning factory buildings and ruins of Stalingrad. Their path must have been the right one, since they met again in the fulfillment of a lofty and painful duty.

All night long the German artillery thundered, and scarcely had the sun risen above the earth plowed by German iron, when forty dive bombers appeared, and again sirens howled, and again a cloud of dust and smoke rose above the plant, covering the ground. The factory buildings, the shattered railway cars, and even the tall factory stacks were lost in a black fog. That morning Markelov's regiment emerged from its hideouts, shelters, and trenches, quit the stone and concrete bunkers, and took the offensive. The battalions moved forward over mountains of slag, over the ruins of houses, past the granite building of the factory office, across a railway track and a suburban garden. They walked past thousands of hideous pits dug by bombs, and overhead was the inferno created by the German aerial army. An iron gale struck them in the face, and still they pressed on. And again a superstitious fear seized the enemy: "Were they human beings, these attackers? Were they mortals?"

Yes, they were mortals. Markelov's regiment advanced one kilometer, took up new positions, and dug in. Only here in Stalingrad do men know what a kilometer means. It means a thousand meters, a hundred thousand centimeters. At night the regiment was attacked by greatly superior German forces. Battalions of German infantry and heavy tanks moved down upon the regiment's positions; German machine guns flooded them with iron. Drunken submachine gunners advanced with the stubbornness of lunatics. The story of how Markelov's regiment fought will be told by the dead bodies of Red Army men, by those who that night and the following day and again the next night heard the tattoo of Russian machine guns and the explosions of Russian grenades. The story of this battle will be told by shattered and burned German tanks and the long lines of crosses topped with German helmets, arranged by platoon, company, and battalion. Yes, they were mere mortals, and scarcely any of them survived, but they did their duty.

On the third day the German planes hovered over the division not for eight hours, but for twelve hours. They remained in the air even after sunset, and from the dark depth of the night sky came the howling voices of the Junkers' sirens and, like the heavy and frequent blows of a sledgehammer, demolition bombs crashed upon the smoking, flaming earth. From dawn to dusk German guns and mortars battered the division's defenses. A hundred German artillery regiments were at work in the Stalingrad area. At times they staged a solid barrage; at night they kept up a methodical, exhausting fire. They were aided by mortar batteries. It was the line of the main attack.

Several times during the day the German guns and mortars suddenly fell silent, and the crushing dive-bombing suddenly ceased. A strange silence would set in. And then observers would cry out, "Attention!" The men at the outposts would reach for bottles of incendiary fluid; tank busters opened their canvas cartridge pouches, submachine gunners wiped their guns with their palms, grenade throwers moved the grenade crates closer. These brief moments of quiet did not mean a respite. They preceded an attack. Soon the clatter of hundreds of caterpillars and the muffled drone of motors announced the approach of tanks, and the lieutenant in command would shout:

"Attention, comrades! German submachine gunners are filtering through on our left flank."

At times the Germans approached as close as thirty to forty meters, and the Siberians could see their grimy faces, their ragged coats, hear their guttural threats and jeers; and after the Germans had retreated, dive bombers would again swoop down on the division, and guns and mortars would resume their fiery blasting with redoubled fury.

Our artillery rendered yeoman service in repulsing the repeated German assaults. Fugenfirov, the commander of one of the artillery regiments, and the commanders of the brigades and batteries stayed with the battalions and companies on the front line. Wireless connected them with the firing points, and scores of powerful long-range guns on the left bank of the Volga lived and breathed with the anxieties, calamities, and joys of the infantry. The artillery worked miracles. It covered infantry positions with a cloak of steel. It worked havoc with the superheavy German tanks that defied the tank busters. Like a sword it cut off the submachine gunners clinging to the armor of the tanks. It came down on the hidden concentration posts, blasted ammunition dumps, and blew German mortar batteries sky high. Nowhere did the infantry feel the friendship and aid of the artillery as in Stalingrad.

In the course of a month, the Germans launched one hundred and seventeen attacks at the regiments of the Siberian Division. There was one terrible day when the German tanks and infantry attacked twenty-three times, and all twenty-three attacks were repulsed. Every day, except three, in the course of the month, German aircraft strafed the division for ten to twelve hours at a stretch; the number of bombs dropped amounting to tens of thousands. And all this on a front one and a half to two kilometers long. The roar was enough to deafen all mankind; the fire and metal were enough to burn, to destroy a whole state.

The Germans thought they would shatter the morale of the Siberian regiments. They thought they had pierced the barrier of endurance of human hearts and nerves. But—an astonishing thing—the men did not bend, did not go out of their minds, did not lose control of their hearts and nerves, but became even stronger and more self-possessed. The taciturn, rugged Siberians grew even more grim and taciturn; their cheeks caved in; their eyes stared gloomily. Here, on the line of the Germans' main attack, in the brief moments of respite, no light banter or song or accordion music was heard. Men were laboring under a superhuman strain. There were times when they went without sleep for three or four days on end, and it was with sinking heart that Colonel Gurtyev, in talking to his men, heard one soldier say quietly: "We've got everything, Comrade Colonel: 900 grams of bread and hot meals brought up in thermoses twice a day without fail, but somehow we don't feel like eating."

Gurtyev loved and respected his men, and he knew that when a soldier says, "I don't feel like eating," it really must be going hard with him. But by now Gurtyev was not worried; he knew that there was no force on earth that could dislodge the Siberian regiments. In the course of these battles, his men and officers had gained a great and cruel experience. The defenses were stronger and more efficient than ever. In front of the factory shops a regular maze of engineering works had sprung up—dugouts, communication trenches, foxholes. Fortifications had been pushed far forward beyond the buildings. The men had learned to perform swift, concerted underground maneuvers—to concentrate or disperse, to pass from the buildings to the dugouts and back by the communication trenches, depending on where the enemy aircraft struck or where his tanks and infantry launched their attacks.

Underground "feelers," "tentacles" were constructed; tank busters made their way along these to the heavy German tanks that stopped within a hundred meters of the buildings. Sappers mined all the approaches to the plant. Men carried the mines in pairs under their arms like loaves of bread. The distance of six to eight kilometers from the riverbank to the factory was completely under fire. The mining itself was effected in complete darkness in the small hours, often within meters of enemy positions. Thus some two thousand mines were planted in the ruins of houses shattered by bombs, in heaps of heavy stones, in craters. Thus men learned how to protect large buildings from the first to the fifth stories by means of a curtain of fire. They set up cleverly camouflaged observation posts under the very nose of the enemy. For defense purposes they utilized bomb craters and the whole complex subterranean sewerage system under the factory buildings. Cooperation between the infantry and the artillery improved daily, and sometimes it seemed as if the Volga no longer separated the canon from the regiments and that the Argus-eyed guns which instantly responded to every movement of the enemy were right there beside the infantrymen.

Together with experience came the inner tempering of men. The division was transformed into a single organism working with singular perfection and astonishing unity. The men themselves were not aware of the psychological changes that had taken place in them during the month they had spent in this inferno, in the forward positions of the great Stalingrad defense line. It seemed to them that they were just what they had always been. In their rare free moments they scrubbed themselves in underground bathrooms; they were brought their hot meals in thermoses as usual, and the heavily bearded Makarevich and Karnaukhov, looking like peaceful village postmen, continued under fire to carry to the forward position in their leather pouches newspapers and letters from far-off Omsk, Tyumen, Tobolsk, and Krasnoyarsk villages. The men spoke of things that had concerned them as carpenters or blacksmiths or peasants. They jeeringly called the German six-barreled mortars "boobies," the dive bombers with their sirens, "screechers" and "musicians." It seemed to them that they had not changed, and only a newcomer from the opposite bank would look at them with respectful awe as men inaccessible to fear; only an onlooker could appreciate the iron strength of these Siberians, their indifference to death, their cool determination to bear the harsh lot of men holding the defense line to the death.

Heroism had become the style and manner of the daily life of this division. Heroism became an everyday affair, a commonplace. Heroism in everything—in the work of the cooks peeling potatoes under a scorching fire of thermite shells. Great heroism marked the work of the Red Cross nurses, high-school girls from Tobolsk, who dressed wounds and brought water to the wounded men at the height of battle. Yes, if you were to look with the eyes of an outsider, you would see heroism in every ordinary movement of the men of this division. It would be seen in Khamitzky, the commander of the Signalers' Platoon, as he sat peacefully on a slope near the dugout reading a novel while roaring German dive bombers were pounding the earth. It would be seen in Liaison Officer Batrakov who carefully wiped his spectacles, placed reports in his dispatch case, and set off on his twelve-kilometer tramp through "Death Valley" as coolly and calmly as if he were going for a quiet Sunday stroll. It would be seen in Submachine Gunner Kolosov who when a bomb burst in his dugout and buried him up to his neck in earth and debris winked merrily at Assistant Commander Spirin. It would be seen in Klava Kopylova—the buxom, red-cheeked Siberian staff typist—who sat down to type the battle order and was buried under debris. She was dug out and moved into another bunker to continue her typing, but was covered with debris again and dug out a second time; undismayed, she moved into a third dugout, finished typing the order, and brought it to the divisional commander for his signature. Such were the people who stood in the line of the main attack.

At the end of the third week the Germans launched a decisive attack on the plant. Preparation for this attack was such as the world has never witnessed before. For eighty hours at a stretch, aircraft, heavy mortars, and artillery were at work. Three days and three nights turned into a chaos of smoke, fire, and din. The hissing of bombs, the screeching roar of shells from six-barreled "boobies," the rumble of heavy shells, the long-drawn-out scream of sirens alone could overwhelm men, but all this was a mere prelude to the thunder of explosions. The jagged flame of these explosions blazed in the air, and the shriek of tormented metal pierced space. This lasted for eighty hours. Then the preparation came to an end, and immediately, at five o'clock in the morning, German heavy and medium tanks, drunken hordes of submachine gunners, and infantry regiments launched the attack proper. The Germans succeeded in breaking into the plant; their tanks roared at the walls of the buildings; they split up our defenses and cut off the command posts of the division and the regiments from the forward position.

It would seem that, deprived of its commanders, the division was bound to lose its capacity for resistance and that the command posts, now directly under the enemy's blows, were doomed to destruction. But an astonishing thing happened: every trench, every dugout, every rifle pit and fortified ruin of a house turned into a stronghold with its own command and its own communication system. Sergeants and privates took the place of disabled commanders and skillfully and efficiently repulsed attacks. At this dire and perilous hour, commanders and staff officers turned their command posts into forts and themselves beat off attacks like soldiers in the ranks. Chamov repulsed ten attacks. The gigantic, redheaded tank commander who defended Chamov's command post, having fired his last round, scrambled out of his tank and attacked the approaching submachine gunners with a shower of stones. The regimental commander himself manned a mortar gun. Regimental Commander Mikhalev, the division's favorite, was killed when a bomb scored a direct hit on his command post. "Our father is killed," said the Red Army men. Major Kushnaryov, who took Mikhalev's place, transferred his command post to a concrete main that ran beneath the plant. For several hours Kushnaryov, Dyatlenko—his Chief of Staff—and six commanding officers fought at the entrance to this pipe. They had several cases of hand grenades, and with these they repulsed every attack of the Germans.

This battle, unparalleled in its ferocity, lasted for several days and nights. It was no longer fought for individual houses and factory buildings, but for every step of a staircase, for a corner in some narrow passage, for a machine, for an aisle between machines, for a gas main. Not a single man in the division abandoned his position in this battle. And if the Germans did succeed in capturing some particular spot, it indicated that not a single Red Army man had survived there to defend it. All fought like the giant redheaded tank driver whose name Chamov never learned, like Sapper Kosichenko, who pulled the safety rings from the hand grenades with his teeth, his left hand having been shattered. It was as if the dead had passed on their strength to the survivors, and there were moments when ten resolute bayonets successfully held an area that had been defended by a whole battalion. Time and again factory buildings passed from the hands of the Siberians to the Germans, only to be recaptured by the the Siberians. In this battle the Germans succeeded in occupying a number of buildings and factory shops. The German attacks attained maximum intensity. Their drive along the line of the main attack reached its highest potential. It was as though, having lifted too great a weight, they had broken some inner springs that were part of the mechanism of their battering ram. The curve of the German pressure began to dip.

Three divisions fought against the Siberians. Their infantry attacks cost the Germans five thousand lives. The Siberians had successfully stood this superhuman strain. . . . They held the line to the death; they did not look back; they knew: behind them was the Volga, the fate of the country. [*November 20, 1942*]

2. THE NEW DAY

On the afternoon of December 16th a high wind sprang up in the northwest. The dark rain clouds lost their vapor and rose, turning to feathery wisps. The fog, freezing, outlined in downy white the wires of the military telegraph and the trees on the riverbank that had been closely cropped by mine splinters. The puddles in the shell craters began to glaze, as films of ice spread over them, and a frost pattern crept across the windshields of the trucks fronting north. Hoarfrost settled lightly on the dark bodies of heavy shells and bombs stacked in the pits near the east pier of the ferry. The earth became resonant, the air spacious. And in the west, above the tattered stone lace of the dead city, the sunset glowed red.

Driven by the wind, pulled by the current, a huge thousand-foot ice floe was moving down the Volga. It crept past Spartanovka, past the ruins of the Tractor Plant defiled by the enemy; then it began to turn slowly about, and close to the "Red October" factory stopped dead, its broad shoulders wedged against the shore ice on the east and west banks of the river.

Carefully pushing aside the stars, the moon rose in a clear sky, and everything white in the world became dimly blue; the moon alone shone brilliantly white, as though it had sucked up all the whiteness of the snow on the steppe. And the wind kept rising, cold and cruel, rejoicing thousands of hearts.

The current, impeded by the floe, sought a path closer to the river bottom, and the surface of the water began to grow a thin, crumbly crust. Within a few hours it was firm and crystalline, and that night Sergeant Titov, a sapper, walked on ice an inch and a half thick that gave and crackled underfoot: he was the first to cross from the left to the right bank of the Volga on foot.

He stepped onto the opposite bank, gazed at the vast plain stretching before him, and began to roll a cigarette. And then, just as Titov was bragging to the soldiers who crowded about him: "How did I get across? Why, I just walked over—it was a cinch," Time turned a great and tragic page in the book of the Battle of Stalingrad. The page had been written by big, strong hands that icy water had chapped, the hands of sergeants, men who loaded cartridges, pontoon builders, members of sapper battalions and motorized units, the hands of all those who for a hundred days had been ferrying back and forth across the dark-gray icy river, all the while looking into the eye of quick, cruel death. Someday a song will be made about those who sleep at the bottom of the Volga. It will be a plain, true song like the work and the death by night among black ice floes suddenly flaring up in the blue flame of exploding thermite shells or under the cold blue eyes of the "Aryan" searchlights.

It is night, and we cross the Volga on foot. The two-day-old ice no longer gives under our tread; the moon lights a network of paths, the countless tracks of sleds. The Red Army messenger who is showing us the way walks ahead of us briskly and confidently, as if he had been using these crisscross paths half his life. Suddenly the ice starts creaking; our guide halts at a wide hole in the ice, and exclaims:

"Oho, we must have gone off the track; we should have turned to the right."

Our guides almost always make this nonchalant remark, no matter where they take us. We bear right and are again on the proper path.

Small round clouds roll smoothly across the moon, and the white Volga darkens, as though strewn with gray ashes. Shell-torn barges are locked in the ice, a blue shimmer bathes the ice-encrusted cables, sterns rising sheer, the prows of smashed cutters and motorboats.

Meanwhile the factories are a battleground. The dark gutted walls are suddenly alight with the white and pink glare of gunfire. The canon reverberates with a hollow booming; the mines explode dryly in resonant waves; spasmodically the Tommy guns and machine guns inject their staccato bursts.

The music of destruction is strangely like the noise of a factory at work in time of peace: the steam hammer flattening steel ingots, rivets being pounded, scrap broken up to be fed into open-hearth furnaces, liquid steel and slag flowing into troughs and flashing a pink light on the young ice of the Volga.

The sounds of night fighting in the factory district also speak of the new page of the Battle of Stalingrad. It is no longer the elemental roar that mounted to the sky, that came crashing torrentially from heaven to earth, that poured over the vast Volga space. Now there is only sniping. The shells and tracer bullets streak in straight flashing lines among the buildings. Here is nothing like the slow, luminous hyperbolas of air warfare. Where the buildings are close together, the streaks are like flashing javelins and arrows hurled by warriors invisible in the darkness. They swiftly flash from the stone walls and they plunge into the cold stone walls, and vanish. Shells and bombs stab at German firing points, hunt out German machine gunners buried in secret, masked dugouts, and like razor blades slash the roofing of deep communication trenches. The sniper is now the hero of the fighting in the factory district, whether his weapon be a trench mortar, a field gun, a hand grenade, or an infantryman's rifle. The Germans have dug themselves into the ground, have crept into stone burrows, have dropped into deep cellars. They have crawled into concrete cisterns, into wells and sewers; they have made their way into subterranean tunnels. Only a sniper's bullet, a hand grenade aimed with precision, a thermite ball, will sting them, pluck them out, burn them out of their deep, dark holes.

It is morning, and the sun rises in a clear frosty sky above the Stalingrad that the Germans have murdered. The sun rises on the yellow sandstone of the steep riverbank. It lights up stone ruins that the shells have drilled, factory yards that were turned into battlefields where regiments and divisions met in a death grapple; it shines on the edges of huge craters punched out by blockbusters. A sullen twilight always broods over the bottom of these terrible pits. The sun fears to touch it. Smilingly the sun peers through the factory chimneys where the shells have torn holes. The sun shines on hundreds of railway tracks, where gutted water tanks sprawl like dead horses, and freight cars, upended by the force of explosions, are piled upon one another, crowded around cold locomotives like a herd in panic clinging to its leaders. The sun shines on piles of iron red with rust, on heaps of metal, the machinery of war and industry that perished in the spasms of explosions and preserved forever the instantaneous convulsion of death. The winter sun shines on mass graves, on improvised monuments, raised where the men who fell on the main line of attack rest.

The men sleep on hilltops, in gulleys and ravines, and near the ruined factory buildings; they sleep where they fought, and as a mighty memorial of their constancy, there are these graves near the trenches, the dugouts, the stone walls with gun emplacements, none of which surrendered to the enemy.

Sacred earth! One wants to remember forever this new city of the people's triumphant freedom that has grown up among the ruins, one wants to absorb it all: these underground dwellings with chimneys smoking in the sun, these interlacing paths and new roads, these heavy trench mortars lifting their muzzles amid the dugouts, all these hundreds of men in cotton-lined coats, cloaks, caps with earlaps, who are busy with the sleepless work of war, who carry bombs like loaves of bread under their armpits, who peel potatoes near the cocked muzzle of a heavy field gun, who hum, swear at each other, talk of last night's grenade fighting, who are magnificently casual in their heroism. How is one to hold lastingly in remembrance all these countless pictures, this marvelous moving panorama of the defense of

Stalingrad, the living moment of today's greatness that tomorrow will become an undying page of history!

But everything changes, and just as today's crossing is unlike yesterday's, as the night sniping in the factory district is unlike the elemental assaults of November, so this day in Stalingrad is unlike the bygone days of October and November. The Russian fighter has emerged from the earth, emerged from the stones; he is standing erect, walks calmly, unhurriedly in bright sunlight across the sparkling, icebound Volga. Swaying from side to side, the soldiers move along pulling sleds; drivers roughly urge on their horses, which step gingerly on the smooth ice. Against the snowy bulge of the left bank are etched the figures of men unloading supplies. A soldier with a leather pouch full of mail saunters along in the sunlight toward battalion headquarters, and up the hill two Signal Corps men carrying thermos bottles of soup walk upright within fifty yards of the German trenches. Yes, the soldiers have won the sunlight, have won the light of day, have won the great right to walk erect on Stalingrad earth under a blue sky. The people of Stalingrad know the cost of this victory, and they smile involuntarily as they watch the movement of troops and machines in the sun. For long months the slightest moving spot, a wisp of smoke by day, a human shape showing for a moment, drew German fire. For months the Stalingrad heavens, dominated by "Junkers" in the daytime, were no longer Russian heavens but a German hell. For months thousands of men awaited nightfall to emerge from their earthen caves and stony holes, to gulp a mouthful of fresh air, to stretch their numb arms.

Yes, everything changes, and those Germans who in September, breaking into a street, made themselves free of the houses and danced to the loud music of accordions, the Germans who drove about at night with headlights blazing and by day boldly carried supplies in trucks, those Germans have now crawled underground, hidden themselves among stone ruins. For a long time I stood on the fourth story of one of the gutted Stalingrad houses with a field glass, looking at the blocks and the factory buildings held by the Germans. Not a wisp of smoke, not a moving figure. They cannot come out into the sun; they have no daylight. They get twenty-five to thirty cartridges a day; their orders are to fire on attacking troops only; their ration is 100 grams of bread and horsemeat. They sit like hairy savages in stone caves and gnaw horsemeat in the smoky dark, among the ruins of the fair city they have destroyed, in the dead buildings of the factories that were the pride of the Soviet land. At night they crawl out of their holes, and dreading the Russian strength that is slowly strangling them, shout: "Hey, Russe, aim at the legs! Why do you aim the head?" "Hey, Russe, I'm cold; let's swap a Tommy gun for a fur cap!"

They destroyed the aqueduct with trench mortars; they hurled five hundred shells at the powerhouse; they burned everything that would burn; they wrecked schools, pharmacies, hospitals, and then they knew terrible days and nights, when, by the law of history and the will of the Russian soldier, it was their fate to meet retribution here, among icy ruins, deprived of the sun and the light of day, in the dark, with only horsemeat to chew on, without water, under the cruel stars of a Russian December night. Yes, everything changes; everything has changed in Stalingrad. The law of history is just and terrible. Unshakable is the will of our Stalingrad armies.

[*December 19, 1942*]

SERGEY ORLOV
(b. 1921)

Pause on the March

The blazing sun has made the armor hot,
Thick on our clothes the dust of the campaign.
Oh, to pull off the coveralls, and sink
Into the shady grass, but first it's plain

We've got to check the motor, lift the hatch;
Let her cool down. No matter how we feel,
Sure you and I can stand up to the worst:
We're human beings, but she's only steel.

1944

ANNA AKHMATOVA
(b. 1888)

From an Airplane

Versts by the hundred, miles by hundreds, hundreds
Of dim kilometers beneath our track:
Reaches of salt marsh, feather grass that billowed;
Beyond, the somber cedar groves showed black.

As though for the first time I saw my country,
And, with a pang of recognition, knew:
It is all mine—and nothing can divide us;
It is my soul; it is my body, too.

1944

YEVGENY DOLMATOVSKY
(b. 1915)

Frost

I wish you'd write me a letter about the frost
(You can't be warm unless there's a frost, you know),
And about the little birch tree, the bashful one,
White as white can be in its cloak of snow.

Write me about the drifts that are piled up
To a giant's shoulders, and tell me everything
About the blizzards that strike so savagely
And kiss so hotly, every kiss a sting.

Write me how thick the ice is in the stream,
And how it sparkles in moonlight; write me all
About the stove, how it crackles cozily,
And how the cricket chirps in a crack in the wall.

Be good and write me about the fire on the hearth,
All the small homely things beyond belief;
I remember how I would hold my wrist to the flame
And it looked transparent as a maple leaf.

. . . Oh, far and far away is my Russia, dressed
In silver, bridal in her bright array,
Here rains run over the sidewalks slantingly,
Spring-fashion, on a January day.

Don't look for blizzards here, don't hope to see
Fresh fallen snow. There is no winter here.
Where men wear rubbers and not thick felt boots,
And capes not overcoats at the end of the year,

Where they have radiators in every room,
Hot baths at any hour, day and night.
But I am lost with nothing to keep me warm.
Send me a snowstorm and I'll be all right.

1946

NIKOLAY ZHDANOV

*

Journey to the Old Home

This story was published in a miscellany that appeared under a Moscow imprint in 1956, when the "thaw" caused by Stalin's death three years previously was at its height. The author's first book came out in 1958.

When he returned to his office after a long and tiring conference, Pavel Alexeyevich Varygin set to examining the official papers that had accumulated in his absence (and had been handed him in a calico-bound folder by his secretary, Nonna Andreyevna). He glanced at several questionnaires and then turned to the telegrams, which usually came from outlying districts and contained various reminders and inquiries. As he read, he marked them with a blue pencil and put them aside, sheet after sheet. Now there was only one communication left, which for some reason had not been opened—obviously owing to Nonna Andreyevna's negligence. Varygin tore the paper seal himself and unfolded the slip.

"Marya Semyonovna died Wednesday the twenty-fourth, funeral Saturday," he read.

He left for the country that very night, on a slow train with two changes: there was an express only every other day, and he would have had to wait a full twenty-four hours.

Varygin's wife saw him off at the door of the apartment, kissed him on the cheek with a mournful air, and said she should perhaps say nothing to the children: they hadn't yet been given their grades for the quarter.

"As you wish," he replied, and as he walked down the stairs in the yellow light shed by the bulbs, he reflected: "For her this is just an annoying unpleasantness, nothing more."

In the train he sat on a bench next the window all the time, looking out through the muddy pane at the grayish strip of earth and the dark silhouettes of the trees rushing past.

The last time Varygin had seen his mother had been about six years earlier. She had come up from the collective farm to get "millit," as his wife mimicked her country speech afterward—she was inclined to look ironically at his country kin.

These six years, it seemed to him now, had gone by without his noticing it. One autumn he had prepared to go to the country, but his doctors recommended that he should take a cure for his heart, and he had gone to Kislovodsk for the waters.

Sometimes, very rarely, a letter came from his mother. It was written at her dictation in a childish hand, and usually on a sheet torn out of a school notebook.

"We aren't making out too good, but we don't complain," his mother would tell him. He was pained, but then it would occur to him that his mother had never had it easy and that the formula, "We make out, we don't complain" essentially sounded quite cheerful.

The train took over twenty-four hours to reach Dvoriki station. The slow November dawn had not yet banished the gray night shadows. They stuck to the low, chilly sky and hid under the station shed, where potatoes, covered with matting, were piled high, presumably awaiting shipment.

He remembered from childhood that just beyond the station there was a thin, marshy forest that stretched for some eight versts, and that beyond that lay half a dozen villages, the last one being their own: Tyurino.* But no trace of the woods remained. Varygin made his way on foot across a swampy lowland, along a fence of blackened poles.

On both sides of the path stood high, neat stacks of peat. They were apparently digging peat here. Beyond the lowland was a macadam road that had not been there before. Varygin waited for a passing truck and rode as far as the village of Lapshino.† From there he walked to Tyurino.

It turned out that his mother's body had already been taken to the churchyard. So he was told at the first hut by an elderly woman in a worn army tunic, who was carrying water from the well in wooden buckets.

"And who might you be?" she inquired, looking at Varygin's sturdy cloth coat.

"Her son," he said.

* *Tyurya* means "mush."—A. Y.
† *Lapsha* means "noodles."—A. Y.

The woman put the buckets down and looked at Varygin again.

"Not Konstantin?" she asked. "I'm Anastasya Derevlyova; you don't remember me?"

"Konstantin died long ago. I'm the other son, Pavel," he explained.

"There, just what I was saying—Konstantin was dead," the woman agreed. "But my daughter-in-law, she wouldn't hear of it, no matter what! But will you find your way to the cemetery? Most likely, you've forgotten your way about. Klashka!" she shouted to a little girl who was picking the cabbage leaves left in the beds after harvest. "Run and show the man how to get to the cemetery—straight across the fields."

Following the little girl as she ran on, Varygin trod the ground frozen hard but not yet covered with snow, stumbling heavily over the hummocks, struggling for breath, and frequently wiping sweat from his face.

They skirted a field of winter crops and walked across a crooked log spanning a stream that meandered through shrubbery. Farther on, the land rose in a gentle hillock, and against the background of the gray sky Varygin caught sight of the old wooden church and the cemetery crosses among sparse, bare trees. He remembered both the stream and the church. But now both were considerably smaller than before. He remembered, too, the water-filled pits that they had passed. Hemp used to be soaked there. The children said that house sprites hid in them.

The cemetery was not fenced, and even from a distance he noticed that someone was standing on the porch of the church.

"I'll go back now, Uncle. All right?" said the little girl, slowing her pace. "The widwife is there: your lodger. Maybe she'll tell the teacher I've been to church. I'll go back, all right?"

"Yes, go ahead," said Varygin.

When he came closer, a young woman ran down the wooden steps of the porch. Her face, reddened by the frosty air, and glowing with health, was wet with tears.

"And we thought you weren't coming," she said, as Varygin introduced himself. "We expected you on the express, at night. We went to the station. We didn't know what to do. You see, perhaps you'll be angry; I, too, am an unbeliever, but Marya Semyonovna insisted on being buried in the old, Christian way. . . ."

Removing his fur cap, and without smoothing the hair that was pasted to his forehead, Varygin entered the church, where several thin candles were burning in the semidarkness and three or four dim figures stood about.

The midwife followed him in and stood near the entrance, but he passed farther on, and suddenly caught sight of his mother's dark face, as small as a child's, lighted by the yellow glow of a candle. He halted, and stood there, motionless, seeing nothing but that face.

The priest who had sparse gray hair and a bony forehead, was reading a prayer in a singsong voice, and seemed to address himself solely to the deceased, who lay motionless, her bloodless lips compressed. The flat faces of the saints painted on the iconostasis were just visible in the darkness. There was the smell of incense, and that smell, like the archaic scriptural phrases that resounded in the gloom, took Varygin back to his childhood when he used to go to this church with his mother and had even sung in the choir. All this was so long ago that it might never have been at all. Once the priest passed very close to Varygin, and from the threadbare old cassock came a whiff of garlic.

When the service ended, the women, who had been hidden by the darkness, closed the coffin, lifted it, and bore it out. Varygin left the church with the others and helped carry the coffin, treading on the limp grass that grew among the wooden crosses, and came to himself only after his mother was buried.

Later he again walked across the crooked log that spanned the stream, which emitted a light mist resembling incense, and again trod the hard ground. It seemed to him that he had just visited a world that, to his mind, had long since ceased to exist.

When they had returned to the village and reached the house, the midwife was the first to run up the steps and, finding the key in her pocket, unlock the door. Varygin remembered the steps and the door with its iron handle. Only the gate leading into the yard was new, and as he passed through it he saw the sign there: "Maternity Station."

Varygin stepped across the threshold. On the left, reaching to the ceiling, was a white stove; on the right, in the corner, stood a wide wooden tub and above it an earthenware washbasin, probably the same tub and washbasin that had been there in his childhood and that he had completely forgotten until that moment.

The ceiling was much lower than before. But the dark rough-hewn beams, slightly bent in the middle, were the same—of that he was certain. Here were the old iron hooks for cradles—three in all. His father had lived here with two married brothers; there were three sisters-in-law in the house, and each rocked her own cradle. He, Varygin, had slept in one of them.

"I stay in the other part of the house mostly," said the midwife, "and see patients there. And your mother lived in this room. Here is her bed, and her towel is hanging where it used to."

Varygin looked at the towel, which was gray with age, and again, not for the first time, the thought that his mother had suffered want struck him painfully.

He took off his cap and coat and wearily sank onto a stool. He wanted to put his head on the table and doze off. The whole family used to eat at this table. In the corner, under the wooden icon, his father would sit. Varygin recalled the smell of cabbage soup and warm bread, with a cabbage leaf stuck to the bottom crust. His mother had often washed the table with hot water and scraped it with a knife that had a broken handle. This knot in the wood with a dark center had always seemed to him like the eye of a horse. Now this table top was yellow and cracked, and the eye had grown blacker and crumbled.

A pile of notebooks lay on the table: "Regional Course in Obstetrics. Abstracts, A. Antonova," he read. The title was penned in the careful schoolgirl hand in which his mother's rare letters had been written.

A. Antonova brought in an armful of wood, lighted a fire in the stove, and put the teakettle to boil. Then she removed the notebooks, fetched a clean towel from a chest under the bookshelves, wiped a cup with it, and poured tea for Varygin.

"I've got to hurry off to Lapshino; I have a delivery there today," she said. "Please excuse me."

He didn't want tea, and he sat there alone, not budging. Life, which had teemed in this house during his early years, had gone elsewhere, and it seemed odd that now there remained only these walls and he—Varygin. But there was nothing for him to do here, and he had to leave. Yet he did not want to think of departure, and was loath to move. Where could he lie down? He turned his head and looked around.

On a bench in the corner stood a superannuated samovar with a loose faucet, leaning foolishly to one side, smirking slyly and looking askance at the bench, as if it wanted to say: "Aha, you too have come apart on the journey. Lie down, brother, beside me!"

Varygin put his hands on the table and leaned his weight on them as he got up, and it seemed to him that the table, too, winked at him with the horse's eye: "So you've come back all the same!"

He went over to the bed and lay down.

A cold, red stripe of sunset glowed beyond the paling and was reflected in the windowpane, when he opened his eyes. The thought suddenly came to him that he had fallen asleep on the bed where his mother had died. He rose and sat down at the table. His coat hung on the wall opposite; on the bench lay his cap. Behind it stood the samovar, grave and gloomy, as though bearing a grudge.

Close by, it must have been just outside, someone was shouting in a shrill, nervous voice:

"They ain't acting in a Party way, that's why I'm squawking! Nobody, I tell you, nobody will let them rush us around; we're village mechanics! Is that according to the law? A person must know, if anything is done against the law!"

"They'll look into it in the District Executive Committee," a restrained, admonishing voice retorted." Be off now—I tell you, the man is resting."

The voices grew faint; apparently the disputants had moved out into the street.

A little later a board creaked on the porch, and a stooped figure in a sheepskin appeared in the doorway.

"You're not sleeping?" a voice came out of the darkness. The switch clicked, and above the table an electric bulb lighted up. Varygin saw facing him a thin old man with small, cheerful eyes.

"Who might you be?" Varygin asked.

"Me? Ilya Moshkaryov. I'm a watchman now, but I used to be a blacksmith. Employed as a watchman because of sickness. I still hang about the smithy. I guard it."

He sat down on a stool at the table.

"I've brought the midwife some firewood, and I saw you were asleep. She must have gone to Lapshino. Zoya Sinyukhina is having another baby."

"And who was that shouting?" asked Varygin, nodding at the wall.

"Pelageya Komkova, the combine driver's wife—she's in charge of fueling motors. They used to be in our kolkhoz, but now they're on the Tractor Station payroll. She kept holding on to the kolkhoz, but only so as not to lose her private plot: two-fifths of a hectare. Now they've dropped her. The reason is that she earned no more than twelve workdays the whole year. Can you keep a worker like that in the kolkhoz? They're taking away her plot, so she's yelling, 'They're unfair to the mechanics!' She came to complain to you. A fat chance of being unfair to her!"

"Aren't mechanics entitled to a plot?"

"Sure thing. According to the law they get three-twentieths of a hectare but the allotment won't come from the kolkhoz acreage; it'll be on vacant land hereabouts. The village soviet decided at a session."

He was silent for a while, and then spoke again:

"So you've come to bury your mama? The last duty. You've done an old person honor. Thanks for not forgetting. Me, I was set to guard the peat, and I was late for the funeral."

The old man stretched out a leg and, leaning back, pulled out of his trouser pocket a quarter-liter bottle of vodka not quite full.

"Here," he continued, growing animated, "if you don't look down your nose at a workingman, let's drink up to your mother's memory what God has sent. Don't think I'm a boozer. Today my niece, Marya Skornyakova, went to register* with Pyotr Dezhurov, from the flax factory. So it's a wedding for them, and my mind is on your mother. I got hold of a bottle, and made off. To each his own."

He rubbed his hands, as if he were cold, looked at the shelf, took down two cups carefully, one after the other, and poured a little liquor into each.

"Your father and me was great friends. Now you're a top man, I hear. Well, people's lots differ. But we are all made the same. Have some?" he asked, stretching out the cup. "Wait, I'll give you a snack with it."

He put his left hand into his pocket, drew forth a dark, pimply cucumber, with his palm wiped off the tobacco crumbs that stuck to it, and broke it in half.

The vodka burned Varygin's mouth; he winced, but did not bite

* I.e., at the Marriage Office.—A. Y.

into the cucumber. The blacksmith downed his drink, too, and ate his half of the cucumber.

"Well, now," he said, with satisfaction, screwing up the sly eyes under his bushy bleached eyebrows. "So you're the leaders, we're—the producers; that's how it is, heh-heh. Let's have the rest, eh?"

He carelessly shook the bottle, which was not quite empty, and they had another drink.

"So it comes to this: some have a funeral, others—a wedding!" said the old man.

Varygin felt a warmth in his chest, and for the first time in three days his spirits rose.

"And how did my mother make out? Well enough, or how?" he asked.

"Not always the same; she managed the way all of us did."

"But still? What about food, for instance?"

"Well, we can't complain. Our own grain lasts only till spring, so we go to Lapshino. Some even ride into town. So the village soviet paid rent to her for the room. The Maternity Station is set up here. She'd get thirty-five a month. And how much did she need? Sometimes she ate white bread, even treated herself to tea. This year, whenever there was sugar at the store, she got some. No, we've nothing to complain about!"

The sound of wheels came from the frozen road beyond the gate, and a cart drove past the house; you could hear the horses stamping and snorting loudly. Then someone started playing an accordion. A gay crowd swept past the house; a girl's shrill voice broke into song, which sometimes became a shout:

> "Because of a field of spring grain,
> Because of a district consumers' co-op,
> Because of a course on the care of bees,
> Darling, I must part from you!"

"Our people are having themselves a time," said the blacksmith. "Do I go and fill up again?" He rose, stuck the empty bottle into his pocket, and vanished, without taking leave.

Varygin, too, rose, put on his coat, and walked out into the yard. It was completely dark by now, and cold stars blazed in a sky swept clean of clouds. He took a few steps near the gate, hunched himself because of the cold, and looked at his watch. The luminous green hands showed only ten past seven. He knew that the express left late at night, and the several hours that remained before his departure appeared to him unpleasantly long and wearisome.

An accordion was playing at the edge of the village, and from that direction came voices, girls' squeals and laughter. Varygin turned and went back to the house. Anastasya Derevlyova was waiting for him on the porch. She was still wearing the army tunic, but her head and shoulders were wrapped in a woolen kerchief.

"I've come to fix you tea," she said in a singsong voice, following him into the house. "Antonina Vasilyevna's worried about you; she sent word from Lapshino. Herself, she can't leave: Zoya's keeping her; the baby doesn't come."

She built a fire on the hearth and set the teakettle to heat.

"It's a shame your mother did not live to see you! What joy it would have given the old one," Varygin heard her say.

"Was she waiting for me?" he asked.

"This year she said nothing. But the summer you wrote that you'd come—she looked forward to it so! She kept saying: Soon, soon! Then she quieted down. But she wasn't sore, no. She understood that it wasn't easy for such a busy man to tear himself away. Of all our local boys you're the one who's gone farthest. There's Afanasy Beryozin from Korkino, too; he's a general somewhere."

Having brewed the tea, she placed a cup before him and sat down at the table.

"But otherwise we've nothing to brag about," she observed. "In the kolkhoz there are only women. We struggle and struggle, and all for nothing. Over in the next kolkhoz everybody got four kilos* again, but on our farm . . ." She waved her hands hopelessly. "Things don't go well with us," she said apologetically. Before such a notable as Varygin she was apparently embarrassed that their kolkhoz was so backward.

"Here's what I'd like to ask you: Did they deal fairly with us or not? This year we sowed seventy-four hectares of hemp. As soon as the *poskon*† blossomed, the spring crops ripened. We reaped them and

---

* Presumably of grain per workday.—A. Y.
† Hemp plants with male flowers.—A. Y.

stacked them, but we were ordered to thresh the grain and make the deliveries to the State. So what happens? From here to the grain-collecting station it's thirty-nine versts and there's two rivers to ferry across, and a long wait at the grain elevator! And if you don't harvest *poskon* in time, don't expect any *matyorka!** But the collection agents insisted: Deliver, deliver! Won't the State wait even a week? we said. We wouldn't have been in arrears. When we'd harvested the hemp we'd have made the deliveries. But no! There just wasn't any arguing with them! And we had no one to appeal to. While we were threshing the grain and hauling it to the elevator we lost the hemp harvest and, uncut, it dropped half of its seeds. True, we got credit for the deliveries —we were among the first. And now we ourselves are without bread again! Judge for yourself: is this right or wrong?"

"She thinks it all depends on me," Varygin reflected in perplexity, trying to recall what *poskon* and *matyorka* were, and what the connection was between them. But he could not remember.

"It's a political question," he said. "With us the State must always come first. Everything depends on the level of the consciousness of the masses."

He broke off, feeling that he was saying the wrong thing. But Derevlyova listened to him with an expression of satisfaction on her face.

"Me, too, I reckon it's a political question," she broke in quickly, obviously pleased that the conversation was acquiring real depth. "That's right, you've explained this fine. Our masses still lack consciousness."

The noise of a motorcycle was heard in the darkness beyond the windows.

"That's her, I reckon," said Derevlyova. "The Tractor Station engineer must have brought her. Comes every Saturday. But she's always busy. Oh, that midwife, she don't know how lucky she is!"

Antonina Vasilyevna entered, followed by a young man with a weather-beaten complexion, high cheekbones, and flaxen hair.

"Well, how are you getting on here?" she asked vivaciously. No trace seemed to remain of her melancholy mood of the morning.

Having washed up, she seated herself at the table, opened a package of sandwiches she had evidently bought at a buffet somewhere and,

* Hemp plants with female flowers; both stalks and seeds are valuable.—A. Y.

348

handing them round, started telling about what a strong, fine baby girl Zoya Sinyukhina had brought into the world.

It was pleasant to look at her milk-white arms, bare to her firm elbows, at her soft, feminine movements as she pushed strands of damp hair behind her pink ears, at her fresh cheeks glowing with color. While she was speaking, she did not once look at the engineer, but she must have felt his gaze on her continually.

"No, she understands how lucky she is," Varygin decided, looking at the girl's eyes, which shone brightly, in spite of all the cares and anxieties of the day. His thoughts went back to his flabby wife, who was always disgruntled and who stuffed the children with food, so that Genya, at eleven, already had a paunch, and Sveta looked like a middle-aged woman with a child's face and fat, heavy legs, and he decided that this engineer was a lucky dog. If long ago his life had taken a different turn, and he had remained in the country, he would now have been a sturdy man in good health and the skin would be drawn tautly over his cheeks, tanned like the engineer's. But you cannot change anything in the past or, apparently, in the future either. And most likely if a young woman with such white arms and a lithe, beautiful, strong body were to fall in love with him now, nothing would come of it anyway.

"Have you been in these parts long?" he asked her.

"Long enough to think of moving on!" She smiled, but a hard light came into her eyes. "Everyone tries to leave the rural districts for the city as soon as possible, for the big centers with their culture and their fleshpots. But they say there's greater need of us here."

She looked at the engineer, as if asking his support.

"Yes, there's a lot to do here," he said. "In our district more than half of the nineteen collective farms are doing badly. Harvests are poor, income is pitifully meager, people work reluctantly, they are undernourished."

Without looking, he took a cigarette from a pouch hanging at his side and began smoking nervously.

"What is the cause of it?" Varygin asked.

The engineer shrugged his shoulders.

"You know better than we. No one wants to work without remuneration."

The midwife silently touched the engineer's hand. He rose from the table and started pacing the room.

Varygin sat there, leaning against the wall and munching a sandwich —he had not eaten since morning. It seemed to him that the engineer was eyeing him in an unfriendly way.

"You are not exaggerating?" Varygin asked hoarsely. "At first I thought you were an optimist."

The engineer walked over to the corner of the room and threw his cigarette butt into the tub.

"Optimism," he said, returning, "is a more complicated thing than it seems at first blush. The country people would be much better off if we had fewer official cheerleaders. Gritting our teeth, we must overcome difficulties, not hush them up. Take our Tractor Station, for instance. There's a lot of things that could be done, but no one really cares! Let's go over tomorrow—you'll see for yourself."

"I'm leaving tonight on the express—business!" said Varygin, and looked at his watch.

The engineer, too, looked at his watch. The fervor with which he had just spoken had abruptly vanished.

"So, I'll be going, Tonya," he said.

She accompanied him into the entry, and Varygin heard them whispering on the porch.

"It's probably time for me to be going, too," he said when she returned.

"Wait a while; there's plenty of time. Mitya will get the Tractor Station to send a car."

Glancing with some embarrassment at Derevlyova, who was quietly washing the dishes in the corner, she broached the subject of the house: did he wish to break the lease and perhaps sell the house, or would he leave things as they were?

"Let everything stay as it was," said Varygin.

Some of his mother's things remained in the dresser. He took two old family photographs that lay on the bottom of the top drawer. He had neither the desire nor the strength to go through the contents of the drawers or to mull over what the engineer had said and what he had seen here during the day.

"Be so good as to see to it all yourself," he said, closing the drawer.

The car came much sooner than he had expected. The midwife

drove out with him so that he wouldn't have to trouble about the ticket himself.

The road as far as Lapshino was abominable, but when they reached the macadamized highway, and the car, its rubber tires softly swishing, rolled swiftly along the gray ribbon lit by the headlights, Varygin's usual equable mood began to reassert itself, and the unpleasant after-taste left by his encounter with the engineer disappeared.

"Of course," he reflected, "our local administration is not all it should be. Sometimes it functions clumsily and harshly; the officials mask their shortcomings by blaming objective factors. But you can't mend matters everywhere at once. Correcting, prompting, comes from above, but the people themselves must take action, too."

"Yes, the people themselves," he returned to the thought in a little while, and he was vexed with himself for not having said this to the engineer.

They reached the station nearly an hour before the express was scheduled to arrive, and, having bought a ticket, sat in the buffet.

The midwife, embarrassed, sipped the port to which he had treated her and kept looking around almost fearfully.

"Why don't you come with me? You could be my secretary," said Varygin in jest.

She choked, spilled the wine on the oilcloth, and blushed so violently that he too felt awkward.

In the train, as he prepared for sleep on the couch in the semidark compartment, where the other passangers were already asleep, he was relieved at the thought that the commotion and unpleasantness of these days were behind him, and he imagined with pleasure how to-morrow he would go into his warm, well-furnished office and sit down in an armchair at his desk.

Nevertheless, a vague sense of guilt haunted Varygin for a long time. Drowsy though he was, he could not get to sleep, and his imagination kept picturing wooden crosses against a gray sky, the familiar house, the long bench against the wall, the old bent samovar in the corner. At the planed table his mother sits, her face small and dark, as it had been in the church; she moves toward him and asks with hopeful expectation, as Anastasya Derevlyova had asked: "Did they deal with us fairly or not?"

ALEXANDER TVARDOVSKY
(b. 1900)

To My Critics

Teach me, would you, my critics, give me a facile
Lesson: yes, according to you
I must be deaf, blind, shape my verses
By what I may and what I may not do.

But forgive me if I foresee a future
Hour, oh, not near, when you'll hector me,
You yourselves, questioning, insisting:
Poet, where were you? What was it you did see?

1958

YURY NAGIBIN
(b. 1920)

The World War interrupted Nagibin's studies at the Cinematographic Institute in his native Moscow. He was attached to the army's section of political education, and after recovery from shellshock became a war correspondent for a newspaper. At the age of nineteen he tried his hand at short fiction, and ever since then he has cultivated the genre assiduously, producing more than a half-dozen books of short stories.

In the Trolley

I was returning by trolley from a suburb of Moscow, where some business had taken me by chance. The car was empty; I walked to the front of the platform and took a seat at the open window. I am very fond of the outskirts of Moscow, the Moscow of my childhood. With a friendly feeling I looked at the little frame houses, their windows that flashed past, ruddy with sunset, at the old trees the foliage of which was the first to take in the timid September twilight, at the hydrants in the shallow puddles reflecting pink clouds. There was a slightly bitter smell of warm earth, fallen leaves, and mushrooms.

When we reached the group of new houses that loomed at the edge of the city like an outpost, two girls came into the trolley. They made the light, gentle noise that usually accompanies the entrance of those who are quick with the freshness and warmth of youth. There was the rustle of clothing—the girls' movements were rapid and jerky—a slight, happy little laugh: they were lucky in getting a trolley; the click of their bags preceding a mild squabble about who would pay for the tickets. The older one won out. Clutching the ribbon of tickets, she walked quickly past me onto the platform, followed by her friend. Two fleeting glances slid over me indifferently, leaving a slight and faintly ridiculous feeling of sadness. The trolley jolted as it turned, the girls collided, or rather the younger one was thrown against the older. The older turned and supported her with a firm, tender, slightly patronizing movement, and they laughed again, as though this were heaven knows how funny. You felt that they loved each other, were glad to be together, and that all the insignificant little details of the occasion gave them sincere pleasure.

The girls were about the same age, and yet you were inclined to call one the older. Not only because, unlike her friend, who wore a school uniform, she was dressed like an adult: a blue blouse, a black pleated skirt, high-heeled pumps, but also because the schoolgirl looked up to her with an enamored gaze. Their relationship was that of older and younger: gently patronizing, on the one hand, and languishingly devoted, on the other.

The older girl was taller and slenderer; she had dark hair, a lusterless skin, soft dark eyes. She belonged to that type of girl who matures early, and in the last year of high school looks retarded, somewhat uncouth and ludicrous. But when they put away all schoolgirl things, they emerge into the wide world in a new, unrecognizable, captivating, guise like chrysalises turning into butterflies. In the other girl, a blonde with reddish hair, pink cheeks, and green eyes, there was still much that was unsettled, puppyish.

Every so often the girls touched each other: the older to set the younger's collar straight, to push a curl off her forehead—in short, to maintain order in her friend's appearance, which was constantly disturbed by the exuberant forces that filled her; the younger girl did so because she simply wanted once more to touch things still forbidden her such as a broach with small pale-blue stones, or mother-of-pearl buttons, or a chamois strap.

These slight contacts, of which they themselves were scarcely aware, did not prevent them from keeping up a confidential and apparently for them very important conversation that had started earlier and that they resumed as soon as they found themselves on the platform. The clangor of the trolley drowned out everything except a few disparate words and the younger girl's stormy exclamations. But you did not have to be especially perspicacious to guess the simple girlish secret the elder was confiding to her friend. It was enough to catch the word *he* that she pronounced sternly and meaningfully, and her friend in a languid and rapturous tone. "And he?" the younger asked, and a moment later: "And you?" and she looked around, not to make sure that no one had overheard them, but because she was bursting with pride: it was no trifle to be the confidante when it came to a real grownup love! You didn't sense any envy in her—nothing but rapture, devotion, adoration. It was I who felt envy—the good kind—of this beautiful girl's friend whom I had never seen. I tried to picture him to myself. For some reason I imagined him to be tall, broad-shouldered, fair-haired, slightly clumsy and shy. But perhaps he was quite homely, shaggy-haired, with a face like a monkey's, yet amazingly attractive, intelligent and kind.

A huge eight-ton truck was moving alongside our trolley abreast of the front platform where the girls were standing. A cast-iron bear gleamed dully on the radiator. When the trolley speeded up, the truck did likewise; when the trolley slowed down, so did the truck. In the cab sat a young driver, broadchested, sunburned, curly-headed, with white teeth, his muscular arm, bare to the elbow, resting on the cross-piece of the wheel. Leaning out of the window a little way, he eyed the girls with frank admiration, and the headwind pressed his tight curls to his tanned, open forehead.

The younger girl whispered something to the older, and, glancing at the driver, gave a low, restrained little laugh. The older girl cast an absent-minded glance at the cab, at the fellow's face, and remarked indifferently, "The brat!"

"But how he looks at you!"

"A lot I care! But he's looking at you, not at me at all."

"Oh, yes, someone will look at me when you are with me!" This was said without envy or resentment, but simply to state a fact.

The trolley made a sharp turn to the left, and the truck bore right into an alley of maples, because the road was not wide enough to let motors pass. For the last time—as he leaned out of the cab—the driver's sunburned face with the broad cheekbones flashed by and disappeared.

"And is it a good thing that your friend is so much older than you?" asked the younger girl, apparently still thinking of the handsome truck driver.

"He's so interesting! He knows so much. He's been everywhere. Imagine, he saw Mayakovsky, even spoke to him!"

"Really?" The younger girl did some mental arithmetic. "Then he's quite old, about like Viktor Stepanovich, remember, our math teacher?" She laughed.

"You little fool, you," the older one said gently. "Viktor Stepanovich looks like a mattress; but *he's* handsome—slim. . . ."

"He is?" Her kindly green eyes grew round. "And you're not scared of him?"

"Why should I be scared?"

"I don't know. I'd be terribly scared. . . ."

"I'm not, not the least little bit. Truly!" And contradicting this proud declaration, a pitiful little grimace of inferiority crossed her beautiful, joyfully animated face.

Something began to be apparent to me. The man was much older than the girl, and dominated her. I recalled fragments of phrases I had caught when the girls first entered the car. "He said, 'call me up' ' "; "He said, 'Come' ' "; "He told me not to . . ." Not once did she make any demand. And, in general, what she said about him suggested no equality, no independence. And the little grimace of inferiority that I had just glimpsed was a reflection, as it were, of that subjection, of which she herself may not have been conscious, but which was an unfamiliar burden on her soul.

I do not know why, but I was pierced by pity for this young, beautiful, defenseless creature. I bent forward slightly. The girls were so preoccupied with their own concerns that the attention with which I followed their conversation could not put them on their guard. But the cobbles again thundered under the rails—we were crossing a square— and all their words were drowned out by the clangor.

To the left of us bricks were stacked high for some building that was under construction. An enormously tall crane, having described a huge semicircle, swung a cage loaded with bricks on an invisible cable. It was far from us, but its openwork arrow, having scratched the lucid, fragile sky, seemed to dart over the square, over the trolley, and send a faint chill to the heart. The younger girl's eyes followed the crane's smooth flight with a joyous and strict attention. The older one did not see the crane or the friend's passing distraction. Her lips continued to move, pronouncing inaudible words. She was entirely absorbed in her own affairs, and a stranger to everything outside it.

The foliage of the trees, singed by autumn, once more flickered beyond the windows. "Beware of fallen leaves!" a wooden sign on a cast-iron post flashed by. The trolley moved more slowly, crushing the dry leaves with a soft crunch, and I could hear the voices of my chance traveling companions once more.

"You'll really, really go away with him?" the younger one asked, pressing her little clenched fists against each other on her chest.

"Yes!" the older girl replied, with a toss of her head.

"And you'll get married?"

"We'll be as man and wife."

"You'll sign the marriage papers?" the younger asked ecstatically. The older girl gave a pitying smile.

"Does that matter?"

"How will it be, then?" the younger girl brought out, shocked. "If you're man and wife, then you must certainly sign. Otherwise how will you be man and wife?" The schoolgirl, who did not yet know the feeling that had swept her friend off her feet, became the senior one, as it were; there were new, sedate, sober notes in her voice. Of course, this evidenced even greater immaturity than had her former naïve, agitated exaltation, and her friend sensed it at once.

"Oh, you don't understand anything!" she drawled, and for the first time there was a touch of disdain in her tone.

The younger girl's lips swelled, trembled. She felt that those words and, above all, the tone in which they were said, had tossed her back, far, far away, into the half-childish world out of which her friend's confidence had drawn her for some brief, sweet moments.

"I'm a fool, for sure," she said humbly. "But why isn't everything in your case . . . the way it is with others?" She blushed with fear that her words might prove offensive.

But the older one did not take offense. On the contrary, her eyes flashed with pride that her friend had at last understood that in her case love was not as it was "with others."

"Do you care about that when you're in love?" she said. "I used to think, too, that if I fell in love with someone, he would become my husband. But did I know that I would meet a man like him? You can't imagine what kind of person he is—absolutely, absolutely extraordinary!" And again the pitiable little grimace of inferiority twisted the corners of her mouth. "Do you know what he said to me? That was when I still didn't understand anything, and thought the way you do. He said, 'He travels the fastest who travels alone!' "

"I . . . I don't understand," her friend mumbled, and something resembling fear showed in her kind, shallow greenish eyes. Of course, she did not understand, but something vaguely dark, secret, hostile, invaded the simple, serene world of her ideas and caused a painful disturbance there. It seemed to me that this fear involuntarily communicated itself to the older girl. The familiar little grimace got stuck to the corners of her lips, but her voice, swayed by something stronger than fear, resounded with pitiful, infirm triumph:

"But I do understand. I can't explain it to you; it is very complicated. Someday you'll understand it yourself."

"You don't understand anything!" I wanted to say to her. "You don't even understand that by that high-sounding aphorism he freed himself in advance of any obligations!"

I looked at her, so pure, fresh, untainted either by doubts or disappointments, so trusting and beautiful, and I asked myself: What but misfortune can come to this girl just entering life at the hands of that experienced man no longer young who knows precisely and coldly what his objective is?

Tall houses and, here and there, old-fashioned mansions appeared, and, caught in the tense, strict rhythm of the traffic, our trolley's free course was restricted: we were sedately moving from light to light. The older girl grew restive. She opened her bag, took out a flat gilt compact with a little mirror and, moving it before her face, examined herself from various angles, touched her eyebrows at the temples with the nail of her little finger, tucked a strand of hair behind her ear, and replaced the compact, clicking the lock of the bag sharply.

"Do you have to get off already?" her friend asked timidly.

"Yes!"

Moved by an obscure, unaccountable impulse, the younger girl turned toward her with a sudden motion of her whole body, and it was difficult to understand what this involuntary movement meant: the desire to protect, to hold back her friend, or to pass on her own disturbed tenderness, her little strength to her. But the older girl did not understand, indeed did not notice her impulse; she was already far away, in the world where there was no place either for this childish friendship or for this frankness: she had already taken leave of her friend. With a faintly repelling movement, she took her hand, pressed it slightly, let go of it, and stepped toward the exit.

The trolley halted sharply at the stop. Before it came to a complete standstill, the girl jumped onto the pavement and receded with it.

As we started off, I had another glimpse of her. With a firm, elastic stride, she moved along the sidewalk, carrying her small, beautiful head high and pressing her bag against her chest. She looked straight ahead and did not see her friend, leaning from the platform, her back twisted so that it looked as though it might break, following her with her eyes.

1956

LYUDMILA TATYANICHEVA
(b. 1915)

"The bear has shifted"

The bear has shifted—lies on his left side now.
Winter will soon be leaving at a trot.
Why must I still keep staring at the window
And wait—oh, will he come or not?

The January night is dark, is bitter.
I do not hear your horse come galloping
Up to the porch. Here on my palm a snowflake
Alights like a wee moon upon the wing.

But I believe in joy. Streams will be ringing
Like bells. And we shall meet, come time and tide.
Let winter rage! Deep in his lair, it's certain,
The bear has shifted—he lies on his left side.

1946

July

Now ripened berries fill
The forest clearing's lap.
Sternly the fir trees watch
Over the valley's nap.

Bright scarlet strawberry juice
Has stained the reindeer's lips;
While, in his antlers caught,
A bluebell swings and dips.

1960

BORIS PASTERNAK
(1890–1960)

Pasternak was born in Moscow into a cultivated Jewish family—the father was a painter and a professor of painting, the mother a musician. His nurse saw to it, he stated, that he was baptized in his early childhood, and he added that "Christian thought" was a decisive influence in his formative years. He received a university education in the humanities and planned a career first in music, then in philosophy, but finally turned to literature. Two books of his lyrics in the vein characteristic of the *avant-garde* poetry of the time appeared when he was in his middle twenties.

After the October Revolution he stayed on in the Soviet capital, and continued to write. He published some short stories and an autobiographical fragment, but devoted himself chiefly to verse. This is couched in a highly concentrated, elliptical language, showing an unusual sensitiveness to verbal texture, a gift for extraordinarily evocative figures of speech, and a penchant for recherché approximate rhymes. Two poems, written respectively in 1915 and 1927, will convey an idea of his matter and manner.

The Urals for the First Time

Without an accoucheuse, in darkness, pushing her
Blind hands against the night, the Ural fastness, torn and
Half-dead with agony, was screaming in a blur
Of mindless pain, as she was giving birth to morning.

And brushed by chance, tall ranges far and wide
Loosed toppling bronze pell-mell in thunder-colored rumbling.
The train panted and coughed, clutching the mountainside,
And at that sound the ghosts of fir trees shied and stumbled.

The smoky dawn was a narcotic for the peaks,
A drug with which the fire-breathing dragon plied them,

361

It is noteworthy that most of the threescore characters who move through the pages are passive victims of the upheavals that overwhelm the country. This applies especially to the figure who holds the center of the stage, Yury Zhivago, physician and poet, in certain respects the author's alter ego. He is the son of a millionaire who had committed suicide, and he marries a granddaughter of another industrial magnate. The news of the downfall of the imperial regime reaches him while he is recuperating from a wound received at the front. He greets the February Revolution with enthusiasm as a divine event, the country's new birth, but in the months that follow the cataclysm he takes a more sober view of it, and though he believes that Russia is destined to be the first socialist state the prospect does not elate him. He is back in Moscow when the Bolsheviks seize power, and the first acts of the government of workers and peasants strike him as "magnificent surgery," expressive of the boldness and intransigence inherent in the Russian national genius.

Busy with his medical practice, he stoically bears the hardships of the first Soviet year, and comes down with typhus. Recovering, he leaves Moscow with his wife and little son for Varykino—an estate that had belonged to her family—near the town of Yuryatin, in the Urals. His hope is that they can weather the storm in that distant retreat. On the journey they encounter the chaos and devastation of the civil war. Zhivago now feels that the revolutionary ideal has been betrayed. The new order, with its reliance on force, no longer commands his sympathy. Far from being a science, he argues, Marxism has no basis in fact.

The little family settles at Varykino, pinning its hopes to subsistence farming. On one of his visits to Yuryatin, the doctor meets Larisa (Lara) Antipova. She is the wife of a high-school teacher who had left her in order to enlist and who, after being reported lost in action, emerged a high-ranking Red commander, renowned for his ruthlessness in fighting the Whites. Zhivago had come to know her as a nurse at the hospital where he was a patient during the war. Before long the two are deeply in love. Tormented by pangs of conscience for his unfaithfulness to his wife, whom he continues to "adore," he decides to give up Lara. Before he can carry out his decision, he is kidnapped by Red guerrillas one evening on his way from Yuryatin. Forced to stay with the band as their doctor, he witnesses scenes of unspeakable brutality, and is confirmed in his disgust with Bolshevism.

After nearly two years he escapes from his captors and makes his way to Yuryatin. He finds that his family has gone back to Moscow. Larisa, however, is in town. And now they are together, united by a passion about which there is "the breath of eternity," a love willed by "the earth under them, the sky above them, the clouds and the trees." But theirs is a doomed and short-lived happiness. For reasons that, like other matters in the novel, are not wholly clear, Lara's absent husband, who had served the Red cause so fanatically, becomes a hunted outlaw. That puts her life in jeopardy too. What with the mass arrests and executions in the region, Yury, who decidedly does not fit into the Communist pattern, is also in a vulnerable position. To attract less attention to themselves, the couple, taking with them Lara's little daughter, remove to Varykino. It is a desolate place, having been visited by raiders who wrecked most of the homes and slaughtered the inhabitants. Yet here their days, filled with homely labors, are a miracle of joy, and during some of the magical night hours poems flow from Yury's pen. Yet the wilderness affords them no safety.

As a high-school girl, Lara had been seduced by a wealthy middle-aged sensualist. He appears on the scene and, declaring that both she and Zhivago are in imminent danger of arrest, offers to take them, as well as the child, across the Soviet border to the Far Eastern Republic, in which he is to hold a prominent post. For the sake of her daughter, Lara accepts the offer, with the understanding that Yury will rejoin her later. He cannot, however, allow himself to be obligated to this man, and so, in the dead of winter, he treks back to Moscow on foot.

He arrives in the capital in 1922, early in the era of the New Economic Policy, "the most ambiguous and fraudulent of the Soviet periods." His wife and two children—the second born while he was with the guerrillas—are in France, and he has lost Lara. A broken man, he is unable to follow his profession or to persevere in any other occupation. He is looked after by the daughter of a former servant of his wife's family. She comes to live with him, and bears him two children. As the years pass, he feels more keenly than ever that the new order is a debasing, life-destroying force. What exasperates him particularly is to see the intellectuals glorify their bondage. He has a theory that the constant hypocrisy to which most of the citizenry are condemned affects their physical health, giving rise to an increase in the incidence of heart ailments.

In spite of his disgust and distress, he decides to take himself in hand. He is eager to live, to make something of himself, to regularize his relations with his two families. By way of preparing himself to rebuild his life, he stays alone for a time, and the room in which he hides becomes "a banquet hall of the spirit." In his solitude he writes, hurriedly, feverishly, revising his old pieces and trying to compose new poems that will convey the exhilarating tumult of the metropolis outside his window. A position on the staff of a hospital has been secured for him by his mysterious half-brother Yevgraf who, on a previous occasion, too, has come to his aid like a *deus ex machina*. But Zhivago never makes the new start. On his way to the hospital to enter upon his duties, he dies in the street of a heart attack.

Lara happens to reach Moscow on the day of the funeral—the plot is a tissue of such fantastic coincidences. Having taken leave of her beloved and the introduction of elections that violated the very principle of free choice.

"And when the war broke out, its real horrors, its real dangers, its menace of real death were a blessing compared with the inhuman reign of the lie, and brought relief because they broke the spell of the dead letter.

"It was felt not only by men in our position, in concentration camps, but by absolutely everyone, at home and at the front, and they all took a deep breath and flung themselves into the furnace of this mortal liberation struggle with real joy, with rapture.

"The war has its special character as a link in the chain of revolutionary decades. The forces directly unleashed by the Revolution no longer operated. The indirect effects of the Revolution, the fruit of its fruit, the consequences of the consequences, began to manifest themselves. Misfortunes and ordeals had tempered characters, prepared them for great, desperate, heroic exploits. These fabulous, astounding qualities characterize the moral elite of this generation." . . .

Five or ten years later, one quiet summer evening, Dudorov and Gordon were again together, sitting at an open window above Moscow, which extended into the dusk as far as the eye could reach. They were looking through a book of Yury's writings that Yevgraf had put together, a book they had read more than once and almost knew by heart. They read and talked and thought. By the time they came to the middle of the book, it was dark and they turned on the light.

And Moscow, right below them and stretching into the distance, the author's native city, in which he had spent half his life—Moscow now struck them not as the stage of the events connected with him but as the main protagonist of a long story, the end of which they had reached that evening, book in hand.

Although victory had not brought the relief and freedom that were expected at the end of the war, nevertheless the portents of freedom filled the air throughout the postwar period, and they alone defined its historic significance.

To the two old friends, as they sat by the window, it seemed that this freedom of the soul was already there, as if that very evening the future had tangibly moved into the streets below them, that they themselves had entered it and were now part of it. Thinking of this the Red cause so fanatically, becomes a hunted outlaw. That puts her life in jeopardy too. What with the mass arrests and executions in the region, Yury, who decidedly does not fit into the Communist pattern, is also in a vulnerable position. To attract less attention to themselves, the couple, taking with them Lara's little daughter, remove to Varykino. It is a desolate place, having been visited by raiders who wrecked most of the homes and slaughtered the inhabitants. Yet here their days, filled with homely labors, are a miracle of joy, and during some of the magical night hours poems flow from Yury's pen. Yet the wilderness affords them no safety.

As a high-school girl, Lara had been seduced by a wealthy middle-aged sensualist. He appears on the scene and, declaring that both she and Zhivago are in imminent danger of arrest, offers to take them, as well as the child, across the Soviet border to the Far Eastern Republic, in which he is to hold a prominent post. For the sake of her daughter, Lara accepts the offer, with the understanding that Yury will rejoin her later. He cannot, however, allow himself to be obligated to this man, and so, in the dead of winter, he treks back to Moscow on foot.

He arrives in the capital in 1922, early in the era of the New Economic Policy, "the most ambiguous and fraudulent of the Soviet periods." His wife and two children—the second born while he was with the guerrillas—are in France, and he has lost Lara. A broken man, he is unable to follow his profession or to persevere in any other occupation. He is looked after by the daughter of a former servant of his wife's family. She comes to live with him, and bears him two children. As the years pass, he feels more keenly than ever that the new order is a debasing, life-destroying force. What exasperates him particularly is to see the intellectuals glorify their bondage. He has a theory that the constant hypocrisy to which most of the citizenry are condemned affects their physical health, giving rise to an increase in the incidence of heart ailments.

In spite of his disgust and distress, he decides to take himself in hand. He is eager to live, to make something of himself, to regularize his relations with his two families. By way of preparing himself to rebuild his life, he stays alone for a time, and the room in which he hides becomes "a banquet hall of the spirit." In his solitude he writes, hurriedly, feverishly, revising his old pieces and trying to compose new poems that will convey the exhilarating tumult of the metropolis outside his window. A position on the staff of a hospital has been secured for him by his mysterious half-brother Yevgraf who, on a previous occasion, too, has come to his aid like a *deus ex machina*. But Zhivago never makes the new start. On his way to the hospital to enter upon his duties, he dies in the street of a heart attack.

Lara happens to reach Moscow on the day of the funeral—the plot is a tissue of such fantastic coincidences. Having taken leave of her beloved in one of the most memorable scenes of the novel, she disappears, and it is intimated that she perishes in one of the "countless" concentration camps. The daughter she had borne to Yury in Siberia becomes a waif, and grows up to be a semiliterate girl who has inherited from her parents nothing but her father's way of smiling. The fate of the couple whose story is the core of the novel is a tragic one. But the two had known the miracle of a love that made them at one with the beauty and joy of all existence. And Yury had left behind a book, presumably a collection of poems—a selection from it is appended to the text of the narrative. In any event, as the pages below indicate, the note on which the novel ends is one of confident serenity.

FROM the Epilogue to Doctor Zhivago

Major Dudorov and Lieutenant Gordon, childhood friends of Zhivago's, meet in the summer of 1943 in a town laid waste by the retreating German troops. Former university instructors, now in the same army unit, they spend the night talking. At daybreak Dudorov, who had dozed off, is awakened by Gordon as he is getting ready to go down to the river to do his laundry. The two resume their conversation:

"Where did you learn to wash clothes like that?"

"From necessity. We were unlucky. We got sent to just about the worst of the penal camps. There were very few survivors. Our arrival, to begin with. We got off the train. A wilderness of snow. Forest in the distance. Guards with rifles, muzzles pointing at us, wolfhounds. About the same time, other groups were brought up. We were spread out and formed into a big polygon all over the field, facing outward, so that we wouldn't see each other. Then we were ordered down on our knees, and told to keep looking straight ahead on pain of death. Then the roll call, an endless, humiliating business going on for hours and hours. And all the time we were on our knees. Then we got up and the other groups were marched off and ours was told: 'This is your camp. Make the best of it!' An open snowfield with a post in the middle and a notice on it saying: 'GULAG 92 Y.N. 90'—that's all there was."

"It wasn't nearly so bad with us; we were lucky. Of course, I was doing my second stretch, which followed automatically from the first. Moreover, I was sentenced under a different article, so the conditions were quite different. When I came out, I was reinstated again, as I had been the first time, and allowed to go on lecturing. And when I was mobilized I was given my full rank of Major, not put into a disciplinary battalion like you."

"Yes, well . . . That was all there was, the post and the notice board, 'GULAG 92 Y.N. 90.' First we broke saplings with our bare hands in the bitter cold, to get wood to build huts. And in the end, believe it or not, we gradually built our whole camp. We put up our prison and our stockade and our cells and our watchtowers, all with our own hands. And then we began our job as lumberjacks. We cut trees. We harnessed ourselves, eight to a sledge, and we hauled timber and sank into the snow up to our necks. For a long time we didn't know the war had started. They kept it from us. And then suddenly there came the offer. You could volunteer for front-line service in a disciplinary battalion, and if you came out alive you were free. After that, attack after attack, mile after mile of electrified barbed wire, mines, mortars, month after month of artillery barrage. They called our company the death squad. It was practically wiped out. How and why I survived, I don't know. And yet—would you believe it?—all the utter hell was nothing; it was bliss compared to the horrors of the concentration camp, and not because of the material conditions but for an entirely different reason."

"Yes, poor fellow. You've taken a lot."

"It wasn't just washing clothes you learned out there; you learned everything there is to learn."

"It's an extraordinary thing, you know. It isn't only in comparison with your life as a convict, but compared to everything in the thirties, even to my easy situation at the university, in the midst of books and money and comfort, the war came as a breath of fresh air, a purifying storm, a breath of deliverance.

"I think the collectivization was an erroneous and unsuccessful measure, and it was impossible to admit the error. To conceal the failure people had to be cured, by every means of terrorism, of the habit of thinking and judging for themselves, and forced to see what didn't exist, to assert the very opposite of what their eyes told them. This accounts for the unexampled cruelty of the Yezhov period,* the promulgation of a constitution that was never meant to be applied,

---

* The half-dozen nightmare years of purges, trials, wholesale arrests that followed the assassination of Sergey Kirov, a high Party functionary, in 1934. Nikolay Yezhov headed the secret police in 1936–1938.—A. Y.

and the introduction of elections that violated the very principle of free choice.

"And when the war broke out, its real horrors, its real dangers, its menace of real death were a blessing compared with the inhuman reign of the lie, and brought relief because they broke the spell of the dead letter.

"It was felt not only by men in our position, in concentration camps, but by absolutely everyone, at home and at the front, and they all took a deep breath and flung themselves into the furnace of this mortal liberation struggle with real joy, with rapture.

"The war has its special character as a link in the chain of revolutionary decades. The forces directly unleashed by the Revolution no longer operated. The indirect effects of the Revolution, the fruit of its fruit, the consequences of the consequences, began to manifest themselves. Misfortunes and ordeals had tempered characters, prepared them for great, desperate, heroic exploits. These fabulous, astounding qualities characterize the moral elite of this generation." . . .

Five or ten years later, one quiet summer evening, Dudorov and Gordon were again together, sitting at an open window above Moscow, which extended into the dusk as far as the eye could reach. They were looking through a book of Yury's writings that Yevgraf had put together, a book they had read more than once and almost knew by heart. They read and talked and thought. By the time they came to the middle of the book, it was dark and they turned on the light.

And Moscow, right below them and stretching into the distance, the author's native city, in which he had spent half his life—Moscow now struck them not as the stage of the events connected with him but as the main protagonist of a long story, the end of which they had reached that evening, book in hand.

Although victory had not brought the relief and freedom that were expected at the end of the war, nevertheless the portents of freedom filled the air throughout the postwar period, and they alone defined its historic significance.

To the two old friends, as they sat by the window, it seemed that this freedom of the soul was already there, as if that very evening the future had tangibly moved into the streets below them, that they themselves had entered it and were now part of it. Thinking of this holy city and of the entire earth, of the still-living protagonists of this story and their children, they were filled with tenderness and peace, and they were enveloped by the unheard music of happiness that flowed all about them and into the distance. And the book they held seemed to confirm and encourage their feeling.

BORIS SLUTZKY
(b. 1919)

Housing Construction

A roof overhead. In the corner a stove that smokes.
But then, there are three more corners, all for you.
Two square windows. At night you will see the dark,
And the sun by day,
                    if you haven't too much to do.
A roof overhead!
                    Off with the right boot! Off
With the left!
                    Into the corner's cozy paradise!
A roof overhead!
A roof overhead!
When there's a roof overhead, oh, but it's nice!

                                        1960

VICTOR NEKRASOV
(b. 1911)

An architect by training, this author was awarded the Stalin prize in 1947 for a fictional work about the Battle of Stalingrad, in which he fought as an officer in the engineer corps. Nekrasov has also to his credit several short stories and a novel dealing with the experiences of demobilized soldiers returning to civilian life from what is officially styled the Great War for the Fatherland. An English translation of a short novel of his appeared under a New York imprint in 1962. He is a member of the Communist Party.

The Second Night

A STORY

Did you ever happen to look for an army unit you needed on a day when an attack began? If not, you are just lucky. You will spend three or four days or more at it, even if you are an experienced front-line soldier returning after a short stay in the army or from a front-line hospital. What is there to say then about a novice who finds himself at the front for the first time? And Lenka Bogorad was just such a warrior. He was eighteen and he was at the front for the first time. One hundred and twenty of them, members of a reserve regiment, traveled from the city of Kamyshin as far as army headquarters under the tutelage of Lieutenant Gurmyza. At headquarters Lenka and Fedka Kozhemyakin were ordered to dig slit trenches near the huts. They dug eight trenches one and a half meters deep, leveled the earth, camouflaged them with grass, and in the meantime their company had left. To cap it all, Kozshemyakin got food poisoning, was taken to a hospital, and Lenka remained all alone. He was forgotten by everyone. An attack opened somewhere on the Donetz; everybody ran about like a madman, and no one wanted to talk to him. Only the cook from the officers' kitchen, to whom he brought four buckets of water, gave him a full mess kit of buttered noodles and advised him to speak to Captain Samoilenko.

"Over there, by the dead willow. A good egg. Ask him to put you in Petrov's division. World-famous general, world-famous division. All through Stalingrad I cooked its porridge."

Captain Samoilenko turned out to be a really good fellow; he did not bawl Lenka out when he dropped his rifle trying to salute, but only laughed and said: "Oh, you yokel," and gave him an envelope inscribed: "To Capt. Pereverzev. Petrov's Div."

"Look for him on the Donetz, near Bogorodichnoye. They are probably there by now." And he called after him, "Make sure you don't lose your bayonet, or you'll catch it!"

Lenka walked out onto the street, turned the bayonet upside down and tied it to the barrel of his rifle, wrapped a rag around the bolt, to keep it from getting dusty, and set out in search of Bogorodichnoye. The day was blithe and sunny; he had a loaf of bread, a sausage, and two bars of millet concentrate in his knapsack, a spoon stuck in his puttee, a mess kit hung from his belt, a tobacco pouch full of shag, and for cigarette paper a whole newspaper—what more did you need? There was no one to boss you now; walk slowly, sit down where you please, and if you get fed up with footing it—there are plenty of cars on the road; jump into any one, it is sure to take you someplace.

So Lenka walked and rode, looking about him. What the devil was going on? He had never seen such a raft of cannon and trucks. They were pushing forward in full daylight, rumbling, raising dust, and all in one direction. Once or twice Lenka passed a party of German prisoners being led somewhere, and he even jumped off a jeep to have a look at a live Fritz—until then he had seen only caricatures of them in papers. He was disappointed. They were like anybody—dusty, tired; only, their knapsacks were about ten times as big as ours, and they kept looking down. Once a Messer' appeared; someone shouted: "Scat!" but before people had time to scatter the Messer' flew away.

Everything was all right—he passed from car to car, from wagon to wagon until the day came to an end; half the loaf and the sausage were eaten, and Bogorodichnoye was still twenty kilometers away, just as it had been when he started out.

Lenka turned off the road, found a bush to shelter him, and lay down, the knapsack beneath his head, the rifle between his knees.

All night long slow planes hummed overhead; somewhere behind the horizon rockets were flaring and field pieces were firing—during the day you did not hear them, but now they boomed incessantly. On the road caterpillar trucks were clanging, voices sounded. Lenka turned from side to side and could not fall asleep. Suddenly he began to feel sorry for himself: there he was, lying under a shrub, while the boys had left and he hadn't said goodbye to a soul—damn those slit trenches!—not to Vanka, nor Gleb Fursov, nor Lieutenant Gurmyza. All the same, he wasn't a bad lieutenant—in two weeks he had bawled him out only once, when he nabbed a chicken; otherwise a decent commander. Then all kinds of thoughts came into Lenka's head. Maria Khristoforovna—the young teacher. How, when he was being taken into the army, she brought him a copybook and pencil that he might write letters. Then he thought of something else, sad too, and of yet something else, and finally dropped off.

2

He woke up—and there was no trace of what had troubled him at night. The sky was blue, the grasshoppers were chirping, larks soared overhead—as though there was no war at all. He ate the rest of the sausage, shouldered the rifle, and was off. From the wounded that he came upon—Lenka looked with respect at these tired men, completely gray with dust, who hobbled along the road—he learned that Bogorodichnoye was on the other bank of the Donetz, a distance of five, ten, maybe fifteen kilometers, but who was there—Germans or our people—no one knew for sure. Nor had anyone heard of the Petrov Division—go and find out which division was where. They added that things were so-so, asked for a smoke, and pushed on.

By three o'clock, straddling rocket-truck shells, he finally reached the Donetz. Not much of a stream—yellow, muddy, one bank low, the other steep. The willow thicket along the road near the bridge was chock-full of cars and wagons. Soldiers sat by the roadside, smoking. Red-faced, sweating lieutenants ran from one to another and drove the men into the shrubs. The soldiers got up reluctantly, walked a dozen paces, and sat down again. Close to the pontoon bridge a young fellow in a tankman's helmet, with a little red flag in his hand, admitted to the bridge in turn a transport of trucks and a detachment of infantry. Dusty. Hot.

Lenka crossed railroad tracks, hung onto some kind of unit, crossed the bridge with it, and no sooner did the thought enter his head, "And what if Fritz comes over now?" than bombs showered from somewhere. Lenka came to under the bridge, up to his neck in the water. How he got there only God knows. He was shaking all over. Somehow he managed to crawl out onto the bank, dragging his rifle behind him, climbed over an upturned cannon, fell, got up, fell again, got up again. Someone was calling shrilly, "Help, help!" A horse was thrashing on the road, its muzzle stretched out. A wagon without a driver dashed by, dropping boxes of some sort.

Lenka started running. He ran, without looking at anyone, hearing nothing, seeing nothing, up the road and on, away from the bridge, damn it. When he reached the edge of a grove, he was exhausted, and sat down. His cap was gone, everything he wore was wet, his shoes squelched. About two hundred paces away several soldiers were cooking something over a fire. Lenka approached them and asked if they knew the whereabouts of Petrov's Division. No, they didn't know; they had just arrived.

He walked on. At the noise of a plane he would turn off the road and walk straight through the shrubbery. The sound of cannon could be heard again. One after another, huge Studebakers, raising clouds of dust, were speeding by with ammunition. Lenka walked on and kept querying the men he met, but no one could give him a sensible answer. Some did not know; others scratched the back of their heads and said, "It seems that on the other side of that grove there are headquarters." Others simply didn't answer. Finally, he came upon a wounded soldier who asked for a cigarette. It turned out that the man was, thank Heaven, from Petrov's Division.

"Which regiment are you looking for?" asked the wounded soldier.

"Not a regiment, but the division headquarters."

"That I don't know," said the wounded man wearily, and started to rewind the dust-blackened bandage on his leg.

"And which one are you from?"

"The Thirty-third."

"Far from here?"

"How should I put it? Kilometers . . . Generally speaking . . . Walk along the road up to that telegraph post—you see it's hanging on the wire? On the left there'll be a ravine. Just follow the ravine; you'll get there."

Lenka sat down—one of his footcloths was all twisted.

"And where's the front? Far?"

The wounded man looked at Lenka's naïve round mug and smiled with his lips alone.

"But it's right here—the front, I mean. . . ."

"How's that?"

"Just so. See that grove? Fritz is in there."

"So why doesn't he shoot?" Lenka was astonished.

"Having supper, so he don't shoot."

There was a pause. Then Lenka asked: "How are things generally? Is Fritz falling back?"

"Not much. He's brought up minethrowers. And he has plenty of mortars. It's a good thing there are no planes yet."

Lenka was nonplussed—how could there be no planes, when he himself had just been through a bombing?

"This a bombing? You haven't seen any bombings yet, my lad." And wearily, but in detail, the wounded man started to spin the usual tale about bombings, about how, alongside him, "why, just like from here to that tree," a bomb had dropped and killed everybody, but he hadn't even been scratched by a splinter. He finished his story, got up, looked at the already darkening sky, thanked Lenka for the shag, and moved on, limping, toward the river. Having taken about twenty paces, he turned round and called, "When you get to the fork in the ravine, bear right, not left, or you'll run into the Fritzes!"

Lenka passed the post, turned off the road, and walked along the bottom of the ravine. It was growing dark fast. Somewhere on the left a machine gun beat a tattoo; then on the right, quite close. Lenka was uneasy. He removed the cartridges from his pouch, stuffed them into his pockets, checked the lock—everything was in order. He reached the fork, turned to the right. Another half a kilometer, and what the devil!—the ravine came to an end. He climbed up the slope, got to the edge, stuck out his head. Emptiness. Up ahead was a dark grove. He had only gone ten steps—a shot, another, a third, and the bullets whistled right over his head. Lenka backed down, and rolled head over heels to the bottom of the ravine. What sort of devilry is this?

And where was he? And where should he go? Forward, back? He decided to backtrack. It had grown pitch dark—not a damn thing could be seen. He reached the fork again. Stopped. From somewhere on the left he heard voices. Lenka felt a trickle of sweat in his armpits. He hugged the ground. Some men, one after another, were coming down the left slope of the ravine. You could hear their heavy breathing, and the loose earth crumbled under their feet.

"Our people," thought Lenka, and just then someone close to him swore under his breath. Lenka raised himself a little.

"Eh, friend . . ."

The lock clicked.

"Who's there?"

"A friend, a friend . . . You're not from the Thirty-third?"

The man put his face close to Lenka's. "No, not from the Thirty-third. What do you want that regiment for?"

"What do you mean—what for? I need to find it."

"What you need is a bullet in your forehead, that's what. You're wandering about in the dark, while your commander has been running his legs off looking for you."

Someone up ahead called in a loud, if stifled, whisper.

"Kravchenko . . . Kravchenko . . ."

"But I'm here. . . ." the soldier answered in the same kind of whisper, and disappeared in the dark. For some time you could hear the earth crumbling into the bottom of the ravine; then all was quiet again.

Lenka sat there a little longer, then decided to come out of the ravine and walk in the direction from which the soldiers had come. Now no one would notice him. The sky became overcast, and neither the stars nor the moon could be seen. It began drizzling. From time to time rockets soared somewhere quite close. Lenka would lie down on his stomach and wait until they died out. The rockets were let off on the left, and Lenka decided to walk to the right, where something like huts or hayricks was discernible.

He had gone about two hundred meters when suddenly someone called from under his very feet, "Maiboroda, that you?"

Lenka started.

"Why the hell did you get lost? Have you found our men?"

Lenka struck against something hard. A horse neighed. A wagon?

"The damn nag," a voice continued from the dark. "Well, did you find them? I'm asking you."

"Who are you looking for?" Lenka asked, squatting, trying to see who was speaking. The voice came from somewhere below.

"How's that? Who are you?"

"And you?"

"Hell!" the invisible man cursed. "May they choke in the world to come, all these Fritzes and Hitlers! Plague take 'em!" And unexpectedly changing to a pleading tone, he said: "Give me a hand, lad. This carrion gets all the shellholes under the wheels . . . Down!"

A rocket soared. By its light Lenka saw a loaded cart leaning to one side, a horse calmly nibbling tall grass, and a soldier with his face flat on the ground.

The rocket died away.

"Give me a hand, friend," the soldier went on. "Maybe we'll pull it out somehow. All you can get Maiboroda to bring is death. I was telling him—drive along the road."

"What are you carrying?" asked Lenka.

"It's those hellish mines—damn the man who invented them."

"Well, all right." Lenka walked around the wagon and felt the wheel. "Eh, man, it's broken."

The soldier delivered himself of a long, elaborate curse, and began explaining that the captain had ordered them to bring the mines as soon as possible and that Maiboroda—he'll always think up something —said that by driving straight across the field they'd save a good kilometer. So there they are, may his mother get the ague. And to top it all, Fritz fires a mortar every twenty minutes.

At that moment Maiboroda himself appeared on the scene out of nowhere.

"Kopytza, where are you?" he asked.

"So you're here. You should have enjoyed your stroll another three hours."

"I've found them. About three hundred meters away."

"I'm much obliged to you. The wheel's broken."

"No-o!"

"No, indeed."

"Hell . . . and the captain is already swearing. There are still two hundred meters, he says, and their tanks are already rumbling."

" 'We'll save a kilometer, we'll save a kilometer'!" the soldier mimicked Maiboroda. "A fat lot of saving you'll do with this nag. How many are there in the wagon?"

"About sixty, I guess."

"Can we make it in ten trips?"

"If we carry six at a time, we'll make it," replied Maiboroda.

"Maybe this fellow will lend a hand. Where are you?"

They started to unload the mines in the dark. It turned out that they were not mortar shells, as Lenka had at first believed, but sappers' mines—big wooden boxes, six or seven kilograms apiece. They had to tie them with wire by twos, and in order not to have the wire cut their shoulders they had to take off their blouses and pad them under the load. They worked at it for a long time—looked for wire in the wagon, tied up the mines. Finally, they were off: Maiboroda first, Kopytzya next, Lenka last. Walking was difficult—the ground was soft, there were many shellholes, it was pitch dark, the rifle was in the way, and at each rocket you had to squat. To cap it all, Maiboroda must have lost his way—they had long since walked more than three hundred meters.

Here and there they stumbled on men who were digging in—the infantry must have occupied the line of defense. They had luck with the mortars—the Germans shifted the firing to the left, so that there was no need to wait.

Maiboroda stopped suddenly.

"It's here, I think." And he set the shells on the ground. "Put them down!"

Lenka carefully put his down and placed them alongside Maiboroda's lot. He was dripping with sweat, although he had walked stripped of his blouse and undershirt.

"Captain . . . eh, Captain!" Maiboroda called in a repressed whisper. No one answered. "Comrade Captain, where are you? We've brought the mines."

"His Honor is over there," came a weak voice out of nowhere, "on the mined field."

"Who's that? Rusinov?" asked Maiboroda.

"Uh-huh."

"Wounded, eh?"

"Something like it. Kirilyuk's done for. Still lying there."

"Where are you? This damned darkness . . ."

"Here, near the shovels . . . And the captain's over there. He's planting mines—instead of me."

"Far away?"

"Oh, no. Some fifty meters. On the right."

"I should report," Maiboroda said uncertainly, and coughed. "No anti-infantry mines planted?"

"No. Don't be afraid to go ahead; you won't be blown up. . . . Any water, boys?"

"The water's in the wagon. Wait till our next trip."

Suddenly a figure emerged from the dark.

"Here, we're here, Comrade Captain," Maiboroda said cheerfully.

The man addressed as captain squatted down.

"Where on earth have you been, you devils? Because of you . . . And who is this—the third man?"

"A soldier, helped us haul the mines. The wagon's busted."

The captain cursed. "How many did you bring?"

"Sixty."

"Hell! We're out of luck. Two men put out of action, and it'll be dawn in an hour." Furious, the captain spat. "Well, all right. Here's what we'll do—Maiboroda and Kopytzya will fetch the mines; they must be here in half an hour. And you—What's your name?"

"Bogorad."

"You'll help Rusinov get to the billets. He knows the way."

"Not necessary, Comrade Captain. I'll lie here in the dugout awhile. Better let him haul the mines."

The captain was silent, then glanced at the luminous dial of his watch.

"Two o'clock already. How time flies!" He got to his feet.

"Soldier, where are you?"

"Over here."

"Take the mines and follow me. Only, be careful."

Lenka crawled to one side, found the mines, shouldered them and, with bent back, followed the captain.

"Put them on the ground."

Lenka did so.

"Now listen carefully." The captain crouched, took Lenka's hand and started passing it over the ground. "Here are little holes dug in the ground. Feel them with your hand. Lay a mine next to one. Four meters farther there'll be another hole; in another four meters, one more hole. Then the second row—the same thing. Understand? That's your job—to place all the mines next to the holes."

The captain spoke in a whisper, but so calmly and unhurriedly that Lenka somehow felt easier. He placed the four mines he had brought and went to get others. When he had placed the twelfth and gone back, Maiboroda and Kopytzya had already brought the next installment—they were making good time now.

All about them it was remarkably quiet. The noise of the motors had ceased. Only somewhere, very far away, a machine gun snorted. It had stopped raining, then it started again—a fine drizzle, pleasant to the overheated body. The darkness and the silence, the fact that he was hauling mines that blow up tanks, things he had never seen in his life—all this was slightly terrifying, but Lenka tried not to think of anything, only to carry and place.

Once, when the dead silence was suddenly torn by a screeching sound and fiery shells with tails swept high overhead, Lenka dropped to the ground, pressing against another man who had dropped next to him. "Scared?" he heard at his very ear, and tried to stop shivering, but could not. "That's nothing, soldier; you'll get used to it!" Lenka recognized the captain's voice. "And why haven't you a blouse on? Maybe that's why you're shivering?" Lenka made no answer, picked up the mines, and walked on.

They finished at daybreak. Once or twice the Germans opened mortar fire, but without effect. They got together the shovels and the boxes with the leftover detonating fuses and moved on to their position. They walked silently, in single file, tired, wet, treading heavily on the sodden black earth. Two men led the wounded soldier; two carried the one who had been killed. All you wanted was to sleep. You didn't even want to smoke. When they arrived, Lenka dropped under the first bush like a stone, without having had a good look at the men with whom he had spent his first night of combat.

3

"Eh, you, wake up. . . . What a gamecock!"

Lenka jumped up and, not understanding anything, looked blank. "How long can you sleep? The boys had breakfast long ago."

A puny, sly-eyed soldier in a discolored blouse stood before him, laughing.

"And where's your undershirt? You were so scared you lost it?"

Lenka looked about him—really, he had only his pants on, no shirt. What a dummy he was—he had left it behind.

The soldier sat down near him.

"You don't recognize me? Maiboroda."

"Ah-h . . ." said Lenka noncommitally, hunching himself; it was rather chilly.

Maiboroda gave him a clap on the back.

"You're a tough one, lad. If I'd known it, I wouldn't have let you go when we were hauling the mines!" He examined Lenka critically from head to foot. The boy was still half asleep. "Go and splash some water on your mug at least. The captain has already asked for you." And again he slapped him on the back. "A bull calf, by God. Come to yourself, now! And I'll look in the wagon—maybe I'll find something."

In a minute he came running with a sports shirt in his hands: "Get into this for the time being; later we'll look into the commissary for something properer."

With difficulty Lenka pulled on the tight bright-orange sports shirt.

"We're off to see the captain. But put on your cap."

The captain was not in his tent. A soldier who sat at the entrance —apparently an orderly—without turning around, grumbled, "Be back right away," and went on scouring a mess kit with sand. Maiboroda pulled out of his pocket a round box containing shag and sprawled at the entrance to the tent. They were in a fresh young grove, with yellow butterflies flying about and a woodpecker tapping overhead.

"We-ell . . . And so it's all over with Kirilyuk," said Maiboroda, and passed the box to Lenka. "Smoke up. And he left two shavers." He looked at Lenka sideways. "Not married?"

"No." For some reason Lenka felt embarrassed.

"And he had two shavers. And he was young too, born in twenty-three. What's your year?"

"Twenty-five," answered Lenka.

"But his was twenty-three. Only two years older than you. All through Stalingrad he was spared, and here . . . We buried him over there under those pines. In the morning I looked at him; it was terrible. Up to here," he passed his hand above his eyebrows, "blown off. The brain dropped out. . . ."

There was a pause. Maiboroda turned to the orderly. "Did the captain go any distance?"

"Do I know?" the fellow answered, without turning around. "They don't report to me yet."

"Is he the battalion commander?" asked Lenka.

"Uh-huh, he's the commanding officer now. Orlik is his name—queer. Used to be acting battalion commander, and when Major Seleznyov was pipped on the Donetz, he became commanding officer."

"A Stalingrad man?"

Maiboroda shook his head.

"No, he's a new one. Came up toward the end of Stalingrad. Straight from a hospital. For a long time he walked with a stick."

From the conversation that followed it became clear that the captain did not get along with the major. The major was not liked by the battalion. He was one of those commanding officers who put on the soft pedal at the front, and in the rear throw their weight around and bawl out their subordinates without reason. That's how the friction started.

"You tell them about Lieutenant Lyashko," the orderly broke in. He was a very young lad who vainly tried to impart a soldierly roughness to his childish voice. He had finished scouring the mess kit and was trying to join in the conversation, but so as not injure his dignity. "The captain settled his hash for him then, didn't he?"

"He did." Maiboroda grinned, turning to Lenka. "One day, you understand, the major got drunk and cursed out Lieutenant Lyashko, commanding officer of the First Company, before everybody—and right in front of the formation. Slacker, he said, called him a loafer, didn't want to fight, and all that. And the captain stood there, listening, red as a beet, his jaws working. And then: 'I'm ashamed of you,' says he, 'before the soldiers, Comrade Major. Lyashko is the best officer in the battalion, and when he's before the formation, no flask sticks out of his pocket.' He snapped his crop, turned round, and was gone. Well, after that things started happening. The major began to pick on him on account of his collar, his boots—and the report, says he, isn't written right, and so on and so forth. . . . Until the war began. And when it did, the major right off grew meek as a lamb. The captain, he was always with the men—on the march, crossing rivers—but not the major. He was mostly in a carriage, or he'd say, 'I'm off to the observation post to see the divisional commander; take charge here, Captain.' Well, it was at the observation post that a stray bullet winged him. It's a pity the wound's a trifling one; it'll heal in a week." Maiboroda sighed heavily. "Yes, with the captain it's somehow more cheerful, by God!" And suddenly he grinned, his black sly little eyes lighting up. "And as for the women pining for him, is it his fault? They stick to him like flies. . . ."

"When we was staying at Chernotroitzkaya—" the orderly began, but Maiboroda interrupted him.

"Don't you butt in. Scour your mess kit, and keep quiet. The whole bottom's black."

" 'Black' . . . 'black.' " The orderly raised his voice, taking offense. "You've been sprawling here like a lord; dropped your lousy butts all over the place. Here comes the captain; he'll teach you manners."

"What are you growling about there?" the captain called to him from a distance.

Tall, slim, his blue cap with its pale-blue trim on his ear, his blouse unbuttoned, he walked with a lazy, slightly waddling gait in his light box-calf boots, slashing leaves from the bushes with his crop.

"So that's what you're like," he said, going over to Lenka and slapping his chest with his crop.

"Bogorad is your name, isn't it?"

"Leonid Bogorad," Lenka answered as smartly as possible, straightening his shoulders and pressing his clenched hands against the seams of his trousers.

"And your patronymic?"

"Semyonovich."

"Well, come in, Leonid Semyonovich; let's talk."

And, stooping, he entered the tent. Lenka and Maiboroda followed him. The captain tossed his crop onto a pile of grass covered with a blanket, turned round, thrust his hands deep into his pockets and, swaying slightly, examined Lenka from head to foot. Lenka stood straight, his bright-orange sports shirt already burst under the armpits, his chest stuck out, his stomach pulled in, filling his lungs with air to seem more robust.

The captain smiled. "Relax. I see you're husky. You know how to dig?"

"What's there to know, Comrade Captain?"

"Flex your arm."

Lenka tensed the muscle. The captain felt it.

"You should have such muscle, Maiboroda, though I don't know what good it would do you. You know only how to work with your tongue."

"What do you want, Comrade Captain? He's young. And I'm already going on thirty. It's easier to make with the tongue than with the hands."

Lenka stood straight, red with the praise he had received, and did not know what to do to give this captain even greater pleasure.

"Have you dumbbells, Comrade Captain?"

"What kind of dumbbells?"

"Ordinary ones. One-pound, two-pound. With one hand I can—"

"All right," the captain interrupted him. "We have no circus here. What we must do is dig. For eight, ten, fifteen hours on end. Before you earn a decoration, you'll sweat a bucketful, and more. This is no infantry—to mount an attack and shout hurrah. Do you understand mines?"

"Mines?" Lenka was confused.

"Yes, sir. The same that you hauled last night—SM, PMD, POMZ. Eh? Your eyes tell me that you hear these names for the first time. TMB? You don't know that?" The captain whistled. "It's a bad job, and I thought . . ."

He paused and looked at Lenka out of the corner of his eye. Lenka stood there red-faced, distressed. He was dying to please the captain, but did not know how to do it, and in his helplessness merely flushed.

"Have you any kind of paper?" asked the captain.

"I do."

"Show it to me."

Lenka pulled a crushed, soiled envelope out of his pocket. "Now I'm done for. He'll send me to the division." The captain read the paper and returned it.

"M-yes . . . So you don't know TMB?"

"No," replied Lenka.

"Fit, but untrained?"

"Why untrained? We were . . ."

"You stabbed a dummy? Stab with a short weapon, hit with the butt from above?"

"Not only a dummy." Lenka took offense. "And how to toss a grenade, assemble and dismantle a machine gun, know the rifle by heart, and how to crawl—"

"To crawl, you say? And do you want to be a sapper?"

"I do."

"Do you undertake to learn all our tricks in a week?"

"I do, Comrade Captain."

"Look at him. People study for years, and he'll do it in a week. . . ." And turning to Maiboroda, he said: "Take him to Lyashko in the first. And find him a blouse. A decent one. And now—about face, forward march!"

Lenka saluted smartly, turned about on his heels, and walked out of the tent with a military step. He liked the captain: so young, and he already has a decoration, and so devilishly handsome—curly-haired, swarthy, black eyebrows, and must be a daredevil; you can see it by his eyes. Generally speaking, all was going well. And Lenka headed for the kitchen to get acquainted with the cook.

4

The engineering battalion in which Lenka found himself was part of a very distinguished division. It received its baptism of fire at Kastornoe, then was at Stalingrad from the beginning to the end of the campaign, and early in March, 1943, was about to move east to be remanned. But then the Germans reoccupied Kharkov, and the division was moved to the Ukraine in forced order, the decision having apparently been made to reman it on the way. When it reached the front line, the Germans had been contained, the battles were over, and there began the "great standing" which lasted three months, if not longer.

The troops were billeted on picturesque Ukrainian villages with poplars, ponds, and other bucolic charms, and they began what in the language of reports was called "battle preparation" and in the language of the rank and file was known as "swelling." The men rested—received reinforcements, studied matériel, engaged in tactical games: "platoon, company, battalion in attack, defense, reconnoitering," and—what was indispensable—they dug no end of fire and communication trenches, digging up all the ground around the villages.

At first they lived in huts; then they built themselves dugouts and supplementary facilities, ate borshch with fresh green vegetables, drank milk. The officers began to play the dandy: they acquired daggers with plastic handles, which dangled like dirks to their very knees, ordered new blouses and riding breeches, displayed newly issued shoulder straps, placed pieces of tin and celluloid under the lining so that the cloth should not get mussed, and fashioned light summer boots from waterproof capes, painting them black, so as not to be caught by their superiors, who forbade improper use of the capes.

In a word, the men rested up wonderfully, although, as is the custom, they grumbled that there was nothing worse than remanning. "It's different at the front—no note-taking, no timetables, no studies— fight and that's all. . . ."

Thus passed April, May, June.

On July 5th planes were flying over the division all day long. Next day the bulletin announced that battles had begun in the region of Kursk. In the evening the division rose and moved south. A few days later, together with other units that were holding the defense, it crossed the Donetz and entrenched on the southern bank.

For thirty-six hours the battalion of engineers covered the crossing, and by the end of the second day was removed from the river and placed on the front line—to lay and clear away mines and dig endless command and observation posts.

Such is the history, in the most compact form, of the unit that adopted Lenka Bogorad. He was issued a machine gun, a new blouse with shoulder straps, stiff English shoes size 41, a sapper's shovel, on which he immediately cut the letters "L. B." with a knife, and on the day's report to the head of the division's engineer unit they increased the figure in the column "Battalion Personnel" by one, without going into unnecessary details.

All at once Lenka became one of the group. In the first place, he was of a cheerful disposition, and that alone meant much: second, he was helpful and easygoing; third, he liked to work—more accurately, he disliked idleness. Furthermore, he had an attractive face —pug-nosed, jolly, with freckles scattered all over it, and even on his ears.

At first they poked mild fun at him, recalling how he had left his blouse at the front, but Lenka took the teasing so goodnaturedly and himself related so amusingly the impressions of that night—how the three of them had been hauling mines and how a minethrower had scared him—that all the witticisms recoiled from him as from armor. And when in excavating the foundation area for a structure to serve a headquarters group with a special assignment, he doubled all the norms indicated in the instructions regarding earthwork, having outdone even a powerhouse like Tugiev, Lieutenant Lyashko himself, who was never amazed at anything, said, "Oho!"

The second day the loudmouthed and quarrelsome cook, Timoshka, from whom you could never get an additional spoonful of porridge, however you begged, threw an extra piece of meat into his mess kit, the officer in charge of the artillery ammunition allowed him to take apart and reassemble a trophy "Walter" and even fire it once or twice, and chubby, pink-faced Musya, the headquarters clerk, coquettishly compressing her lips, said, "You look very, very much like a very, very good friend of mine," and, within the limits of her ability, smiled enigmatically. Even Major Kurach, the serious, bespectacled deputy political instructor, liked Lenka, though Lenka was no more at home in politics than in higher mathematics.

In a word, everybody loved Lenka, and even if he took advantage of it, he did not do so often or injure anyone thereby. Generally speaking, he felt free and easy with everyone, and only the devil knows why he was embarrassed by Captain Orlik. The captain would come over, stand there, a mocking look in his black eyes, and his cap slightly to one side over his forelock, put his hands in his pocket and ask: "Well, how are you, Leonid Semyonovich, not fed up with digging? Shall we perhaps have a smoke?" He would sit down, light up; the fellows would laugh, joke, but Lenka wouldn't say a word. Or Orlik would call him to his tent and start asking him something relating to sapper's work, as if examining him. In two days Lenka learned the names of all the mines and how to charge them and how to light a Bickford cord, but when it came time to show off before the captain—everything dropped from Lenka's hands, matches refused to light, broke. What the devil!

In short, Lenka fell in love with the captain. He fell in love the way schoolboys fall in love with their older comrades. He even tried to imitate his way of smoking, his gait, but could he walk that lightly in his heavy boots? And the captain did not notice him, or made believe that he did not, and Lenka could only dream of the day when he would distinguish himself in combat or, better still, save the captain's life at the risk of his own. Then he would see of what Lenka was capable. But this occasion did not present itself; the battalion was currently engaged in the prosiest of all front-line occupations—it made dugouts and cut logs for roofing—and he could save the captain from no one except perhaps staff officers; every one of them demanded that his own bunker be built first and roofed not with two, but four layers of logs.

Battles developed on the southern bank of the Donetz, at Izyum and points east. A little later Information Bureau bulletins described them as local engagements showing a tendency to grow into large-scale battles. The division to which the battalion belonged, having skirted Bogorodichnoe on the left, fought its way over several more kilometers, found itself before the village of Golaya Dolina, and halted there. The Germans dug in, improved their equipment, and even attempted a counterattack, which, while it ended unsuccessfully, arrested our movement forward for a fairly long time.

In the course of the engagement one of the division's regiments succeeded in capturing a German battery of heavy artillery—six huge 154-millimeter howitzers. The regiment was officially congratulated, but the commander, having the foreboding that the Germans would try to retake the cannon, demanded a company of engineers to mine the battery area, at least against tanks.

The first company of the battalion was just about to finish camouflaging the dugouts for a headquarters group with a special assignment, when Shelest, Orlik's orderly, came running, out of breath, and announced that the captain had ordered the men not to start work on another dugout but return at once to their position.

On the way Lenka tried to get chummy with Shelest.

"Are we goin' to attack?"

"Sure, not retreat," Shelest answered evasively. He was not a bad fellow, but as a man who stood closest to the brass and was the first to get all the news, he was inclined to put on airs.

"They say the Twenty-seventh has captured some battery or other?"

"They say."

"Well, and what does the captain say?"

"He says he has a bellyache."

"Oh, quit it! I'm asking you like a human being."

Shelest himself was dying to tell the latest news, but you must raise your price. So, he held out for another five minutes and finally said that we had taken Bogorodichnoe, but had lost many men and that Fritz had no end of mine throwers and that some kind of "Tigers" and "Ferdinands" had turned up—must be some new tanks. No projectile can pierce them, they say.

"And do mines blow them up?"

"Mines?" Shelest did not know the answer, but not to lose face replied that mines do smash them, but not fast. He did not figure out what "not fast" might mean, but this detail in itself seemed to him perfectly plausible.

"By the way, the captain was telling Lieutenant Lyashko that he should pay some attention to you."

"What d'you mean—'attention'?" Lenka pricked up his ears.

"Well, he should teach you a thing or two. 'The fellow's not very brainy,' he said, 'so you teach him a thing or two, because we'll soon be sending him out on missions, and I'm afraid he'll get blown up by a mine.' "

"That's what he said: 'not very brainy'?"

"Yes, that's how he put it."

"You're lying!"

"I got other things to do than lie. 'Such a clumsy bear,' says he; 'today he almost blew my head off with a practice grenade.' "

"That's just what he said to the lieutenant?"

"That's just how he put it. And the lieutenant thought and thought, then said . . ." For a minute Shelest halted, to think up the lieutenant's answer.

"Well?"

"So he says to him, 'Perhaps we were wrong taking him into our battalion.' "

"And the captain?"

"Don't interrupt me, damn it! 'Maybe we ought to turn him over to some regiment of sharpshooters,' says he, 'so we'll have less trouble with him?' "

"Well, and the captain?"

"The captain mumbled something and then said: 'Maybe we'll get rid of him. We'll try him out with the first mission,' says he, 'and find out if he's up to the mark or just shit.' "

"Now you're lying—'shit' he didn't say."

"Maybe he said something worse."

"Go to hell!" Lenka took offense, and walked off. "You made it all up. . . ." But he was disgusted and bitter.

He would return from the first mission, after destroying this same "Tiger" or whatever you call it, and would say nothing about it to anyone. He would return and go to sleep. And next day all the talk throughout the battalion would be: Who destroyed the "Tiger"? But not a syllable out of him. Tugiev? No. Sergeant Koshubarov? No. Maybe, Lieutenant Lyashko himself? Not him either. Who then? The explanation was that no one in the battalion saw that he had done it; only the sharpshooters saw it. So they would tell their commanding officer, he would tell his, and so on, up to the top: "Private Bogorad, from the Eighty-third Regiment, destroyed the 'Tiger.' " And so the general would summon him. . . . No, the general wouldn't take the trouble to summon him on this account; he would simply send a message to the battalion: "For such and such a feat I congratulate Private Leonid Semyonovich Bogorad." And the captain would flush, he would begin snapping his crop on his boot, and he'd ask: "Why didn't you say anything, Bogorad?" And then he would answer: "Why should I say anything, if they want to expel me from the battalion and consider me shit?" And the captain would . . .

At this point Lenka stumbled against something and ran into a man who was right in front of him.

"Are you crazy or what? Haven't you eyes in your head?"

Lenka did not answer, and stepped aside, but the thread of the fantasy was broken, and what the captain said in reply has remained unknown.

5

The men ate their supper hurriedly and set off at once. The battery was four or five kilometers away, and Lieutenant Lyashko hoped to be able to mine at least part of the area before dawn. But at the front things don't always happen the way you want them to. Lyashko decided to save time by going through the woods instead of following the road—one of the most unreliable ways when you are in a hurry —and as a result they reached the battery when it was already quite light. The mines, dispatched in four wagons, had long been waiting for them on the spot. The chief of the regimental staff, Major Sutyrin, redheaded, sweaty, completely worn out, was furious.

"Why didn't you get here next week, damn you? Your command posts and your observation posts for the brass have spoiled you completely, and nobody can bring you up to the front line for love or money."

Lyashko scratched his unshaven chin with two fingers—it was hard to make this man lose his temper—listened to the major calmly, and when the latter paused to fill his lungs, inquired, "Who'll show me the directions the tanks are likely to take?"

The major burst out again: "Show him the direction! There! There! There! The directions are everywhere." He pointed in all directions. "The tanks may show up any minute now. What are we going to do then? I'm asking you—What are we going to do? Well, why don't you speak?"

Lyashko fully understood the major's condition. He had been in the war from the beginning, had been in all sorts of messes, had known more than one superior officer; he sympathized with the unhappy man—he had known him since Stalingrad—and calmly, without unnecessary talk, he waited until the major finished blowing off steam. But five minutes earlier the major had been reproved by the division's chief of staff for being late with a report, and he would have gone on bawling out Lyashko and his company and his battalion and all sappers generally for a long time, if, as Lyashko's luck would have it, the regiment's engineer Bogatkin had not approached them. No longer young, his temples graying, his left arm in a sling, he walked over unnoticed and stopped beside Lyashko, winking at him. The major turned to him at once.

"Here, Engineer, are your vaunted sappers! Do what you please with them. I'm fed up with all this. They were enjoying themselves in the woods, you see, while we here were fighting to keep these damn howitzers."

The engineer smiled wearily. "You are wanted on the telephone. Forty-one."

"Don't they have a man on duty there? It always has to be Sutyrin."

"All right, all right, go."

The major cursed, and ran into the dugout.

The engineer smiled again.

"The old man is all in, by God. Otherwise he's a fine fellow. How many men have you brought?"

"The whole company. They asked for a company."

"Too many, of course, but that's nothing; we'll get through sooner. Where are the men?"

"They're shaking the apple trees."

"Order them to stop. The quartermaster has lost two men already on account of the apples. It's hot, and there's a shortage of water, so they shake trees all day long."

"And what's this?" he pointed to Lyashko's bandaged arm.

"It's nothing. Grazed by a bullet. Their snipers haven't had any practice, not like in Stalingrad."

Somewhere quite nearby a mortar crackled, and almost immediately several shells exploded in the orchard. Apples showered from the trees. Instinctively Lenka hugged the ground, but seeing that the soldiers were crawling about in the orchard and collecting apples, paying no attention to anything, he, too, not to lag behind and seem a coward, stuffed his pockets with little apples that were still perfectly green.

"Get rid of the apples!" Lyashko shouted from a distance, and walked over to the soldiers. With him were the engineer and a sergeant.

"Petrenko, take your platoon and go with this sergeant," said Lyashko, and seeing Lenka, added, "Well, Bogorad, congratulations on your holy baptism."

"I won't let you down, Comrade Lieutenant!" Lenka felt his mouth going dry.

Lyashko took a watch out of his side pocket; it was as huge as a locomotive machinist's.

"By five, zero, zero everything must be ready, Petrenko. Is that clear?"

6

Lenka long remembered that morning. It was an early July morning with the edge of the sun just peeking from behind the apple orchard, with dewdrops trembling on blades of grass, with a field mouse which scurried at his very feet, turned around, looked at him, and whisked into a hole known to it alone and to no one else on earth. He remembered the stout apple tree, on which someone had already cut out with a knife "B. R. S. July 1943," and how the sergeant rolled the last cigarette, obligatory before every mission, and how his hand shook slightly, so that he dropped the shag and started picking it up from the ground. Then a bullet whistled overhead, and Lenka bowed, whereupon Private Antonov said: "You're bowing easily, Lenka." It wasn't a bullet that whistled, but a bird—there is such a scoundrelly bird that whistles like a bullet. Then Petrenko said, "We're off," and everyone, groaning and swearing, got up and moved on, but Kasatkin, of course, forgot his shovel and had to go back for it.

At first, they crossed the orchard, then descended into a gully and walked along its bottom. First went Petrenko, in command of the platoon, tall, broad-shouldered, with a big, pockmarked face; he was followed by Antonov who stepped along with his customary clumsy, bearish gait; Lenka bore up the rear. He strode, looked at the back of Antonov's neck, which was red and the hair of which had been freshly trimmed, and wondered when that devil had found time to get a haircut—only yesterday he was shaggy. Then they emerged from the gully and found themselves in a brushwood thicket. They crossed it, and as they came out of it Petrenko commanded, "Down!" All dropped to the ground: on the right of Lenka—Antonov, on the left, lanky Suchkov, who at once produced bread from his pocket and began munching.

"It's a good thing Antonov is along," thought Lenka; "he's an old hand at this mining business, a fellow who has been through a lot." Antonov glanced at Lenka out of the corner of his eye—he was cleaning the screws on the machine gun with a chip—and reflected in his turn: "So far so good; he's not in a funk." Then Lenka stuck the chip into his cap and, propping his head on his hands, for lack of any other occupation began to examine the meadow in front of him.

"Here's the field glass"—Antonov nudged him—"have a look at the Fritzes."

Lenka took it, pressed his eyes against the eyepieces, and began to turn his head from side to side. A grove, a stand of pines, a meadow, again a grove, a stand of pines, a meadow.

"Well, found them?"

"No. . . ."

"Look straight ahead."

Lenka looked straight ahead and saw—the devil, right before his nose—two soldiers running. One dropped behind, squatted, then got up and ran after the other. You could even see their rifles, and that they did not wear blouses and that their sleeves were rolled up. Lenka turned his head and saw another soldier. He sat in a tree, as if on a platform, and he too was peering through a field glass.

"O, look, look, an observer!"

"Don't yell! Pleased?" Antonov took away the binoculars.

Lenka stared without using the field glasses and could not make out anything. What a devilish business! A Fritz sits in a tree and probably sees Lenka. Now he'll say something to somebody, and they'll open fire on him. But he calmed down at once: the sun was shining behind them, and the Fritzes couldn't see them.

Petrenko crawled up, and showed him, Antonov and Suchkov, where to lay the first row of mines. They brought the mines, and began digging holes. The Germans did not shoot; the ground was soft; the work went fast, Lenka was digging holes—one, two, three, and a hole was ready—Antonov planted the mine, and Suchkov covered it with sod and strewed twigs over it. "Come on, come on, Suchkov, don't dawdle—only five pieces left."

And suddenly it began—it began exploding everywhere at once! Shells, mines, the devil knows what else! Lenka had barely time to jump into a trench—it was lucky that someone had dug them there—pressed his face against the earth, squeezed his ears between his knees and crouched like that, contorted, his eyes shut tight, his teeth clenched, and kept counting: "One, two, three, four, five, six . . ." Then he even stopped counting.

Lenka came to, because someone booted his back. Freeing his head from his knees, he looked up and saw Antonov's face. He was shouting, but there was no making out what he was saying. Lenka climbed out of the trench. Two steps away lay Suchkov, his legs wide apart, his head in his arms. And why's he lying so stupidly? A little way off, Antonov too was lying, and his back was shaking. He turned around for a second; his face was red, lips compressed. He waved his hand, meaning "Lie down!" and turned away again. Lenka ran up to Antonov, lay down alongside him, and only then noticed that he was shooting. Up ahead Germans were running straight toward them— ten or twenty men, maybe more. Lenka pressed the machine gun against his cheek and fired a round, then a second, a third. The Germans ran, shouted, and perhaps fired, then started dropping; then the mines started going off, and they ran back.

"Ah-h-h!" Lenka shouted suddenly to his own surprise, and jumped up.

Antonov hit him painfully on the leg with the butt of the sub-machine gun.

"Lie down, you fool!"

Lenka plunked down on his stomach, and Antonov hit him again, this time on his head, above the ear.

"Why are you hitting me?" Lenka snapped.

"Keep mum; be glad you're alive. Still got cartridges?"

Lenka felt the extra disk that hung in a bag from his belt, took it off and laid it by his side. He looked askance at Antonov, then at Suchkov. The latter lay just as before, his legs wide apart, his arms around his head. "He's done fighting," flashed through Lenka's head, and he turned away. The sound of firing was still coming from the right; then it ceased.

"They've failed so far." Antonov laid the machine gun aside and looked at Lenka. "Well, how are you?"

"All right." Lenka tried to smile.

Antonov suddenly made a face.

"Eh, boy, you've been . . . What's above your ear?"

Lenka felt it—sticky. Looked at his hand—red. Blood . . .

At that moment Petrenko called, "Finish up the rows, while it's quiet," and Antonov and he began to plant the remaining mines.

By six o'clock the company succeeded in mining five fields, one more than Sutyrin wanted. Two of them were the work of Petrenko's platoon. Antonov and Lenka were in the lead—together they laid sixty-four mines. Lenka felt like a hero. His head was bandaged, and he answered the men's questions with, "It's nothing, just a scratch." Lieutenant Lyashko said to him: "If I had a camera, I'd snap you—you look like a real hero." And the engineer with the gray temples, hearing that Lenka, the novice, had set so many mines, said: "Keep on outdoing the oldsters, so they don't get stuck up." Lenka beamed and flushed and out of modesty kept saying that it was all Antonov—without him he was a zero without a digit. And he was sorry, oh, how sorry, that Captain Orlik wasn't there. . . .

Only the death of Suchkov, taciturn, lanky Suchkov, did not let him savor his triumph. They had not been friends; furthermore, Suchkov was the only man in the battalion Lenka had quarreled with, and Lenka had always been irritated by the fact that Suchkov was continually munching bread and that when he was at work he would have a smoke every five minutes; but he was the first man Lenka knew whom the Germans had killed. Just a while ago they had been talking; Suchkov had asked him for a scrap of newspaper in order to roll a cigarette, and he gave it to him, and Suchkov had said, "Good paper, doesn't tear," and now he was lying, his arms stretched out, his eyes closed, and the men were digging a grave for him. And when the first clod of earth fell on his body, wrapped up in a waterproof, Lenka felt a lump in his throat, and blinked his eyes rapidly.

7

The mission had been accomplished, the minefields planted, they could go home. But Major Sutyrin, who was fearful of tanks—they did not come, and he kept waiting for them—persuaded Lyashko to leave one platoon until evening.

"You understand," he said in a begging, wheedling tone entirely different from that he had used in the morning, "there is another lousy road here. If tanks go into action, they are sure to use this road, you'll see. Now it's light, and nothing can be done. Leave the boys here till night, and they'll do what's needed in a jiffy. And I'll issue them a nightcap."

Lyashko scratched his chin as he had in the morning and, sighing heavily, began teasing the major.

"I have no right, Comrade Major. I understand it very well, but I have no right. The order is for all the men to return to headquarters after carrying out the assignment."

The major clasped Lyashko under the arms—he was a head shorter than the lieutenant and could not reach his shoulders—and did not stop begging.

"Well, don't be revengeful, don't be revengeful, Lyashko. This morning I lost my temper, I know, but have a heart. I'd send my own men, but you know yourself, there are hardly any of them left, and they're out in various battalions. But you have eagles, that's it— eagles; before you know it, they'll finish the job. And I'll give them dinner and supper, and a double portion too!" And he looked imploringly into Lyashko's eyes. "Well? Agreed? Eh? Don't make it tough for me."

In the end the major managed to persuade Lyashko, after giving a sworn promise—"I swear on the holy cross," and he crossed himself fervently three times—"that by midnight the platoon will be back."

The other platoons had left. The one that remained occupied the former German artillery dugouts and hit the hay. Lenka alone, excited by the events of the night, could not fall asleep. First he pestered Antonov with questions, then Petrenko; they mumbled something unintelligible in reply, and ended by simply cursing him out, and Lenka began to loiter about the battery, passing his hands over the cannon, until he was chased away. He got into the orchard, gorged himself on sour apples till his teeth were on edge and there was a rumbling in his stomach, and finally buddied up with the regiment's scouts, daredevils in wide gay trousers, unbuttoned blouses, with daggers in their belts. The previous night they had gone scouting, held up a German truck that had lost its way, brought in the chauffeur as an identification prisoner and spoils of war in the form of two chests. Now, settled in one of the dugouts, they were playing cards, using the trophy watches and other trash as stakes. Lenka staked his sole possession, a combination pocketknife, with twelve gadgets, and within an hour won two watches—one with a black, the other with a yellow dial—a fountain pen with a green design on it and a razor in a white plastic box. Then the scouts treated him to devilishly strong cognac, and it all ended by his falling asleep there without even noticing it.

When he woke up, it was getting dark. The scouts had gone to carry out a mission, and in the dugout there was only a master sergeant who was looking over the platoon's equipment. Lenka, in a funk, thinking he had overslept, ran over to his unit, and there Petrenko pounced on him:

"Where the devil have you been? We searched the battery, the orchard, we've been run off our feet—and you get plastered too. Breathe!"

Lenka breathed.

"I thought so. You've been in the battalion less than no time, and you get into trouble already. Is this a reserve regiment or a combat unit? The captain was asking for you. What shall I tell him?"

Lenka stood there, his arms along his trouser seams, and was silent. And he had to get involved with those daredevil scouts just when the captain came. He was out of luck, simply out of luck!

"Ah, the vagrant has turned up," came a voice from behind his back. Lenka started, recognizing the captain's voice. "Where on earth were you?"

"With the scouts near here. Dropped in on them," Lenka answered in the most innocent tone he could muster.

"You swilled vodka with them, eh?"

Lenka felt himself blushing.

"Don't be bashful. Did they treat you to vodka?"

"Cognac . . ." Lenka answered in a scarcely audible whisper.

The dugout nearby went to pieces with the outburst of laughter.

"Was that to keep you from getting a headache?" The captain pointed to Lenka's bandage and sat down on a box of shells. "Can I get a drink? Only, not cognac."

Several hands were reached out to the captain.

"Here are good apples, tart."

Petrenko slapped one of the hands, so that the apples were scattered.

"Throw them away! To the devil with them! As it is, you've all spoiled your stomachs. You're squatting in the shrubbery all the time. Maiboroda, bring some water; there's a barrel over near the cannon."

The captain got to his feet. "All right. Joking apart. How many men have you got, Petrenko?"

"Ten. With me."

"Take six—that will be more than enough—and give me Antonov, Tugiev and . . ." The captain looked around the dugout, fixing his gaze on each of the men in turn. He turned to Lenka. "Did you get it bad on the head?"

"Oh, no. Just a—"

"All right. Eyesight good?"

"All right."

"You see well at night too?"

"Yes."

"So, these three—Antonov, Tugiev, Bogorad—are coming with me. Take the others on the mission. Only, you must all be back by twelve."

"We'll get through in an hour." Petrenko rose. "We'll eat supper in our own quarters."

"That's all. Get the men together. And you three—follow me!"

The captain climbed out of the dugout, looked around, and made his way to the apple orchard. The sun had set and there was dampness in the air. A group of soldiers, settled under a cannon, were singing a Ukranian song below the breath. Drawers and shirts were drying on the cannon. From far away came the sound of an accordion.

"Let's sit down, boys," said the captain. "Light up." He seated himself under an apple tree, the same on which the letters "B. K. S." were cut, and produced a package of Kazbek.

Antonov went so far as to click his tongue. "How did you come by that, Comrade Captain?"

"Don't ask; light up. Kind folks made me a present of them."

Antonov winked at Lenka, meaning: We know who those folks are.

"You'll have to wrap this up in something," the captain said, pointing to Lenka's bandage.

"I could take it off altogether."

"Don't take it off; wrap it up, I said. In the dark it would shine like a lantern. Now we'll make our way to the Germans. Straight into their lair. You've never seen them at close range, have you? We must have a look at them, mustn't we?"

"We must," Lenka replied, without much conviction.

The captain smiled. "Well, we won't go exactly to the Germans, but, in general, close to them. A small operation is planned for tomor-

399

row, and you and I have to check two areas to find out if the Germans have laid mines. And we must work fast, so the second company has time to make a passage through those areas. Burlin will arrive by midnight—so we have three, at most four hours. Clear?"

"Clear," replied Antonov. "And how far must we go?"

"You'll find out presently. You'll take Tugiev, I—Bogorad. Your sector is the road to Golaya Dolina; mine is to the left between the two groves. The distance between the front line and the Germans is about three hundred meters; therefore the minefield must be two hundred to two hundred and fifty meters away. We ought to be able to get through in three hours. Each one is to take two grenades and check the automatic guns. Take Finnish daggers too. We meet in fifteen minutes at this apple tree. Forward, march!"

All three returned to the dugout.

"Watch the captain," Antonov whispered to Lenka. "You know how he is. He's sure to be up to something."

"How do you mean?" Lenka was puzzled.

"Oh, he'll think up something. He'll want to bring in a prisoner, or something like that. So don't let him. Tell him time is getting short, and the company's waiting."

"But he knows it's waiting."

"Yes, he knows, but I know him. You think he was ordered to go? No, at headquarters they said to send an officer, that's all, and he decided to go himself."

When they returned to the apple tree, the captain was sitting there as before, but he had a map on his knees and was measuring something on it with a pair of compasses.

"Well, is everything ready?"

"Everything, Comrade Captain."

"Then we're off."

"That's for you." Antonov handed him two grenades. "Brand-new, still smell of paint."

The captain hung the grenades on his belt, straightened his blouse, and shook hands first with Tugiev, then with Antonov.

"Good luck."

"The same to you." Antonov smiled. As always, Tugiev was silent. "And remember, Burlin will be here at midnight."

"I remember. But why?"

"Oh, nothing. Just like that." Antonov smiled again, and shook Lenka's hand. "You had your hands full today."

On parting they walked in different directions: Antonov and Tugiev past the cannon on the road, Lenka with the captain straight through the shrubbery.

8

Why Orlik had chosen Bogorad, instead of one of the more experienced men, he himself did not know. When he was on his way from the battalion to the front line, he had firmly decided to send Antonov with Tugiev, and Petrov with Vakhrushev. They had been on a scouting mission more than once, all experienced men, Stalingraders. He himself had no intention of going. The divisional engineer said (Antonov was right): "Send some company commander, or, no, a platoon commander, but a brainy one." But when he came into the dugout and looked at Bogorad, the thought popped into his head: "Why not send him? By God, maybe he'll turn out to be a pretty good scout—he is a bright, efficient fellow, plainly no coward; there is a shortage of scouts now, and of the privates only Vakhrushev and Tugiev remain. We must prepare successors for them. I'll send him."

At the same time he himself suddenly felt a desire to go. "I'll watch Bogorad to see how he handles the situation. Besides, I'm fed up with all these dugouts and shelters for the brass, damn them." And so he decided to take Bogorad with him, and to send Antonov with Tugiev.

They were walking through the shrubs, about a kilometer from the front line, and somewhere grasshoppers, invisible, were chirping away and overhead swallows were darting impetuously.

"Messers . . ." Lenka smiled. "Maybe it'll rain, they are flying so low." And after a few more steps he added: "There hasn't been any rain in a long time. See how cracked the earth is."

Indeed, it had not rained for a long time—ever since the night when Lenka entered the battalion. The grass was burned; it had become dry and yellow. Lenka bent down, took a handful of earth, and rubbed it between his fingers.

He reached his hand to the captain and poured out on his palm earth as dry as powder.

"Even the worm too has got skinny. Look at it. Shall I give it a drink from the water bottle?"

Orlik glanced at his watch.

"Let's sit down. Let's wait till it's quite dark." He felt that Lenka had lost his usual tenseness and he wanted to talk to him.

"Sure, let's wait. . . ." Lenka readily agreed and sat down under a shrub cross-legged.

Orlik seated himself beside him and, pulling off a boot, began to rewind a footcloth.

"How quiet it is, eh?" said Lenka, whispering, obviously in order not to break the quiet. But at that moment, as if on purpose, a mortar clicked close by and a shell, having whistled over their heads, went off somewhere behind them.

The captain looked at Lenka out of the corner of his eye.

"Not scared any more?"

"Of what?"

"Of shells."

"Of shells?" Lenka shrugged his shoulders, then asked, "And you?"

The captain smiled. "I've been acquainted with them a long time. Right here," he slapped his leg, just above the knee, "I treasure three splinters. . . . But the first weeks at the front I ducked regularly."

"Have you been fighting long?"

"From the beginning. From June, 1941."

"And now you're not scared at all?"

"Of what?"

"Why, right now, going on a mission?"

Orlik smiled again. "You're smart; I see you're counterattacking. How shall I put it?" He looked for an appropriate explanation, but was unable to find one. "It's yes and no, somehow. . . ."

"That goes for me, too. Just now I was walking along and thinking: 'A man doesn't want to die, does he?' And if that's so, then it means that he's scared. Isn't that it?"

"Well, let's assume that it's so. . . ."

"But we must go, the way you and I are doing now. And maybe we'll be killed or crippled, but we go all the same. And generally speaking . . ."

Lenka suddenly fell silent, caught an ant, and began to examine it.

"Generally speaking, what?"

402

"Well, anyway, generally speaking . . . There you are fighting, fighting, and you don't know against whom. . . ."

"How's that—you don't know?" Orlik was completely taken aback. "We've been fighting for two years, and you don't know—"

"Well, not that I don't know. . . . Of course I know. I know that there's Hitler, there are fascists, that they want to seize all Russia and the whole world. . . . But before, say a hundred or two hundred years ago, it wasn't like this, was it? Two armies met and fought. He fought you, and you fought him—and one got the upper hand. But now . . ." Lenka blew the ant off his palm and watched it fall. "Just now Suchkov, in our battalion, was killed. When we were laying mines. You know him, a tall fellow, from our platoon. A shell came flying and killed him. And he never saw a live Fritz closer than three hundred meters. I didn't either. . . ."

"Well, that pleasure you'll have," said Orlik, forcefully thrusting his leg into a box-calf boot, but he pulled it out at once. "Give me your famous pocketknife," he said. "There's something sticking out there, a nail or something. . . ."

Lenka produced the knife, pulled out the screwdriver, and handed it to the captain.

"This will do it."

The captain began fussing with the nail, and Lenka fell silent. And he wanted to talk about many things. Now, what kind of a war is this? Everything arrives by air. For instance, now: around you everything is quiet, beautiful, swallows are darting, all kinds of bugs are crawling, and suddenly a piece of metal comes flying out of no one knows where—and straight into you. And you don't even know who fired. . . . Or a minefield . . . You hide little boxes with toluol in the ground and you carefully, carefully camouflage them with grass, different twigs, and it's all a fraud. And then we ourselves get blown up, the way it happened two days ago in the Thirty-third. And generally speaking, who invented war? And when was the first, the very, very first war? A thousand years ago, or two, or more? And what started it? And Lenka also wanted to talk about something else. About this: that here he is now going on his first mission with the captain and that, of course, he's scared, but the captain need not worry, he'll carry out any order of his over and above the line of duty, and if they clash with any German . . . Let there be, let there be a clash with them;

he even wants this—he won't let him down; he'll get the better of any Fritz; on his way to the front, in some village, he'd seen partisans hanged by the Germans, five people, among them a girl, a young thing, seventeen or eighteen years old, no more. . . . And Lenka wanted to talk about much else, just here, in the woods, when he was all alone with the captain, but the captain did not pay attention to him; he was carefully thrusting his leg into the boot. Then he got up and said in his cheerful voice:

"Well, philosopher, shall we go?" And he held out the knife, the famous combination pocketknife with twelve gadgets. "A good weapon, Where did you get it?"

Lenka put the knife in his pocket.

"Back in Sverdlovsk, at the secondhand market. I got it in exchange for sugar."

For several minutes they walked in silence—Lenka in front, the captain behind. He had dropped behind on purpose. Lenka walked along quietly pushing aside the shrubs, holding the machine gun in his right hand to keep it from knocking against the reserve magazine. He looked like one of the regulars—footcloths reaching no higher than the calves, his blouse short and tight, a sailor's belt with an anchor on the buckle, got by barter from the scouts, a small cap on his very ear—a woolen one, in spite of the heat—for swank. If he had a couple of medals, too, who would say the fellow had been at the front less than a month?

Lenka turned around and suddenly said, "May I ask you a question, Comrade Captain?"

"Why not? Go ahead."

"Is it true that you don't drink vodka?"

"Oh, really!" The captain gave a laugh. "Where did you get that?"

"The soldiers say."

"The soldiers, the soldiers . . . Well, in your opinion should I do my drinking in front of them, eh? And, anyway, why does it interest you?"

"Oh, just so . . ."

"What do you mean, just so?"

"Well, simply . . ." Lenka hesitated slightly. "I don't know; maybe a private isn't permitted to drink with an officer, but I'd like very much, Comrade Captain, to have a drink with you . . . honest."

The captain laughed gaily and threw his arms about Lenka's shoulders as he walked along.

"It isn't permitted?" asked Lenka.

"Why not? Everything is permitted, private of the Guards. Just wait till we get to Berlin."

Somewhere up ahead and to the left trench mortars made a gnashing sound, and fiery comets, racing each other, though slowly, flew across the sky, which in the west was still a transparent violet. Then a rumbling noise came from somewhere in the rear.

"The swine!" Lenka cursed, and halted. They had come to the end of the shrubbery. "Now what?"

"Now the dagger between your teeth, on your stomach—and follow me."

Afterward Lenka could not recall how long they had been crawling —an hour, two hours, perhaps all night. Nor could he recall what he had been thinking about and whether he was scared. He crawled along, and that was all—the captain in front, he behind. But his heart pounded so loud he was afraid the captain would rail at him later, and so he tried to check his breathing in the hope that this would quiet his heart, but it kept pounding and pounding in his chest, in his head, his arms, his legs—his whole body. Once they found themselves in a little swamp, got wet, and the captain said, in a scarcely audible whisper, "Bear left," and they turned left. Then they got into a grove, probably the same he had once looked at through a field glass.

"Gee, how far we've gone!" flashed through Lenka's head. Crawling was disagreeable: unaccustomed to it as he was, his knees and elbows ached; because of his knife, he had a cramp in his jaws; the grenades and the reserve magazine were in his way. He kept on crawling, afraid of dropping behind the captain, moving his arms and legs steadily, swallowing his saliva, and listening to the surrounding quiet.

At last, thank goodness, they turned back.

They had discovered no mines anywhere. Nor any Germans. What the devil had become of them? There weren't even any rockets.

They reached the familiar swamp, and skirted it. Up ahead, in the dark they could make out the vague shapes of two pear trees split by shells. So they were near their own front line. And suddenly . . .

The captain stopped. Lenka's nose almost bumped into the captain's boots. He held out his hand, and froze in that position. To the right, a score of paces away, voices were heard. Someone was speaking in a subdued whisper; someone answered. Then they fell silent. Lenka stared so hard into the darkness that green circles swam before his eyes. It was as though someone were smoking. A light flickered and went out. Lenka felt everything in him contract and grow tense. His heart was no longer pounding—it too kept quiet. His mouth went dry. He took the Finnish dagger out of his mouth, pulled up his right leg, then his left; noiselessly he crawled close to the captain. The latter, without turning his head, found Lenka's hand and pressed it hard. Lenka understood. Slowly, holding his breath, he crawled in the direction of the light.

Lenka lay on the grass and stared with wide-open eyes at the sky—it was black, without a single star. His neck ached. His left thumb was sprained and swollen, a knife slashed his blouse and even his undershirt from top to bottom. The knife slid over his chest and stomach, but, oddly enough, made only a slight scratch that did not even bleed. The German proved very strong, and Lenka struggled with him a long time before he grew altogether quiet.

The captain had gone somewhere to report on the results of the reconnaissance. It was quiet all about—the pines murmured gently overhead and from far away came the neighing of a horse. Lieutenant Lyashko had left with his men long ago. Lenka remained alone. It was not his regiment; except for the scouts, he knew no one, and generally speaking he didn't want to see anyone now. For some reason he was shivering constantly in a sickening fashion. And his neck ached. It was hard for him to turn his head.

A soldier passed by. Lenka hailed him and asked for matches. He lighted one and, shielding the flame with his palms, again carefully examined the Finnish dagger. No, there was no blood. When he had hit the German, he must have struck the rucksack or the gas mask attached to it. Nevertheless he struck it into the ground several times, then wiped it carefully with the edge of his blouse. . . . The German had knocked the dagger out of his hand almost at once. Then for a long time they had rolled on the grass. Then . . . Lenka started shivering again. He got up and, shouldering his machine gun, walked into the forest. After taking about twenty steps, he came upon the captain. It was dark, but the captain recognized him at once.

"Where are you going?"

Lenka did not answer.

"I was coming to get you. I've made my report, sent Burlin back with Antonov and Tugiev, and now you and I can catch our breath." The captain poked Lenka in the back. "Let's go."

Lenka did not ask where they were to go, deciding that it would be to their billets, but having passed the battery the captain turned right, toward the artillery dugouts.

"Who goes there?" a hoarse voice was heard in the darkness.

"All right, all right, friends." The captain did not even slow down. "This damn darkness . . . Where's the engineer's dugout? Is this it?"

After the pitch-black darkness of the forest, the dugout seemed almost dazzlingly bright. In the far corner, at a little homemade table, his blouse unbuttoned, sat Captain Bogatkin, leafing through a magazine. In another corner the signalman was snoring.

"Here he is, our hero," Orlik said gaily, as he entered. "Leonid Semyonovich Bogorad. Be kind and gracious to him."

"We're already acquainted." The engineer smiled wearily and got up. "He does look the hero."

Only now did Lenka recall that his blouse was torn, and he started hurriedly stuffing it into his trousers.

"Hold on, hold on, hero!" the engineer came over to him and passed his finger over Lenka's hard, downy abdomen. "What are these—battle wounds? Let's paint them with green stuff. We have everything here."

He wound some cotton on a match, dipped it into a vial, and painted a bright green stripe on Lenka's body from clavicle to navel.

"Your luck, my boy. You've kept your innards. They'll come in handy. Now button up and sit down."

Lenka drew his blouse together like a dressing gown and stuffed it into the trousers. He removed the grenades and the reserve magazine from his belt and laid them in a corner alongside the machine gun.

"Stop fussing there," Orlik called to him. "Come here. Have a look at your new acquaintance."

Still busy stuffing his blouse into his trousers, Lenka went over to the table.

"Recognize him?" Orlik held out a photograph.

A small snapshot with scalloped edges showed a pug-nosed, smiling, blue-eyed lad with a forelock, wearing an unbuttoned white shirt. Orlik threw two more photographs on the table. One was the same fellow, in shorts, sitting on a beach, his arms clasping his knees, and next to him was a girl in a swimming suit and a bathing cap. The other picture was of an old man with a high collar, an old woman, and the same fellow with the same girl—he wearing a jacket and tie, his hair neatly combed, with no forelock; she was in a light-colored dress, with a flower in her hair.

Lenka lifted his eyes to the captain's face. The latter looked at him gaily and, putting the photographs together, held them like a fan in his outstretched hand.

"Johann Amadeus Goetzke, corporal. Born in the city of Mannheim in 1925. Killed on the Russian front in 1943, in the region of Golaya Dolina, on the night of . . . What's the date, Bogatkin?"

"The 25th," said the engineer.

"On the night of July 25th killed by the Soviet soldier Leonid Bogorad. . . . Do you recognize him now, soldier?"

Unable to tear himself away, Lenka stared at the snapshot, at the smiling, cheerful, pug-nosed face. There, on the field, near the pear trees smashed by shells, he had not seen this face. But that strong, round neck . . . He turned aside, he could not look.

Orlik was jovial and talkative. After all that had happened, he was excited, and now he wanted to talk, to be active.

"Come on, man, don't be stingy, don't be stingy. Dump everything you have on the table."

Quickly and deftly he cleared the table of papers and folders and spread a newspaper on it.

"You should have an orderly like him, Bogatkin, eh? Take him on; you won't be sorry."

Bogatkin was known in the division for his refusal to recognize what he called "the institution of orderlies." He sewed on his own undercollar, washed his own socks and handkerchiefs. Now he took a towel and wiped a glass, the cover of a flask, and a shaving mug, then got two bottles of cognac from under the table and, having wiped them with the towel, put them on the table. Orlik began to examine the labels with the air of a connoisseur.

"Your sappers aren't much, old man. They could have got French stuff. But, hell, we've drunk all kinds. . . ." With two deft blows he knocked out the corks and smelled the necks of the bottles. "No, not so bad. And the snacks?"

Bogatkin put on the table a bar of chocolate in a brown and gilt wrapper and a flat sardine tin. Orlik clicked his tongue.

"We're living it up, Bogorad. We've a whole International here: Hungarian cognac, Swiss chocolate, Portuguese sardines. Did you ever taste sardines? Own up. You'll lick your fingers. But tear yourself away from these photos. Lost in admiration of golden-haired Gretchen?"

Without a word Lenka held out the pictures.

"A hot number, this wench, eh?" Orlik, screwing up one eye, examined the photograph. "The late lamented seems to have known a tasty dish when he saw one."

Lenka gave the captain a sullen look and dropped his eyes.

"You mustn't, Comrade Captain . . ."

But the captain did not catch Lenka's words, or made believe that he did not, went up to the table, took the glasses, and held one out to Lenka.

"To your fiery baptism, Leonid Semyonovich! To your second night of combat!"

Lenka stood silent, his head lowered.

"On the first one you got acquainted with mines. And with us. On the second—with this Goetzke . . . Well, why so crestfallen?" The captain took him by the chin. "Drink, you'll cheer up!"

Lenka shook his head.

"Are you sick? Bogatkin, your thermometer. I swear, he's ill."

"May I have your permission to leave?" Lenka asked very quietly.

"Where will you go?" Orlik stood before Lenka, holding the glass in one hand, the shaving mug in the other, both full to the brim. "Where to?"

"Nowhere . . . I'll wait for you outside."

"But last night when we were on our way to carry out the mission, you yourself . . ."

Lenka raised his head and looked the captain in the eye.

"May I have your permission to leave, Comrade Captain," Lenka repeated, just as quietly and urgently.

The captain turned round abruptly, went up to the table, put down the glasses, stood there for several seconds, then, without turning, said, "Go," and when Lenka had left, gulped a full glass, not clinking it with his host's.

Orlik stood over sleeping Lenka for a long time. Rolled up into a ball, he lay under a bush, his machine gun pressed between his knees, both his palms under his cheek in a childlike fashion. In his sleep he moved his lips, shivered. Around him on the grass, in the shrubbery, in twos or threes, lay other such boys, covered with overcoats or padded jackets, pressed against each other, and all of them dreaming, all of them muttering and sighing in their sleep.

It was past three o'clock; day was breaking, but the birds were not yet singing; the planes had not appeared. And although it was now time for them to head for their battalion, Orlik was sorry to wake up the sleeping boy, who lay there with the machine gun pressed hard between his knees. And perhaps he was not only sorry to wake him, but simply delayed the moment when the boy would open his eyes and look at him.

"Chirp. Chirp. Chirp." The first bird awoke.

Lenka huddled up, smacked his lips, turned over on his back, scratched his bare stomach, then wiped his nose, yawned, and opened his eyes. And in these eyes there was now only childhood, only the sky, only an incredible desire to sleep. "Chirp. Chirp. Chirp."

1960

YURY KAZAKOV
(b. 1927)

Like not a few young writers, this author, a native of Moscow, is an alumnus of the Gorky Literary Institute in the capital. A student of music, he has been a member of an orchestra. He was not published until he was thirty, and so far the short story has remained his medium. Some critics have commended his work for its veracity, its depth, its insight into the human heart. Others have attacked it—specifically the first story printed below—as decadent and therefore alien to the spirit of Soviet art. The more discerning sector of the public has been reading Kazakov eagerly.

The Outcast

Worn out by the heat of the day and gorged with half-raw, insufficiently salted fish, Yegor, the buoy keeper, is asleep in his hut.

The hut is new, bare. There isn't even a stove. True, a part of the floor has been cut out for it, and there is a pile of bricks and moist clay in the entry. Tow sticks out from the crevices of the timbered walls; the window frames are new, the panes are not puttied; they rattle thinly when the steamboats whistle, and ants crawl on the windowsills.

Yegor wakes up at sunset, when the air is filled with hazy brightness, while the river turns into a mass of motionless gold. He yawns, yawns in sweet torment, writhes, and violently tenses his muscles. His eyes still closed, he hurriedly rolls a cigarette with nerveless hands and lights it. He inhales deeply, passionately, making a sobbing sound with his lips, clears his throat with relish, vigorously scratches his chest and sides under his shirt with his hard nails. His eyes grow moist, assume a tipsy look; the body is flooded with hearty, soft languor.

Having had a smoke, he goes into the entry and just as avidly as he smoked, he drinks the cold water, smelling of leaves, roots, and setting his teeth pleasantly on edge. Then he fetches the oars, the kerosene lanterns, and goes down to the boat.

His boat is stuffed with crumpled sedge, and what with the water in it, it is heavy. Yegor reflects that he ought to bail out the water, but he is too lazy. He sighs, glances at the sunset, as well as up and down the stream, spreads his legs apart, and, straining more than is necessary, pushes the boat into the water.

Yegor's duties are by no means onerous. He has to place lighted lanterns on four floats, two downstream from his hut, two upstream. He always takes a long time to decide whether to row first downstream or up. On this occasion, too, he lapses into thought. Then, settling down, he fusses with the oars, treads down the sedge, kicks the lanterns, and begins to row against the current. All this is fiddle-faddle," he thinks, limbering up, rowing jerkily, quickly, bending backward and straightening up, glancing at the reflection of the banks that are growing dusky or pink in the calm water. The boat leaves a dark wake on the gold of the water and neat spirals on the sides.

The air grows cool; swallows dart right above the water and cry shrilly; close to the banks the fish splash, and at each splash Yegor makes a face as if he has long known that particular fish. From the banks comes the odor of strawberries, hay, dew-drenched shrubs, from the boat—that of fish, kerosene, and sedge, and already a scarcely visible mist is rising from the water, which gives off the odor of depth and secretiveness.

Yegor lights red and white lanterns in turn and places them on the floats. Lazily, ostentatiously, scarcely using the oars, he floats downstream and lights the lanterns there. They burn brightly and are seen from afar in the thickening dusk. Yegor's return trip is hasty. Back home he washes up, examines himself in the mirror, puts on his boots, a clean shirt, sets his navy cap at an angle, rows to the opposite bank, ties up the boat in the bushes, proceeds to the meadow, and with an alert eye looks westward.

The meadow is already misty and smells of dampness. The mist is so thick and white that from a distance it looks like a flood. Yegor walks, floats, as in a dream, the mist up to his shoulders, and only the tops of the hayricks are visible, only the black strip of the forest showing far off under the hushed sky, the sunset that is growing dim.

Yegor stands on tiptoe, cranes his neck, and finally espies a pink kerchief far off above the mist.

"E-eh!" he hails in a rich tenor.

"A-ah!" comes a weak call.

Yegor quickens his step, then stoops and runs like a quail along the path. Turning off it, he lies down, the grass staining his knees and elbows green and, his heart pounding, he stares in the direction in which he had glimpsed the pink kerchief. A minute passes, two minutes, but no one appears, no sound of steps is heard, and, no longer able to bear it, he gets to his feet and stares above the mist. As before, he sees only the trace of the sunset, the strip of forest, the peaks of the hayricks—everything is hazy and dim around him. "She's hiding!" he decides with impatient rapture, again he dives into the mist, and walks stealthily westward. He holds his breath, the blood, swelling, floods his face, his cap feels tight. Suddenly he notices quite close by a dim, shrunken little figure, and starts with surprise.

"Halt!" he yells savagely. "Halt, or I'll kill you!"

And, stamping his boots, he chases her, and she, squealing, runs away from him, laughing and losing something from her bag. He quickly overtakes her, together they drop onto soft molehills smelling of fresh earth and mushrooms, and firmly and happily embrace in the mist. Then they get up, look for what she had dropped from her bag, and slowly stroll toward the boat.

As before, only their heads are visible above the mist, and now it seems to both of them that they are floating somewhere as in a dream, drunk with the ringing of the blood in their ears.

2

Yegor is young and already a drunkard. His wife, too, was a drunkard. A loose woman, seedy, much older than he, she was drowned in the autumn, as the ice was forming on the river. She had gone to the village to get vodka, had drunk some on her way back and grew tipsy. She walked along, bawling songs, and when she reached the river opposite their hut she shouted:

"Yegor, you plague you, come out, look at me!"

Yegor came out in high spirits, his sheepskin coat over his shoulders, his bare feet in ragged shoes. She was striding on the ice, swinging her bag, and when she reached the middle of the river she started a jig. Yegor wanted to shout to her to hurry up, but it was too late: before his eyes the ice broke under his wife, and she sank instantly. Throwing off the sheepskin and his shoes, with nothing on except a shirt, he ran barefoot on the ice, and as he ran the ice under him kept cracking, heaving gently, settling. He tumbled down, crawled on his stomach to the hole, but only looked at the black steaming water, only howled, screwed up his eyes, and crawled back. Three days later he boarded up the hut and went off for the winter to his village, three versts away on the other side of the river.

One day at floodtime in the spring he was ferrying young Alyonka, who hailed from Trubetzkoe, and when she started getting out the money to pay him, all of a sudden he said hurriedly:

"Well, all right, all right . . . It's all fiddle-faddle. . . . Drop in some time at my place: I live alone; it's boring. And there's things to be washed, too—without a woman there's no fightin' the cooties. And I'll let you have fish."

When, a fortnight later, toward evening, Alyonka, returning to her own village, dropped in on him, Yegor's heart pounded so hard that he got scared. For the first time in his life Yegor made a fuss over a girl. He started a fire outdoors between bricks, set up the soot-covered teakettle, questioned Alyonka about her life, suddenly stopping in the middle of a sentence, embarrassing her to the point of tears and feeling embarrassed himself. He washed up and put on a clean shirt in the entry, ferried her across the river at night, and walked with her in the meadows.

Now Alyonka often comes to him and always stays two or three days. When she is with him, he treats her negligently and makes fun of her. When she is not there he is bored, frets, everything drops from his hands, he sleeps a lot and has bad, disturbing dreams.

Yegor is stocky, has a prominent Adam's apple, is rather flabby, somewhat clumsy. The expression of his large-featured, hooknosed, doughy face is sleepy and blank. The sun and wind have tanned his skin almost black; and his gray eyes look blue. His character is odd, unbalanced; he's aware of it and suffers from it. "I'm half-baked-like," he complains in his cups. "The devil knocked up a drunken goat, and here I am."

He spends May Day in his hut. Why he has not gone to the village, as he had wanted to at first, he himself does not know. He lies in the mussed, unmade bed, and whistles. From the opposite bank comes a thin shout:

"Yeg-o-or!"

Yegor gloomily strides to the edge of the water.

"Yeg-o-or, they want you to come."

"Who wa-ants me?" Yegor shouts after a pause.

"Uncle Va-sya and Uncle Fe-e-dya . . ."

"Why don't they come to my place?"

"They can't co-ome; they's dru-unk. . . ."

Yegor' face wears a look of depression.

"Tell 'em I've work to do, wo-ork!" he shouts, though, of course, he has no work whatever to do. "They're havin' themselves a time in the village!" he thinks bitterly, and pictures to himself his mother, his kinfolk, all drunk, the tables loaded with snacks, the pies, the girls all dressed up, flags on the houses, movies at the club, the accordions going all the time, and he recalls the yeasty taste of home-brewed beer. Gloomily he spits into the water and climbs up into his hut.

"Yeg-o-or . . . co-ome . . ." the enticing voice responds from the opposite bank, but he does not listen.

His attitude toward everything is one of indifference and mockery, and he is inordinately lazy. He has a good deal of money and makes it easily. There is no bridge in the vicinity, and he ferries people across, charging one ruble a trip, and when he is irritated, even two. The job of buoy keeper, which is light, old man's work, has completely spoiled, demoralized him.

Sometimes a vague uneasiness seizes Yegor. This usually happens at night. Lying next to the sleeping Alyonka, he recalls his service in the Navy. He thinks of his pals—of course, he lost all contact with them long ago—recalls their voices, their faces, even the talk, but vaguely, apathetically. . . . How are they now? Where do they live, and do they remember him? He recalls the low, gloomy shore, the North Sea, the eerie northern lights in the winter, the crippled bluish dwarf firs, the moss, the sand, the dazzling, shimmering brilliance of the lighthouse at night.

He thinks about all this with unconcern as of something very distant. But sometimes a weird idea comes to his head and makes him shiver. He imagines that the shore is the same as it used to be, that there are barracks on it with slate roofs; at night the lighthouse shines, in the barracks there are seamen, two-tier berths, the crackling of the radio, talk, letter writing, smoking. But, oddly enough, it seems to him that he never was there, that he had not been in the service, that all this is a dream of his, a trick of the devil.

He gets up, makes his way to the bank, seats himself or lies down under a bush, wrapped in his sheepskin. He strains his ears, and stares into the darkness at the reflection of the stars in the river, the distant lights of the buoys. At such times there is no one around to whom he could pretend, and his expression is sad and thoughtful. His heart is heavy; he is troubled by a vague desire—to go away, to live differently.

Far off a deep, velvety three-tone whistle slowly comes into being and just as slowly dissipates. A little later a brightly lighted steamer heaves into view, its paddlewheels splashing rapidly, the steam hissing; and it whistles again. The noise it makes is resoundingly echoed by the woods. Yegor watches the steamer, and his depression deepens.

He imagines the young women, smelling of perfume and traveling no one knows where, who sleep in the cabins. Near the engine room there is a warm smell of steam, polished brass, machines. The decks and railing are covered with dew; a yawning officer of the watch stands on the bridge at the helm. On the upper deck lone passengers in overcoats stare into the dark, at the lights of the buoys, fishermen's red bonfires, the reflection of the lights of a factory or a power station, and all this seems wonderful to them. And someone is sure to be asleep on a bench, his jacket over his head, his legs drawn up.

Life is passing him by! What entices him and disturbs him so in the dead of night? And why is he so depressed, taking no joy in the dewy fields and the quiet river, in the easy work?

And yet his native place is beautiful—these dusty roads, familiar since childhood; these villages, each with its own ways, its habit of speech; his own village, where on many an evening, hiding in the rye, he had kissed one girl or another, where he had fought till he blacked out; beautiful is the bluish smoke of a bonfire on the river-bank, and the lights of the buoys, and the spring with the violet snow on the fields, with the vast turbid floods, the chilly sunsets spread over half the sky, the piles of last year's leaves in the ravines! Beautiful is autumn also, with its boredom, rain, the odorous night wind, the special coziness of the hut! Why, then, does he wake up at night? Whose call reverberates along the river: "Yeg-o-or!"? He is terrified, chilled; the distance summons him, cities, noise, lights, work, real work that can bring happiness!

And, dragging his coat, he returns to the hut, lies down next to Alyonka, wakes her, and clings to her, pitifully and hungrily, presses against her, feels her only like a child on the point of crying. Screwing up his eyes, he rubs his face against her shoulder, kisses her neck, growing weak with joy, with love and tenderness for her, feeling her quick and tender kisses on his face. He no longer thinks of or desires anything else, wishing only that this should go on forever.

Then they whisper, although they could speak aloud. And, as always, Alyonka tries to persuade him to settle down, to give up drink, to get married, to move away, to get real work, so that he should be respected and that they should write about him in the papers.

Half an hour later—calmed, lazy, sarcastic—he mutters his pet phrase, "fiddle-faddle!" but he mutters the phrase absentmindedly, inoffensively, secretly wishing that she would go on whispering and trying to persuade him to turn over a new leaf.

3

Often travelers who go up and down the river in motorboats, canoes, and even on rafts spend the night in Yegor's hut. Each time the same thing happens: the wayfarers turn off the motor and one of them goes up to the hut.

"Hello, master of the house!" says the traveler with assumed heartiness.

Yegor is silent; breathing heavily, he is tinkering with a creel made of withes.

"How are you?" the traveler says, somewhat discouraged.

Still not a word out of Yegor, who is wholly absorbed in his work on the creel.

"How many of you?" he asks, after a long pause.

"There are only three of us. . . . We'll make out somehow," the traveler says with timid hope. "We'll pay, don't worry. . . ."

Apathetically, slowly, with long pauses, he asks the man who they all are, where they come from, where they are going. And when the subject has been exhausted, he consents with obvious reluctance:

"Well, all right, you can spend the night."

Then they all get out of the boat, pull it ashore and turn it over, carry their rucksacks, canisters, pots, and the motor to the hut. It gets crowded and begins to smell of gasoline, boots, the road. Yegor perks up, shakes hands with everyone, grows cheerful, anticipates a drinking bout. He begins to fidget, to talk without stopping, mostly about the weather; now and then he shouts at Alyonka, builds a great fire outdoors. And when the vodka is being poured out, his eyes shimmer through his drooping lashes; he breathes quietly and slowly; he is tormented by the fear that he'll be passed over. Then he takes the glass in his strong dark hand with its broken nails, says firmly and gaily, "To acquaintance!" and tosses it off, his face turning stony.

He gets drunk quickly, easily, joyously. He gets drunk, and starts telling lies with conviction, with delight. His tall tales have to do chiefly with fish, because for some reason he is sure that the travelers are interested solely in fish.

"We've got all kinds of fish here," he says cautiously and, as it were, reluctantly, munching a snack. "True, they're getting scarce, and . . . but"—he hawks, pauses, and lowers his voice—"but if you know how . . . By the way, yesterday I caught a pike. Truth to tell, not a big fellow, only about sixty pounds. In the morning, when I was on my way to the buoys, I heard him splashing about near the bank. I cast my line right away, and while I was busy with the buoys he took the bait; the hook got into his very belly."

"Where is this pike, then?" he is asked.

"I took him to the workers' settlement right then and there and sold him," he replies without blinking an eye, and describes the pike in detail.

And if someone voices a doubt—someone always does, and Yegor waits for it impatiently—he flushes violently, and this time, as the master of the house, reaches for the bottle, pours himself a full glass, downs it quickly, and only then directs his tipsy, vacant gaze toward the skeptic, and says:

"If you like, we'll go over tomorrow! What do you bet? What kind of motor have you?"

"M-72," he is told.

Yegor turns around and stares at the motor leaning against the wall in the corner.

"That one? Posh!" he says scornfully. "Slavka has a Bolinder; it's mine, I brought it to him from the Navy, put it together myself. A

418

wonder, not a motor: twenty kilometers an hour! And against the current . . . Well, I bet the Bolinder against your knickknack! Well? A fellow like you had an argument with me—and lost his rifle. Want to see mine? A made-to-order Tula job, a killer. Last winter"—he hesitates for a second and his eyes glaze—"I brought down 350 hares! Well?"

The nonplussed guests, to needle him, ask, "Why don't you get yourself a stove, fellow?"

"A stove?" Now Yegor is shouting. "And who'll build it? Can you? Go to it. There's clay, bricks, all the makin's, in a word. Build it, and I shell out a hundred and fifty in a lump sum on the spot. Well? Build it!" he insists stubbornly, knowing that no one will call his bluff and that therefore victory will be his again. "Well? Build it!"

Noticing that there is some vodka left and that the guests are laughing, he retires to the entry, puts on his Navy cap, unbuttons his collar so that his undershirt shows, and returns to the room.

"Allow me," he brings out with tipsy, exaggerated deference, and reports: "Seaman of the Northern Fleet, at your command! Permit me to congratulate you on the anniversary of the holiday of communism and socialism. Fling at the enemy all the forces of the camp of peace! And on this occasion won't you stand me a drink?"

They treat him, and Alyonka, painfully ashamed on his account, starts making up beds for the company. Hot tears well up in her eyes and she waits with impatience, almost with fury, for Yegor to start amazing the guests. And he does.

Overcome by complete torpor, he suddenly sits down on the bench, leans against the wall, twists his shoulders, moves his legs about, trying to settle himself comfortably, clears his throat, lifts his head, and breaks into song.

At the first sounds of his voice conversation stops instantly— astonished, frightened, all look at him! He does not sing popular jingles or modern songs, although he knows them all and hums them constantly—he sings in the old Russian manner, drawlingly, reluctantly, as it were, a bit hoarsely, the way the old men he had heard as a child used to do. He sings an old song, long-drawn-out, with endless o-o-o's and a-a-a's that tug at the heartstrings. He sings quietly, somewhat playfully, almost coquettishly, but there is so much power and feeling in his voice, so much that is truly Russian, in the age-old tradition of epic balladry, that in a minute everything is forgotten—Yegor's coarseness and stupidity, his drinking and bragging, forgotten the trip and the fatigue. It is as though the past and the future are at one, and only the extraordinary voice resounds and eddies and befogs you, and you want to listen endlessly, holding your breath and letting your tears flow, your body bent, your head propped on your hand, your eyes closed.

"You belong in the Bolshoi Theater! Bolshoi Theater!" all cry at once, when Yegor finishes, and everyone, excitedly, with shining eyes, offers him help; all want to write to the papers, to call someone up. . . . All, jubilant, feel festive, and Yegor, happy with the praise, tired, already slightly cooled off, is again negligent and sarcastic, and his heavy face is again devoid of expression. He pictures to himself vaguely the Bolshoi Theater, Moscow, a dashing team of horses, light between columns, a shining auditorium, an orchestra—he saw it all once in a movie—stretches lazily, and mutters:

"It's all fiddle-faddle . . . them theaters. . . ."

But people take no offense: so great is his power, so incomprehensible and mighty he seems to his guests.

But this is not the peak of glory for him.

4

His glory reaches its peak when he is "dragged down," as he puts it. This happens once or twice a month when he is particularly out of sorts and depressed. The fit of blues begins in the morning, and he starts drinking in the morning, too. True, he drinks a little at a time and now and then says lazily:

"Well, now . . . Let's do it, no? I mean . . . Eh?"

"Do what?" Alyonka makes believe she doesn't understand.

"Let's sing . . . have a dooet, eh?" Yegor says indolently, and sighs.

Alyonka smiles scornfully and makes no reply. She knows that the time hasn't arrived, that Yegor isn't yet entirely "dragged down." And she keeps busy, tidies the place, washes something, goes down to the river to do some laundry, returns. . . .

Finally the time comes. This usually happens toward evening. Yegor no longer talks of a "dooet." He gets up, disheveled, morose, looks out of one window, out of the other, leaves the hut, drinks some water, then thrusts the bottle of vodka into his pocket, and picks up his sheepskin.

"Are you going far?" Alyonka asks guilelessly, but she begins to tremble all over.

"Let's go!" Yegor says rudely, and steps clumsily across the threshold.

He grows pale, his nostrils dilate, the veins on his temples swell. Alyonka, coughing a little and muffling her throat with her kerchief, walks beside him. She knows that Yegor will get to the top of the steep bank, glance up and down the river, grow pensive, as if not knowing where to settle, and then make his way to his favorite spot— beside a leaky, overturned, flat-bottomed boat at the very edge of the water in the birch grove. And there he will sing with her, but not at all as he had done for the guests: somewhat negligently, a little play-fully, not with his full voice.

And, indeed, Yegor halts on the top of the bank, pauses for a while, then walks to the flat-bottomed boat. He spreads out his coat, sits down, leaning against the side of the boat, and stands the bottle between his legs.

The sunset is beautiful; the mist on the fields is like a flood; the strip of distant forest is black, and so are the tops of the hayricks. The branches of the birches overhead are motionless; the grass is damp, the air quiet and warm; but Alyonka is chilly and snuggles up to Yegor. He takes the bottle with a trembling hand and swallows a sip or two, hawking and writhing. His mouth is full of sweet saliva.

"Well . . ." he says, turning his neck, clears his throat, and warns her in a whisper: "Mind you support me!"

He fills his lungs with air, grows tense, and opens up mournfully in a tremulous tenor of utmost purity and sharpness:

"Up-on the se-ea,
    the blu-ue se-ea . . ."

Alyonka screws up her eyes, trembles painfully, waiting for her turn, and comes in, her voice low, sonorous, and true:

"A swa-an flo-oats with his ma-ate."

But she no longer hears her own low, lusterless, passionate voice— how can she? All she feels is how softly and gratefully Yegor's hand squeezes her shoulder; all she hears is his voice. What joy the song is, and what torment! Yegor, his voice now softening, now tightening,

421

now husky, now metallically sharp, keeps uttering the marvelous words, so extraordinary, so familiar, as if they had been singing them for a hundred years:

"The swa-an floats, so smo-othly, oh-h!
Nor ever grazes
The fine yellow sand. . . ."

Oh, but what is it? How painful and familiar all this is, as if she had known it all her life, as if she had lived somewhere long, long ago and had been singing just like this and listening to Yegor's marvelous voice! What distant lands had she traveled through, what seas had she sailed? It was with him, with Yegor that she had walked across a meadow under a sunset sky, under stars, in a mist, as in a dream, intensely joyous, drunk without having had a drink!

"Whence did a blue-ue eagle come?"

Moaning and weeping, straining his ears, half turned away from Alyonka, Yegor surrenders himself wholly to the singing. His Adam's apple trembles; his mouth is mournful. Oh, this blue eagle! Why, why did he throw himself upon the white swan, why did the grass droop, darkness pervade the world, why did the stars fall and the sea turn rough? Oh, for an end to these tears, this voice!

And they sing, feeling only that suddenly their hearts will burst and they will drop dead on the grass—and they want no resurrection after such bliss and such torment.

And when they finish, worn out, devastated, happy, when Yegor silently lays his head on her lap and breathes heavily, she kisses his pale cold face and whispers, choking:

"Yegor, darling . . . I love you, my marvelous one, my golden one. . . ."

"It's all fiddle-faddle," Yegor wants to say, but says nothing. His mouth is dry, and on his tongue there is a sweet taste.

1959

Autumn in Oak Woods

I took the bucket to fill it with water at the spring. This was a happy night for me, because she was coming by in the night launch. But I knew what happiness was like; I knew that it was uncertain, and that is why I took the bucket on purpose, as if I did not hope she would come and was just going to fetch water. Somehow things were turning out altogether too well for me this autumn.

This late autumn night was slate-black, and I didn't like to go outdoors, but all the same I did go out; I took a long time putting a candle in the lantern, and when I had done this and lighted it, the glass grew misted for a while and the faint spot of light blinked and blinked until at last there was a full flame, the mist vanished, and the sides became transparent.

I had not put out the light in the house, and the lighted window was clearly visible while I was walking down the road, flanked by two rows of larches, toward the Oka. My lantern cast a wavering light all around, and you might have taken me for a switchman, except that heaps of maple leaves and larch needles moistened by the night air made a dull noise under my boots. Even in the dim light of the lantern the needles had a golden tint, and barberries showed red on leafless shrubs.

It is eerie to walk alone at night with a lantern! You alone make the leaves rustle with your boots; you alone are in the light and exposed to view; everything else is hiding and watching you.

The road descended a steep slope, and the light in my window soon vanished. Then the road came to an end, and I found myself following a path among scattered shrubs, oaks, and firs. Tall stems of late daisies, tips of fir branches, bare twigs, kept clicking against the bucket. A booming sound, now muffled, now clear, came from afar.

The path sloped downward more sharply and grew more winding; every so often the white trunks of birches began to emerge from the dark. Then the birches disappeared; stones started turning up on the path, and I became aware of a freshness in the air. Though nothing was visible beyond the circle lighted by the lantern, up ahead I sensed a broad expanse—I had reached the river.

Just then the distant buoy on the right came into view. Its red light was duplicated, reflected in the water. Then the buoy which is nearer my bank became visible. It blinked faintly, and I could see the river.

I walked down, over the wet grass, between osier bushes and along the edge of the water, toward the spot where the launch usually docked to let off a passenger. The spring muttered monotonously and gurgled in the dark. I set down the lantern, went over to the spring, filled the bucket, drank some water, and wiped my mouth with my sleeve. Then I stood the bucket next to the lantern and looked in the direction of the distant pier.

The launch was already at the pier, the red and green lights on the rails were dimly visible. I sat down and lighted a cigarette. My hands were cold, and trembled. Suddenly it occurred to me that if she was not on the launch, and if they noticed my lantern, they would think that I wanted to cross the river and would come over. I put out the lantern.

Dark fell swiftly; alone the buoys shone, as if through holes pricked by a needle. The quiet was clamorous. At that late hour for miles along the river I must have been the only one on the bank. And in the dark village on the heights which lay beyond the oak forest, everyone had long been sleeping, and only in my house was there a light.

Suddenly I pictured to myself the long road she was traveling on her way to me, how she had journeyed from Archangel, slept, or sat wakeful at the window of the railroad car, and perhaps spoke to someone. How all these days she had been thinking of our meeting, just as I had. And how she was now sailing down the Oka and looking at the banks, about which I had written her when I asked her to come to me. How she came out on deck, and the wind, wafting the odor of moist oak forests, blew in her face. And how she spoke to people down in the warm lounge, behind misted windows; how they told her where to get off, and where she should spend the night, if no one met her.

Then I recalled the North, my wanderings there, and how I had lived at the fishery and the two of us had speared wolf fish on white nights. The fisherman would sleep heavily, snoring and moaning a little, and we would be waiting for low tide and put to sea in a rowboat. She rowed noiselessly, and I peered into the deep, at tangled seaweed, looking for shapes of fish. Quietly I lowered the spear, plunged the white tip into the neck of the wolf fish, with an effort lifted it out of the water, and the fish, splashing our faces, struggled savagely on the spear, opened its terrible jaws wide, coiled itself, and then straightened out like a spring, looking like a triton. And afterward when it lay on the floor of the boat, for a long time it rustled, quivered, and fastened a death grip on whatever came its way.

And I recalled what a blissful year it had been for me, how many stories I had succeeded in writing, and I thought of the other stories I would yet write in the remaining quiet, lonely days by this river, where on winter's threshold Nature was already quenched.

Night surrounded me, and the cigarette, when I inhaled, lighted up my hands, face, boots, but did not prevent me from seeing the stars—and this autumn there was such a dazzling multitude of them that their ashy glow shone on the river, the trees, the white stones on the bank, the black squares of the fields on the hills.

And it also occurred to me that the chief thing in life is not how long you will live: thirty, fifty, eighty years—because in any case the time will be too short and in any case it will be terrible to die—the chief thing is how many such nights there will be in your life.

The launch had already left the pier. It was still so far away that you could not perceive its motion. It seemed to be standing still, but it was not at the pier, and that meant that it was sailing upstream toward me. Soon there was the high-pitched sound of the diesel engine, and suddenly I was seized with fear that she was not coming, that she was not on the launch, and that I was waiting for nothing. I thought of the distance she had to cover, of the time she had to spend in order to get here, and how unsubstantial my plans were for a happy life here together.

"Can it be!" I said aloud, and stood up. I could no longer sit quietly, and I started pacing the riverbank. "Can it be!" I repeated helplessly from time to time, and kept looking at the launch, meanwhile reflecting how outrageous it would be for me to have to return alone with my bucket of water and how empty my house would be. Can it be, I asked myself, that luck is against us, and after so many days and so many failures to get together, we shall not meet, and everything will go to pieces?

I recalled how three months earlier I had left the North to return home, how she had unexpectedly come to the village from the fishery to see me off, how she had stood on the gangplank while I was getting into the motorboat, to be taken out to the steamer anchored far away in the roadstead, and how she had kept saying the same thing: "So you are going away, darling! Oh, you don't understand anything! So you are going away, darling!" And how I, already in the motorboat and distraught by the hubbub of the leavetaking and other noises, by the crying of the women and the shouting of the men, I already grasped that it was childish of me to leave, and I was faintly hoping to set things right in the future.

The launch was close to the bank now, and I no longer was pacing there, but stood at the very edge of the black water, staring fixedly at the boat, narrowing my eyes and breathing noisily with excitement and hope.

Suddenly the sound of the motor dropped in pitch, a searchlight flared up in the wheelhouse, and a smoking slant beam slashed the bank, skipping from tree to tree. The launch was looking for a place to dock. It kept sidling to the right; the beam hit me in the face; I turned aside, then looked again. A sailor stood on the upper deck and was opening the gangway to drop the companion ladder onto the bank. Next to him, in a light-colored coat, stood she.

The prow of the launch dug softly and deeply into the bank; the sailor pushed the companion ladder forward, and helped her off, and I grabbed her suitcase, set it next to the bucket, and only then slowly turned around. The searchlight was blinding me, and I could not manage to get a clear view of her. She was walking toward me, casting a huge, unsteady shadow on the top of the wooded slope. I wanted to kiss her, but changed my mind, not wishing to do it in the glare of the searchlight. And we simply stood there next to each other, shading our eyes from the light with our hands and, with strained smiles, gazed at the launch. It went into reverse; the beam of the searchlight crept to one side, then vanished; the diesel engine again struck up its song, and the launch, with the long row of lighted windows in the lower cabins, started moving off rapidly upstream. We were alone.

"Well, greetings!" I said in embarrassment. She stood on tiptoe, grasped my shoulders so hard that it hurt, and kissed me on the eyes.

"Let's go!" I said, and coughed once or twice. "It's devilishly dark; wait, I'll light the lantern."

I lighted the lantern, and again it got misted at first, and we had to wait until there was a full flame and the glass dried and became transparent. Then we were off: I up ahead with the suitcase and lantern, she with the bucket of water.

"It isn't too heavy for you?" I asked after a while.

"Go on, go on!" she said huskily.

She had a husky, low-pitched voice, and she was strong and firm-fleshed, and for a long time I did not love that in her. For in women I wanted softness. But now, here, on the riverbank, at night, as we walked toward the house one behind the other, after so many days of anger, separation, letters, and strange, threatening dreams, her voice and her sturdy body and rough hands, her northern accent—all this was like the whiff of a bird that was a stranger to these parts—a wild, gray-feathered bird that had got separated from the autumnal flock.

We bore to the right, moving into a ravine, along which lay a short, steep paved road, narrow, overgrown with nut trees, pines, and mountain ash. We started ascending in the dark, served only by the dim light of the lantern, and overhead the narrow river of stars was flowing and black pine branches were floating on it, in turn hiding and revealing the stars.

Out of breath, we reached the road between the larches and began walking abreast.

I was overcome with the desire to show her everything and tell her about this place, the people, the various small happenings.

"Just smell it," I said. "What a smell!"

"Winy," she responded, rather out of breath from walking. "I already smelled it when I was on the steamer."

"It's the leaves. And now come this way."

We left the things on the road, jumped over a ditch and got into some shrubs, lighting our way with the lantern.

"It must be somewhere around here," I muttered.

"Mushrooms," she said in amazement, from behind. "They're Russulas."

At last I found what I was looking for. It was the white feathers of a young chicken scattered over grass, pine needles, and yellow leaves.

"Look," I said, throwing light on the spot. "There's a chicken farm in the village. The grown chickens have been allowed to leave the yard—and so the fox comes here every day and sits in the shrubs. When the chickens wander out into the woods, it catches one. And gorges itself on the spot."

I pictured this fox to myself, with white bristles on its dark snout, how it licked its chops and huffed to blow the down off its nose.

"It must be killed!" she said.

427

"I have a gun; we'll wander through the woods, and perhaps luck will be with us."

We returned to the road, and went on. My lighted window came into view, and I began to think what it would be like when we got there. Suddenly I wanted a drink. I had some rowanberry brandy at the house. I had made it myself. It was pleasant to pick the berries in the woods, take them home, squeeze them so as to get a foamy yellow liquid and then strain it into a bottle of vodka.

"Up our way it's winter!" she said, surprised, as it were. "The Dvina is frozen; only in the middle icebreakers cut a passage. Everything is white, and the passage is black . . . and it steams. And when a ship moves through the channel, dogs run beside it on the ice. And for some reason there are always three of them."

I pictured the Dvina to myself, and the steamers, and Archangel, and the village on the White Sea from which she had come. Tall, two-story cottages, empty, black walls, silence and seclusion.

"Is there ice yet?" I asked. "At sea?"

"It's drifting in," she said, and she, too, seemed to be remembering something, perhaps what she had left behind. "On my way back there'll be need of reindeer, if . . ."

She broke off, and I waited, listening to her breathing and her footsteps, and then asked, "If—what?"

"Oh, nothing," she said more huskily and slowly than usual. "If more ice piles up, that's what!"

After stamping our feet on the porch, we entered the house.

"O-oh!" she exclaimed, looking about and removing her kerchief. Whenever she was surprised or happy, she uttered this low-pitched, slow "O-oh" of hers.

The house was old and small: I had rented it from a man in Moscow who occupied it only in the summer. There was almost no furniture except old beds, a table and chairs. Beetles had gnawed the logs, and the walls were sprinkled with white powder. But there were a radio, electric light, a stove, and several fat old books, which I liked to read evenings.

"Take off your things!" I said. "We'll light the stove right away. . . ."

I went outdoors to cut some brushwood for the stove. But I was almost ill with happiness; there was a ringing in my ears; my hands trembled, I felt weak, and I wanted to sit down for a while. Stars were sparkling thinly and sharply. "There'll be a frost—the first frost!" I thought. "And by morning the leaves will be gone."

A melodious three-tone whistle slowly floated over the river, and for a long time the echo reverberated in the hills. A tugboat was making its way somewhere down below, one of those old steam-driven tugboats, few of which are left nowadays. The new launches and tugboats have a short, high-pitched, nasal whistle. Waked by the whistle, several cocks on the chicken farm crowed in falsetto.

I cut some branches, gathered an armful of firewood, and went indoors. Coatless, she stood with her back to me, and was getting something out of her suitcase, so that there was a rustle of newspaper. She wore a bright dress that was too tight, and were I to go visiting with her, or take her to a club in Moscow, people would smile covertly, and this was certainly her best dress. And I recalled that at home she ordinarily wore pants tucked into high boots, under an old, faded skirt, and that there this was all right.

I put the teakettle on, and started to light the stove. Soon it began to roar; the brushwood crackled, and the smell of smoke and burning wood filled the room.

"This is for you!" she said, standing behind me.

I turned round, and there on the table was a salmon—magnificent, of a dull silver color, with a broad dark back and lower jaw curved up. The house smelled of fish and the sea, and again I was seized by the longing for travel.

She was a native of the White Sea littoral; she had even been born at sea in a motorboat, on a golden summer night. But she was indifferent to those nights. Only a newcomer to the place is driven out of his mind by them because of the quiet and the loneliness. Only when you are a stranger there, torn away from everyone and forgotten, as it were, by all, only then are you unable to sleep at night, and you keep thinking and saying to yourself: "Well, well! That's nothing, it's only night, and you're not here forever, and why fret about the night; let the sun slink along the edge of the sea—sleep, sleep. . . ."

And she? At the fishery she would sleep soundly behind a cotton print curtain, because at dawn she had to get up and, together with husky fishermen, row out, remove the fish from traps, then cook fish chowder, wash the dishes. . . . And that's how it was every summer until I came.

And now on the bank of the Oka, we are drinking rowanberry brandy, eating salmon and talking, recalling all sorts of things. How, on white nights, we used to put out to sea in order to spear wolf fish, how we would haul traps with the fishermen during a storm and swallow bitter water and feel sick, and how we would go to the light-house to fetch bread, and how one night we were sitting in a village reading room with padded jackets off and in our stocking feet, going through the newspapers and magazines that had come in during the days we had spent at the fishery.

I spread my greatcoat, fur side up, on the floor near the stove; we put the candy next to the teakettle, took our cups, and lay down on the coat, looking now at each other, now at the pink firebox and the embers from which little flames flared up now and then. In order to lie there longer, I would sometimes get up and add fuel to the fire; then the brushwood crackled, and we would move away from the heat.

At about two in the morning, unable to sleep, I got up in the dark. It seemed to me that if I fell asleep she would go off some-where and I would no longer sense her presence. What I wanted was for her to be with me always and for me to be aware of it. "Take me into your dreams, so that I may always be with you!" I wanted to say. "For we must never be parted for a long, long time."

Then I thought to myself that people who leave us and whom we no longer see die for us. And we for them. Queer thoughts come into your head at night when you can't sleep, either for joy or for anguish.

"Are you asleep?" I asked quietly.

"No," she answered from her bed. "I'm comfortable. Don't look; I'll get dressed."

I walked over to the corner where the radio was hanging against the wall, and turned it on. I tried to find some music amid the crackling of static and the patter of the announcers. I knew that it was there, and I found it. A man's velvety voice said something in English; then there was a pause, and I concluded that the next thing would be music.

I was startled, because at the very first note I recognized the melody. I recall this jazz melody whenever I am in high spirits or, on the contrary, depressed. It is alien to me, but I am drawn to it by

430

the secret thought that rings there—I don't know whether it is a happy or a mournful one. I often think of the melody when I'm traveling.

I pulled the coat over to the radio and we sat down on the coat, embraced. All these months my heart had been oppressed by a sense of loss, but now I was in possession of what I thought I had lost, and what I recovered was even better than I could have supposed.

The double bass muttered elegiacally, groping in the dark for contrapuntal melodies, wandering among insoluble riddles, rising and falling, and its slow movement reminded me of the starry sky. Listening to it greedily, the saxophone was complaining of something; again and again the trumpet soared to incredible heights, and from time to time the piano moved in with its apocalyptic chords in E. And the drummer, like a metronome, like time itself, rendering the rhythm dynamic by syncopation, dominated the ensemble with a soft hollow tattoo.

"Let's not turn on the light, all right?" she asked, looking up at the greenish dial of the radio and at its gleaming little eye.

"All right," I agreed, and I thought that perhaps I would never have such a night again. I was sorry that three hours of it had already gone. I wanted it to start all over again from the beginning, wanted to go out again with the lantern and wait, wanted us to reminisce again, and later again be afraid of parting in the darkness.

She got up to fetch something, glanced out of the window, and said huskily, "Snow . . ."

I too got up and looked into the darkness beyond the window. Snow was coming down silently: the first real snow this autumn. In the morning there would be mouse tracks around the piles of brushwood in the forest, tracks of rabbits near the acacias, which they love to gnaw at night; and I remembered my gun and I was happy, I shivered with ecstasy. Lord, what joy! How wonderful that it was snowing, that she had come and that we were alone and that there was music and that we had our past and our future, which perhaps would be better than the past, and that tomorrow I would take her to my favorite places, show her the river, the fields, the hills, the forest, and the ravines. The night was passing, but we could not sleep; we spoke in whispers and embraced, afraid to lose each other, and we kept feeding the fire in the stove; we looked at its ruddy jaws and its heat baked our faces. We dropped off at seven in the morning, when the windows had already turned blue, and we slept a long time, because there was no one to wake us in our house.

While we slept, the sun rose and everything thawed a little, but later everything froze over again. After we had our tea, I took my gun and we went outdoors. We felt momentary pain: the intensely white wintry light struck our eyes, and the air was so pure and sharp. There was no more snow, but everything was crusted over with ice. The crusts were lusterless, semitransparent. An odorous vapor escaped from the cowshed; the calves were jostling each other nearby, and the clatter they made was as loud as though they were stamping on wooden planks. This was because the liquid dung had not hardened under the frozen mud. Some were munching the hoary winter crops with gusto and were urinating frequently, lifting up their tails, spreading apart their legs, and showing the curly hair on the groin. And when they urinated emerald spots appeared on the wet young rye.

At first we walked along the road. The ruts had frozen over, but under the ice there was muddy water, and when our boots broke the crust, brown mud sprinkled the ice. And in the woods late dandelions, already jaundiced, stuck out through the ice. Leaves and pine needles were frozen into the ice; the last mushrooms stood crusted with ice, and when we kicked them they broke off and, jumping up noisily, went rolling over the ice for a long time. The ice gave way under our feet, and there was a great crackling and clattering around us.

From afar, the fields on the hills were a smoky green and sprinkled with flour, as it were. The hayricks had turned black; the woods were transparent, black and naked. Alone the birches' white paling stood out sharply; the trunks of aspens shone softly with a velvet green, and here and there on the hills the red crowns of trees that had not yet lost their foliage were blazing. Through the trees you could see the river for quite a ways, and it looked cold and deserted. We walked down the snow-covered ravine, leaving deep tracks, at first muddy, then clean behind us, and drank from the spring near the aspen that had been cut down. The bottom of the little hollow in front of the spring was lined with a layer of blackened leaves, maple and oak; a cold, bitter

432

odor came from the aspen that lay on the ground, and where the trunk had been cut it was the color of amber.

"Good?" I asked, glancing at her, and was astonished: her eyes were green.

"Good!" she said, looking around avidly and licking her lips.

"Better than the White Sea?" I pursued.

She looked at the river and the slope again, and here eyes were even greener.

"Well, the White Sea . . ." she said vaguely. "We have . . . We have . . . But here there are oaks," she interrupted herself "How did you manage to find such a spot, darling?"

I was happy, but also somewhat ill at ease and apprehensive: everything had been arranging itself too well for me this autumn. To calm down, I lighted a cigarette, and was wreathed in smoke and vapor. A tugboat appeared on the Oka; it speeded downstream, raised waves, and we followed it with our eyes in silence. A thick stream of vapor poured from the engine and another spurted from a hole in the side just above the water line.

When the tugboat vanished from view behind a bend in the river, we walked up the path among sparse trees in a clear grove, to have one more look at the Oka from a height. We walked quietly, in silence, as in a white dream in which we were at last together.

1961

YEVGENY YEVTUSHENKO
(b. 1933)

"I lie upon damp earth"

I lie upon damp earth and hug
A spade, and let the minutes pass,
A blade of grass between my lips,
A rather sourish blade of grass.

In ground so devilishly hard
Spades break before they can strike deep;
And how I long to fall asleep,
But you are not allowed to sleep.

"You can't
          get on your legs at all?
Just look at the poor dear!" she hoots:
A girl in a blue sleeveless shirt,
Her overalls stuck in her boots.

As luck will have it, she strikes up
A song that lilts, a lilting song:
"I'll find my love, and when I do
Won't I torment him all day long!"

Boldly she flashes her blue spade,
Jangles her earrings, for a stunt
Flings out a sudden word so raw
Even the boys look up and grunt.

They laugh, the lot!
                "Eh, what a snake!"

"Well, Anka,
            how she hands it out!"
The currant bushes and the stars
May know, as I know without doubt

That, past the intoxicated bushes,
Pushing
         the towering grass
                    aside,
She enters the night woods with me,
Moving as with a drunken stride,

And that she drops her swarthy arms,
Clumsy as if her pulses failed,
And in the darkness speaks to me
Beautiful words, and veiled.

N. MELNIKOV

This author, whose real name is Melman, is a journalist, short story writer, and literary critic. In the late forties he was a victim of the campaign against "kinless cosmopolites," which was a manifestation of obsessive Soviet chauvinism with overtones of anti-Semitism.

The Komsomol at Work

A DOCUMENTARY

The man look as if he were suspended from the sky. He waved to me, leaning back as far as the safety belt permitted, and shouted:

"I'm going to Moscow soon!"

I recognized Kolya Yenikeyev, the repairman. That he was going to Moscow I had heard from him already. But apparently not alone on the ground but also up in the air he didn't stop thinking about it.

"How do you get to Park Street there?"

"The subway will take you."

"And is it far to Luzhniki?"

"Quite near."

Kolya had forgotten that he had already questioned me about Park Street and Luzhniki. He must have forgotten it in his excitement. For the repairman this was a red-letter day: a job that normally took a week they nearly finished in two days. All that was left to do was to change the last flanges, screw the last nuts, and the network of pipes would be in working order. Then they would get leave and Kolya would pay his first visit to Moscow.

Then Raya Yefimova, secretary of the Komsomol [Communist League of Youth] Committee, came along. "What's this—you want to write up Yenikeyev?" she asked. "Don't be in a hurry."

"What's the matter?"

"Come to headquarters in the evening, and you'll find out. We'll have a bone to pick with one or two members."

These days the heat rose to 104 degrees. People stood still at street corners hoping for a breeze. But from morning till evening Yenikeyev stayed up there under the incandescent sky, handling a heavy wrench. He was in charge of the thorough repair of the aerial gas pipes. He had been written up in the local Komsomol newspaper. Of evenings Kolya would sit down on a stool outside the common living quarters and quietly play the accordion.

I told Yefimova that, of course, I would come to headquarters, but that, to my mind, Yenikeyev was a good egg.

"I used to think so too," Raya answered dolefully, as if sorry for herself.

"And what else will come up?"

"Why, something even worse than the Yenikeyev case!"

She said this angrily, looking me severely in the eye, and involuntarily I thought: "Is she getting ready to pick *me* to pieces?"

"We'll discuss Shainurov's immoral behavior," she brought out. Shainurov headed the Komsomol Building Office,* and I decided that Yefimova was pulling my leg.

"Stop joking, I'm asking you in earnest."

"And I'm answering you in earnest."

"But what's he done?"

"Come tonight, and you'll hear for yourself. So long for now. See you in the evening."

She was off, her gait hurried and businesslike, and I went to look for Shainurov. During the three weeks that I spent on the construction site we had struck up quite a friendship, and it seemed to me that I had the right to ask him frankly: What had happened?

But it isn't so easy to find Shainurov. I looked into the Building Office—a padlock on the door. At the bureau of the Party Committee they said that he had been there but had left. Preparations were being made for the opening of the butyl plant, and the place was probably swarming with construction workers and future operators. Shainurov must surely be there too. But the approaches to the new building were in the hands of the roadbuilders. At every step there were signs: "Road closed," "Don't walk." And if you poked your nose into a forbidden area, you were stopped with a rude word. Somehow, with

---

* The activities of the Communist League of Youth include participation in building railroads, canals, power stations, blast furnaces, oil refineries, factories.—A. Y.

pieces of asphalt sticking to my soles, I managed to reach the door of the building. On all the stairways there was the slap of painters' brushes, and in order to avoid them you had to be on your guard. I did not get into the individual shops. Special commissions for the acceptance of equipment were at work there. No matter whom I asked if Shainurov were there, I got the same answer. "Stepped in, but left." There was nothing for me to do but to wait till evening.

In the street I was almost knocked down by Krasnov, the head of the construction board. He greeted me and dashed on.

Not so long ago I had witnessed a glum conversation between Alexander Ivanovich Krasnov and Shainurov, after which the Komsomol Office placed on the bulletin board an "urgent notice" reading: "Comrade Krasnov is imperiling the plan for starting the plant." That day I dropped into Krasnov's office with Shainurov. A typewriter was clattering in a businesslike fashion; the safe jutted impressively from the wall. The chief himself was seated at a large desk in his spacious study. He nodded to us wearily, wearily reached out his hand.

"Bear in mind," he said turning to Shainurov, "that your 'urgent notice' hits the whole Trust on the rebound. Haven't you gone too far?"

"Your board isn't the whole Trust," Shainurov retorted. "And the Trust isn't the whole Soviet Union."

The secretary dashed into the study and started talking rapidly, tears in her voice.

"You'd better discharge me, Alexander Ivanovich. I was sitting and working when suddenly someone stuck his insolent head in at the door and started jeering at me. 'Aren't you fed up, dear citizeness,' says he, 'with imperiling the plan for starting the plant?' That's the limit! Whether you like it or not, I have placed a long-distance call to Tiraspol. They didn't answer our wire, so they'll have to tell us over the phone if they'll finally ship that damn Mettlach tile. And you," she turned to Shainurov, "go to my flat and take up the tiling in my kitchen and the bathroom, only leave us alone. . . ."

Having delivered herself of all this, she vanished as suddenly as she had appeared.

"Well, are you satisfied?" Krasnov asked Shainurov.

"I am. It seems we'll get the tiles."

Then Shainurov inquired about bricks. Krasnov promised to help.

He added, however, that the Council of National Economy didn't allot building materials every day, and it might be that they simply wouldn't listen to him, but that he would do what lay within his power.

"You must forgive me," said Shainurov. "Your secretary is worked up, but not you, in my opinion. What has planned allotment of materials to do with it? The building project needs bricks!" He got up and headed for the door. "I'll wait for you downstairs," he said to me, and left.

I, too, rose. In taking leave of me, the chief said: "Shainurov has brains. The Komsomol Office is too small for him. He belongs on the Regional, or at least on the District, Committee."

I decided that Krasnov was sly. He simply thought that as a noted administrator it did not befit him to take offense at a youngster. It was much more diplomatic to commend him.

In the street Shainurov voiced his distress:

"Honestly, I never thought that Krasnov would pay no attention to our denunciation. We expected that he would kick up a row, get the allotment revised, would at least demand the removal of the 'urgent notice' from the bulletin board. Krasnov has done nothing. Well, then, I'll have to call on the Council of National Economy myself." And suddenly Shainurov exploded:

"At the grand opening of the butyl plant, I bet Krasnov will be elected to the presidium!"

A broad staircase led to the office of the Council. Shainurov stopped and suggested we have a smoke. "Can it be that he has cold feet?" I wondered. Well, why couldn't he have cold feet? He was twenty, short, puny—a mere boy, wearing a checked shirt and a belted jacket. Not a very impressive exterior—no wonder the janitor looked at him askance.

In the waiting room we were met by the secretary, a polite-looking young man. Visitors, singly or in pairs, sat on sofas. Here the telephones did not ring but buzzed gently, steps were deadened by a runner, people spoke in whispers or quietly, as though over there, behind the velvet curtain, lay someone gravely ill. And though I was certain that no such person was there, Shainurov's voice (he did not know how to speak quietly) jarred on me.

He began by introducing himself, then introduced me, then got down to business. The construction project with which the Komsomol was concerned could not continue on a pittance, he said; it needed fifteen to twenty thousand bricks a day. The secretary replied prissily that the plan for the deliveries had been approved long ago and that in this matter anything not arranged for, unauthorized, was out of the question. In short, the same tune that we heard from the chief of the construction board. Restraining himself, Shainurov continued to attack stubbornly:

"The men do piecework. They want to work, eat, make money, dress well, go to the theater."

Speaking in the same doleful voice, the young man said, "I cannot help you."

At this point Shainurov could no longer restrain himself:

"But I don't ask for any help from you personally. What I demand is that you list me among those who wish to be received by your chief."

"I don't list people who come on business like yours."

Shainurov examined the secretary with a long, appraising look, apparently figuring out what else the secretary deserved to be told.

"Isn't it clear to you," he began, rasping out each word, "that it isn't me who needs the bricks?" And he supplied the answer himself: "No, it isn't clear to you. You don't care a damn about our construction project—that's why it's not clear to you."

Everywhere and in everything Shainurov divided people into two categories: those who helped the project—they were good, and those who didn't—they were bad.

We left. On the landing we were hailed. The secretary was hurrying toward us.

"You're a fool, that's what you are," he said to Shainurov, this time without a trace of civility. "Well, suppose I do put your name on the list of people who want to see the chief, he won't receive you before Saturday. And this is Tuesday. Will that suit you?"

"No, it won't. Let me see him at once."

"Did you see how many people were waiting?"

"I did."

"They'd tear me to pieces."

"And it would serve you right."

The young man was a little older than Shainurov, and now that the conversation assumed an informal character everything became simpler.

"You know Vaska Maslov?" asked the secretary. "He's been with you from the beginning."

"I see him every day."

"Give him my greetings—Smorodinov is my name. We graduated from the Building Institute the same year. He was given a construction job; I was sent to this place. I'm fed up with it up to here!" He drew the edge of his palm across his neck.

"About time you stopped wearing out the seat of your pants."

Confidentially the secretary informed us: "They gave me living quarters. It's awkward to throw up the job right away."

"We don't live in shacks either," said Shainurov, with a smile.

"I'll attend to your bricks myself. I'll take it up with the chief today."

We were returning to the construction site by a quiet lane. Five-story houses on the right stared with all their windows, as it were, at the vacant lot across the street. Soon the land would be built up, but in the meantime it was the delight of little boys who were playing soccer.

After a long pause Shainurov suddenly started speaking gaily: "I have an interesting idea: What about getting Smorodinov to join our Office? That would be great!" But instantly his enthusiasm vanished. "No, it won't work. Utopia." Instead of being enthusiastic about his idea, he was now indignant. "The devil knows what enters a man's head! You'd think that the Council of National Economy has only one solitary construction project."

And he plunged into the controversy that agitated the little boys who were playing soccer on the vacant lot. God alone knows when he had time to discover which side was right and which wrong. The controversy was over a goal: the ball lay on the goal line, but the team that had lost claimed that the redhead who had scored the goal was out of the field of play. The redhead was about to burst into sobs. Shainurov announced that the goal had been scored correctly, that he had seen it clearly from the side. The verdict was accepted, but at this point the goalkeeper of the defeated team rent the air with lusty wails. He had to be replaced. I believe that if I had not been with him. Shainurov would have started kicking the ball in complete self-forgetfulness. But this would not have prevented him from appearing the following day before the Supreme Soviet to plead for his bricks.

In fact, this is exactly what he did. The important comrade on the Council of National Economy was a deputy of the Supreme Soviet. As a voter, Shainurov called on him and not only was duly received but obtained a promise that the plan for the delivery of building materials would be revised without delay.

That very week two brick yards started shipping twenty thousand bricks daily to the construction site.

At six in the evening, I arrived at headquarters, where, as Yefimova, secretary of the Komsomol Committee, had said, "Shainurov's immoral behavior" would be discussed and where they would have words with Yenikeyev, the repairman. Of course, there are no saints on earth, and everyone may go wrong. But I couldn't imagine how Shainurov had misbehaved and what Yenikeyev's transgression was.

The Komsomol Office and the Komsomol Committee occupied rooms that opened onto the same passage of a small one-story house. All the doors and windows were wide open, to make it easier for people to breathe. Toward evening the temperature dropped, but only very slightly. Instead of 104 degree, it was only about 100.

Raya Yefimova, deep in thought, sat before the telephone at Shainurov's desk but not in the seat which he occupied as chairman.

"I've been waiting for a long-distance call from Barnaul a good hour—and not a sound," she complained. "The fixtures factory has let us down. What are they thinking of? They keep disregarding our orders. Shainurov wanted to take a leave of absence and go out there by train. We are turning into fixers."*

"Still, what are you going to haul him over the coals for?

"You mean Shainurov?"

"Why, yes."

"And I bet you wanted to write a whole article about him?"

I answered that this was beside the point but that I simply didn't believe Shainurov was capable of an immoral action.

Yefimova answered: "And if a man takes the bride from under the bridegroom's nose? What would you call that?"

*Tolkachi. A tolkach arranges, among other things, prompt delivery of goods in ways often illegal.—A. Y.

"Shainurov took her?"

"Exactly. Do you know Galya Khasanova from the methylsterol shop?"

"Sure."

"He took her away from Fedya Blokhin, the fitter. The Committee was preparing a Komsomol wedding for them. We managed to get them a dinner service, a sofa. The Construction Committee and the Factory Committee promised to give them a room in a new house, and Shainurov went and upset everything. He snatched away the bride. Is that honorable?"

In reply I asked what kind of a bride she was if you could snatch her away. So everything was for the best.

"I see, you're smiling, but I'm ashamed to look people in the eye. We pestered the Construction Committee and the Factory Committee to death. Picked out a dinner service, ordered a sofa . . . It isn't as if Galya were the only girl in the world."

And to my surprise, and perhaps to her own, Raya confessed: "By the way, I was in love with Shainurov too. Now it's finished."

The telephone rang. A long-distance call.

"Hello!"

It was Shainurov who had introduced me to Galya Khasanova. She was standing before an instrument panel. Overhead a huge spiderweb of steel pipes. The air vibrated with an impatient, demanding hum, as if a huge bee had flown in and had no way of getting out. This muffled noise sounded like an echo of the mighty work of pyrolytic furnaces.

Galya's eyes were glued to the tiny window in which a pen was tracing on white graph paper the curve of the temperature of the furnaces, which resembled a cardiogram.

Shainurov asked Galya to explain to me the meaning of methylsterol, and went off.

"Methylsterol," said Galya, her eyes fixed on the little window, and lapsed into silence.

Without another word, she went over to a small table, opened a drawer, took out a batch of pamphlets, and handed them to me.

"It's all written there," she said, smiling slyly, and returned to her work.

It was a broad hint, but I took no offense. I merely cursed Shainurov who had so deftly got rid of me. . . .

"Hello!" Yefimova shouted into the receiver. "Who is speaking?
I want Committee Secretary Timchenko. . . . Went to a movie? How's
that—to a movie? In working hours? No wonder we aren't getting any
of your fixtures." Suddenly she turned to me and whispered: "I forgot
that their time is three hours ahead of ours!" Then she spoke into
the mouthpiece again: "Listen, friend, to whom am I talking? Nikishin? Well, Comrade Nikishin, this is to inform you that if you don't
fill our order within the next few days we'll write a collective letter to
Komsomol Pravda. What, what? You'll write it yourselves? How is it
that we're not in the plan? Listen, Nikishin, on what date will you
start shipping? The 20th? Have Timchenko wire us. All right? Well,
so long. No, no, wait! What movie is showing in your town today?
Again you're behind the times. *Russian Souvenir* was showing here
long ago. Good luck!" Raya put down the receiver, opened the record
book, and made an entry. "In a moment," she said, "another bridegroom will present himself here. You'll see what kind of bird he is.
He has written to this Committee." She handed me a paper. "Read
it. He thinks we're a lot of boobies here. . . ."

The application stated that *he* and *she* had loved each other a long
time, and begged the Committee to arrange a Komsomol wedding.
They also begged the Committee to take account of the fact that you
cannot start a family outdoors. . . .

"You understand!" Raya stormed. "What they're after isn't a family
but a room. Not a living soul has ever seen them together. They know
that at a Komsomol wedding the newlyweds are handed the key to a
room, so they've decided to try their luck—you never can tell. And
then—divorce, and they'll exchange the one room for two. He'll be
here in a moment; you'll see for yourself."

Sure enough, the fellow soon arrived. A cigarette between his teeth,
a leather jacket thrown over his shoulders in spite of the heat, pants
tucked into his boots. On the threshold, without even greeting us,
he asked gaily, "Well, secretary, are we going to get up a little
wedding, eh?"

Raya glared at the fellow gloomily and slowly rose from behind the
desk.

"Is this a barroom?"

The fellow snatched the cigarette from his mouth and hid it behind his back.

"Sorry. I'm young, I'll mend my ways. But I only came to ask."

Raya sighed, sat down again and, without looking at the fellow, observed: "The Komsomol Committee doesn't believe in this love of yours. It's all bunk, not love. You've got to go to the office and take your bride along. And now off with you."

The fellow did not leave at once; he lingered awhile as if he were sort of offended!

"I only came to ask, and you're sending me to the office right away. You could have said no, and that'd be the end of it."

"No, that won't be the end of it. You'll answer for lying. Both of you."

The fellow left without saying anything more, and Raya took a long time calming down.

"Well, tell me, isn't he a character? 'Are we going to get up a little wedding?' Just as if it was a question of buying a half-liter of vodka."

In came Grigoryev, a demobilized sailor. For several days he had been haunting the plant and the construction site; he looked, he figured—he couldn't make up his mind whether to stay here or push on somewhere else. In the morning he would appear in one or another section of the building under construction; then he'd spend the day dropping in on the Komsomol Committee and at the office. He still wore his Navy uniform. Maybe he wanted to show off or hadn't bought a civilian outfit yet.

"Aren't you fed up with loafing?" Yefimova asked him.

Grigoryev sat down, produced a steel cigar case, and began playing with it.

"You can't decide things like this offhand," he said. "Before I served in the Navy I was a submachine gunner of the sixth rank, and here I must start as an apprentice. Of course, it's a new technique; there's no harm learning it. Still, it hurts. . . ."

Raya retorted that it was silly to feel that way, and if a man has a head on his shoulders and a pair of hands where they should be, he won't be a learner for long.

"Today I stepped into your mess hall," Grigoryev continued unhurriedly; "the grub ain't bad, and it's civilized-like, generally speaking."

"And you thought we ate with our fingers, eh?"

Grigoryev held his peace. Then he informed us that at the ship's amateur shows he wasn't the worst: "I'd sing a number, and they'd split their sides."

To this, Raya responded, not without venom: "So why come here? Apply at the Philharmonic Society."

In short, the sailor suffered defeat on all scores, and soon lapsed into silence.

The meeting opened in spite of the absence of some of the members. There was no helping it: the evening belonged to soccer. Already in the morning people were asking me if I was going to the soccer game. When I said that I wasn't, they stared at me, and somebody said, "But we're playing Syzran today!"

Raya said that Shainurov would be late because he had been summoned by the Regional Committee of the Komsomol and that he had asked them to start without him. And I thought, "Can it be that the business about the wedding has reached the Regional Committee too?"

Two men whom I had not met were present: the brigadier* of the decorators, Mukhin, or simply Petya, as Raya introduced him to me, and Krylov, a foreman from the furniture factory. Yefimova introduced him to me dryly, giving only his surname.

As soon as Petya saw Krylov, he pounced on him. "You cheat, you palm off shoddy wares on us!" Petya shouted.

"Don't get up on your hind legs. I'm no private craftsman; why do you single me out for attack?"

Yefimova raised her voice, demanding silence. Petya sat down, turning his back on Krylov. Someone suggested that the radio, which emitted the thrilling hum of the stadium, should be turned off. The representative of the motor depot, Vasya Kharitonov, reluctantly rose, went over to the radio and, before turning it off, listened for a moment and drew a heavy sigh.

---

* In Soviet usage, with its predilection for military terminology, a *brigadier*, man or woman, is the head of a *brigade*, a group of workers performing the same type of labor.—A. Y.

446

The discussion was started by asking Vasya Kharitonov if the truck drivers were going to work on Sunday clearing the area of the plant. It was pointed out that the day of the grand opening of the butyl shop was at hand. Kharitonov declared that he could not guarantee this, that the boys were working two shifts and that if you don't rest up on Sunday you'll fall asleep at the wheel on Monday.

"You're breaking our hearts," said Raya, "Get the activists together and make a speech to the boys. Remember when you addressed the transport workers. After that, how many people volunteered to haul equipment from the station on their off days!"

"That's a matter of the past," Vasya said. "You'd better ask me how many people I had to grab by the scruff of their neck to make them volunteer. The devils applauded me, but then started shouting, 'We can do without your equipment!' "

Next to Kharitonov sat Khalida Fattakhova, the brigadier of the women masons. Everyone knew that one of these days she and Kharitonov were going to drop in on the Registry Office to record their marriage. Meanwhile Khalida did not spare her future husband.

"What can you expect of him?" said Khalida. "You see, he doesn't know how to talk to people, so he's likely to use his fists."

"Well, do what you please," Yefimova said to Vasya; "get together the most active members, take people by the scruff of the neck, but we must have the trucks."

She reported her conversation with Barnaul, and broached the subject of a mass outing, but at that moment a fellow from the brigade of repairmen ran in, all out of breath, and announced that the boys wouldn't be able to meet the deadline because ten flanges turned out to be defective, and the storehouse was locked up.

"That's the careful preparation for repair work!" someone grumbled.

Vasya Kharitonov, though he had no car, was dispatched to find the man in charge of the storehouse. Petya and Krylov, forgetting their feud, went over to the repair shops. Grigoryev, the sailor, tagged along. Yefimova ran over to the common living quarters to look for metalworkers. Thus the meeting, scarcely begun, broke up so that pipes would be repaired on time. At ten in the evening the gas from the oil refineries was scheduled to flow through the pipes again to the functioning shops of the Synthetic Alcohol plant. I remained alone with Khalida Fattakhova. She spread a clean sheet of paper on the desk and began to compose an "Urgent Notice" that denounced the metalworkers.

One Saturday evening there was a lecture "On Love" at the auditorium in the municipal park. Khalida and Kharitonov sat on a bench behind me. Soon after the beginning of the address the crowd in the hall began to dwindle rapidly. The lecturer argued that before the October Revolution a woman had every reason to be unfaithful to her husband, for that was a defiance of the Czar's autocracy. Examples: Anna Karenina and Katerina from Ostrovsky's play *The Storm*. But now that the old world was done with, there were no grounds for such actions.

It was impossible to understand where the park administration had dug out this moth-eaten expert on ethical problems.

Not far from me a fellow got up noisily. "Not for us," he said loudly, and made for the exit.

Khalida and Kharitonov were having a whispered argument.

"It's either he or me!" Vasya declared firmly.

"It's ridiculous," Khalida answered.

"I'm not responsible for myself," Vasya raged. "It's about people like him that lectures should be given."

I thought that he was referring to a rival, but afterward I discovered that he was speaking not of a rival but of Khalida's great-grandfather, his worst enemy.

Within half an hour's ride from the young city of oil workers and chemists the miserable shacks of an old workers' settlement were living out their last days. One evening Kharitonov drove me out in his three-ton truck to see the place. Along a wretched road stood several ramshackle little houses flattened against the ground. It looked as though you could pick them up with a shovel and toss them into the body of the truck.

"That's where he lives," said my driver.

At one time Vasya had been proud of his future kinsman, and assured people that Khalida's great-grandfather had been all but personally acquainted with Pugachev.* But now he could not bear to hear the ancient mentioned.

"The man is over 120," Vasya stormed. "And how puffed up he is, the shameless nationalist."

* Leader of the peasant uprising under Catherine II.—A. Y.

Old man Fattakhov's pride consisted in his refusing to give Khalida his great-grandfatherly blessing; in other words, he forbade her marriage to Kharitonov. Russians, Ukrainians, Armenians, and Tartars were represented in the vast Fattakhov clan. The great-grandfather had a good time at all the weddings of his grandchildren and great-grandchildren, but in this instance for some unknown reason he balked. Either he felt the approach of death and wanted to show his mettle for the last time, or he was taken by a sudden whim. At the family council it was decided to humor the old man and to have a quiet wedding.

Apparently it was not easy to find the man in charge of the storehouse. Kharitonov was a long time in coming back. Petya, Krylov, and the sailor looked into all the repair shops without any results. Raya brought two metalworkers from the brigade that was making flanges, but they both asserted that the flanges in question were unusable, that new ones had to be cut, but that perfect ones, they were sure, were in the storehouse. Someone proposed to break the padlock, but then the storehouse keeper himself appeared, convoyed by Kharitonov. The metalworkers were right—all the necessary items were in the storehouse, and as punishment for slipshod performance the metalworkers were forced to help with the repair work. Furthermore, Khalida suggested that they themselves should place the "Urgent Notice" denouncing them on the bulletin board. But this they refused to do.

The meeting was resumed. Petya again turned his back on Krylov. Raya again took up the projected outing in the woods, reported her negotiations with the restaurant trust. The latter undertook to supply patties, fruit juices, pastry.

"Beer wouldn't be amiss," Kharlamov remarked quietly, but was opposed by the women present. The men held their peace.

A girl in a magnificent red skirt, a white blouse and white high-heeled slippers, appeared in the doorway. A large, gaudy bag hung from her arm.

"May I?" she asked with a coquettish smile, confident of being irresistible.

"Come in," Yefimova dryly granted her request.

Kharitonov waved his hand at her. "Greetings, Natasha."

Grigoryev, the sailor, was visibly smitten by Natasha's beauty.

"It's simply *parlez vous français*," he whispered in my ear.

"What brings you here?" asked Raya.

Natasha explained that she was three months behind in paying her Komsomol dues, but she begged to be forgiven because with this devilish exchange of living quarters she had completely lost her head and didn't have a free moment.

"If you only knew the amount of red tape," Natasha said to Raya. "Hundreds of papers, a thousand explanations, why you change and what for."

"And as a matter of fact, why did you make the change?" asked Yefimova.

"I wanted a balcony and sunlight—the old flat was dark all day long. So that meant a lot of painting, whitewashing. You know Sonia Kovalyova? Imagine, I decided to give her a chance to make a little money on the side: I engaged her to do some painting evenings, but she botched the job so, it turns my stomach to see what she's done."

"You should have done the work yourself," said Raya. "Or have you forgotten how to hold a brush?"

Apparently Natasha decided that Raya was joking. She smiled, rummaged in her bag, got out her Komsomol card and the money, and put both on the desk before Raya.

"But hurry up, please, we're going to the theater this evening. Have you seen the Moscow company yet? People say they're exceptionally good."

"Do you have orchestra seats or balcony?" Kharitonov inquired.

"Orchestra, Vasya dear. They always reserve the same seats for us. It's positively boring. . . ."

"See here," said Raya. "I'm not going to accept your dues."

"Oh, Raya dear, but I don't know when I can manage to drop in again."

"I won't accept your dues even when you come again," said Yefimova.

"How's that—you won't accept?"

"I can't take this money. It isn't yours. You haven't earned it. It comes to this, that your husband pays your Komsomol dues."

"So what? Are you sorry for him?"

"I'm not sorry for him. But is it possible you don't understand that it isn't your rent or your electricity bill you've come to pay. Komosmol dues you pay with your own money. And besides, what kind of Komsomol member are you? There are signs at every corner saying that both the plant and the building under construction are desperately in need of hands, and you have a trade. But you don't give a damn. You made Sonia Kovalyova work for you, and she, the fool, agreed."

Drops of perspiration appeared on Natasha's powdered face. Obviously she did not know what to do. Run away? Make a scene? Burst into tears? She ended by compressing her lips maliciously; her eyes blazed, her nostrils dilated.

"So you think I'm some kind of a sponger or zoot-suiter?"

Now Kharitonov joined in: "Really, who are you? Here I'm looking at you and wondering, Who are you and what do you want a Komsomol card for?"

Most likely, no one had ever put such a question to her, and she did not know how to answer it.

"Honestly," Kharitonov continued, "at first I was glad for you. 'There, she got married,' I thought; 'she'll go to school; it'll be easier for her than for others.' But you neither work nor study."

"But I will," Natasha brought out.

"What will you do?" asked Raya.

"I'll study."

"I don't believe you."

"I will. I'll take up foreign languages."

"That's what everybody says who doesn't want to do anything. I don't understand; it's as though you *are* one of us and you aren't. To whom were you bragging about a flat with a balcony, and orchestra seats? Well, we haven't any apartments with balconies yet, and we buy tickets for the cheapest seats. What of it?"

"As a matter of principle, I never buy expensive tickets either for the movies or the theater," said Kharitonov. "I'd rather have a mug of beer in the lobby."

Natasha stood silent and motionless. Her aplomb had completely vanished. She stood as though rooted to the spot.

Heavy drops of rain struck the windowsill.

"Rain! At last!" Several voices were heard at once.

"What about our repairmen?" Yefimova fretted. "Are they still hanging on the steel framework?" She took Natasha's card and money from the desk and handed them to her. "Go, you'll be late for the theater. I'll take the matter up with the District Committee. Let them decide. We need no ballast."

Natasha put the card and the money into her bag, turned around, and left without saying goodbye.

"Why did you have to chase her out into the rain?" asked the sailor.

The downpour was raging. Caught up by the wind, it was swirling on the ground like dust. Through the window we could see Natasha. Stumbling, making no effort to avoid the puddles, she was running toward the trolley stop.

Thinking aloud, someone said, "Natasha will return to construction work."

A car rolled up to the house, and Shainurov jumped out of it. He walked hurriedly down the passage. Then he stopped in the doorway, said, "Greetings!" and walked over to his seat at the desk. His gloomy, anxious look spoke for itself. Apparently clouds were gathering over the head of the chief of the Komsomol Office. He looked long and attentively at the representative of the furniture factory, pulled something out of his pocket and placed it on the desk. It turned out to be a door handle.

"Since when are door handles nailed rather than attached with screws?" Shainurov asked Krylov.

"They're supposed to be screwed on," said Krylov.

"But your handles are all nailed on."

"Again 'my handles'! Why attack me? I'm not working in the Section of Technical Control, you know. I have deadlines to meet. It never occurred to me to check. As it is, the shop superintendent says to me, 'Do you get your wages from the factory or from Shainurov at the Komsomol Office'?"

"That isn't all," said Petya, who had apparently decided to finish Krylov off. "Not a single door is properly varnished. We ourselves had to run to get varnish. They're already designing the posters with the slogans for the grand opening of the butyl plant, and we run to get varnish."

Krylov sat there, looking gloomy, his head drooping. "Tomorrow at the operational meeting I'll have them over the coals," Krylov promised. "You had better come too," he said to Shainurov.

"Are you a minor?"

"Well, don't come; I'll do it alone."

"I have to make a trifling announcement," Shainurov said. "The Regional Committee of the Komsomol has decided to nominate me secretary of the District Committee."

"You're being promoted!" the sailor exclaimed. Apparently he already considered himself one of the group.

Shainurov smiled mirthlessly, and said: "Comrades from the Trust are putting themselves out. They're fed up with me. There's nothing to discharge me for, so they have decided to promote me. Their figuring is simple: the District Secretary has a whole district to think of; one buliding project is nothing to him. And I have no trump card to play. You must grow, they say."

I recalled how Krasnov had lavished praise on Shainurov. But at the time I attached no importance to his words.

"We won't let you go," Yefimova snapped. "You can't leave us. Is is possible that you agreed? I'll go to the Regional Committee myself!"

She seemed to have forgotten the Komsomol wedding Shainurov had broken up, her own discomfiture, and was ready to run headlong to the District Committee at once.

It was already dark when Kolya Yenikeyev, wringing wet, dirty from head to foot, barged into the room. He dropped into the first chair he came upon and stretched out his legs. "Finished!" he ejaculated just one word and closed his eyes. Then he opened them again and stared at Yefimova. "Tell me right away why you summoned me, or I'll lie down here and won't get up."

"Feast your eyes on him!" Yefimova urged us, pointing to Yenikeyev. "The Committee asked him to provide accordion music for the mass outing. So he demanded that we pay him at the rate we pay artists whom we invite. Look at the artist!"

"But I was joking, Raya dear."

"You're lying. Aren't you ashamed to look us in the eye?"

Nearly two days and nights Yenikeyev had worked somewhere up in the air under the mercilessly blazing sun, and just now in a downpour. You'd imagine he would unburden his soul and send them all to hell. But he sat and looked at Raya good-naturedly, blinking his singed carroty eyelashes guiltily.

"I *am* lying. I asked for money. Thought an extra ruble would come in handy in Moscow. Well, generally speaking, I've made a fool of myself."

Now and then I recall August, 1943, the first days of our offensive on the Western front. The battalion to which I belonged had thinned considerably. We were waiting for an order to move on Yelnya at any moment. The town was before our eyes; we spoke of nothing else; it was as if we all hailed from Yelnya.

A very youthful soldier, apparently just called up, approached the battalion commander. I remember distinctly his smart, irreproachable appearance: the rifle with fixed bayonet set against his leg, the roll on his back, a gas mask at his side, a pouch, a shovel, a mess kit, a spoon in his boot . . . and in his eyes, tears.

The commander asked him what the matter was. He explained that he had been slightly wounded, obtained permission to leave the field hospital, and for the second day was unable to find his unit. He showed his Red Army papers and Komsomol card. The commander ordered that he be given something to eat. The soldier cheered up, and an hour and a quarter later he was killed.

Years passed, but I can't forget him. He suddenly appeared before my eyes in a remote spot of the Siberian forest where a paper mill was being built, in the Kazakhstan steppe where a blast furnace was being erected. And today I saw him again: he dashed in here at the Komsomol Building Office and anxiously reported the breakdown in the repair work.

I have not informed the reader where, in exactly which region, the lights are burning late into the night in the windows of the Komsomol Building Office and the Komsomol Committee Office, headed respectively by Shainurov and Yefimova. I haven't done so because the girl I call Raya Yefimova told me roundly: "Don't write about us yet; we've only started." Besides, she hasn't authorized me to relate within everyone's hearing the story of her unrequited love.

It is still uncertain what will be the end of this affair of nominating the head of the Building Office for the post of District Secretary. "I like it fine right here. I don't care to go anywhere else. We'll put up a fight yet," he told me that very evening.

VICTOR KOCHETKOV

"The battle raged"

The battle raged. Earth seethed
With fires, fiercely bright.
The world was narrowed to
The groove of the gunsight.
But we,
Resolved, armed with strong faith, we hurled
Forward, and gave back its old
Dimensions to the world.

1960

Quatrain

Posted where all alarms converge, how vainly
I look for respite that the times deny.
As if one man alone were answerable
For the whole planet, and that man were I.

1960